The Hermeneutics of Social Identity in Luke–Acts

The Hermeneutics of Social Identity in Luke–Acts

Nickolas A. Fox

FOREWORD BY
Thorsten Moritz

PICKWICK *Publications* • Eugene, Oregon

THE HERMENEUTICS OF SOCIAL IDENTITY IN LUKE–ACTS

Copyright © 2021 Nickolas A. Fox. All rights reserved. Except for brief quotations in critical publications or reviews, no part of this book may be reproduced in any manner without prior written permission from the publisher. Write: Permissions, Wipf and Stock Publishers, 199 W. 8th Ave., Suite 3, Eugene, OR 97401.

Pickwick Publications
An Imprint of Wipf and Stock Publishers
199 W. 8th Ave., Suite 3
Eugene, OR 97401

www.wipfandstock.com

PAPERBACK ISBN: 978-1-7252-7863-9
HARDCOVER ISBN: 978-1-7252-7864-6
EBOOK ISBN: 978-1-7252-7865-3

Cataloguing-in-Publication data:

Names: Fox, Nickolas A., author. | Moritz, Thorsten, foreword.

Title: The hermeneutics of social identity in Luke–Acts / by Nickolas A. Fox; foreword by Thorsten Moritz.

Description: Eugene, OR: Pickwick Publications, 2021 | Includes bibliographical references.

Identifiers: ISBN 978-1-7252-7863-9 (paperback) | ISBN 978-1-7252-7864-6 (hardcover) | ISBN 978-1-7252-7865-3 (ebook)

Subjects: LCSH: Bible. Luke—Criticism, interpretation, etc. | Bible. Acts—Criticism, interpretation, etc. | Group identity—Religious aspects. | Identification (Religion)—Biblical teaching. | Hermeneutics.

Classification: BS2589 F69 2021 (print) | BS2589 (ebook)

Unless Otherwise indicated, all Scriptures are from the ESV® Bible (The Holy Bible, English Standard Version®), copyright © 2001 by Crossway Bibles, a publishing ministry of Good News Publishers. Used by permission. All rights reserved.

03/17/21

To Angela:

*I could not have done this without your support;
it means the world to me.*

Contents

List of Tables | ix
Foreword by Thorsten Moritz | xi
Preface | xiii
Acknowledgments | xvii
Abbreviations | xix

Introduction | 1
    The Genre of Luke–Acts   3
    The Dating of Luke–Acts   4
    Luke's Prefaces   5
    The Authorship of Luke–Acts   7
    Luke's Purpose(s)   9
    Scholarly Precedent   11

Chapter 1: Social Identity in the Early Church | 13
    Cultural Memory and the Early Church   14
    Social Identity: A Survey of the Scholarship   16
    Social Identity Theory   27
    The Social Function of Group Beliefs   34
    Group Beliefs in Acts   36
    Narrative and Intertextuality   46
    Conclusion   52

Chapter 2: God-Fearers as Luke's Audience | 53
    God-Fearers in Acts   54
    God-Fearers in Scholarship   58
    Minor Characters and Decentralization   63

The Critic-Response Type-Scene   78
Conclusion   88

Chapter 3: The Gospel and Decentralization in Luke–Acts | 89
The New Exodus in Luke–Acts   91
The Rhetorical Use of Names in Luke–Acts   93
Promise and Fulfillment in Luke   95
Promise and Fulfillment in Acts   129
Conclusion   141

Chapter 4: Luke's Use of Prototypes and Exemplars | 142
What is a Prototype?   143
Prototypical Figures in Acts   144
Minor Characters   158
Excursus: Angels and Visions in Luke's Writings   165
Sinai and Pentecost: Forming a New Covenant   168
Exemplars and Anti-Exemplars   170
Conclusion   181

Chapter 5: Luke's Identity-Forming Rhetoric and the Speeches in Acts | 183
Rhetoric in the First Century   187
The Use of Names in the Historiograpical Speeches in Acts   192
Stephen's Identity-Forming Rhetoric   194
The Rhetorical Function of The Land   208
Stephen's Critique of the Temple   216
Rhetorical Method in Paul's Speech   219
Conclusion   231

Conclusion | 232

Bibliography | 239

Tables

Table 1: References to God's Arm in the LXX | 101

Table 2: Similarities Between Jesus and Stephen | 151

Table 3: Antagonistic Uses of Ἰερουσαλήμ/Ἱεροσόλυμα in Luke–Acts | 154

Table 4: Decentralizing Uses of Ἰερουσαλήμ/Ἱεροσόλυμα in Luke–Acts | 155

Table 5: Encounters with Angels in Luke–Acts | 166

Table 6: Similarities Between Sinai and Pentecost | 168

Tables

Table 1: References to God's Arm in the LXX | 101

Table 2: Similarities Between Jesus and Stephen | 151

Table 3: Antagonistic Uses of Ἰερουσαλήμ/Ἱεροσόλυμα in Luke–Acts | 154

Table 4: Decentralizing Uses of Ἰερουσαλήμ/Ἱεροσόλυμα in Luke–Acts | 155

Table 5: Encounters with Angels in Luke–Acts | 166

Table 6: Similarities Between Sinai and Pentecost | 168

Foreword

ONE OF THE MORE intriguing omissions in New Testament scholarship has been the question of the performance of Jesus' core personnel (the Apostles and other significant leaders in the early church). To be fair, Mark's brutal attention to the failures of the disciples—replicated to a significant extent in the other Gospels—has received a fair amount of attention on the level of narrative criticism. However, scholars have typically refrained (1) from drawing the obvious, yet painful theological lessons from this state of affairs and (2) from pursuing rigorously the remarkable storyline of the Acts of the Apostles in which the latter are, to be frank, astonishingly ineffectual and for the most part quite simply absent!

Nick Fox does not set out to rectify this situation as such. He does, however, end up offering an examination of the speeches in Acts that advances the above-mentioned discussion considerably. How so? Part of the answer is found in his particular approach (Social Identity Theory); another in his attention to the role of God-fearers in Acts, that is, a loosely defined group of potential and actual Gentile believers who—by definition!—start at the opposite end from the Apostles. Whereas the latter were fellow-Jews, coached by Jesus to carry the gospel forward into the Roman empire, it is actually the former that succeeded in doing so, alongside other "minor characters." That expression captures well the contrast between the actual achievers in Acts (including Gentiles) and those who were *supposed* to achieve (Jesus' Jewish disciples as the major characters in the Gospels)—but who failed almost comprehensively, with a few exceptions in the very early chapters of Acts (eleven of the Twelve) and Peter, albeit only in the first half of Acts. To be clear, whereas Fox neither focuses on the Apostles' failures "to show up" when and where most needed, nor on the evangelistic role of the God-fearers per se, both of these are implications of Acts that serve well to frame the relevance of his discussion, not least because the manner and circumstances of their inclusion calls for the implied audience to capitalize on said inclusion for purposes of joining—and thereby advancing—the story of God's kingdom throughout the Roman empire.

The question, then, becomes, what can Social Identity Theory (SIT) contribute to the theological concerns surrounding the social storytelling of Acts? SIT has increasingly entered the field of New Testament studies. Since Luke–Acts engages so vividly the role of God-fearers and perceived outsiders in the early Christian re-centering of God's people around the person and faith of Jesus, Luke's two-volume work has been among the first in the New Testament to attract the attention of SIT. By developing and using a modified version of SIT, Nick Fox addresses directly Luke's decentralizing of ecclesial formation in the wake of the early Christian proclamation of the risen Christ. While others (Joel Green, Holly Beers, Luke Timothy Johnson) have noticed this phenomenon in Luke–Acts before, a fuller treatment of Luke's particular narrative strategies pertaining to the inclusion of outsiders was needed. The outward movement inherent in Luke's concept of God's people far transcends the merely geographical (Temple, Jerusalem, land) and personality-based (Apostles and other leaders in Jerusalem) and encompasses nothing less than the surprising inclusion of the "minor characters" who are now the SPIRITually empowered ones to transform the very core of what it means to be communities of God's people beyond Israel.

Thorsten Moritz, PhD

Preface

THE CHANCE TO RESEARCH and write on Luke–Acts has been a great privilege. It has been seven years since I started writing a research proposal, and those years have seen a lot of change: personal and academic growth, spiritual formation, deepened relationships, and certainly a few gray hairs.

The dissertation writing process is one that devotes rigorous attention to expanding scholarship in certain ways. However, if one is lucky, some of that good biblical flavor rubs off in the process, which has certainly been the case for me. I would like to quickly share three things that became much clearer to me while writing this book on Luke–Acts. These are more reflections of a Christian minister than of a Luke–Acts scholar, but sometimes those worlds overlap. In other words, if the reader might seek to gain devotional payoffs from reading this scholarly work, these might be good places to look.

1. The Holy Spirit empowers mission

I have heard people say so many times in the Church, "We don't want to get ahead of God." It is usually said to encourage prudence, wisdom, and patience among God's people when they are trying to make a decision or discern God's will. And those things—prudence, wisdom and patience—are good things. We humans can be an impulsive, foolish, and impatient lot.

And yet, the picture is quite different in Luke–Acts, particularly when it comes to outreach and new missionary initiatives. Jesus ministers to tax collectors, Gentiles, Roman Centurions, prostitutes, and lepers long before the disciples seem ready to follow suit. Likewise in Acts, the Holy Spirit seems unwilling to wait for the apostles to get with the program of outward expansion and instead uses "whosoever will" (i.e., Stephen, Phillip, etc.) to accomplish the mission. In fact, much of the first half of Acts shows the disciples trying to catch up to what the Holy Spirit is already doing!

It is a good reminder to us. Perhaps, rather than reign in our eager expectations in wait for God, we would do well to look for what the Holy Spirit is doing in venues outside of our comfort zones and seek to join (or more likely catch up) with that work.

To put it another way, I heard someone counter the question of the skeptic, "Where is God working in the world today?" with "Where is God *not* working in the world today?" This response is truer than we think; we only need eyes to see the Holy Spirit's work and presence in uncommon and possibly uncomfortable places.

2. God is more interested in radical inclusion than we are

We in the twenty-first century cannot fully comprehend the truly radical nature of a respected Jewish Rabbi partying with tax collectors, calling one of them to be his disciple (alongside a zealot), praising the faith of a Roman Centurion, and touching a leper. Likewise, for early Christians to enter the home of a Gentile, baptize an Ethiopian Eunuch, and declare the Jewish faith open to all people is a kind of iconoclastic change that sent ripples through the Middle East.

Pentecost lists fifteen nations that were represented at what is often considered the birth of the Church. Diversity, it seems, is the opening note. This continues through the middle of Acts, which is perhaps the most reorienting section of the New Testament, opening the faith to all people. And the final third of Acts is then devoted to Paul's missionary journeys in Gentile worlds and the trials that take him before a multiplicity world leaders.

While some people may be tempted to suggest that race and racism in the twenty-first century world is overblown or that good, Bible-believing Christians should not engage in such discussions, they have not considered Luke–Acts. Few topics are as ubiquitous as inclusion of outsiders, particularly across racial lines. Luke does not let us forget that God's heart is for the outsider.

3. Jesus' decentralizing statements about Jerusalem are shocking

As I was finalizing this work for publication, my wife and I got the chance to travel to the Holy Land for the first time. We hung out at the Sea of Galilee; visited the synagogue in Capernaum, where Jesus does his first miracle in Mark 1; climbed to the cliff of Nazareth, where the synagogue members attempt to throw Jesus off in Luke 4; and saw baptisms at the Jordan River. The best thing, though, was traveling to Jerusalem and hearing the stories of Jesus' last week in the actual locations where they happened. To remember his prayer in the Garden of Gethsemane, the Olivet discourse from the Mount of Olives, and all the teaching (and cleansing) he did on the Temple Mount made these stories with which I was very familiar come alive in a new way.[1]

The Talmud teaches that God gave ten measures of beauty to the world; nine were given to Jerusalem, and one to the rest of the world.[2] Jerusalem—the Holy City, the City of David. Imagine the shock when Jesus predicts its destruction. Imagine the

---

1. As it were, I have begun leading trips to Israel so others can have experiences like we had. See www.holylandventures.net if you're interested in more information.

2. *Kiddushin* 49b. The New Testament writings predate the Talmud, but it is likely that this sentiment reflects a real stream of thought dating back to the first century and before.

impact when Jesus, in the role of a prophet, calls out the corruption of its leadership and the wickedness of its religious leaders.

One of the benefits of research and contextual study is to try, as much as possible, to hear the text the way the original readers would have heard it. Jesus as a radical first century Jewish prophet is a lens we have too scarcely applied to him in the western Christian faith tradition. I'm afraid we miss a substantial level of shock when we read the scriptures without that lens. Focusing on Jesus' decentralizing of Jerusalem helps clarify and intensify the meaning of the story.

In the end, I hope this work contributes to the scholarly world of Luke–Acts by offering a new way to understand both Luke's aims for God-fearers and the decentralization that happens through his two volumes. I also hope that this work challenges you devotionally. I hope you are inspired to open Luke's gospel and reread some of the stories and narrative elements you may have missed before. I hope you are drawn to the characters in Acts who model what an uncommon, radical life in the Way looks like and whom it seeks to welcome. I hope you are moved by a religion that invites any who desire to commit to the mission and the community of faith, regardless of their nationality, skin color, family, or occupation.

I know I was.

N. Fox, July 2020

Acknowledgments

I am thankful to so many who assisted me and made this endeavor possible. This is *anything but* an individual achievement.

To God, who inspires, empowers, loves, and calls.

To my wife, Angela, who has been patient and supportive through years (and years) of advanced education. This is dedicated to you.

To Thorsten Moritz, who provided supervision and guidance throughout this process. It was not always easy, but it was always good and generative and helpful.

To Diane Holmquist for reading and editing an early draft of this, and to the other co-workers who checked in and offered support these last several years, particularly Gregg and Jeff, my brothers and prayer warriors.

To the wonderful people of South Metro Vineyard Church and the SG:Skyline small group who have been supportive with prayer, community, and fun. Nikki Bloom was kind enough to do some editing late in the process, which I greatly appreciate.

To supportive parents, for always cheering me on.

This would not be possible without you all.

Thank you.

Abbreviations

All abbreviations not listed here can be found in the *Society of Biblical Literature Handbook of Style* (Atlanta: SBL, 2014).

BangTF	*Bangalore Theological Forum*
BDAG	Bauer's Lexicon
IstanMitt	*IstanbulerMitteilungen*
ITQ	*Irish Theological Quarterly*
JHistSex	*Journal of the History of Sexuality*
JITC	*Journal of the Interdenominational Theological Center*
JOTT	*Journal of Translation and Textlinguistics*
JSQ	*Jewish Studies Quarterly*
NE	New Exodus
PRSt	*Perspectives in Religious Studies*

Introduction

My thesis is that Luke–Acts was written primarily for the purposes of creating identity for a God-fearing audience within the New Christian Movement of the first century CE. Social identity is typically formed by leveraging cultural memory in the audience through group beliefs, promise and fulfillment, prototypes and exemplars, and the tools of rhetoric. Methodologically, I will be looking for evidence of these elements in the text. For instance, group beliefs are an ongoing concern for Luke, although he will rarely state these beliefs explicitly. He primarily communicates them through narrative implications and character representations that the reader is attuned to. Constructing norms by story-telling, implications, and character representations is a powerful strategy for instilling group beliefs. Examining these elements will require particular attention to how the author connects the past with the audience's present. I will also look for promise and fulfillment patterns, taking special note of instances where Luke roots his story in the history of Israel. These patterns are strategically presented throughout the introductory material, vis-à-vis the canticles. These songs surrounding the birth of Jesus result in a trajectory of inclusion. Additionally, I will explore Luke's use of characters to further appreciate his creation of cultural memory through emulatable characters (prototypes and exemplars), noting how these characters engage the imagination of the audience. Again, Luke's method is not to state explicitly group norms for the audience, but to demonstrate them powerfully through narrative characterization. Lastly, I will be sensitive to the tools of rhetoric Luke uses to accomplish his goal of building social identity. These tools occur prominently in the speeches given in Acts 7 and 13 where Stephen and Paul recount a Jewish salvation history that extends to all people, paying careful attention to the mention of the names of important figures. It is necessary to view these speeches from two perspectives: first, their appeal to God-fearers (chapter 3) and secondly their rhetorical brilliance (chapter 5). We will see that rhetoric is a key way Luke builds a connection between his audience and characters for the purposes of building social identity.

In the case of Luke–Acts, the role of God-fearers seems crucial, as will be shown later. Methodologically, this raises the question of the relationship between any inherent claims of the text on a literary level and what may or may not have plausibly happened historically. Since God-fearers are only available to us as a literary phenomenon, the main focus of this study will be on Luke–Acts as literature. Any references to Luke's community are really references to the community projected by the text. However, there are some places where this literary approach will intersect with history. These are opportunities to use historical content as interpretive guardrails. In short, it will be crucial to distinguish conceptually between the literary and the historical, while being aware that the latter can serve as checks and balances for our reconstruction of the former.

Social Identity Theory is a relatively new but helpful approach to understand the social dynamics of human group behavior as well as what is happening socially in the biblical world. Chapter 1 lays the foundation for this theory and why it matters for identity formation in Acts. This primarily happens through the recounting of cultural memory and through prescribing norms, values, and behavior for the God-fearing audience. There is an ethic of behavior that Luke establishes for the early church that is central to building social identity.

Luke's focus for this task of identity formation is the God-fearing reader. The implied author's hope was that the implied audience would be willing to identify with the positive protagonists in the narrative, that is, the God-fearers. The "God-fearers" are Gentiles attracted to the synagogue and the God of Israel, but who have not taken the final step of conversion, i.e., circumcision. The historical question of the existence of God-fearers is a subject of much debate. Chapter 2 is a thorough exploration of the empirical evidence for God-fearers in the first century with a specific focus on their role in Acts. In addition, the role of God-fearers in Acts is part of a larger movement of decentralization that runs throughout Luke's two volumes. This decentralization is a movement away from the power structures of Judaism and a movement toward the inclusion of outsiders. Chapter 2 traces decentralization throughout the two-volume work of Luke–Acts.

Once it is clear that Luke is primarily attempting to create social identity in God-fearers in Luke–Acts, we must ask: if God-fearers are Luke's focus, why is he so concerned with connections to Israel and the Hebrew Scriptures? Chapter 3 examines these roots and reevaluates "the gospel" in a decentralized and robust way that considers God's activity in the Hebrew Scriptures (promise), including Israel's history as well as the current and future inclusion of all peoples (fulfillment). Luke sees Jesus' movement through an Isaianic lens, which lays the groundwork for the identity of God's people in Luke–Acts.

Having established Luke's inclusive aims rooted in Israel's history, it will be important to focus on his use of the tools of social identity theory to create social identity for God-fearers. A key feature in the creation of social identity is the utilization of prototypical characters and exemplars to prescribe belief and behavior to the target group. This strategy creates clear models for prospective members to emulate. Chapter

4 examines the use of prototypes and exemplars in scholarship and in Luke–Acts, including the primary prototype for God-fearers, Cornelius.

Finally, the task of communication is essential for the process of creating social identity. How will this information be communicated to the group? Chapter 5 looks at rhetoric in the ancient world as well as the rhetorical elements in Acts that help the reader develop social identity. Key to this end are the speeches given by Stephen and Paul in Acts 7 and 13 (respectively) that tell the story of Jewish salvation history through the lens of the New Christian Movement for the creation of social identity in the God-fearing readers.

Furthermore, a project like this lends itself to several important chapters where the author's strategy is clearly on display. For this project, the key chapters are Acts 5–8, 10, and 13. These chapters contain climactic scenes for us. However, Luke's gospel will be explored robustly, as it creates expectations for what will happen in Acts. It is necessary to delimit the project's scope to the first half of Acts, though, as most of the second half deals with Paul's extended trials. Some elements from the second half of volume two will be referenced, but only as they relate to my core argument.

Typically scholars have focused on issues such as genre, the prefaces, authorship, and purpose. Part of my contribution is to consider the question of God-fearers and social identity in a hermeneutically more refined manner. The differentiation between literary and historical aspects of interpretation is crucial in this regard. However, attending to these historical questions matters precisely to the extent that they affect interpretation.

The Genre of Luke–Acts

Many would agree with Pervo that, "Genre is one of the most hotly contested topics in the study of Acts."[1] The primary challenge comes from the nature of Luke–Acts being a two-volume work, for if they are considered volume one and volume two of a single work, as most scholars agree, the genres of the different volumes affect one another. "It is not obvious," Burridge says, "how a single work can have two volumes in two different genres."[2] Despite much discussion, three primary schools of thought emerge. The first is historiography. In this camp are scholars such as David Aune, Martin Dibelius, Colin Hemer, and Craig Keener.[3] There are certain variations of this understanding (i.e., historical monograph, rhetorical history, etc.), but each falls generally within

---

1. Pervo, *Acts*, 14.

2. Burridge, "Genre," 4. Not all agree these should be treated as a single work. See Pervo, "Genre"; Parsons and Pervo, *Rethinking*; Walters, *Unity*. In response to these objections, see Green, "Narrative Unity," 4.

3. Aune, *Environment*, 77–115; Dibelius; Hemer, *Acts*; Keener, *Acts*, 1:89: Some scholars prefer to be more specific, delineating this work as historical monograph. See Palmer, "Historical Monograph"; "Ancient Historical Monograph"; Plümacher, "Luke"; *Lukas*; *Geschichte*; "Stichwort"; Bovon, *Theologian*; Eckey, *Die Apostelgeschichte*.

the scope of historiography. The second category, perhaps one step removed from historiography, is novel or epic. Key scholars representative of this view are Richard Pervo and Dennis MacDonald.[4] This designation is mostly due to skepticism of Luke's trustworthiness as a historian, and an attempt to place him in another, less historically rigorous category. The third view is Acts as ancient biography. Key scholars taking this approach are Charles Talbert, Richard Burridge, Sean Adams, David Barr, and Judith Wentling.[5] Burridge's take is interesting in that he sees Jesus as the feature character of volume one of the biography, and the church as the feature character of volume two.[6] Each of these contributions has managed to enrich the discussion of the genre of Luke–Acts by highlighting specific elements of the text that cannot be ignored. Each of these theories allows for the implied author to create social identity in his implied reader, the God-fearer. As such, genre concerns are secondary to this thesis. However, it is noteworthy that the primary elements observed in ancient histories are battles and speeches,[7] the latter being a key focus of this monograph. In addition, Luke's strategic and dynamic use of characters suggests either biography or history as the most appropriate designations. Understanding Luke–Acts as a two-volume work of ancient historiography allows us to see Luke as both concerned with the rules of rhetoric and the narrative strategy of identity formation.[8] Thus, this thesis will proceed with the view of the majority of scholars, that Luke–Acts is historiography. However, even if one of the other theories were pursued, it would not negate the understanding of Luke forming social identity for his audience.

The Date of Luke–Acts

Dates proposed for the composition of Luke–Acts range from the Sixties in the first century into the second century. Most arguments for an early date see the author as a companion of Paul, and since there is no mention of Paul's letters, an early date is typically preferred.[9] However, these issues do not necessarily require an earlier

4. Pervo, *Profit*, 114; MacDonald, *Homer*.
5. Talbert, *Patterns*; *Genre*; Burridge, *Gospels*, 275–79; Adams, *Collected Biography*; "Genre"; Barr and Wentling, "Conventions."
6. Burridge, *Gospels*, 277.
7. Gempf, "Public Speaking," 261.
8. Keener, *Acts*, 1:116–47. For discussion of how ancient historians can be seen to be writing from different perspectives, see Keener, *Acts*, 1:148. Another compelling option that straddles the historiography and biography labels is Sean Adams's suggestion of "collected biography." This shares many of the benefits of history/historiography that are important to Luke–Acts, such as "opening features, mode of representation, metre, scope, sources, methods of characterization, setting, style/register, audience and purpose" (Adams, *Collected*, 170). Collected biography allows us to retain these features, but account for the fact that though Luke's gospel focuses on Jesus as the main character, Acts has several, and seems to focus on the presentation of these characters.
9. Longenecker, *Acts*, 31–34. For a discussion of whether the author was a companion of Paul, see section below, "The Authorship of Luke–Acts."

date of authorship. Even if the author was a companion of Paul, he could easily have written later.[10] The discussion of the Temple in Luke 21 seems to suggest that the work comes after its destruction in 70 CE.[11] In addition, most scholars see Luke using Mark's gospel as a source, following Papias, which is likely around that time, also pushing the date after 70 CE.[12] Pervo and others date Luke's writing later than 90 CE, suggesting that he used Josephus as a source.[13] This seems extreme, and an earlier date that fits within the majority view of 70–85 CE is preferable.[14] However, since this thesis makes a literary argument, certainty about the date is not as crucial to the task as some scholars assume.

Luke's Prefaces

The preface (also sometimes called "prologue") of Luke's corpus (Luke 1:1–4) as well as the parallel preface to volume two (Acts 1:1) have been of particular interest to scholars.[15] Many include discussion of Luke's preface with the considerations of genre or purpose, and these are noble quests, as it allows us to consider all of the information and allow the prefaces to provide clues for shedding light on these other matters. However, the interpreter must take care not to overburden the prefaces. Their role was to bring the reader to the narrative, not to foreclose it. Rather we must let the whole narrative drive the purpose. The preface itself does not yield enough information in isolation from the later dynamics of the text to determine the purpose. For example, "Theophilus" could be seen as symbolic representative of God-fearers.[16] This does not mean that "Theophilus" is necessarily historical or, by contrast, fictitious. Either of those options could be correct. There is nothing inherent in the author's vocabulary to overcome the interpretive ambiguities of the text. The preface itself is not sufficient to answer the central question of my work. The narrative dynamics of the entire Lukan corpus should inform our reading of the preface rather than the other way around. Of course the original reader encountered the preface before reading the whole narrative, but this allows for the preface and the narrative to hold a tension as

---

10. Johnson, *Luke*, 2.

11. Gaventa, *Acts*, 51.

12. Papias frg. 3.15. Also, see Brosend, "Means."

13. Pervo, *Dating*, specifically sees Luke's references to Theudas and Judas the Galilean on the lips of Gamaliel as sourced in Josephus, *Ant.* 18–20. Also, see Pervo, "Dating Acts"; Tyson, "Dates"; *Marcion*.

14. For scholars who date Luke–Acts in the 70–85 range, see Twelftree, *Spirit*; Johnson, *Luke*, 2–3; Brosend, "Means," 358; Windisch, "Case."

15. Robbins, "Claims"; "Prefaces"; Alexander, "Greek Preface-Writing"; *Preface*; "Formal Elements"; Adams, "Preface"; Brown, "Prologues"; Moessner, "Prologues"; Callan, "Preface"; Higgins, "Preface."

16. Alexander, *Preface*, 188, disagrees, seeing "Theophilus" as a real person, not as a purely symbolic name. Johnson, *Luke*, 28, by contrast, holds that "Theophilus" could be a representative title.

the reader explores the whole story. The narrative dynamics are specific enough to be far less ambiguous than the vocabulary used in the preface. Nonetheless, since the preface is such an important aspect of studies in Luke–Acts studies, it is worth some attention in this introduction.

Ancient writers included introductions as an essential feature of their works.[17] Introductions were seen as rhetorically sophisticated and handbooks advised including them.[18] Luke is the only gospel writer who includes a preface, and by doing so he thereby allows comparisons with others in the ancient world.[19] For Alexander, one of the foremost experts on the Lukan prefaces, Luke's version does not fit with the normal pattern in ancient history.[20] Adams challenges this, seeing the conventions as more fluid, and rightly looks beyond this feature to the larger work.[21] Elsewhere, Alexander concludes that Luke's prefaces "help us to resolve some long-standing questions about the genre of the two works."[22] Alexander's points stands, but to suggest that the preface carries enough weight to settle questions of genre without consideration of the narrative content of the book would be misguided. For Bovon, the preface sets forth "the motivation, purpose, and method of his work."[23] It helps establish Luke's goal of confirming the certainty (ἀσφάλειαν) of what his audience had been taught and providing an orderly (καθεξῆς) account.

The preface of Acts is shorter, with the author quickly switching to narrative after only a few words. Surely the implied audience of volume two is supposed to make connections back to volume one and use these as an interpretive frame for volume two. The focus of this preface is on the work as a whole, with a particular emphasis on the end of Luke (24:39–53).[24] Luke's second preface can afford to be brief since his intention is mostly to create a strong perception of literary unity. The mental activity of fleshing out the sense of unity is left up to the readers, therefore engaging them more fully. From this point forward the reader is effectively conditioned to reconstruct the author's intended narrative dynamics of both volumes. Arguably, if the second preface succeeds in doing so, it will have made a significant contribution to the reading or listening experience.

---

17. Josephus, *Ap.* 2.2; Polybius, *Polyb.* 3.1.3–3.5.9; Virgil, *Aen.* 1.1–6.

18. *Rhetorica ad Alexandrum* 29, 1436a.33–39; Dionysius of Halicarnassus, *Thucydides*, 19; Lysias, *Orationes*, 24.

19. Alexander, *Preface*, 23–41.

20. Alexander, *Preface*, 26–34.

21. Adams, "Preface," 190–91.

22. Alexander, *Acts*, 42.

23. Bovon, *Acts*, 16.

24. Chance, *Acts*, 34; Aune, *Literary Environment*, 135; Parsons, *Departure*, 189–90; Marguerat, *Les Actes*, 48.

INTRODUCTION

The Authorship of Luke–Acts

With our focus on narrative dynamics, we need to move beyond scholarship's preoccupation with empirical authorship. Having said that, given the prevalence of these questions in scholarship, they cannot be avoided. This work aims at reconstructing the world projected by the author. While most scholars interpret "author" as a reference to the empirical person who wrote the text, it is far more important to understand the implied author projected by the text. Of course, to the extent that knowledge of the empirical author helps in reconstructing the implied author, it should be pursued. Curiously, most scholars who ask the empirical authorship question do little to advance any reconstruction of the implied author. This seems hermeneutically weak because, for purposes of actual interpretation of the text as it stands, we must engage the implied author. Not doing so would mean to compromise interpretation, not least because it would fail to use implied authorship for purposes of checks and balances in speculating about the empirical author.

The notions of the "implied author" and the "implied audience" are clearly distinct from the "empirical author" and "empirical audience."[25] Lundin, Walhout, and Thiselton discuss this differentiation in *The Promise of Hermeneutics*.[26] They distinguish between *reference*, "the relationship of the language of the text to the world that is projected by the language," and *mimesis*, "the relationship of the fictional world projected by the text to the actual world that we inhabit."[27] Texts create models of reality, which the authors call "thought-systems" or "world-pictures" that are different than actual, historical reality. However, they go on to suggest that the audience must have some prior notion of reality, asking "How is it possible to identify what fiction gives us as a world-picture unless we have some idea of what a world-picture is? The only source of and basis for that prior idea is the actual world we encounter in our experience."[28] Thus, while my argument is about the implied author and the world projected by the text, at times the empirical realities of the first- and second-century worlds will serve to critique or validate our interpretations of Luke's narrative projections.[29]

Given the very limited data available to us, we need to be extremely cautious about drawing major conclusion from speculations about empirical authorship. Also, "the fictional text is not to be thought of as a carbon copy or mirror of the world, but it is nevertheless anchored in the world."[30]

---

25. See Booth, *Fiction*, from whom I am borrowing the term "implied author." Also, Krieger, "Empirical Reality"; Juhl, "Implied Author."

26. Lundin et al., *Promise*. Also, see Iser, *Reading*, 68; Todorov, *Poetics*; Ellis, *Theory*; Riffaterre, *Semiotics*; Moritz, "Critical."

27. Lundin et al., *Promise*, 74. For more on the history of mimesis, see pages 18–19.

28. Lundin et al., *Promise*, 75–76.

29. These points will be God-fearers in chapter 3 and Rhetoric in chapter 5.

30. Lundin et al., *Promise*, 79, suggest, "The fictional text is not to be thought of as a carbon copy

"Virtually everyone recognizes authorial unity" in Luke and Acts.[31] That a man named Luke is the author was "a long-standing tradition" that dates to the oldest extant manuscript of the Gospel of Luke.[32] Many scholars have connected this with the character mentioned in Philemon 24, Colossians 4:14, and 2 Timothy 4:11. The most interesting of the internal evidences are the "we" passages (Acts 16:11–17; 20:5–15; 21:1–18; 27:1–29; 28:1–16),[33] which some see as placing the author as an eyewitness of the events and a companion of Paul.[34] Others suggest that the "we" passages in Acts are a mere literary convention, seeing all seemingly historical evidence as a way to "heighten its appearance of authenticity . . . to give [the] work credibility and 'tone.'"[35] Other scholars understand the "we" passages as the reflection of a convention for sea travel.[36] Finally, still others hold that they are the result of using a travel journal as a source.[37] Regardless of the empirical author, the implied author seems to be writing from the perspective of an eyewitness in these few chapters.

Most scholars identify Luke as a Gentile,[38] while others suggest that the author was either Jewish[39] or a God-fearer.[40] For the majority, the author was a Gentile.[41] Most of the arguments used against Luke being a Gentile are pertaining to his knowledge of the Hebrew Bible and the Jewish world. A God-fearing identity would solve that problem. If the reference in Colossians 4:14 is to the implied author of Luke–Acts, he is a Gentile, as in 4:11 the author suggests a different subset of people as the only Jewish Christians he considers co-workers. Also, Acts 1:19 refers to the Field of Blood

---

or mirror of the world, but it is nevertheless anchored in the world."

31. Powell, *Acts*, 6. Some scholars who dispute common authorship between Luke and Acts are Argyle, Clark, and Wenham.

32. Fitzmyer, *Acts*, 50.

33. This is the list espoused by Porter, *Paul*, 42–46, and narrowly defines the "we passages" as explicitly including "we." Others, such as Campbell, *We Passages*, 406, and Keener, *Acts*, 3:2350, see a more expanded list that includes 20:16–21 and 27:30–44. For more on the "We" passages, see Porter, "Excursus."

34. Fitzmyer, *Acts*, 50; Plümacher, "Historian"; Campbell, *We Passages*, 90–91; Dupont, *Sources*, 164–65; Rackham, *Acts*, xv–xvii; Neil, *Acts*, 22–23; Munck, *Acts*, xliii; Thornton, *Der Zeuge*, 83–85; Arrington, *Acts*, xxxii; Jervell, *Apostelgeschichte*, 66, 82; Hemer, *Acts*, 312–14; Schnabel, *Acts*, 669; Gilchrist, "Eyewitness Reporting."

35. Pervo, *Profit*, 57, 115–38.

36. Robbins, "Land."

37. Barrett, *Acts*, xxvii–xxx. For a full discussion of the travel journal view, see Dupont, *Sources*, 113–65. This last view, that the implied author is writing as an eyewitness and companion of Paul for these sections, has the most scholarly support.

38. Bock, *Luke*, 1:6.

39. Denova, *Things*, 230–31; Malina and Pilch, *Acts*, 7; Ellis, *Luke*, 52–53.

40. Tuckett, *Luke*, 63; Ray, *Narrative Irony*, 165–70. Some entertain both possibilities of a Jewish or a God-fearing author, such as Jervell, *Theology*, 5; *Apostelgeschichte*, 50–51; Sterling, *Historiography*, 328.

41. Fitzmyer, *Luke*, 1:42–47; Pesch, *Die Apostelgeschichte*, 27; Hotze, "Christi Zeugen," 29–35; Doohan, *Acts*; Pervo, *Acts*, 7. While most scholars do not consider the implied author, their reasoning can nonetheless be used for reconstructions of the implied author, at least to some extent.

that Judas's body fell into as Ἀκελδαμάχ "in their language." The strongest argument would support the assumption of a Gentile with considerable knowledge of the LXX and the Jewish religion, whether or not he was a God-fearer.

Luke's Purpose(s)

Although I am arguing that Luke's primary purpose is to create social identity for a God-fearing reader, "most authors give a combination of [purposes for Acts] because of the complexity of the problem."[42] Thus, we need not be limited to one stated purpose at the exclusion of the others. It is also important to consider both volumes (Luke and Acts) for any purpose claims, although because of the uniqueness of Acts in the New Testament, it often receives more attention in deciding a purpose for the two-volume work.

One possible purpose is that Luke is interested in describing the spread of Christianity from Jerusalem to Rome.[43] If so, the focus is on the reporting of history, and it does recognize the geographic move away from Jerusalem. There is certainly a sense that Luke is communicating history to his audience.[44] However, this does not give due weight to the author's narrative movement beyond Jerusalem nor does it fully understand the strategy employed from a social identity perspective.[45]

Another consideration is that Luke is writing with a missionary motive.[46] This view has some merit and intersects with my work nicely. Unnik notes the particular importance of the term σωτηρία in Luke's writings.[47] Dibelius states that the purpose is "to acknowledge in adoration what the gospel is and how it conquers men."[48] I will argue that Luke's aim is the creation of a social identity for a God-fearing readership, which includes evangelism as part of that process, but sees God-fearers as recognizing Christianity as part of Israel's story.[49] Nonetheless, Luke's emphasis on evangelism can hardly be questioned, as this may be the reason for the surprise ending of Acts,

---

42. Unnik, "Confirmation," 42. Also, for other surveys of purposes, see Schneider, "Der Zweck"; Maddox, *Purpose*; Powell, *Saying*, 13–19; Keener, *Acts*, 1:435–58.

43. Unnik, *Confirmation*, 39–40.

44. Consider the prefaces (Luke 1:1–4; Acts 1:1), where the communication of historical information seems central, as well as reference to historical figures (Luke 1:5; 2:1–2; 3:1–2; 13:1; 23:1–3; 25:13; 26:30; Acts 4:6; 5:34; 11:28; 12:1; 13:7; 18:2, 12; 22:3; 23:24, 26; 24:24, 27; 25:1, 13, 26). Also, see Bruce, *Acts*, 22; Maddox, *Purpose*, 21, 186.

45. See chapters 2 and 3 on God-fearers and Decentralization.

46. Unnik, *Confirmation*, 40. Unnik also speaks of a "preaching" motive, 41–42, which is unclear how he differentiates a missionary motive from a preaching motive. Also, see Larkin, "Recovery"; Liefeld, *Interpreting*, 31. Some counter this idea that Luke intends to convert Theophilus, as the preface suggests that he has already been instructed in the gospel tradition (Luke 1:4). See Stanton, *Preaching*, 29–30; Maddox, *Purpose of Luke–Acts*, 20.

47. Unnik, *Confirmation*, 50–53.

48. Dibelius, *Aufsätze*, 117.

49. See chapter 3, "The Gospel and Decentralization."

seeing the gospel go forth unhindered.⁵⁰ That is, the author expects the reader to take up the call of discipleship and continue the ministry of the characters in Acts.⁵¹ Other possible reasons for the surprise ending include the belief that Luke planned to write a third volume,⁵² that his purpose for writing had been accomplished by the end,⁵³ or that he did not want to end on Paul's martyrdom, possibly to avoid potentially inappropriate parallels with the death of Jesus in volume one.⁵⁴ However, the emphasis on continued mission is the best choice.⁵⁵

Other options for the purpose of Luke–Acts are that he was writing an apology for or a defense of Paul, Christianity, or the Gentile mission.⁵⁶ Unnik notes the neutral or favorable reaction of many Roman officials,⁵⁷ compared to the reaction of Jewish authorities. He suggests correctly, though, that this can only be a secondary motive, as many features cannot be explained away if this is the primary purpose of Luke–Acts.⁵⁸ Related to this idea is the suggestion that there is an anti-Jewish purpose to Acts, however, Unnik rightly rejects this idea quickly, as the Jewish people remain central to the Christian movement throughout.⁵⁹ We find in Luke–Acts the aim to place Jesus and Christianity within salvation history.⁶⁰

Finally, it has been suggested that one of Luke's purposes was instruction or edification.⁶¹ There is undoubtedly an element of instruction in Luke's writings. Adams, for example, mentions that this is the one word (διδάσκω) present in the first verse

---

50. Keener, *Acts*, 1:437. It should be noted that though this seems like a surprise ending to many, including some ancient readers, open endings were common in the ancient world. See Adams, *Collected Biography*, 233–42; Lee, *Sense*; Marguerat, "Enigma," 304; "'Et quand'"; *La première*, 333; *Historian*, 216–16.

51. For more on this challenge to the reader to continue the unfinished mission, see Karris, *Invitation*, 15; Goppelt, *Apostolic*, 9; Rosner, "Progress," 232–33; Willimon, *Acts*, 192; Backhaus, "Im Hörsaal."

52. The theory that Luke planned to write a third volume seems to ignore the narrative aim of Luke–Acts, and the emphasis on characters, speeches, and fulfilled promises that we see in the two volumes. There is just one unresolved element in Acts, that is the fact that Paul remains in prison. It does not foreshadow future events, as Luke 21:12–19 does for Acts. For arguments suggesting a planned third volume, see Winandy, "La finale"; Zahn, *Die Apostelgeschichte*; Ramsay, *Traveler*, 184. For criticisms of this view, see McGiffert, *Apostolic Age*, 418n1; Rackham, *Acts*, xxxviii; Bock, *Acts*, 757.

53. Bailey, "Why"; Spivey et al., *Anatomy*, 267.

54. Spencer, *Acts*, 241; Aune, *Literary Environment*, 118; Trompf, "Declined."

55. For an overview of views on the ending of Acts, see Omerzu, "Das Schweigen."

56. Unnik, *Confirmation*, 40–41. For defense of Paul, see Tannehill, *Acts*, 329. Also, see Donfried, "Attempts"; Hengel, *Acts*, 60; Kent, *Jerusalem*, 17; Downing, "Law," 148; Bruce, "Apologetic"; Puskas and Crump, *Introduction*, 143–46; Rothschild, *Rhetoric*, 65–66.

57. He points to Acts 16:35–40; 22:25–29; 23:29–35; 26:30–32; 28:18–22.

58. He cites, for example, the story of Ananias and Sapphira, which I discuss in detail in chapter 4.

59. Unnik, *Confirmation*, 41. For example, Paul regularly returns to the synagogue to preach even after he separates himself from the Jews (Acts 13:46; 18:6; 19:9). See also Klausner, *From Jesus to Paul*.

60. Wright, *People*, 373–75; Larkin, "Recovery"; Miller, *Empowered*, 42–43.

61. Unnik, *Confirmation*, 41.

and the last verse of Acts.[62] However, Unnik criticizes this view, asking, "how did these materials serve the purpose?"[63] In other words, if Luke intends to teach, what is he teaching and how does that serve a larger purpose? I argue that the instruction of norms, ideologies, goals, and values are an attempt to create social identity in an outgroup looking to become an ingroup.[64]

Scholarly Precedent

As a final word of introduction, this monograph operates under the notion that Luke's primary concern is to connect with a God-fearing audience. Other scholars have previously made this argument, most notably John Nolland. This project seeks to leverage those arguments and move to the important work of seeing the difference that this understanding makes in the way we encounter the text. I am moving beyond Nolland by focusing on seeing Luke–Acts as a two-part work written to create social identity in a God-fearing audience. However, a short summary of the argument is appropriate here.

Nolland makes the case that the ideal reader for Luke–Acts is a God-fearer because "Luke [makes] considerable use in his argumentation of reader-assumptions which could only be true for people whose religious values had been considerably shaped by first-century Judaism."[65] He argues that many of Luke's arguments would be unintelligible to Hellenistic Gentiles.[66] More positively, he notes the great lengths Luke goes to in order to counter the claim that Jesus is a false Messiah, present Jesus and his death in the tradition of the Old Testament prophets, and highlight the universal scope of God's plan that embraces both Jews and Gentiles.[67]

The advantage of Nolland's approach is that it preserves many of the traditional reasons for assuming Luke was writing to Gentiles, while better explaining the remarkably Jewish nature of Luke–Acts.[68] It helps demonstrate why the mission in Acts continues to both Jews and Gentiles, and also the rejection by some Jews.[69] It is God, the Spirit, who "overcomes the solidly conservative scruples of the early Christians

---

62. Adams, *Collected Biography*, 244. See also Pervo, *Dating*, 36.
63. Unnik, *Confirmation*, 41.
64. See pages 34–46.
65. Nolland, *Luke*, 1:xxxii; Nolland, "Luke's Readers," 241.
66. For example, he mentions Luke 21, the "Temple logion," as a specific polemic that could only be understood by "people familiar with the Jewish thought world" and who "identify themselves with the fortunes of the Jerusalem Temple." This is also contra the common notion that Luke–Acts is to a Gentile readership with a focus on God's shifting interest from Jews to Gentiles. See Nolland, "Luke's Readers," 1–128, 241.
67. Nolland, "Luke's Readers," 242.
68. Nolland, "Luke's Readers," 3.
69. Nolland, "Luke's Readers," 244. Nolland notes that this was common in Jewish history and actually accelerates the advancement of the Gospel.

about the acceptance of Gentiles."[70] Furthermore, Nolland claims that Christianity is evaluated in Luke–Acts using the norms of early Judaism, something that is best explained by a readership composed of God-fearers.[71]

Nolland concludes, "[God-fearers] may not have been the only people for whom he wrote, but it is clear that he wrote with them very much in mind."[72] Likewise, Luke may well have a wider agenda than simply a God-fearer focus, but "the suggestion here proposed should not be taken in a limiting way but should only be considered to the degree that it provides focus for important strands within Luke's project."

We will proceed assuming that Luke wrote primarily for an audience of God-fearers and for purposes of creating social identity for this group. Chapter 2 will elaborate in greater depth the background of God-fearers as a group and examine relevant scholarship.[73]

---

70. Nolland, "Luke's Readers," 243.

71. Nolland, "Luke's Readers," 245.

72. Nolland, "Luke's Readers," 245.

73. As I was preparing this work for final publication, it came to my attention that Coleman Baker, author of *Identity, Memory, and Narrative in Early Christianity*, had been convicted of criminal charges. I immediately took steps to minimize his presence in this work and removed all references to him except where it was absolutely necessary in footnotes for reasons of intellectual property. The reader should also note that Baker's work is no longer in print.

1

Social Identity in the Early Church

SOCIAL IDENTITY TELLS US who we are. It comes from the process of connecting an individual with a group as well as distinguishing that person from other groups. Social Identity Theory may be defined as "that *part* of the individual's self-concept which derives from their knowledge of their membership of a social group (or groups) together with the value and emotional significance attached to that membership."[1] As such, they adopt the stories and narratives of those groups and share them as their own. This process forms social identity. "Remembering [the past] creates a history that provides a coherent continuity out of the discontinuities of all human experience."[2] For Lieu, "remembering" is closely connected with the stories we tell as individuals and groups.[3]

Henri Tajfel and John Turner were the leading authorities in the early days of social identity theory. In researching categorization and intergroup conflict, comparing their findings against other research in the 1960s and 1970s,[4] Tajfel and Turner laid out an early definition of Social Identity Theory: "Social groups . . . provide their members with an identification of themselves in social terms . . . [which are] relational and comparative: they define the individual as similar to and different from, as 'better' or 'worse' than, members of other groups."[5] Thus, we see here early versions of three elements of social identity that defined Tajfel's contributions for years to come, that is, that social identity contains a cognitive (self-awareness of group membership), an evaluative (positive or negative value coming from group membership), and an

---

1. Tajfel, *Social Identity*, 5.

2. Lieu, *Christian Identity*, 62.

3. For example, in *Christian Identity*, 62–63, Lieu says, "For individuals, this remembering is often expressed through one's 'story,' a self-narrative that gives meaning to the present, although such stories can never be entirely separated from the norms and expectations of the particular social context. . . . In some contexts, of course, the individual's story will be inseparable from that of the group of which s/he is a member."

4. For example, the Realistic Group Conflict Theory (RCT) of MuzaferSherif and D. T. Campbell. See Tajfel and Turner, "Integrative Theory," 33.

5. Tajfel and Turner, "Integrative Theory," 40.

emotional component (emotion about ingroup or outgroup).⁶ In short, Social Identity Theory is a social science that studies group membership, attributing value and worth to individuals through their participation in an ingroup, over and against other outgroups. It proposes that a person's sense of who they are depends on the groups to which they belong. This is the foundation of a trajectory of scholarship that would continue to grow and develop over decades.⁷

It was in the early 1990s that Social Identity Theory was first applied to the Bible. Philip Esler describes a "eureka" moment when, having encountered the work of Tajfel and Turner, he was "amazed and delighted by the potential for fresh interpretation of the New Testament evident in Tajfel's ideas."⁸ This led to Esler's paper at the British New Testament Conference in 1994.⁹ Thus, the relationship between the Bible and Social Identity Theory is relatively new. Meanwhile, the theory has grown and expanded to the point where there are numerous tools and scholars each bringing their influence and expertise to the world of Social Identity Theory.

Cultural Memory and the Early Church

Within the landscape of Social Identity Theory, there is a stream of scholarship that represents something unique and helpful for this project. Liu and László represent a leading edge of research on the creation of social identity among groups, and particularly the key role that stories play in identity formation. "Studying how people tell

---

6. Esler, "Group Norms" 159.

7. Although not exhaustive, this provides a somewhat chronological reading list of some of the developments in Social Identity Theory that pertain to this work over the course of the last fifty years. This first group of texts may be thought of as the early years, when the theory was emerging out of the 1970s and early 1980s: Barth, *Ethnic Groups and Boundaries*; Tajfel, "Social Categorization," 61; "Le Categorisation Sociale"; *Differentiation*; "Experiments"; *Intergroup Relations*; *Human Groups*; Turner, "Cognitive Redefinition"; Tajfel and Billig, "Similarity." Notably, in 1986, Tajfel and Turner published their co-authored piece "The Social Identity Theory of Intergroup Behavior," significant because it highlighted the differing biases between personal identity and social identity. By this point, Social Identity had become a legitimate player in the marketplace of psychological and sociological studies. This might be thought of as the golden age of the theory: Tajfel and Turner, "Social Identity Theory of Intergroup Behavior"; Turner, "Current Issues in Research"; Turner et al., "Self and Collective"; Wattenmaker et al., "Linear Separability," 159; Smith and Zarate, "Exemplar and Prototype Use"; Bar-Tal, *Group Beliefs*; *Shared Beliefs*, 5. As a new millennium approached and dawned, a new generation of scholarship engaged in the world of Social Identity Theory, which would eventually make its way into biblical studies (see note 8): Brewer and Brown, "Intergroup Relations"; Brown, *Group Processes*; Lamont and Molnár, "Study of Boundaries"; Douglas, *Purity and Danger*; Fuller, "Contesting Boundaries"; Liu and László, "Narrative Theory," 87–88. While some of the theory is now somewhat dated, enough progress has happened within the discipline to make Social Identity Theory crucial for interpretation.

8. Esler, "Group Norms," 148.

9. Subsequently published; see Esler, "Group Norms," 147, where he adds an introduction explaining the story of encountering Social Identity Theory. For other examples of Social Identity Theory and the Bible, see Esler, *Conflict and Identity*; "Prototypes"; "Outline"; O'Loughlin, "Sharing Food."

and understand stories, including performances of their own history or mythology, enlightens us about the process of how a group creates a social reality."[10] They quote Assmann, who distinguishes between cultural and communicative memory. Communicative memory is "from the proximate past, shared with contemporaries. . . . Cultural memory, on the other hand, goes back to the supposed origins of the group. Culture objectifies memories that have proven to be important to the group, encodes these memories into stories, preserves them as public narratives, and makes it possible for new members to share group history."[11]

Both of these types of memory are at work in the communities of the early church. On the level of history, it appears that those who followed Jesus during his public ministry shared their personal stories, which found their way into the culture of the early church and the Gospels. Some key features of this story appear in the sermons in Acts. Since the early church met mostly in small house communities, we can expect that telling stories of these shared communicative memories played a key role in their fellowship.[12] Many people who had encounters with Jesus during his public ministry and were a part of the early Christian community would have shared in this communicative memory. However, this may have faded rather quickly, as these people are beginning to die.[13] Within a few decades the church would have been removed from the teachings and life of Jesus, marking the end of the span of communicative memory.[14] So how did later converts, those who did not know Jesus during his earthy ministry, and those who did not even share in the Jewish customs, share in the story? In light of our empirical assumptions, what do we make of the "God-fearers," the group of Gentiles in Acts who are attracted to the God of Israel, but have not converted to the Jewish faith (the presumed implied audience of Luke–Acts)? This is where the process of cultural memory comes in. Cultural memory makes it possible for later group members to share in the identity-forming experiences through group narratives. This is key for social identity formation and allows for ongoing group membership generations after the foundational events took place. Cultural memory preserves these stories for future generations.

The question I am addressing here is this: how did the God-fearing readers of Luke's narrative experience social identity in a world where they were outsiders to both the Greco-Roman world and the Jewish religious system of the day? Hogg and others, in writing about "Uncertainty Identity Theory" (a theory conversant with the

---

10. Liu and László, "Narrative Theory," 87–88.

11. Liu and László, "Narrative Theory," 88; Assmann, *Das kulturelle Gedächtnis*. Also, see Volf, *Memory*. Assmann suggests that communicative memory dies out with the people who experienced those memories. In other words, communicative memories are the memories that never become cultural memories.

12. Banks, *Community*, 35–36; Gehring, *House Church*.

13. "A characteristic example is generational memory that emerges in time and decays with the death of its carriers" (Liu and László, "Narrative Theory," 88).

14. Liu and László, "Narrative Theory," 88.

Social Identity Theory of Tajfel and Turner), suggest that when self-related uncertainty is high, the need to belong to a well-defined group is also high, as belonging to a group is one of the most effective ways to reduce self-related uncertainty.[15] Perhaps the people with the most acute need for a greater certainty of identity in the Roman Empire in the first century were the God-fearers, making them adesirable target for social identity formation by Luke.[16] Note the words of Nolland: "Such a God-fearer would have experienced the ambiguity of his situation in Judaism: welcomed, but at the crucial divide still considered to be an outsider to the promises of God. . . . He has not fully found his way into Judaism, and now he stands at the crossroads."[17] Thus, Luke's audience is among those who most need to have their identity shaped through group membership, and make our question of how this identity is formed in the text of Acts all the more relevant.

How might the social identity-forming process show itself in the book of Acts? Since this group of God-fearers was largely not among the group that had followed Jesus during his ministry, this group's social identity is constructed through cultural memory, rather than their own personal stories of first hand experience.[18]

Social Identity: A Survey of the Scholarship

Although much of the work done in the twenty-first century focuses on the identity of self in a western context, it is important to distinguish this from my work. When we begin to talk about the study of identity, we observe a major watershed in the literature. Identity work in the twenty-first century mostly has to do with the ego and the identity of the self, rooted in a western, individualized context. It aims to address agency, life-stages, cultural assumptions, and the like.[19] That is outside of my interest in this project. My research is not focused on personal, psychological identity, but on social identity as is mediated through groups and is extended to individuals by means of group membership. This delimits the options for research and methods. Social Identity Theory, on the other hand, offers another branch of identity creation to explore that, although it has mostly been focused on modern, western identity

15. Hogg et al., "Uncertainty," 74.

16. I will establish, I believe Luke is primarily writing to a God-fearing audience to create social identity, which makes this point all the more acute.

17. Nolland, *Luke*, 1:xxxii.

18. Perhaps some examples of Gentile followers of Jesus do exist in the gospels, such as the Canaanite Woman (Matt 15:22) or the Centurion in Luke 7 and Matthew 15, although Luke does not mention if these people were ever part of the Christian community during Jesus' ministry, and furthermore, they are not God-fearers. It is possible that a public Rabbi such as Jesus drew a large enough crowd that some God-fearers may have heard Jesus teach during his ministry, but it seems rather unlikely that they had extensive experiences with him. Luke seems to present the Ethiopian Eunuch and Cornelius as the first of this type of convert in the early church. Thus, we do not know of a prominent God-fearing experience with Jesus before Acts 8.

19. See Cote and Levine, *Identity*.

formation and groups, applies quite well to an ancient, communal culture.[20] Before the work of Henri Tajfel, for example, the focus of identity research was very individualistic and personal in nature.[21] His ideas were radical at the time, as they suggested that the cognitive processes of categorization played a role in the way people judged themselves and others.[22] Thus, groups offer identity to their adherents. Liu and László came in the next generation of scholars who are writing on and interacting with these issues, standing on the shoulders of Tajfel, Turner, and others. The unique contribution of their work is on incorporating historical narratives in the way they understand social categorization and identity formation. Considering the way that historical narratives affect social categories is an important step forward in the exploration of this scholarship. "Historical narratives are stories that communicate symbolic and practical meaning over and above the 'bare facts' of history."[23]

Liu and László offer the most integrative explanation of the relationship between narrative/textual cultures with the use of story and social grouping in identity formation. They provide a schema for how identity is formed through cultural memory. Furthermore, they represent a non-Western take on the overlap of these topics.[24] The global perspective they bring, combined with a specific interest in the issues relevant to my research of the first-century new Christian community (i.e., identity, story, narrative, and groups) make them the most significant voice for our purposes. They combine history, the social/group nature of identity, and narrative in a helpful and unique way. Liu and László's definition of cultural memory provides a helpful starting point for developing a method for evaluating the construction of identity in the book of Acts. Note these elements, as they provide an outline for the work here:

---

20. Another important distinction to make is that there is a branch of scholarship that discusses narrative identity from an individual perspective, rather than a group perspective. For this perspective, see McAdams, "Narrative Identity," 99–115. Consider also Burke and Stets, *Identity Theory*, 3, who suggest, "the individual and society are linked in the concept of identity."

21. See Adorno et al., *Authoritarian Personality*; Sewell, "Golden Age." Also note that Tajfel's journey started in observing racism as a Jew in World War II Europe, but his work quickly influenced identity studies.

22. Tajfel stood on the shoulders of those who came before him. For example, see Mead, *Mind, Self, and Society*; "Nature"; Adorno et al., *Authoritarian Personality*; Festinger, *Cognitive Dissonance*; "Social Comparison"; Sherif, *Intergroup Conflict*. For Tajfel's works, see Tajfel, "Le Categorisation Sociale"; *Differentiation*; "Experiments"; *Social Identity*; *Human Groups*; Tajfel and Billig, "Social Categorization"; Tajfel and Turner, "Social Identity Theory."

23. Liu and László, "Narrative Theory," 87.

24. Janos László was an eastern European from Hungary, and a faculty member at the University of Pecs and has written and studies extensively on the overlap of story and identity. See http://pszichologia.pte.hu/prof-janos-laszlo?language=en. James Liu, while born in Taiwan and educated in America, describes himself as a "Chinese-American-New Zealander." Liu is the Co-Director of the Center for Applied Cross-Cultural Research and Professor of Psychology at Victoria University of Wellington, New Zealand and remains a world traveler and scholar. See http://www.victoria.ac.nz/cacr/about-us/people/staff/james-liu.

Cultural memory

 a. "goes back to the supposed origins of the group" and

 b. "objectifies memories that have proven to be important to the group,

 c. encodes these memories into stories,

 d. preserves them as public narratives, and

 e. makes it possible for new members to share group history."[25]

Liu and László identify some very important issues. Some authors, such as Aaron Kuecker, have previously applied these tools to the New Testament and the book of Acts.[26] Kuecker aims to present the Spirit as the creator of superordinate identity. I will also use the work of Smith and Zarate heavily, especially in the study of prototypical characters.[27] The work of these scholars, combined with social identity theory, provides a language and a context that serve my work of exploring the social identity creation in Luke–Acts.

What is lacking in these approaches, as helpful as they are, is focused attention on the literary nature of the text, especially the dynamics between the implied author and implied audience. It is here that I aim to enhance the methodological moves made by these scholars. It will be important to distinguish between the implied world projected by the text and the empirical world of the historical realities[28] in the first century of the Christian movement. As interpreters, our primary concern should be the former, that is, the projected world of the text. However, there are places where it will be necessary to consider the historical realities that informed the text's first-century perspectives, in order to show the plausibility of claims I will be making about the implied world of the text and the transformative aims of the implied author. We need to move back and forth between implied to empirical for purposes of checks and balances. Putting it differently, attention to empirical, historical realities should help delimit our interpretive options as we seek to reconstruct the text's projected world. Consequently, we have to work interdisciplinarily by combining the science of social identity formation with historical research into an ancient culture.

Once again, the concept of mimesis is important here. Plato and Aristotle were the first to discuss this literary feature, that is, the referential relationship between art and reality. The term became elusive in ancient philosophical literature and in modern

---

25. Liu and László, "Narrative Theory," 88.

26. Kuecker, *Spirit*. Another seminal author in the field is John C. Turner, a contemporary of Tajfel. See Turner, "Experimental"; "Henri Tajfel"; *Rediscovering*; "Social Comparison"; "Current Issues"; Turner et al., "Self and Collective." See also Baker, *Identity*.

27. See chapter 4.

28. This includes the empirical author, the intended audience, the cultural realities of the day, and the like.

scholarship.[29] Its discussion in ancient western philosophy gave rise to a rich tradition of commentary over the last two thousand years.[30] Defining mimesis as denoting that relationship between the implied and the empirical is relatively straightforward. Much more complex alternative definitions have been suggested.[31]

The work of Lundin, Walhout, and Thiselton helps solidify the accepted use of this term in modern times. They clarify that texts create world-projections that are distinct from the associated historical realities. Having said that, some connection between the projected world of the text and the real world must be assumed, for, as Walhout puts it, "if the text produces in our minds 'models of reality' or 'world-pictures,' how would we recognize these models unless we had some prior notion of reality or of a world?"[32] To put it another way, "The language of the text is used to project and thus to refer to an imagined world. And this imagined world stands in a certain relationship—a mimetic relationship—to the actual world outside or behind the text."[33]

Thus, over the course of this book there are three areas where it will be important—not least for purposes of check and balances—to look "behind the text" into the historical realities of the first century. The first area relates to God-fearers. They play an important role in Acts, and this work seeks to highlight and understand that role in order to determine more accurately how Luke engages what is likely a God-fearing audience.[34] For this to happen, we need to establish the actual likelihood of a group that we call "God-fearers" having existed in the first century, a question that has been much debated in scholarship.[35] Furthermore, attention to the historical evidence assists us in better determining the merits of a variety of scholarly claims. Chapter 2 explores these historical questions about God-fearers.

Secondly, this work examines the rhetorical tools used by Luke in the formation of his two volumes, as well as the rhetoric displayed by his characters, specifically Stephen and Paul. Understanding the role of rhetoric in the first century will help establish the likelihood that Luke was utilizing these tools in his argumentation. Chapter 5 is devoted to these matters.

---

29. Lundin et al., "Promise," 71. For more on the usage of this term by Plato and Aristotle, see Potolsky, *Mimesis*; Gebauer and Wulf, *Mimesis*. The modern work that seeks to create a unified theory of representation is Auerbach and Said, *Mimesis*. Plato discusses the concept primarily in *Ion* and *Republic* (II, III, VI, X) and Aristotle in *Poetics*.

30. Dautenhahn and Nehaniv, *Immitation in Animals*; Halliwell, *Aesthetics*; Lacoue-Labarthe, *Typography*. Gebauer and Wulf trace the history of the theory from Plato to more modern times.

31. Potolsky, *Mimesis*, 1, for example, suggests that Mimesis can appropriately mean "emulation, mimicry, dissimulation, doubling, theatricality, realism, identification, correspondence, depiction, verisimilitude, resemblance," and that "no one translation, and no one interpretation, is sufficient to encompass its complexity."

32. Lundin et al., "Promise," 75.

33. Lundin et al., "Promise," 76.

34. Nolland, "Luke's Readers," 3; *Luke*, 1:xxxii.

35. For the history of scholarship on the discussion of God-fearers, see pages 58–63 and the notations there.

Lastly, questions as to whether the persecution and martyrdom of Stephen may serve as a prototype for readers facing persecution will be addressed. This involves consideration of the historical evidence for the persecution of Christians in the first century.

Origins: "Cultural Memory Goes Back to the Supposed Origins of the Group."

Origins matter in the creation of social identity.[36] They matter even more for the creation of groups, as this is a key way the purposes and values of the group are understood and formed. Origin stories have a tribal quality to them, in that those on the inside feel a sense of ownership of the origin story of the group.

A great example of an origin story that goes back to the supposed origin of the group is the story of the exodus in Scripture. The phrase "supposed origin" is important here. Most entities have a multiplicity of points of origin. Is the point of origin of a business when the vision statement is written, or when land for the building is purchased, or when it makes the first sale? Likewise, there are many origin points in the formation of God's people that may be suggested, but the exodus is an iconic event that is referred back to again and again.[37] VanSeters states, "The birth of the nation [of Israel] was the exodus from Egypt."[38] This origin point situates God's people as freed and rescued because of the work of their God in a remarkable fashion, which Jesus will emulate in his ministry in Luke. The account of the exodus is an origin story of God's people that creates cultural memory.[39]

Watts employs the language of "ideology," which relates to origins.[40] He defines ideology as "that all-pervasive interpretive framework by which a group not only understands itself, but also justifies and projects itself over against other groups."[41] For Watts, "ideology is a function of the need of a group to provide a rationale for its existence.[42] He demonstrates persuasively that this can be seen in both the Old and New Testament narratives. The exodus has gone through the transforming filter of the book of Isaiah,

---

36. Lieu, *Christian Identity*, 14.

37. Other potential origin points could include the calling of Abraham, the life of Jacob, Joseph saving his brothers, the kingship of Saul or David, and others, although it seems clear that the Exodus works best as the example in this discussion.

38. VanSeters, *In Search of History*, 359. Also, see Watts, *New Exodus*, 3, who calls the Exodus Israel's "founding moment."

39. More will be said on the identity-forming elements of the exodus origin story later in the chapter.

40. Watts, *New Exodus*. Watts is doing similar work regarding Isaiah and identity as it relates to a gospel, in this case, Mark. Luke–Acts, although in two volumes, is also a gospel. See more on the genre of Luke–Acts at the end of this chapter.

41. Watts, *New Exodus*, 36.

42. Watts, *New Exodus*, 37.

who predicts the "New Exodus," which is to come.[43] The New Testament writers see the events of their day as effectively amounting to a New Exodus, and write accordingly.[44] There is an obvious correlation between cultural memory and this language of ideology. Thus, Watts can provide a helpful example and commentary of the process of detecting cultural memory in the New Testament Scriptures.

Any origins discussed regarding the early Christian movement must connect to Israel, the parent religion, in some way. Origins of the Christian story must have continuity with Israel and her story. This continuity with Israel is worth noting, and will be a consistent focus through this work. For Gillis, "The core meaning of any individual or group identity, namely a sense of sameness over time and space, is sustained by remembering, and what is remembered is defined by the assumed identity."[45]

While it might be assumed that the origins of Christianity are the formation of the church at Pentecost (Acts 2), or Jesus' birth (Luke 2) or the beginning of his ministry (Luke 4),[46] our starting point has to be Luke's attention to how the new community relates to the history and narratives of Israel. Joel Green says, "The proper 'beginning' for his narrative is *there,* in the past, in God's redemptive purpose as set forth in the scriptures. Luke is not introducing a *new* story, but continuing an old one,[47] as if the real 'beginning' were the Septuagint. He roots the coming of Jesus and the universal Christian movement in God's purpose, continuous as one divine story."[48] In addition, "Without that historical continuity any answer to the identity question can only be invented rather than discovered."[49] Lieu's words remind us that while Christianity was a new movement and seen by the early Christians as a new era in salvation history, it is unavoidably tied to Israel and her history, prophets, and message. For the God-fearer, then, to connect fully with Christianity, there is a certain familiarity needed with these elements of Israel's story. Judaism, like Christianity, is a story with rituals, identity markers, beliefs, and practices that go along with it. Luke sees this continuity with Israel as very important and seeks to preserve that in his works. "For the reader sensitive to the echoes, that means for the inside reader who knows her scriptures, or at least is familiar with their story, the narrative of Jesus from his birth, and of the church, shares much with and runs in continuity with that of Israel in the past."[50] It will be necessary to look for places where storytelling connects the past to the audience's present.

43. Watts, *New Exodus*, 4.

44. See New Exodus in chapter 2.

45. Gillis, "Memory and Identity," 3.

46. Note that both Israel and the church share a similar difficulty in pinpointing a single origin point.

47. The role of Israel's story as a key part of Luke's presentation of the gospel will be fleshed out in great detail in chapter 2.

48. Green, "Beginning," 66.

49. Lieu, *Christian Identity*, 97.

50. Lieu, *Christian Identity*, 93

There are multiple ways Luke connects Christian origins with contemporary narratives about Israel.[51] In the ancient world, antiquity was thought to be necessary for the authentication of a movement.[52] "Luke's emphasis on continuity with the biblical heritage was important to a movement that claimed ancient Israel's scriptures as their own as well as for a world that made antiquity a basic criterion of authenticity."[53] The first-century Roman world tended to be suspicious of new fad religions, and Luke does what he can to remove this stigma from Christianity. Keener adds, "It is the genius of [Luke's] story that he seeks to do so in a way that both affirms new revelation about the uncircumcised Gentile mission (throughout Acts) and grounds it in Israel's story (and especially the prophecies of Isaiah).[54] And, "[Early Christianity] apparently saw itself as following Israel's faith and certainly Israel's true king."[55] Thus, summarizes, Lieu, "More important for Christian identity, then, was this prior history that found its climax in Jesus than any subsequent one that took its start from him."[56]

Another way Luke creates continuity between the early Christian movement and Israel is with his genealogy. Jesus' baptism and beginning of his ministry affords Luke the opportunity to trace Jesus' heritage through important historical figures. Nolland points out several keys to understanding Luke's use of Jesus' genealogy here, two of which are helpful for our purposes: (1) Tracing Jesus' ancestry through David's son Nathan rather than Solomon, as Matthew does, and (2) the genealogy extending to Adam and ultimately to God, as opposed to Matthew who stops at Abraham.[57] Luke's identification of Jesus with Adam, the first human, and then calling him the son of God, fits nicely with Luke's emphasis on Jesus being the son of God, as well as the universal nature of Jesus' mission to all people in Luke. Luke also appears to be less concerned than Matthew with establishing Jesus' royal lineage, as shown through his tracing the lineage through Nathan and bypassing the kings of Judah.[58] Nolland notes that Luke is "less positive generally about the history of Israel [than Matthew]."[59]

Yet, Luke still includes a genealogy, and is thus clearly interested in connecting Jesus to his Hebraic roots. The genealogy not only creates identity for Jesus by connecting him to key figures such as Adam, Abraham, and David, but also speaks to the God-fearing reader of the text, showing, however subtly, that Jesus is the savior of all

---

51. We have good reason to assume that these narratives are available to God-fearers mostly through the mediation of synagogues.

52. Furthermore, the oldness of Judaism may have been what attracted God-fearers to the synagogue and the Jewish faith to begin with.

53. Keener, *Acts*, 1:459.

54. Keener, *Acts*, 1:459.

55. Keener, *Acts*, 1:467.

56. Lieu, *Christian Identity*, 94.

57. Nolland, *Luke*, 1:170. Nolland also comments on the location of the genealogy in Luke and "the identification of the beginning (ἀρχομένοι) referred to in v. 23."

58. Nolland, *Luke*, 1:170.

59. Nolland, *Luke*, 1:170.

people (Adam), not only Israel (Abraham and David). "Narrative connects individuals to a collective through symbols, knowledge, and meaning."[60] Adam, for example, is the first created human in Genesis and the father of all mankind, Gentiles included. Abraham is the first Hebrew, the father of the nation of Israel and of the coming Messiah. David is the great king of Israel whose line God establishes forever, creating a royal lineage, which Jesus belongs to.

Furthermore, each of these characters represents a duality in some way. Adam's two sons, Cain and Abel, both offer sacrifices to God.[61] Because Abel's sacrifice is better, Cain kills him. Abraham also has two sons who feud, Ishmael and Isaac, from different women.[62] One is chosen and one is not. David represents a duality of values. On the one hand, he symbolizes what is good about humanity as well as God's commitment to righting the wrongs of this world.[63] On the other hand, he also makes mistakes and wars with his descendants.[64] We see something of a continuation with this duality in all of the kings. The key criterion is whether they want to participate with God's narrative. Israel, too, lives in something of a duality. It represents the contrast between desirable and undesirable humanity, the struggle between the desire to be selfish, versus the call to be sacrificial. Luke presents a duality in Israel as well, between Jesus and those following him on the one hand, and the Pharisees, circumcision group, and other opponents on the other hand.[65] Thus, these are more than simply names on a genealogical list. Rather, they are symbolic representations of Israel's narrative reality, which extends all the way back to Adam and is for the whole world. Although I have only mentioned here briefly what will be fleshed out more fully in chapter 3, Luke's origin of the Christian movement does not start with Jesus, but with Adam, flowing through Israel. Jesus is the culmination of human history, especially with respect to Israel's salvation history and its fulfillment in Christianity.

Stories: "Cultural Memory Objectifies Memories That Have Proven to Be Important to the Group and Encodes These Memories into Stories."[66]

The origin story and other information worth remembering go through a process of objectification, where the stories, having something of a life of their own, leave the realm of personal stories and become objectified as group stories. It is no longer personal and relative, but shared, public, and living. These stories are at least somewhat

60. Liu and László "Narrative Theory," 87.
61. Gen 4:1–12.
62. Gen 16:1; 17:15–22.
63. 1 Sam 16–18.
64. 2 Sam 11–24.
65. Luke 5:21, 30; 6:2, 7, 11; 11:39–43; 12:1; 13:1; 15:2; 16:14; 19:39; Acts 4:5–7; 5:17–18; 15:5, 21–23, 27–42.
66. Liu and László, "Narrative Theory," 88.

shapeable by the community as they are retold.⁶⁷ An excellent example of this is the case of the four Gospels, where stories are shaped and arranged to fulfill the goals of the author, although the main story remains essentially the same. Another example is the way that the faith of the early church exists on collective and personal levels through the realm of shared events and experiences, but then, at some point, is codified into doctrine and shared with a wider group. In a similar way, cultural memories become official stories that can be shared among the group. We do not have reliable access to the memories that predate the formation of these stories, nor do we even have access to the shared stories, but only to the public performances and codified narratives of these stories (see below).

With an iconic event like the exodus, cultural memory is working on multiple levels. First, the memory is objectified in an official way, as it becomes the basis for the Passover meal. To the extent that the Passover meal was scripted and liturgical among all the people, it served this function as an encoded story.⁶⁸ It comes complete with a script, rituals, and imagery that help the Hebrew person relive the event in a ritualistic way every year. It also works on the level of national story. Although more on this will be delineated in chapter 2, specifically regarding Luke, two examples of how this ideology of the exodus functions among the New Testament writers will be helpful in the discussions of the codification of origin stories.

Markan Motifs

As we are exploring the role of cultural memory in social identity formation, it is hard to ignore the important work done in Markan scholarship. Irrespective of source theories about the literary relationships of the Gospels, the fact remains that these are first-century documents that offer us insight into the role of cultural memory. Our awareness of such texts that contain similar dynamics can also add plausibility to our reconstruction of Luke's purpose. Likewise, organizational schemas present in Mark can also be observed in Luke. For example, Watts points out that the Gospel of Mark is organized around several motifs that recall the exodus as reminders to the readers and hearers. He sees Mark 1:21—3:6 as covering the "sea motif," reflecting back to the passage of Israel through the sea and a place of deliverance.⁶⁹ There are six references to the sea, the lake, or water in the first three chapters of Mark. Mark 3:13—6:6 reflects

---

67. An example of the shapability of these stories might be seen in the way the exodus is understood and shaped for the New Testament writers in light of the Isaianic program. Since our minds tend to understand the new in terms of the old, we would expect the writers of Isaiah to see things in terms of the national event of the exodus, shaping the story as they did, and likewise the New Testament writers. See Watts, *New Exodus*, 38.

68. Watts, *New Exodus*, 37.

69. Watts, *New Exodus*, 19. In this section of the text, Watts is interacting with a number of other scholars regarding Mark's relationship to the Old Testament. See Piper, "Unchanging Promises"; Hobbs, "Mark and the Exodus"; Schulz, "Altes Testament"; Bowman, *Mark*; Schneck, *Isaiah*.

the Sinai event as it opens with reference to "the mountain" and involves longer teaching sections of Jesus, as well as the election of a new community.[70] At the end of this section (6:1–6), the rejection of Jesus at Nazareth echoes the golden calf incident from Exodus 32.[71] The next section, Mark 6:7—8:21, is reminiscent of the wilderness with sections discussing God's provision, guidance and testing, and the people's rebellion. Lastly, Watts sees the last section of Mark 11:1—16:8 as the Temple section, which represents "Mark's use of the Temple's fate to symbolize the failure of the Jewish mission (e.g., 11:12–25) and the success of the Gentile one (e.g., 12:1–12)."[72]

Passover

Watts introduces the practice of the Passover Haggadah as the second example of ideology from the exodus in the New Testament, calling it exemplary. "Here the community's history is retold, the values, energies, and ideals enshrined in its founding moment inculcated, and the community re-constituted through succeeding generations."[73]

As stated above, the Passover meal works so well as an ideology because it comes with a script, rituals, and imagery, which all help the Hebrew person reenact their history and relive the event of the exodus every year. The Passover is a national story to be passed on to children and future generations, passing on traditions, memories, and identity as God's people. It is no accident, of course, that in all four Gospels, this is the last meal Jesus eats with his disciples, albeit with certain changes made to center the ritual on Jesus, which are to be repeated.[74] The disciples are not only to remember their origin as the people of God when they practice the meal, but they are to remember their Messiah. This becomes an identity-forming ritual in the early church, as all who participate in it share in the origin moment of the church, created in the upper room.[75]

Public Narratives: "Cultural Memory Preserves Them as Public Narratives."[76]

These stories become public narratives when they are shared with the group. They become public in various ways, including orally, such as in public performances and speeches, as well as narratively through writing and the codification of stories in text

---

70. Watts, *New Exodus*, 19.
71. Watts, *New Exodus*, 19.
72. Watts, *New Exodus*, 20.
73. Watts, *New Exodus*, 37.
74. Matt 26:17–25; Mark 14:12–21; Luke 22:14–23; John 13:1–30.
75. Once again, multiple origin points could be suggested for the church, including perhaps the most common, the falling of the Spirit at Pentecost. See more under section on Origins below.
76. Liu and László, "Narrative Theory," 88.

form. The role of public performances in the first-century Roman world is well established.[77] Some even suggest that entire books of the Bible were written to be read aloud in public performances, as Greek Tragedies would have been.[78] Others, like Maxwell, simply note the audience's responsibility to fill in the gaps of the speaker.[79] More will be said on speech giving in chapter 5 on the use of rhetoric.[80]

New Members: "Cultural Memory Makes It Possible for New Members to Share Group History."[81]

Finally, once the key events and memories of the group are objectified into stories and shared publicly, new members are allowed to participate in the group history, even though they were not present for the origin. Converts to Judaism, for example, would have the benefit of being a part of the synagogue and participating in the tradition of interpretation that sees the exodus as central to the way they understand their history. Thus, they become members of the group by sharing in that history, although they were not a part of it. The past becomes the participants' present. This is normal with most origin stories. Consider, none of the Hebrew people were a part of the exodus after the original generation died out, yet that remains central to the identity formation of Israelites. The sharing of the tradition and language with new members allows them to be a part of the exodus story.[82]

This section begins the process by discussing the origins of the group (section a from Liu and László above) and the effect that lineage and origin have on the community of the early church. It will also explore Social Identity Theory and the mechanics of how identity is formed in groups, with the specific task of looking for evidence in the text of group beliefs. Chapter 2 examines the empirical data surrounding God-fearers and the focus on decentralization that runs through Luke's two volumes. Chapter 3 traces the thread of the Old Testament narrative through Luke–Acts and demonstrates how the important elements of promise and fulfillment became part of the Christian

---

77. See, for a few examples, Gempf, "Public Speaking"; Winter, "Official Proceedings"; Satterthwaite, "Acts in the Background"; Mirhady, "Oath-Challenge"; Halliwell, "Comic Satire." More will be discussed on this topic in chapter 5.

78. See Bilezikian, *Liberated Gospel*.

79. Maxwell, "Audience."

80. I am focusing on the role of speeches as a method of identity formation. I do not do redaction criticism, but rather, focus on the speeches as they are. My hope is that my approach is truer to the text as it stands. For more on redaction criticism in the speeches, see Gempf, "Public Speaking," 263; Mellor, *Tacitus*, 116; Porter, "Thucydides."

81. Liu and László, "Narrative Theory," 88.

82. Some important works to consider here are Riesner, *Jesus als Lehrer*; Gerhardsson, *Memory and Manuscript*; Riesenfeld, *Gospel Tradition*. While these volumes all represent elements of memory and transmission of the stories of early Christianity, they are important to be aware of, but they are different than my work. These arose as responses to form criticism. My concern is not source critical (for or against) but rather seeking to work with the narrative product.

story (sections b, c, and d). A key part of new members sharing ingroup history (section e) is establishing "a surface structure empathy hierarchy" and opens the way for "participatory affective responses."[83] Luke will use characters to engage the imagination of his audience. This is discussed in depth in chapter 4 on prototypical characters and exemplars. Last, chapter 5 offers an in-depth exploration and summary of how Luke uses the tools of rhetoric to strategically formulate identity in his audience, particularly using speeches.[84] These speeches connect the dots of Jewish salvation history for God-fearing readers and allow them to share in the cultural memory.

Social Identity Theory

Social Identity Theory provides a helpful set of tools to help evaluate identity formation in Luke–Acts. Social Identity Theory seeks to explain "intergroup discrimination and conflict, on the basis that 'individuals seek to differentiate their own groups positively from others to achieve a positive social identity.'"[85] "Social identity will be understood as that part of an individual's self-concept which derives from his [sic] knowledge of his [sic] membership of a social group (or groups) together with the value and emotional significance attached to that membership."[86]

There are three areas where Social Identity Theory will lend its terminology and thought process to this study of identity in Acts. Two of these, (1) the relationship of subgroups and superordinate groups and (2) group beliefs will be discussed here. The third, (3) prototypes, is discussed at length in chapter 4.

Subgroups and Superordinate Groups

It is well established in scholarship that people categorize themselves and others according to group belonging. Indeed, Tajfel describes the situation of two individuals from specific groups meeting as though "the plot is laid down before the actors ever step on the stage."[87] Esler adds, "No instances can be found in real life in which two people encountering one another would not be affected by their allocating one another to various social categories about which they had some preconceived ideas and attitudes such as gender, nationality, profession, and so on."[88] These categories help people make sense

---

83. Liu and László, "Narrative Theory," 96.

84. Another element that could be considered here is the boundary crossing rituals of first-century Christianity (i.e., water baptism, Spirit baptism, etc.). Although it falls outside of the scope of this present work, for a fuller discussion of these boundary-crossing rituals, see Lieu, *Christian Identity*; Calpino, "Opened."

85. Esler, "Outline," 24, quoting Turner, *Rediscovering*, 42.

86. Tajfel, "Social Categorization," 63.

87. Tajfel, "Intergroup Behavior," 423.

88. Esler, "Outline," 17.

of life as they break the world into smaller realities, smaller categories that are easier to conceive of. It has been said that human brains are cognitive misers—"they simply take well-worn shortcuts because they cannot always deal with other people in all their complexity."[89] That is to say, our brains save mental energy whenever possible. Evaluating people based on social groups helps preserve this precious mental energy. People are no longer experienced as billions of complex, unique individuals but are members of larger groups that are easier to comprehend.

Another reality present here may be the narrative substructure of the human mind. People tend to think in narrative categories, so arranging people in groups with narratives of origin and cultural memory serve this narrative mindset better. Liu and László, for example, suggest that narrative is a "universally human mechanism of communication and cognition."[90] From the perspective of the neuroscience of the brain, the "internal narrative" of the human mind cannot be overestimated.[91]

As an example, a traveler in the first century may encounter a man wearing a robe with tassels, and a long beard. This traveler is able to make a number of assumptions about this person on sight. First, the person is a male, which places him in a category with about half the people in the world and the attitudes and assumptions that go with being male in the patriarchal first-century world. His beard and tassels tell the traveler that he is Jewish, one of the children of Israel. This results in a much more specific classification. The Jews[92] were not a monolithic people by any means, but this man's appearance certainly separates him from the many other tribes and races who call the Middle East their home in the first century. The traveler is now able to make some broad assumptions about what this man believes religiously (monotheism) and certain rituals he keeps (Torah, purity laws, etc.).

Perhaps the man identifies himself as a Pharisee of the house of Hillel. The man has now been classified quite specifically according to his theological alignment, who his colleagues would be, and even the stances he likely takes on certain theological issues of the day. All of these assumptions allow the traveler to categorize this man whom he meets. He is no longer a random person, but he is part of a people and a tribe and a specific community that has a robust narratival heritage, complete with certain customs and norms. Even within this somewhat narrow classification, there is still much that is unknown and vast amounts of complexity remain with this man—his attitudes and

---

89. Fiske and Taylor, *Social Cognition*, 37.

90. Liu and László, "Narrative Theory," 87.

91. For modern interactions with this, see Siegel, *Mindsight*; Cozolino, *Human Relationships*; Scheib, *Pastoral Care*, 3–4. However, there is a rich history of this work that goes back several decades. For more, see McAdams, *Stories*; *Person*; Mink, "Narrative Form"; Sarbin, "Root Metaphor"; Spence, *Narrative Truth*; Howard, *Two Stories*; Linde, *Life Stories*; Damasio, *Feeling*; Roser and Gazzaniga, "Automatic Brains"; Brunner, *Actual Minds*; *Acts of Meaning*; Polkinghorne, *Narrative Knowing*; MacIntyre, *After Virtue*; Giddens, *Modernity and Self Identity*; Cohler, "Personal Narrative."

92. I am using the phrase "The Jews" exclusively in line with New Testament usage and therefore in a strictly sociological sense.

opinions on certain topics, what kind of father he is, what he likes to do for leisure, his moods, his family etc.—but the few assumptions the traveler has made and his knowledge of the culture help him to know better how to interact with this man.

What is more, in the honor and shame culture of first-century Palestine, the traveler may need to know how to show due honor to this man as he encounters him. Is he allowed to greet this man publicly as they pass on the road? If, for example, the traveler is a Samaritan woman, communication is not possible without breaking social norms.[93] This sort of group identification happens by people everywhere and at all times and can help us shed light on certain aspects of identity formation in the New Testament.

As mentioned previously, God-fearers are dealing with many social challenges in the first-century religious landscape. They are caught between the culture and religious traditions of the Jews on the one hand, and their own Greco-Roman heritage on the other. It is likely that God-fearers would perceive themselves as religiously inferior to the Jewish people—as Nolland says, "an outsider to the promises of God."[94] Tucker suggests that there are three ways in which a subgroup that perceives itself as inferior can respond. "First, the inferior group can, through action and reinterpretation if its characteristics, become more like the superior group. This will entail the assimilation of the group as a whole into the superior group (meaning the boundary between the two groups is removed and the first group disappears)."[95] Some God-fearers chose to take this path, get circumcised, and become proselytes (i.e., converted Jews), thus doing away with the class division.[96] Although this did not happen with many God-fearers, it was an option for some.[97]

Second the inferior group may reinterpret its characteristics in a new and more positively valued ways. Third the inferior group can invent new characteristics that establish a positively valued group distinctiveness.[98] Thus, perhaps God-fearers in the first century, though they may perceive themselves as inferior to the Jews at the synagogue on religious grounds, could take solace and identity from their higher wealth, or their greater education, or their social standing among the merchants in their village. Seeing things this way would allow them to identify themselves with the group of

---

93. As is the case with Jesus in John 4. Also, see Crook, "Honor"; Georges, "Shame to Honor"; Richards, "Honor/Shame Argument"; McVann, "Reading Mark Ritually"; DeSilva, "Noble Contest."

94. Nolland, *Luke*, 1:xxxii.

95. Esler, "Outline," 21.

96. It should be noted that though the conversion ritual of circumcision only applies to men, women can be seen to be included as well when considered in the context of household language. These references and categories of Jew, Gentile, and God-fearer appear in a patriarchal world that puts a high emphasis on the household, as evidenced by the narratives of Lydia (Acts 16:13–15) and the jailer (Acts 16:29–34). No gender disconnect was observed based on circumcision. It appears to have not risen in people's minds.

97. For example, Nicolas from Antioch, mentioned in Acts 6:5.

98. Esler, "Outline," 21.

wealthy merchants and gain value, which would help lessen the feelings of low value from their inferiority in their association with the synagogue.

The true solution to this division between groups, however, is for the members of these groups to overcome their differences by entering into close community. This creates a separate, superordinate identity in which both the Jew and the God-fearer are equally valued in terms of claims to honor and access to resources. This identity, rooted in Jesus, is what Christianity has to offer the God-fearer from a social identity perspective.

However, recategorization into a new superordinate group does not require that the subgroups and all of the meaning they carry be destroyed. Gaertner suggests that when "both the superordinate and the sub-group identities are salient"[99] form the most effective types of common ingroups.[100] Furthermore, promoting a common superordinate identity without threatening the original subgroup identities has been the most effective, according to research.[101]

Kuecker concurs and claims that this method, which he calls "superordinate identity with retention of subgroup alliance,"[102] is "the phenomenon most evident within the Spirit-formed communities described in Acts."[103] Thus, the members of the new Christian community would likely maintain a good portion of what makes their subgroup unique, whereas other elements would need to change. Jews would likely still avoid certain types of food (pork, etc.), whereas they would eat and fellowship with Gentiles.

Francis Watson, drawing on the insights of Ernst Troeltsch, makes another sociological proposal about group relations in the early church.[104] Watson suggests that new movements often start as reform movements within the parent group, not intending to break off and become their own movement, but simply to reform the mother religion. When opposition is encountered, a common option is to become a sect, "a closely-knit group which sets up rigid and clearly defined barriers between itself and

---

99. Turner, *Rediscovering*, 54, defines salience thusly: "Salience refers to the conditions under which some specific group membership becomes cognitively prepotent in self-perception to act as the immediate influence on perception and behaviour." In other words, the group membership you become aware of at the moment.

100. Esler, "Outline," 29, quoting Gaertner and Dovidio, *Intergroup Bias*.

101. "Further research confirmed that the development of a new ingroup identity was more likely to be achieved when the original subgroup identities were not threatened in the process. Thus Matthew Hornsey and Michael Hogg have suggested that the most effective way to improve relations between groups 'is to promote awareness of a common superordinate identity, while at the same time preserving the integrity of valued subgroup identities'" (Esler, "Outline," 30).

102. Kuecker, *Spirit*, 33.

103. Kuecker, *Spirit*, 33.

104. In addition to Troelsch, Watson comes from a long line of scholars who have done work on sectarianism and reform movements in early Christianity, including Max Weber, Robin Scroggs, Wayne Meeks, and John Gager, to name several.

the parent community."[105] At this point, the sect goes through a three-stage process of separation, which includes (1) denunciation of the parent group, (2) antithesis, where the group values and the groups themselves are contrasted against one another, the parent group seen as dark and in error and the sect is associated with light and truth, and lastly (3) reinterpretation, where the religious traditions of the community are claimed by the sect and the sect is declared to be "the sole legitimate heir to those traditions."[106] Watson sees this model clearly played out in the life of the early church, particularly in Paul and his writings, as the local group of Christians finds themselves at odds with the local synagogue.

One cannot help but see these elements in the book of Acts. While followers of Jesus start out inside Judaism, attempting to spread the message of Jesus as Israel's Messiah, the story of Acts deals with this rejection by Judaism and the subsequent turn to the Gentiles.[107] Christianity then begins to become a sect. Watson sees an "essential difference" between reform movements and sects as the former has a hopeful attitude toward society and the hope that the parent religion will be reformed, whereas a sect adopts a more hostile view of society.[108] Certainly, the New Testament has a range of authors and characters that relate to Judaism and the world in various ways. Paul, for example, becomes the apostle to the Gentiles, but first-century writings attributed to him suggest he maintains hope that his own people will see the light.[109] In Acts, although the trend is toward Jewish rejection, the majority of Christians in Acts are still Jewish and these believers play a key role in the continuation of the church. Nonetheless, Watson offers a key framework in understanding sectarian movements and the social dynamics of the book of Acts, and three of his points deserve special comment.

First, Watson speaks of the process of going from a reform movement to a sect where "all distinctions of rank and status which seem so important to society at large fade into insignificance by comparison with the fundamental distinction."[110] This is clearly the case in Acts, as connection to Jesus becomes that fundamental mark of differentiation. The Pentecost scene offers a remarkable transformation in the community as "Jews from every nation under heaven" gather,[111] the Spirit comes upon the people, and the result is mass conversion, which has the effect of these people having everything in common and selling their possessions to give to the poor.[112] Later in the

105. Watson, *Judaism*, 19. Also, see Aune, *Literary*, 11; Jewett, "Impulses"; Stendahl, "Introspective Conscience"; Minear, *Obedience*; Dahl, *Studies*; Wilckens, *Der Brief*; Davies, "People of Israel"; Sanders, *Paul*.

106. Watson, *Judaism*, 20.
107. Acts 7:59—8:1; 13:46; 18:6.
108. Watson, *Judaism*, 39.
109. Rom 10.
110. Watson, *Judaism*, 39.
111. Acts 2:5.
112. Acts 2:44–45.

narrative, the leaders of the movement claim that they are mortals, "just like you."[113] This elimination of distinction can be seen throughout the rest of Acts as well, as outsiders are included, former enemies of the church are transformed, and God-fearers and Gentiles are converted.[114]

Another interesting contribution by Watson is his claim that sectarian movements place trust "in a future eschatological vision."[115] He sets this against the desire to transform society and placing hope in an "irresistible divine power." Eschatological hopes can be seen throughout the book of Acts in the claims made by Jesus in Acts 1 and activity of the Spirit throughout. Despite the struggles and persecutions Paul and the other apostles face in Acts, the hope for transformation seems to persist. Acts, for example, ends with a hopeful statement that the gospel went forth unhindered. Nonetheless, Paul is in prison and many important witnesses to the gospel have been killed (i.e., Stephen, James, etc.). Thus, we see here a combination of evidence on both sides of Watson's categories (i.e., hopefulness on the one hand and lack of hopefulness on the other).

Lastly, Watson mentions that as a reform movement becomes a sect, it becomes at odds with the parent movement as "salvation is to be found exclusively through membership of the sect."[116] Watson also stresses alienation from society here as well. There are elements of this in Acts. Salvation in Acts is both inclusive (open to all) and exclusive (found only in Jesus).[117] The exclusivity of salvation in Jesus is seen early on, as in Acts 4:12, Peter says, "There is salvation in no one else, for there is no other name under heaven given among mortals by which we must be saved." This is a consistent message through the book and is stressed in many passages both inside and outside the book of Acts.[118] Thus, in these ways, early Christianity looks largely like a reform movement, which starts to break with the parent movement of Judaism and become its own sect, creating differentiation in various ways.

However, there is scholarly discussion on multiple sides of this issue. Burridge, for example, holds that to speak of Paul's "conversion" in Acts 9 is misguided, as it "suggests (wrongly) that he changed from being a Jew into a Christian."[119] However, by contrast, Segal disagrees and prefers the language of conversion.[120] Many more scholars are involved in this discussion,[121] and even Watson's own thinking

---

113. Acts 14:15.
114. Acts 1:8; 2:5, 44–45; 8:4–40; 9:1–43; 10:1—11:18; 13:26–40; 14:15; 15:1–29.
115. Watson, *Judaism*, 39.
116. Watson, *Judaism*, 40.
117. Acts 2:21; 4:12.
118. Acts 15:11; 16:30–31; Matt 1:21; Luke 2:30; 1 Thess 5:9.
119. Burridge, *Imitating Jesus*, 84.
120. Segal, *Paul the Convert*, 6, 62.
121. Stendahl, "Call"; Davies, *Paul*; Bruce, *Paul*; Sanders, *Paul*; Becker, *Paul*; Donaldson, *Paul and the Gentiles*; Engberg-Pedersen, *Beyond*; Corley, "Interpreting Paul's Conversion."

has changed over the different editions of his book.[122] In the end, the language of a sectarian relationship of Christianity to Judaism as well as the multi-step process Watson lays out is helpful for understanding what Luke represents in his two volumes, as there are clearly elements of opposition, conversion, and reinterpretation in the early days of the church.

An Example From Acts: The Ethiopian Eunuch

As a case study, we will explore the story of the Ethiopian Eunuch. This character has more significance in the discussion of God-fearers and decentralization, so chapter 2 will offer a more thorough look into this character. The section there includes the scholarly discussion about the identity of this figure, whether Jew, God-fearer, or Gentile. Here he is a helpful example of social identity in the New Testament.

Acts 8 records the encounter between Philip, one of the seven chosen for leadership in Acts 6, and the Ethiopian Eunuch. Although this story comes earlier, Peter's experience with Cornelius, who is the prototypical God-fearer, is the encounter that shifts paradigms. The conversion of the Ethiopian Eunuch is a remarkable story in its own right. Philip is a minor character,[123] but he becomes a change agent in the book of Acts. He is proclaiming in Samaria (in the north) to an Ethiopian (from the south) Gentile before the famous Cornelius episode with Peter.

The eunuch is an outsider to the things of God. According to the Law of Moses, as a eunuch he must be excluded: "No one whose testicles are crushed or whose penis is cut off shall be admitted to the assembly of the Lord."[124] He is certainly not allowed to be part of God's people, Israel. Thus, he has found himself interested in the God of Israel, but remains an outsider to the promises of God. In this way he represents the insecurities of the implied audience.

What are the groups that this Ethiopian belongs to? He is a male, Ethiopian, wealthy, foreign, and an outsider due to both his nationality and in his sexuality.

The only option for this man is for new categories of inclusion to be created. There must be a new superordinate identity that welcomes him into the plan of God. There are hints at this reality. Isaiah 56 suggests with regard to eunuchs, "I will give them an everlasting name that will endure forever."[125] While there is no direct reference of this

---

122. Watson offered a major rewrite of this book in 2007 with the new title *Paul, Judaism, and the Gentiles: Beyond a New Perspective*. The most significant changes were his engagement with the evolution of "The New Perspective on Paul" theology, which goes beyond the scope of this work. His sociological work on sects and reform movements became less of a focus in this subsequent work, but the basic building blocks cited here remain basically unchanged.

123. More will be said on minor characters in chapter 2.

124. Deut 23:1. Also, see Wilson, *Unmanly Men*, 13–49, who argues that the eunuch is selected as a way to refigure masculinity in the Greco-Roman world, using other examples as well, such as Zechariah's inability to speak.

125. Isaiah 56:5b.

passage in Luke's corpus, Luke does rely heavily on Second Isaiah[126] and would, for that reason, presumably be familiar with this statement about the role of eunuchs in God's future kingdom. In that way, the Ethiopian Eunuch works as a beautiful fulfillment of Isaiah's prophecy for Luke.

As the story closes, Philip discusses the Scriptures with him, shares the gospel, leading to conversion and baptism, and the scene ends abruptly (and miraculously). There are some unanswered questions we are left with regarding the Ethiopian Eunuch, as the reader is left wondering about the impact on identity. His identity as an Ethiopian, a eunuch, and a servant to the Ethiopian queen need not be threatened or changed by his conversion to this new faith. What did change was his inclusion to the people and the plan of God, and this new superordinate identity is big enough to include both Philip and the one "who has been emasculated."

The Social Function of Group Beliefs

"Group beliefs" represents another area of Social Identity Theory that can help us understand the dynamics of the identity formation in Acts. A large part of the identity formation of group membership comes from participating in the shared beliefs and behaviors of the group. "Sharing beliefs is one of the basic elements for the expression of common social identity, because beliefs with particular contents prototypically define a group. Defining themselves as group members, individuals adopt these beliefs as part of their social identity."[127] As individuals begin to adopt the claims of the group and live in new ways that are consistent with the behaviors practiced and prescribed by the group, they identify socially with the group and social identity is formed.

Discussion of beliefs is a somewhat neglected area of Social Identity Theory.[128] The exception is Daniel Bar-Tal, who is a leading voice in the role of beliefs in identity formation as it relates to Social Identity Theory. He suggests that group members "share group beliefs that characterize them and differentiate them from other groups."[129] Bar-Tal discusses four categories of group beliefs, which are widely used by behavioral scientists. These are norms, values, goals, and ideology.[130] These elements are not necessarily unique to Acts or to the early movement of the Way, as many of these group beliefs could be present in other subgroups and movements as well. However, for the purposes of the Lukan corpus, there is an effort to craft social identity around these issues, as discussed below.

---

126. See pages 91–93 on the New Exodus in Luke–Acts in chapter 3.
127. Bar-Tal, *Shared Beliefs*, 5.
128. Esler, "Outline," 34.
129. Bar-Tal, *Group Beliefs*, 5.
130. Note that Bar-Tal's use of the term "ideology" is similar but also somewhat distinct from Watts's use of the same term above. More on this below.

Norms

The first group is norms, defined as "shared standards that guide group members' behavior... norms tell group members what they should and should not do, prescribing appropriate behavior and indicating inappropriate ones."[131] Not only do norms regulate group members' behavior, but they also "provide criteria for judging it."[132] Examples of common areas that group norms regulate include things like food, clothing, rituals, and relations with outgroups. Thus, norms tend to be concerned with specific patterns of behavior.[133]

Values

Values are defined as "an enduring belief that a specific mode of conduct or end-state of existence is personally or socially preferable to an opposite or converse mode of conduct or end state of existence."[134] Bar-Tal distinguishes here between the former category of instrumental values and the latter category of terminal values. In addition, values have less to do with behavior than norms, but rather deal with the abstract relation to certain ideals to which group members aspire. Some examples include freedom, truth, tolerance, individualism, or equality. The author suggests these can be formally expressed in writing, or they may never be formally defined and "carried latently through the social processes of socialization and influence."[135] The author's examples come from formal written accounts, such as mission statements and credos, as tracing and evaluating values that were never formally defined would be harder to extract. However, these might be observed through the stories they tell as a group. Values will become most helpful to us as we begin to look into the text of Luke–Acts and find specific examples of Luke identifying positive values for his readers, which is done in a further discussion below in this chapter.[136]

Goals

Bar-Tal defines his third category as group goals, meaning "valued or desired future specific states for the group."[137] All groups have goals in some form. Where goals play a significant role in the life of the group, they function as group beliefs, especially

---

131. Bar-Tal, *Group Beliefs*, 49.

132. Bar-Tal, *Group Beliefs*, 49.

133. As an example, Bar-Tal talks about the norms of Amish society, including separation and nonresistance. See Bar-Tal, *Group Beliefs*, 49–51.

134. Rokeach, *Nature*, 5.

135. Bar-Tal, *Group Beliefs*, 51.

136. See page 40.

137. Bar-Tal, *Group Beliefs*, 53.

where groups are formed with certain goals in mind. "Subsequently, goals are often considered a raison d'etre for group formation, frequently keeping group members together, provide a basis for solidarity, and give direction for activity."[138] More so than norms and values, the goals of a group are often quite explicit, as "they increase the identification of group members with their group and define the boundary for group membership."[139] Additionally, March and Simon state, "The greater the extent to which goals are perceived as shared among members of the group, the stronger the propensity of the individual to identify with the group and vice versa."[140] Thus, goals are among the most important group beliefs that Bar-Tal categorizes, as shared beliefs offer the highest identity payoff for group members. As an example, the author cites a number of political interest groups who have clear, explicit, and practical goals that are their reasons for existing.

Ideology

The last item in Bar-Tal's outline of categories of group beliefs is ideology.[141] Sometimes thought of as the mental characteristics of the group, Bar-Tal defines ideology as "an integrated set of beliefs constituting a program, a theory of causes and effects, and premises on the nature of man and societal order."[142] Shared ideology usually flows from the group members' shared experience and contributes to the groups cooperation, morale, and rationale for their behavior. It forms identity in the group as well, and it "describes its exclusivity." Shared group ideology is oftentimes more important to political, social, and religious groups.[143]

Group Beliefs in Acts

Having introduced Bar-Tal's categories, are these elements of shared social identity present in Acts? There is partial overlap between these categories and what we see in Acts. Two elements missed in Bar-Tal are narrative and intertextuality. They will be discussed below. To the degree that these elements are demonstrated in Acts and are shared by the God-fearing reader's experience, cultural memories are formed around association with the projected group of the Way and social identity is created.

138. Bar-Tal, *Group Beliefs*, 53.
139. Bar-Tal, *Group Beliefs*, 53.
140. March and Simon, *Organizations*, 66.
141. This is not to be confused with Watts's usage of the term ideology referenced above.
142. Bar-Tal, *Group Beliefs*, 56. Note the similarity to the definition Watts, *New Exodus*, 36, offers which was posted above, "that all-pervasive interpretive framework by which a group not only understands itself, but also justifies and projects itself over against other groups."
143. Here Bar-Tal uses the Italian Fascist Party and their practice of ingraining the shared ideology of the state as supreme over the individual, starting as early as school age children, as an example. See Bar-Tal, *Group Beliefs*, 56–57.

Norms

First-century Judaism was ripe with group norms of all kinds, including food laws, clothing expectations, rituals and relations with outgroups all included in this prescriptive (but at times unspoken) set of norms. In addition, the Judaism of this period was very diverse. Jewish groups each had their own set of norms and values, operating under different calendars and convictions. For example, the isolationist Essenes, with their desert communities and priestly inclinations differ from the Sadducees that control the wealth of the Temple tax.[144] However, despite this diversity, some general trends of norms and values can be observed. Many of these norms continued throughout early Christianity. However, there are norms that are created by the early Christians and that are identified by Luke.[145]

An example of norms among the Christ group in the first century occurs in the summary statement in Acts 2:42–47. The norms of shared possessions,[146] shared meals,[147] and meeting together in each other's homes and the Temple courts[148] are present in the community from early on in the narrative. The assumption is that Christians will share possessions with one another, meet together, and share meals with one another. These help regulate normative behavior and provide criteria for judgment. As the audience participates in these group norms, they identify with the early Christians.

Some of the elements that exist as norms show up in other ways as well. For example, a value (the next category) of the early Christian community is generosity, whereas the norm associated with that value is shared possessions.[149] This norm is modeled by the leaders and practiced by the people. Kuecker states, "Luke's interest in the use of possessions by the new community is unquestionable."[150]

An interesting, and perhaps dark example of this is seen in the story of Ananias and Sapphira. We are told at the end of Acts chapter 4 that Barnabas "sold a field that belonged to him, then brought the money, and laid it at the apostles' feet."[151] Kuecker suggests that Barnabas is an exemplar for new community generosity because of his behavior here.[152] In the next verse, we are introduced to two new characters Ananias

---

144. See, for example, Kalimi, "Day of Atonement," which approaches the Day of Atonement with these different groups in mind. Also, see Regev, *Sadducees*.

145. This topic of Jewish norms that are abandoned in Christianity will be discussed more fully in chapter 2 on decentralization, and again the modeling of new prescriptive norms will be discussed in chapter 4 about prototypes and exemplars.

146. Acts 2:45; 3:1–8; 4:32–35; 4:36—5:11; 10:2. Also, see Kwong, "Everything in Common."

147. Acts 2:42–46; 10:1—11:18; 20:7, 11.

148. Acts 2:46; 3:1–10; 5:20–21, 42; 10:32; 16:15; 18:26; 21:16; 22:17; 28:7.

149. Acts 2:45; 3:1–8; 4:32–35; 4:36—5:11; 10:2.

150. Kuecker, *Spirit*, 136.

151. Acts 4:37.

152. Kuecker, *Spirit*, 139. For more on exemplars, including this scene, see chapter 4.

and Sapphira, who also sell a field, but keep some of the money for themselves and are dishonest about it. The result is that both he and his wife are struck dead because of their dishonesty and greed. The author is making a bold statement about possessions and honesty, which are prescribed norms in the early Christian community. However, perhaps there is another, more subtle statement being made by the author about the ownership of land in the Jewish community no longer being central to what it means to be a Jew. Certainly with the Diaspora, many Jews did not own land in Palestine, though many others still did, and they likely saw this as central to their identity as children of Israel.[153] In the shifting norms of the early Christian community, Luke appears to be making a statement here that it is no longer ownership of land in Palestine that gives identity, but commitment to Jesus alone. Thus, Ananias and Sapphira's unwillingness to part with their field (i.e., land) is a strong statement to Jewish Christians tempted to hold onto and draw identity from their land ownership.[154]

Other norms in the early Christian community are the rituals they partake in together. Baptism as a common ritual in the book of Acts and the word appears twenty-one times in its verbal forms.[155] The normative pattern in the book of Acts is that baptism follows fairly quickly after repentance.[156] Another ritual in the early Christian community is the Lord's Supper. Although the ritual of the Lord's Supper is specifically spelled out in Luke 22:14–20, in Acts it is only referenced in summary statements.[157] However, it does fit the larger topic of meals together, which are common in Acts.[158] Meals together become a norm for the early Christian community.[159]

---

153. Blomberg, *Jesus*, 49.

154. Barnabas is said to have sold a *field* (ἀγρός). Ἀγρός appears in the New Testament thirty-seven times, only here in Acts, but ten times in Luke. Ananias and Sapphira have sold a piece of *property* (κτῆμα). Κτῆμα appears four times in the New Testament, twice in Acts (once in Matt; Mark), each time talking about the redistribution of wealth and selling of property. Interestingly, the other two occurrences are from the account of the rich young ruler who is asked to sell all he has, and goes away sad because he has many possessions (κτήματα). Later they are each questioned about the *land* (χωρίον). Χωρίον appears ten times in the New Testament, seven times in Acts (once in Matt; Mark). Six of the seven times this word is used in Acts it occurs in the suicide of Judas in chapter 1 (three times) or in this account (four times, counting the reference to the church selling houses or land in 4:34 that introduces this story). The most obvious and significant word the author could use to make this point about land would be γῆ, used two hundred fifty-two times in the New Testament, including twenty-six times in Luke and thirty-three times in Acts, but it is not used here. For a more robust discussion of land, see chapter 5.

155. The noun form βάπτισμα is also used five times.

156. Acts 2:38, 41; 8:12–13, 36–38; 9:18; 10:47–48; 16:15, 33; 18:8; 19:5; 22:16. For more on water baptism, see Beasley-Murray, *Baptism*; Cullman, *Baptism*; Jeremias, *Infant Baptism*; Larere, *Water and Spirit*; Porter and Cross, *Baptism, and the Church*; Porter and Cross, *Dimensions of Baptism*.

157. Acts 2:42; 20:7. Not all agree that this is referring to the Lord's Supper here. See Twelftree, *Spirit*, 131.

158. For more on communal meals in Luke–Acts, see Finger, *Of Widows and Meals*; Heil, *Meal Scenes*; Just, *Ongoing Feast*; Mittelstadt, "Hospitality"; Moxnes, "Meals"; Moritz, "Dinner Talk"; Smith, "Table Fellowship."

159. Acts 2:46; 16:34; 20:7, 11; 27:35–36.

The other interesting situation regarding shared meals in the book of Acts is the shifting norms with respect to who can eat together and what food laws need to be followed. Acts 10 opens the doors for the Jews to eat any kind of food they desire, ending the strict food laws of the Old Covenant. Chapter 11 continues this radical shift in the accepting of Gentiles into God's people, which also includes fellowship and community meals. Thus, while this norm of meals together exists in Judaism for more than a millennium, it sees radical shifts in the book of Acts.[160]

In Acts 15, we see norms spelled out in a very clear way in the letter that the Jerusalem disciples send to the believers in Antioch. The requirements they give regulate the emerging food restrictions, which have been all but abolished, and provide criteria for judgment. Acts 15:28–29 reads: "It seemed good to the Holy Spirit and to us not to burden you with anything beyond the following requirements: You are to abstain from food sacrificed to idols, from blood, from the meat of strangled animals and from sexual immorality. You will do well to avoid these things."

A final norm worth mentioning is the infilling (or baptism) of the Holy Spirit. After the prophecy in Acts 1:8 of the coming Holy Spirit, the infilling of people by the Holy Spirit becomes a regular experience throughout the rest of the book of Acts.[161] Both groups and individuals experience the infilling of the Spirit, while others are said to be full of the Spirit.[162] Sometimes individuals are filled in order to accomplish a specific purpose, as Paul in Acts 13:9, or to give a speech, as Peter in Acts 4:8. Engagement with the Holy Spirit, in one form or another, seems to be a norm in Acts.[163] The Spirit is a sign of holiness and inclusion in Acts,[164] and it speeds up the identity-forming process.[165]

---

160. A larger discussion about shared meals will be discussed in chapter 4.

161. The key initiation stories in Acts that involve characters participating with the Spirit are Peter (2:4); Peter's Sermon at Pentecost (2:38); Samaritans (8:12–16); Paul (9:17–18); Cornelius (10:43–48); the Ephesians (19:1–7). For a full list of the other elements involved in each initiation scene, see the chart in Graham Twelftree, *Spirit*, 97.

162. A full list of the use of this language in Acts, broken into three categories (general statements, individuals, and groups), is as follows: (1) General Statements: prophesy of the coming Spirit (1:8); the Holy Spirit is given to those who obey (5:32); (2) Individuals: (regular filling or for a specific purpose) Stephen described as full of the Holy Spirit (6:5; 7:55); Paul (9:17); Barnabas (11:24); (specific purpose) Peter filled for a Speech (4:8); Paul for miracle (13:9); and (3) Groups: Pentecost (2:4); Apostles' prayer (4:31); Samaritans (8:15–17); Cornelius's household (Gentiles) (10:44); Iconium (13:52); Ephesus (19:6).

163. For more on scholarly discussion regarding the "baptism of the Holy Spirit," see Cartledge, *Tongues*; Ervin, *Conversion*; Esler, "Glossolalia"; Fee, "Baptism"; Menzies, *Development*; Turner, "Significance"; Turner, "Spirit Empowerment."

164. Tannehill, *Acts*, 135, calls holiness "the extreme opposite of the unclean."

165. This is especially true with Cornelius, who will be discussed more in future chapters.

Values

One of the normative values of the early church according to the book of Acts was generosity. In addition to the summary statements and stories told about the life of the early church, this value also appears in the speeches in the book.[166] One of the major ways this generosity played itself out was through the sharing of possessions.

Furthermore, community was another value that was present in the early church. This is related to the norm of meals together and can be seen in the summary statements as well, such as, "They broke bread in their homes and ate together with glad and sincere hearts, praising God and enjoying the favor of all the people."[167] We also see the community coming together in times of hardship and persecution,[168] as well as for prayer.[169]

Closely related with community prayer are the phrases like "the will of God" and "the word of God"/"word of the Lord." This language has a ubiquitous role in the book.[170] Pao, for example, suggests that the word of God is a main actor in the conquest sections of the book and that its goal is to establish a community of the word.[171] We also see obedience to God's Spirit and his will as central in various points of the narrative, as when Paul insists on traveling to Jerusalem in the face of persecution and death: "When he would not be dissuaded, we gave up and said, 'The Lord's will be done.'"[172] Thus, obedience and response to God's word and will is a value in the early church.

Goals

What are the future-oriented goals of the early church? Three clear future-oriented goals of the community in Acts essential to the narrative are the outward expansion of the gospel,[173] the reconstitution of God's people, and the future eschatological hopes of the early church. Starting with the outward expansion of the gospel, the last words of the book of Acts suggest this as the hopeful future realized: "For two

---

166. Acts 2:45; 4:34–35; 11:29; 20:35.

167. Acts 2:46b–47a.

168. Acts 4:23–31; 5:41–42.

169. Acts 1:14; 3:1; 4:24–31; 6:6; 8:15; 12:12; 13:3; 14:23; 16:13, 25; 20:36. Community prayer is so common in the book of Acts it might rightly be considered a norm of the early church.

170. Word of God: 4:31; 6:2, 7; 8:14; 11:1; 12:24; 13:5, 7, 46; 17:13; 18:11; 20:32. Word of the Lord: 8:25; 13:44, 48, 49; 15:35, 36; 16:32; 19:10, 20; 20:35.

171. Pao, *New Exodus*, 155. Pao goes on to suggest three points on the word of God: (1) The central character of the travel narrative is the word of God; (2) the nature of the travel of the word of God is one of conquest as the word prevails in the midst of opposing forces; and (3) the word's journey is a linear one, as it does not return to the same city twice. See Pao, *New Exodus*, 156.

172. Acts 21:14.

173. By gospel, here, we mean conversion to the new Christian community as seen in the book of Acts. More will be said about the nature of the Gospel in chapter 2.

whole years Paul stayed there in his own rented house and welcomed all who came to see him. He proclaimed the kingdom of God and taught about the Lord Jesus Christ—with all boldness and without hindrance!"[174] Similarly, Acts represents a dynamically fast-growing community because of this goal being realized in the narrative. Luke reports on three different occasions that the Lord "added to their number," once noting that three thousand were added to their number in a single day.[175] Other statements show the daily growth of the Christian community.[176] These statements of outward growth allow the reader to participate in the goals of the movement by helping facilitate growth and conversion, and at the same time, increase their own social identity within the group.

The goal of outward expansion of the gospel is clearly seen in the programmatic verse in Acts 1:8. As noted by many scholars, this verse sets a geographical outline for the advancement of the gospel that the book seems to follow,[177] as the movement starts in Jerusalem, spreads to Judea, involves kingdom expansion in Samaria,[178] and continues on to the ends of the earth. While this last phrase, "the ends of the earth" has been debated, some say that, for Luke, the conversion of the Ethiopian Eunuch amounts to the fulfillment of Jesus' prophecy.[179] However, throughout Acts, there will be many more points of fulfillment. It would appear to be premature to put the point of fulfillment solely on the eunuch. On the contrary, kingdom expansion continues to be seen throughout the book, with the new Christian community seeing continual conversion and growth.[180] The last verses of Acts seem to suggest this is Luke's expectation for the future as well.

Related to the advancement of the gospel is the goal of expansion and reconstitution of God's people. Acts 2 becomes something of a Sinai moment for the followers of Jesus, as the church is born.[181] The idea of the Pentecost scene in Acts 2 as a type of new Sinai moment is credited to Jacques Dupont.[182] His argument is that (1) Pentecost was a celebration of the giving of the Law in the time of Luke's writing, (2) the numerous illusions in Acts to Sinai, and (3) that Acts 2:33 is a reference to

---

174. Acts 28:30–31.

175. Acts 2:41.

176. Acts 2:47.

177. Keener, *Acts*, 1:575; Tannehill, *Acts*, 9; Witherington, *Acts*, 106; Marguerat, *Les Actes des Apôtres*, 20; Molthagen, "Geschichtsschreibung," 166.

178. Acts 2; 8:1; 5, respectively.

179. Unnik, "Der Ausdruck"; Tannehill, *Acts*, 109. This view is not universally held. Keener, *Acts*, 1:708, for example, suggests that Luke uses the phrase as the LXX does to talk of universality. Also, see Johnson, *Acts* (who cites Deut 28:49; Ps 134:6–7; Isa 8:9; 48:20; 49:6; 62:11; Jer 10:12; 16:19; 1 Macc 3:9); Lake and Cadbury, "Commentary," 9.

180. Acts 2:47; 5:14; 6:1, 7; 9:31; 11:21, 24; 16:5; 28:30–31.

181. This point will be discussed again in chapter 4.

182. Dupont, "La nouvelle," 193.

Psalm 67:19.[183] If Luke intends us to understand the Pentecost scene as a type of Sinai moment, the implications are that this is a reestablishing of God people. This is a fairly radical shift. For one, the event is said to include Jews from "every nation under heaven," a statement about unification of Diasporic Jews. References are made to "all Israel" and "fellow Jews and all you who live in Jerusalem,"[184] which seem to stress this point. What is more, though, is that this scene is loaded with hints that more than just Jews are included in this new formation of God's people. The diversity of the audience and the language miracle both suggest the universality of God's plan.[185] Tannehill suggests that perhaps these Jews function as representatives of their homelands, including Gentile inhabitants.[186] What is more, statements are made as in 2:39 that suggest the promise is for "you and your children and for all who are far off—for all whom the Lord our God will call." Lastly, the quotation from Joel is universal in nature in multiple ways, referring to the pouring out of the Spirit on πᾶσαν σάρκα, "all people/flesh," the young and old, men and women, slaves, and ultimately "everyone who calls on the name of the Lord will be saved."

The conversion of the eunuch, spoken of above, also works to reestablish God's people. Suffice it to say that the old boundaries of who was allowed in have been abolished, as shown by the conversion and baptism of this man into the family of God. He who was once excluded is now welcomed. This is emphasized again with the conversion of Cornelius and his household in chapters 10–11. The community of God's people is once again expanding by breaking down barriers that are over a thousand years old.[187]

Another "desired future" for the new Christian community has to do with the expectation of last things.[188] The eschatology of Acts seems to include a belief that they

---

183. Dupont, "La nouvelle," 193. Menzies, *Empowered*, 189–90, summarizes the argument more fully: "(1) By the time Luke penned Acts, Pentecost was regarded as a feast commemorating the giving of the Law on Sinai; (2) the Pentecost account contains numerous literary allusions to Sinai and therefore was shaped with this event in mind; (3) Acts 2:33 is based on Ps 67:19 (LXX) and should be interpreted in light of the Psalm. Whereas the rabbis interpreted Ps 67:19 with reference to Moses who, at Sinai, ascended into heaven to receive the Torah in order that he might give it to humanity, in Acts 2:33 the Psalm is applied to Jesus who ascended to the right hand of God, received the Spirit, and poured it out on the disciples." This issue will be dealt with in more depth in chapter 4, but an introduction to the tension here is necessary. Although Menzies summarizes this view well, he ultimately argues against it (*Empowered*, 190–201). For an exposition and argument against Menzies's points and toward a Pentecost-Sinai connection, see Estrada, *Followers*, 200–203. For more support of Pentecost as a new Sinai, see Turner, *Power*, 267–316.

184. Acts 2:36, 14, respectively.

185. Tannehill, *Acts*, 27.

186. Tannehill, *Acts*, 27.

187. Much more will be said on the story of Cornelius and his family in chapter 4 on prototypical characters.

188. Regardless of the eschatological beliefs of this group, those shared beliefs create social identity for the members.

were in the last days.¹⁸⁹ Peter's response to the accusations of drunkenness on the day of Pentecost includes the opening quotation from Joel: "In the last days, God says, I will pour out my Spirit on all people."¹⁹⁰ Peter suggests that the last days have come, using a pesher interpretation to apply Joel to what he is witnessing.¹⁹¹ Keener states that since Peter has inserted the phrase "last days" into the Joel quotation in place of "afterward," he has in mind "the period of Israel's restoration, which Jewish hopes now fixed in the eschatological time."¹⁹² What is more, Peter seems to suggest at times that the last days are quite imminent, as in Acts 3:19–21. "Peter still appears to anticipate (or at least hope for) a quick repentance and restoration of Israel."¹⁹³

However, there may be some tension among the eschatological expectations of the disciples with regard to the apparent delay of the parousia.¹⁹⁴ This, of course, depends on what Luke has in mind when the characters in Acts expect Jesus' return. One option is that the early Christians expect a future, physical parousia of Jesus that is not realized at the end of Acts. This is perhaps strengthened by the statement by the angel in verse 11: "This Jesus, who has been taken up from you into heaven, will come in the same way as you saw him go into heaven." "The delay of the eschatological time remained a problem not only for early Christians but for other Jewish thinkers as well."¹⁹⁵ However, "in the same way" could be understood as the mode of presence, that is, the risen state of Christ, rather than the mode of arrival.¹⁹⁶

Another option is that Luke presents the activity of the Spirit at Pentecost in Acts 2 is the return of Jesus, followed by subsequent returns in chapters 4, 8, 9, 10, and others. The kingdom and the Spirit were closely linked in the disciples' minds.¹⁹⁷

---

189. Acts 2:17, 33; 3:19–21; 10:45. This is certainly the case in other parts of the New Testament, though it is impossible to know what, if any, level of familiarity Luke had with these documents. Nonetheless, the expectation that Luke's audience was in the last days is incumbent in the verses above. For other examples throughout the New Testament, see 2 Tim 3:1; Heb 1:2; Jas 5:3; 2 Peter 3:3. These other documents show that it is plausible to read first-century documents as projecting an implied audience that believes they are in the last times, including Luke–Acts.

190. Acts 2:17a.

191. Keener, *Acts*, 1:878.

192. Keener, *Acts*, 1:877.

193. Keener, *Acts*, 1:879.

194. Despite the evidence that the disciples expect a quick return, such as Acts 2:17, 33; 3:19–21; 10:45, the book ends without a physical parousia realized. Some also see an element of political expectation in the disciples' question in 1:6, perhaps expecting Jesus to triumph over Caesar and Rome. Questions of "who was Lord over the world" are common among the ancient Jews (Bauckham, *Revelation*, 8). However, the degree to which the disciples' question and Jesus' response are rooted in history is debated. See Derrett, "Luke's Perspective"; Stauffer, *Christus*; Cassidy, *Jesus*; Geldenhuys, *Luke*; McKnight and Modica, *Jesus is Lord*. For a survey of the relevant literature, see Aland, "Das Verhältnis."

195. Keener, *Acts*, 1:685. Keener mentions a number of Jewish and early Christian writings that reflect this, including *4 Ezra* 7:74; *Gen. Rab.* 67:4; cf. 2 Peter 3:9; and others.

196. In Greek (emphasis added): οὗτος ὁ Ἰησοῦς ὁ ἀναλημφθεὶς ἀφ᾽ ὑμῶν εἰς τὸν οὐρανὸν *οὕτως ἐλεύσεται ὃν τρόπον ἐθεάσασθε αὐτὸν* πορευόμενον εἰς τὸν οὐρανόν.

197. Keener, *Acts*, 1:682.

There is a close connection between the outpouring of the Spirit and the eschatological expectation of Israel's restoration,[198] both in the Old Testament and in the New Testament.[199] Keener says "any talk about the Spirit's outpouring was de facto eschatological in character."[200] Thus, the robust focus on the Spirit's outpouring in suggests a form of realized eschatology for Luke and could fulfill the promise of chapter 1. This, too, is a desired future shared by the new Christian community, as the Spirit ushers in the new era of fulfillment and restoration.

Regardless of the way Luke intends his readers to understand these categories of eschatology, return, restoration, and hope, the shared expectation creates social identity among that group and allows for new members to share in those expectations as well. However the specifics of the fulfillment are to be understood, Jesus represents the culmination of the early Christians' eschatological hopes.

Ideology

What are the shared ideologies, mental characteristics, and rationale of the community in Acts? Three elements surface: the centrality of Christ, theology in speeches from the early Christians, and an optimistic morale.

A shared ideology that is seen throughout the text of Acts is commitment to Christ. In the Gospel of Luke, we see Jesus redefine a number of important Jewish symbols around himself. Blomberg sees the most important of these symbols as the Temple, the land, and the Torah, suggesting, "Jesus challenged the adequacy of all three of these institutions as they stood seeing them instead as fulfilled in himself."[201] As much as these symbols were identity creating for Jews in the first century, Jesus was becoming the thing around which Christian identity was to be centered.[202] In addition to these, one could add the keeping of the Sabbath, following dietary laws, and circumcision. Jesus challenged the idea of Sabbath as it stood in Jewish thought of the time.[203] Although the other Synoptic Gospels talk of the ending of the dietary laws,[204] Luke's Gospel does not do so, at least not explicitly.[205] The most important statement made in the New Testament regarding dietary laws occurs in Acts 10–11, and although circumcision is not mentioned by Jesus, the council in Acts 15 as well as the ministry of Paul make clear that circumcision as an identity marker of God's

---

198. Keener, *Acts*, 1:682.
199. See Isa 42:1; 44:3; 59:21: Ezek 36:24–28; 37:14; 39:29; Joel 2:28—3:1; Matt 12:28.
200. Keener, *Acts*, 1:682.
201. Blomberg, *Jesus*, 49.
202. These issues will be discussed more fully in chapter 2 and again in chapter 5.
203. Luke 6; 13:14–16; 14:1–6.
204. Matt 15; Mark 7.
205. Uncleanliness in Luke primary has to do with unclean spirits. See Luke 4:33, 36; 6:18; 8:29; 9:42; 11:24; Acts 5:16; 8:7; 10:14, 28; 11:8.

people is antiquated.[206] Instead, the new movement becomes entirely centered on Jesus. It is possible that there is a sense of a redefinition of the remnant going on as well, where the disciples represent faithful Israel. The lone criterion for this new remnant becomes commitment to following Jesus.

One of the places we see the centrality of Jesus is in the speeches in the book. Marion Soards says, "Within the worldview assumed by the speeches in Acts one finds the distinctive, repeated and debated bold assertion that God's will and work for salvation are brought to a realization in Jesus Christ."[207] Soards also offers a few interesting emphases that emerge from the speeches and sermons in Acts, including the operation of God's plan, divine authority, and the importance of witnesses, all of which have a Christological focus.[208]

A third element of shared ideology is located on the level of morale of the group. Acts presents a movement of people who face intense persecution, but do so with a certain level of optimism and grit. For example, several times in Acts, characters show joy in the midst of persecution. The disciples rejoice after flogging because they are counted worthy to suffer for the name,[209] Stephen responds in the face of death as Jesus did, by asking forgiveness for his executors,[210] and Paul and Silas sing hymns while in prison, leading to the conversion of the guard.[211] These examples establish a shared morale of optimism and joy in the midst of persecution and suffering.[212]

Narrative Seams

Another interesting way that the author assists in social identity creation for his readers is in the use of narrative seams. Luke–Acts is told by an extradiegetic narrator who has access to the entire narrative and even "inside views" into the character's thoughts. Thus, Luke is commenting on the story in various ways to maximize the experience for his reader. This perceptibility of the narrator in the book of Acts, says Steven Sheeley, can be seen in several ways. The most obvious of these is self-conscious narration, which is seen in the preface, Acts 1:1–3.[213] Second, the narrator defines terms five dif-

---

206. Paul's, on his missionary journeys, despite starting in the synagogues preaching to Jews and God-fearers, focuses on the conversion of the Gentiles. Acts makes clear that Gentiles need not be circumcised but are welcomed as God's people. For these elements in Paul's ministry, see Acts 13:46–47; 14:27; 15:3–19; 18:6; 21:19–25; 22:21; 26:17; 26:20–23; 28:28.

207. Soards, *Speeches*, 186.

208. Soards, *Speeches*, 184–94. For more on the connection between ideology and speeches, see Kennedy, *New History*, 16, 41, 62, 128, 140; Burridge, *Gospels*, 29, 155; *Imitating Jesus*, 2, 136–37, 169, 208, 372. Also, see Winter and Clarke, *Literary Setting*.

209. Acts 5:41–42.

210. Acts 7:59b; 60.

211. Acts 16:25–34.

212. For more on suffering in Luke–Acts, see Tabb, "Salvation," 43–61.

213. Sheeley, *Narrative Asides*, 157.

ferent times for the audience.[214] Third, several times the author offers commentary on the story or on the characters.[215] Last, Sheeley points out one instance of inside view, as the narrator reveals what Peter is thinking in 12:9.

In those instances where the author translates terms for the audience, it is clear that he is communicating with readers who do not have a full grasp of the Hebrew or Aramaic languages (i.e., translating Barnabas etc.). This fits with the claim made by this work that the primary audience is God-fearers,[216] who may have some knowledge of Judaism, but likely are not fluent in Hebrew or Aramaic. The commentary sections mentioned above may reveal important elements of the author's agenda. For example, four of the five comments identified by Sheeley are in chapters 10 or 11, which is a major transition point in the narrative with the conversion of Cornelius and Peter's defense of this to the Jews.[217] The most noteworthy of these narratival comments are when the author is praising a character in the story. The two occurrences Sheeley points to are comments about Cornelius and Barnabas, who are both important characters in Luke's purpose and have prototypical elements to them.[218]

Narrative and Intertextuality

Social Identity theory is still relatively new. Only recently have scholars applied these insights to ancient texts like the Bible. While Bar-Tal presents a helpful outline for evaluating the formation of group beliefs, there are two areas that need more development. These are narrative and intertextuality.[219]

Narrative

Narrative plays a part in every one of Bar-Tal's categories mentioned above. In fact, stories are vehicles for values. Stories are the context of all life, including both thoughts and actions, and they construct the way people approach the world. Thus, they are involved in the way we share group beliefs in various ways.

One of the most obvious ways that narrative is involved in the elements of shared beliefs above is in the use of rituals. Rituals have a story connected to them to give them meaning. As people reenact rituals, they tell a story. This is certainly true with

---

214. Acts 1:19; 4:36; 9:36; 13:8; 14:12.

215. Sheeley, *Narrative Asides*, 157, identifies five of these (10:2, 36; 11:24, 26; 17:21).

216. See chapter 2.

217. It should be noted that only two of these fall specifically within the discussion of Cornelius and the aftermath. 11:24, 26 come right after this scene. 10:36 is debatable. Sheeley appears to see the phrase οὗτός ἐστιν πάντων κύριος as a comment by Luke rather than part of Peter's speech.

218. More will be said on prototypical characters in chapter 4.

219. Bar-Tal does use the term narrative in evaluating the social identity of Jews in response to the defense of Masada, using Josephus as a narrative source, although it is brief and does not take a large enough role in his work. Bar-Tal, *Shared Beliefs*, 58.

the rituals seen in the New Testament. As mentioned above, baptism and the Lord's Supper both tell stories. These are rooted in Judaism, which has "always been characterized by a sense of time and history."[220] There is a long history of ceremonial washing in Jewish life.[221] For New Testament Christians, there is the more recent history of John's baptism[222] and baptisms that happened during Jesus' ministry.[223] Thus, this practice has a dual context.[224]

The Lord's Supper, too, has imbedded narrative connections. The immediate connection is to Jesus and his last meal with his disciples before the crucifixion. However, there is a much stronger connection with the Passover and exodus event, as the Passover Seder was the context for Jesus' last supper.[225] "In a sense the function of the Seder is to elicit recitation. . . . The goal of the Seder is to make generations existentially aware of the Exodus."[226] The narrative connections here point back over thousands of years. Jesus does what countless Jews have done throughout generations, but he takes it a step further and adds elements that point to himself. It is this narrative richness that gives the ritual its meaning. Jesus' closing words of the ritual in Luke—"do this in remembrance of me"[227]—highlight the continued story nature this ritual is to have for future generations. Again, to the degree that the God-fearing reader participates in these rituals, cultural memories are formed and social identity in the Christ group is strengthened.

Norms exist in the realm of narrative as well. Groups create norms by the stories they tell. The example above of the story of Barnabas, when contrasted with the story of Ananias and Sapphira, shows this practice well. Another example is the repetition of baptism as an important part of conversion. Baptism has a narrative connection in that, as a ritual, it looks back to what it rehearses, but it also has a narrative existence in that the normative nature of baptism is reinforced and kept alive by the stories of conversions

---

220. Harris, *Exodus and Exile,* 2.

221. Fike, *Mikveh.* Also, see Webb, *John the Baptizer.*

222. There are five references to John's baptism in Acts (1:22; 10:37; 13:24; 18:25; 19:4).

223. The only reference to Jesus and his disciples baptizing in the gospels is the statement in John 4:1–2: "Now Jesus learned that the Pharisees had heard that he was gaining and baptizing more disciples than John—although in fact it was not Jesus who baptized, but his disciples."

224. There is no full narrative explanation of baptism in Luke–Acts. Presumably the implied author expected the implied audience to know the significance. The closest we have to a description of the imagery and narrative connection of baptism in other early Christian writings is in Romans 6:3–4: "Or don't you know that all of us who were baptized into Christ Jesus were baptized into his death? We were therefore buried with him through baptism into death in order that, just as Christ was raised from the dead through the glory of the Father, we too may live a new life." However, it is unclear whether the implied audience would have been expected to be aware of these writings.

225. Luke clearly displays the last supper as the Passover meal, as Luke 22:15 shows. However, some debate has existed about the nature of the last supper and its connection with the Passover feast. See Evans, *Mark,* 372.

226. Harris, *Exodus,* 20.

227. Luke 22:19b.

that involve baptism. Values relate in a similar way. Principles are valued to the degree that they are repeated and shared as narratives among people. Values are reinforced to the extent that stories are told to praise them, and they decline as they are no longer the subjects of shared stories, or as they are spoken against and opposing values are narrated. Thus, we can see narrative as crucial for each of Bar-Tal's elements.

Third, groups project their goals as desired futures through the medium of story. These may be short narrative snippets as in vision statements, or they may be more elaborate. This is seen in Acts in a dramatic way through the prophet Agabus, who seeks to avoid an undesirable future by tying himself up with a belt as a picture of what will happen to Paul in Jerusalem.[228]

There is also a sense where salvation has a future dimension to it in the book of Acts, and to this extent, can be seen as a narrative driven future goal. Witherington sees a future oriented element of salvation in two texts in Acts (2:21; 15:11).[229] He connects these references to the eschatological view of the "Day of the Lord," a rich Old Testament idea which is being evoked in each of these verses, but seen most clearly in the Joel quotation. "In the future, salvation means entering God's Dominion and being a participant in the messianic banquet when the Lord returns."[230] This vision of the future is the ultimate climax to the story for those participating in God's plan, and thus, it serves the role of desired future.

Intertextuality

Another important element to combine with Bar-Tal's work is intertextuality. Bar-Tal's work on group identity and group beliefs does not explore the world of texts and written narrative nearly enough.[231] Similarly, Liu and László, while dealing with texts, do not consider intertextuality sufficiently. Narrative and intertextuality are intertwined.[232] Intertextuality refers to the interconnectedness of texts as they refer to one another, or a dialogue of texts. As Moyise puts it, "No text is an island. . . . It can only be understood as part of a web or matrix of other texts, themselves only to be understood in light of other texts,"[233] or Alkier, "Every text is written and read in relation to that which is already written and read."[234]

---

228. Acts 21:10–14.
229. Witherington, "Salvation," 160.
230. Witherington, "Salvation," 61.
231. Bar-Tal could approach this as the "written histories" of a group, or the documents that groups share. There seems to be important research to be done here regarding texts and their effect on group formation and identity sharing.
232. I'm aware that some approach intertextuality from a source critical perspective. However, I am using narrative and intertextuality to focus on the final document.
233. Moyise, "Intertextuality," 23.
234. Alkier, "Intertextuality," 4.

Intertextuality has been an emerging topic in the discussion of interpretation over the last fifty years, finding its start in the work of Bulgarian scholar Julia Kristeva as she was studying in Paris in 1965.[235] Intertextuality has become a way to move beyond structuralism and give texts a dynamic life. More importantly, it reveals an important dialogue that is taking place between biblical authors that we do well to pay attention to. Hays sets up the situation quite well:

> The question, so formulated, is a question about *intertextual narration as a culture forming practice*. Communities form and maintain their identities through the stories they tell about their origins, history, and future destiny. When a particular retelling of the community's story becomes sufficiently revisionary, the practice of reading becomes *countercultural*: It challenges or transforms accepted readings in the service of a revisionary vision for the community's life, "giving people a new past to live with" that can change their future indefinitely.[236]

For Luke–Acts, Hays notes how intentional and skillful the author is at connecting the story of Jesus seamlessly to Israel's story.[237] He mentions a number of ways this can be seen in the early part of the Gospel of Luke, which will be discussed more in chapter 3, but he also discusses the use of intertextual quotations that create a countercultural community among the Christ group in Acts.[238]

At times, the intertextual nature of Luke–Acts is quite obvious because the quotation is made plain. For example, Hays discusses the communal prayer in Acts 4, in which the disciples reference Psalm 2, and then immediately apply it to their context "in virtual *pesher* style."[239] The quotation is taken word for word from the LXX of Psalm 2:1–2,[240] and is very easy to recognize. In other places, however, the reference to Jewish Scriptures is more subtle. For example, as discussed above, shared possessions and generosity are an important focus for Luke. Hays connects the phrase "there were no needy persons among them" in the summary statement in 4:34 to Deuteronomy 15:4, "However, there need be no poor people among you, for in the land the Lord your God is giving you." "The intertextual connection suggests that the community of Jesus' followers is the true covenant community of Israel."[241] Truly, as we see in cases

---

235. Alkier, "Intertextuality," 4. See Kristeva, *Revolution,* 59–60. For a robust discussion on the history of intertextuality, see Beers, *Servant,* 6–30.

236. Hays, "Liberation," 102.

237. Hays, "Liberation," 103.

238. Hays also lists seven tests for intertextuality that are helpful in determining if a certain text is referring to the Old Testament, sometimes called an echo. See Hays, *Echoes in Paul,* 29–32, and for a Lukan application of these elements, see Hays, *Echoes in the Gospels*; Adams, "Framing."

239. Hays, "Liberation," 115.

240. With the exception of διάψαλμα/Selah at the end of verse 2.

241. Hays, "Liberation," 116.

like this, the community of the early church matches the dream of what the community of Israel should have been.

The Passover meal, rooted in narrative connections as mentioned above, also has an important intertextual dimension. The statement by Harris above that the goal of the ritual of the Passover meal is to make participants existentially aware of the Exodus is at the core of the intertextual relationship.[242] Not only does the reader encounter this phenomenon in the upper room with Jesus and his disciples where the ritual is redefined by Jesus to refer to himself, but the reader encounters shared meals regularly over the course of the rest of Luke–Acts. The most explicit of these is the scene after the discussion with the travelers on the road to Emmaus. Jesus, whose identity is still veiled, sits down for a meal with them, gives thanks and breaks bread with them, echoing the words from the Lord's Supper just two chapters before.[243] It appears to be this breaking of bread that enables the travelers' "eyes [to be] opened" and recognize him.[244] The characters become cognizant of what the reader knew all along. What is curious about this, though, is that it appears to be only the apostles present at the Last Supper,[245] although they are not present with Cleopas and the other traveler (for after Jesus disappears, they go and find the eleven).[246] The fact that the Lukan corpus only mentions two occasions where Jesus broke bread, which are with different groups of people, but that this becomes the key to the travelers recognizing him after the resurrection, is significant. By highlighting two type-scenes involving different people, it becomes the readers' responsibility to see the connections. The reader remembers the breaking of bread in the upper room and the words Jesus spoke regarding the bread of his sacrifice and the cup of the new covenant.[247]

The mentioning of breaking bread and community meals will continue throughout Acts. In the summary statement in chapter 2, this appears to be a key feature of the new community.[248] Paul will continue the practice as well.[249] With each occurrence of these community meals, the reader is reminded not only of Jesus talking about the New Covenant in the upper room the night he was betrayed, but also of the historic Exodus event, the connotations of the end of slavery, and the liberation that God brings. We see here intertextuality working not only on the level of Luke and the book of Exodus, but between the different scenes in Luke's Gospel and the interplay between Luke and Acts.[250] The readers are invited to break bread with other believers

---

242. Harris, *Exodus*, 20.
243. Luke 22:19.
244. Luke 24:30–31, 35.
245. Luke 22:14.
246. Luke 24:31–33.
247. Luke 22:19–20.
248. Luke 2:42–46.
249. Acts 20:7, 11; 16:34; 27:35.
250. Twelftree, *Spirit*, 131, hints at this reality when he says, "It seems right to conclude that, by the

in their communities, thus enacting the identity forming nature of these texts that are working intertextually, making them like the early Christians and like Israel. Furthermore, the reader is granted special insider information before the participants in the story become aware of it. This connection to the past and the ongoing reminder of this narrative-driven ritual helps create social identity in a reader.

Intertextuality of shared community texts builds social identity in three specific ways. First, it references current group realities in the language of an important community document. Jewish Scriptures were crucially important to the disciples and the new Christian community. There are few things that would create the uniqueness of the group than to declare that the events foretold in the Scriptures were the very events taking place among them. The new Christians were living out the dreams of the prophets. As the new community forms its own distinctiveness, it does so as an interpretation of community texts.[251]

Second, it contrasts the distinctiveness of the current communities against other communities, which is rooted in the text. Luke presents the new community as the New Israel. This creates distinctiveness with Judaism in the first century. They find ways to disassociate themselves from the Roman Empire. In the example from Acts 4 above, Pilate and Herod, along with the Gentiles and Jews who oppose the current move of God, are connected with the raging nations and the wicked kings who come against God's anointed. The tactic of a group seeing itself as standing for holiness against many forces that seek to destroy it results in a high level of group cohesion.

Third, intertextuality creates social identity by reinforcing the group's origin, history, and future destiny. Each of these elements is rooted in the Old Testament Scriptures. Luke sees the origin of the church in the story of Israel.[252] He sees the history of the group intersecting with the prophets and the promises made to Israel in the Old Testament. The future destinies of the group mentioned earlier—outward expansion of the gospel, reconstituting God's people, and eschatological hopes—are all in some way rooted in the Old Testament Scriptures. Thus, references to and interplay with these Scriptures reinforce these future expectations.[253] As readers enact the norms, behaviors, and rituals they see in Luke–Acts, they participate with previous generations in identity forming ways.

---

term 'breaking bread,' Luke is referring not to the Last Supper but to the Jewish act, including prayers, that began, yet was distinct from, the meal proper. From Luke's perspective, therefore, every meal in which the followers of Jesus participated after Easter was now a joyous recollection of meals they shared before Easter." For more on shared meals in Luke–Acts, see Finger, *Of Widows and Meals*; Heil, *Meal Scenes*; Just, *Ongoing Feast*; Moxnes, "Meals"; Smith, "Table Fellowship."

251. For more on the use of intertextuality in biblical texts and oral texts, including case studies in other biblical books, see Huizenga, "Intertextuality and Allegory"; Meek, "Intertextuality"; McKay, "Political Reading"; "Status Update"; Nicholson, "Cultural Studies"; Evans and Johnston, *Searching the Scriptures*.

252. This point was discussed earlier in this chapter.

253. For other examples of working with intertextuality and identity, see Hacham, "Maccabees"; Leim, "Glory"; Venter, "Canon"; Davis, "Crossed Texts."

Throughout the rest of this work the intertextual connections of Luke–Acts with the Hebrew Scriptures will be central. Luke finds vindication for the Christian community in the history of the Jewish faith. These are key social identity markers for him. Thus, in order to do justice to the identity-forming nature of Luke's writings, we must attend to the intertextual cues.

Conclusion

Social Identity Theory offers a methodology and language by which to understand the identity-forming nature of Luke–Acts. By participating in cultural memory, new members are able to share in the group's history and benefit from the social identity the group affords its members. The book of Acts is interested in two groups, Jews and Gentiles, the latter with a specific focus on God-fearers, coming together under the superordinate identity that Christ offers. Luke's corpus achieves a sense of improved identity by incorporating prescribed group beliefs, ideals, values, and norms. This allows the observant reader of Acts to notice the social identity-forming nature of Luke–Acts. These prescribed elements are richly embedded in Luke's narrative and are working intertextually with the Septuagint. Before exploring the heavily intertextual nature of Luke's work more deeply (chapter 3), such an exploration facilitates an in-depth look at our primary subjects and the ideal audience of the book of Acts, the God-fearers. Examining God-fearers in history, scholarship, and Acts is needed, as this has been a popular discussion in Acts scholarship. To these issues we now turn.

2

God-Fearers as Luke's Audience

My key claim is that God-fearers are the ideal audience for Luke–Acts, as they are the primary target of the author's transformative illocutionary intent of identity formation. God-fearers, who are "Gentiles who become adherents of the Jewish God without becoming proselytes,"[1] cannot be subsumed under existing categories of the Jews or the disciples, and they stand in tension with these groups.[2] There is tension because although they are attracted to Judaism and the synagogue, they have not become converts, so they "presented a great opportunity for Christian Evangelists."[3] They stand in a notable gap, with attractional forces on at least two sides (the Jewish establishment and Greco-Roman culture), and they play an important role in the Acts narrative.[4] Thus, they have been a topic of particular intrigue for scholars.

Note Nolland's words:

> The presence of God-fearers in the synagogues seems to have been of particular interest to Luke (Acts 13:16, 26; 14:1ff; 17:4,12,17; 18:4). Nowhere else in the NT do we hear of them at all. If the name Theophilus is symbolic it would suit God-fearers well. The assumption of a God-fearer readership allows the traditional reasons for regarding the first readers as Gentiles to retain much of their force, while opening up a new possibility for explaining the many Jewish

---

1. Levinskaya, *Diaspora*, 52. Trebilco, *Jewish Communities*, 145, offers a more detailed description: "a group of pagans who attended the synagogue regularly and adopted some Jewish customs such as Sabbath observance and food laws but who were not circumcised and so were not full members of the Jewish community in the way that proselytes were."

2. Cheng, *Characterization*, 232

3. Barrett, *Acts*, 501. Barrett mentions here that the God-fearers were attracted to Jewish ethics, theology, and worship. Bruce, *Acts*, 203, suggests that the Jews' "simple monotheism" as one of the attractive points. There also may be some character connections, for example, that Samson can be seen as a Hebrew version of the Greek hero Hercules. In addition, Judaism is much older than the other mythologies and mystery religions of the day, complete with the Hebrew Scriptures that date back over one thousand years from the first century, and this could be a big reason why Gentiles were attracted to it.

4. "Their response to the Word throughout Acts, negative or positive, subtly contributes to the plot" (Cheng, *Characterization*, 232).

features of Luke–Acts: Christianity would need to defend itself as faithful to Judaism, as much to the God-fearer as to the Jew.[5]

Since God-fearers comprise a large part of the current study, an analysis of the group in Acts along with the diversity present in the early church will set the stage. Second, a review of significant literature on God-fearers in the first century is needed for an accurate understanding of Luke's context as it relates to his transformative agenda. Next, we will encounter two ways that the text considers the God-fearing audience, minor characters and decentralization. Lastly, I will demonstrate Luke's identity-forming agenda in highlighting God-fearers as key figures in his narrative.

God-Fearers in Acts

Luke devoted a substantial part of Acts to God-fearers.[6] Scholars debate how to understand two key Greek phrases in Acts.[7] The words in question are οἱ φοβούμενος τὸν θεὸν ("the ones fearing God" or "the God-fearers") and οἱσεβομένοι τὸν θεὸν ("the ones worshipping God" or "the God worshippers"), used eleven times in Acts.[8] Here are the eleven occurrences, broken down by scene.

Cornelius

- Acts 10:2: εὐσεβὴς καὶ φοβούμενος τὸν θεὸν σὺν παντὶ τῷ οἴκῳ αὐτοῦ, ποιῶν ἐλεημοσύνας πολλὰς τῷ λαῷ καὶ δεόμενος τοῦ θεοῦ διὰ παντός.

    "He was a devout man who feared God with all his household; he gave alms generously to the people and prayed constantly to God."

- Acts 10:22a: οἱ δὲ εἶπαν. Κορνήλιος ἑκατοντάρχης, ἀνὴρ δίκαιος καὶ φοβούμενος τὸν θεόν, μαρτυρούμενός τε ὑπὸ ὅλου τοῦ ἔθνους τῶν Ἰουδαίων.

    "They answered, 'Cornelius, a centurion, an upright and God-fearing man, who is well spoken of by the whole Jewish nation . . .'"

---

5. Nolland, "Luke's Readers," 3. For a thorough examination of Luke's introduction, see Adams, "Preface," 177–91.

6. Levinskaya, *Diaspora*, 120.

7. A review of the scholarly debate is below.

8. Finn, "Reconsidered," 76. Levinskaya, *Diaspora*, 120, claims there are eight references and for some reason ignores the three in chapter 10 about Cornelius (despite treating him as a God-fearer and his story as key in understanding God-fearers [121]). Boer, "God-Fearers," notices how these terms are never used for Jewish piety in Luke, but reserved for Gentiles. For pious Jews, he uses the word λατρεύω (Luke 1:74; 2:37; 4:8; Acts 7:7, 42; 24:14; 26:7; 27:23). It is also important to note that the phrase in Acts 2:5, sometimes translated "God-fearing Jews," is Ἰουδαῖοι, ἄνδρες εὐλαβεῖς, using a completely different Greek word.

- Acts 10:34b–35: ἐπ' ἀληθείας καταλαμβάνομαι ὅτι οὐκ ἔστιν προσωπολήμπτης ὁ θεός, ἀλλ' ἐν παντὶ ἔθνει ὁ φοβούμενος αὐτὸν καὶ ἐργαζόμενος δικαιοσύνην δεκτὸς αὐτῷ ἐστιν.

    "I truly understand that God shows no partiality, but in every nation anyone who fears him and does what is right is acceptable to him."

Paul in Pisidian Antioch

- Acts 13:16: Ἀναστὰς δὲ Παῦλος καὶ κατασείσας τῇ χειρὶ εἶπεν· ἄνδρες Ἰσραηλῖται καὶ οἱ φοβούμενοι τὸν θεόν, ἀκούσατε.

    "So Paul stood up and with a gesture began to speak: 'You Israelites, and [others who fear God/Gentiles who worship God/you who fear God], listen.'"[9]

- Acts 13:26: Ἄνδρες ἀδελφοί, υἱοὶ γένους Ἀβραὰμ καὶ οἱ ἐν ὑμῖν φοβούμενοι τὸν θεόν, ἡμῖν ὁ λόγος τῆς σωτηρίας ταύτης ἐξαπεστάλη.

    "My brothers, you descendants of Abraham's family, and others who fear God, to us the message of this salvation has been sent."

- Acts 13:43: λυθείσης δὲ τῆς συναγωγῆς ἠκολούθησαν πολλοὶ τῶν Ἰουδαίων καὶ τῶν σεβομένων προσηλύτων τῷ Παύλῳ καὶ τῷ Βαρναβᾷ, οἵτινες προσλαλοῦντες αὐτοῖς ἔπειθον αὐτοὺς προσμένειν τῇ χάριτι τοῦ θεοῦ.

    "When the meeting of the synagogue broke up, many Jews and devout converts to Judaism followed Paul and Barnabas, who spoke to them and urged them to continue in the grace of God."

- Acts 13:50a: οἱ δὲ Ἰουδαῖοι παρώτρυναν τὰς σεβομένας γυναῖκας τὰς εὐσχήμονας καὶ τοὺς πρώτους τῆς πόλεως

    "But the Jews incited the devout women of high standing and the leading men of the city . . ."

---

9. The three versions offered for translation of the phrase (NRSV, NIV11, ESV) show the range of ways this term has been understood.

Lydia

- Acts 16:14: καί τις γυνὴ ὀνόματι Λυδία, πορφυρόπωλις πόλεως Θυατείρων σεβομένη τὸν θεόν, ἤκουεν, ἧς ὁ κύριος διήνοιξεν τὴν καρδίαν προσέχειν τοῖς λαλουμένοις ὑπὸ τοῦ Παύλου.

  "A certain woman named Lydia, a worshiper of God, was listening to us; she was from the city of Thyatira and a dealer in purple cloth. The Lord opened her heart to listen eagerly to what was said by Paul."

Paul in Thessalonica

- Acts 17:4: καί τινες ἐξ αὐτῶν ἐπείσθησαν καὶ προσεκληρώθησαν τῷ Παύλῳ καὶ τῷ Σιλᾷ, τῶν τε σεβομένων Ἑλλήνων πλῆθος πολύ, γυναικῶν τε τῶν πρώτων οὐκ ὀλίγαι.

  "Some of them were persuaded and joined Paul and Silas, as did a great many of the devout Greeks and not a few of the leading women."

Paul in Athens

- Acts 17:17: διελέγετο μὲν οὖν ἐν τῇ συναγωγῇ τοῖς Ἰουδαίοις καὶ τοῖς σεβομένοις καὶ ἐν τῇ ἀγορᾷ κατὰ πᾶσαν ἡμέραν πρὸς τοὺς παρατυγχάνοντας.

  "So he argued in the synagogue with the Jews and the devout persons, and also in the marketplace every day with those who happened to be there."

Paul in Corinth

- Acts 18:7: καὶ μεταβὰς ἐκεῖθεν εἰσῆλθεν εἰς οἰκίαν τινὸς ὀνόματι Τιτίου Ἰούστου σεβομένου τὸν θεόν, οὗ ἡ οἰκία ἦν συνομοροῦσα τῇ συναγωγῇ.

  "Then he left the synagogue and went to the house of a man named Titius Justus, a worshiper of God; his house was next door to the synagogue."[10]

---

10. Another verse that fits with the pattern we have seen, but does not use the word, is Acts 14:1, where Paul and Barnabas convert Greeks in a synagogue:
Ἐγένετο δὲ ἐν Ἰκονίῳ κατὰ τὸ αὐτὸ εἰσελθεῖν αὐτοὺς εἰς τὴν συναγωγὴν τῶν Ἰουδαίων καὶ λαλῆσαι οὕτως ὥστε πιστεῦσαι Ἰουδαίων τε καὶ Ἑλλήνων πολὺ πλῆθος.
"The same thing occurred in Iconium, where Paul and Barnabas went into the Jewish synagogue and spoke in such a way that a great number of both Jews and Greeks became believers."

The Cornelius scene introduces the reader to the term οἱ φοβούμενος τὸν θεὸν and the paradigmatic convert. The concept is repeated numerous times in the ministry of Paul throughout the rest of the book. "The references to God-fearers cover a wide geographical area including Caesarea, Pisidian Antioch, Philippi, Thessalonica, Athens, and Corinth."[11]

Each usage falls between Acts 10 and 18. However, despite this concentration of occurrences, the concepts of diversity and decentralization are central in the entire two-volume work. The idea of God-fearers is not new with Cornelius in Acts 10, though he is a major part of moving Luke's agenda forward. He follows the stories of the Centurion in Luke 7 and the Eunuch in Acts 8, in addition to many other minor characters,[12] not to mention the availability of the Spirit to those outside the main stream. Thus, the appearance of the God-fearers works as a climax to Luke's narrative trajectory. This chapter examines these narrative elements of diversity, minor characters, and decentralization. We now turn to the diversity in Luke's second volume.

In Acts we find a range of cultural diversity as it pertains to people groups. Luke reports a diverse church in Jerusalem for Pentecost in chapter 2, as verses 9–11 offer an unusually precise account of a number of the different nations represented,[13] thereby expanding 1:8. The diversity of languages and geography of Jewish people fits with the trajectory of outward expansion and inclusion. Thus, Luke is establishing early on in volume two the diverse nature of those who participate inactivity of God and the multinational context in which the Spirit first appears. This sets the stage for the inclusion of outsiders, which will be a major part of Acts.[14] Furthermore, within Judaism there are a variety of groups presented in Luke–Acts (Pharisees, Sadducees, Zealots, the Circumcision group, etc.), ranging in response to Jesus and to the New Christian Movement from fully committed discipleship to outright rejection and opposition. For example, Brawley notes that although Luke presents the Pharisees as clashing with Jesus, they are presented more positively in Luke–Acts than in the other Gospels.[15] By contrast,

---

11. Levinskaya, *Diaspora*, 120.

12. Philip (Acts 6:5; 8:5–40), Stephen (Acts 6:5—8:1), Barnabas (Acts 4:36; 9:27; the missionary journeys in chapters 11–15), Ananias and Sapphira (Acts 5:1–11), the other Ananias (Acts 9:10–19), Lydia (16:14, 40), Titus Justus (Acts 18:7), Apollos (Acts 18:24–28), Eutycus (20), Paul's traveling companions (Silas in 15:40, the list of characters in chapter 20), Felix (23:24—24:27), Festus (25:1-12), and many others.

13. "Parthians, Medes, Elamites, and residents of Mesopotamia, Judea and Cappadocia, Pontus and Asia, Phrygia and Pamphylia, Egypt and the parts of Libya belonging to Cyrene, and visitors from Rome, both Jews and proselytes, Cretans and Arabs—in our own languages we hear them speaking about God's deeds of power" (Acts 2:9–11). See Gilbert, "Nations."

14. Davies, "Inclusion." Some may suggest that Luke's emphasis on Jewish diversity undermines his mission to God-fearers. However, Luke, in his focus on God-fearers, has an outward trajectory of decentralization in mind, which is both personal and geographical. The diversity surrounding Pentecost is fully coherent with Luke's purposes. See discussion on decentralization below.

15. Brawley, *Conflict*, 84–106. Also, see Hakola, "Friendly Pharisees," who affirms this point as well, looking at it through the lens of Social Identity Theory, and offers a history of the discussion about whether Luke is anti-Jewish. Despite this being the consensus of scholarship for many years,

the Sadducees engineer his execution.[16] Moreover, there is a distinction made between the Hebrew speaking Jews[17] and the Greek speaking (Hellenistic) Jews.[18] In addition to God-fearers,[19] who are connected in some way with the synagogue, there may be another distinction to be made between Gentiles who are interested in God[20] and Gentiles who are far off.[21] Thus, the God-fearers appear in Luke–Acts amid complex diversity. They stand in a middle ground between the Jews who are already welcomed into the church and the Gentiles who will only become such as the narrative of Acts unfolds. God-fearers play a key role in the narrative with the conversion of Cornelius providing the paradigmatic shift. Before attending to this shift, the history of scholarship with regard to God-fearers needs to be consulted.

God-Fearers in Scholarship

Having established the diversity of the groups in Acts, which includes God-fearers, a survey of relevant literature is necessary. Jakob Bernays opened the discussion by publishing an article in 1877 that wrestled with a passage from Juvenal[22] that seems to introduce a classification of people who keep the Sabbath and abstain from pork, but do not keep the rest of the Law.[23] Then, in 1933, Lake continues what he calls "a long and complicated discussion" and argues that the term God-fearers could be used of Jews or Gentiles who were pious, and concludes, "There is no suggestion that the word has a technical sense."[24] Some years later, this sentiment continued in the work of Feldman who seeks to demonstrate that the term is used of a pious person and does not become a technical term until the mid-second century.[25] While some believed that Luke was presenting evidence of Gentiles who were attracted to the synagogue, many still believed it was the work of a "theologically inspired imagination"[26] that explained

---

Jervell's argument in 1972 shifted the view for most. See Jervell, *People of God*. For an earlier treatment of the issue, see *Jervell*, "Das gespaltene."

16. Tyson, "Opposition."
17. Acts 6:1.
18. Acts 6:1; 9:29
19. Acts 10:2, 22, 34–35; 13:16, 26, 43, 50; 16:14; 17:4, 17; 18:7.
20. This is, admittedly, a difficult category, and perhaps could be enfolded into "God-fearers." The Ethiopian Eunuch is interested in things of God and some scholars call him a God-fearer, but he represents a different kind of diversity than Cornelius.
21. Acts 17:18–21; 19:17–20.
22. Juvenal, *Satire* xiv.96–99.
23. Bernays, "Die Gottesfürchtigen."
24. Lake, "Proselytes," 88; Gempf, "God-Fearers," 445. Also, see Overman, "God-Fearers."
25. Feldman, "Jewish 'Sympathizers.'"
26. Hemer, *Acts*, 447.

why a primarily Jewish religion had become so Gentile. The discussions that continued for decades largely confirmed prior findings.[27]

By the sixties and seventies, God-fearers had become a hot topic in the world of New Testament studies. The *Encyclopedia Judaica* defined the term and estimated the numbers in the first century as high as "perhaps millions."[28] Flusser and Hengel agreed about the large numbers of God-fearers and commented on the diversity of Judaism during this time.[29] The discussion at this point was "overwhelmingly literary"[30] in nature, with a focus on the references in Acts and "isolated references" from classical literature.[31] The acknowledgment of this group and the scholarly interest had never been higher.

The 1980s saw a flurry of discussion around God-fearers, and some resistance to a growing consensus that Luke was using a technical term and signifying an official group in the culture. Wilcox states, "Whether the term οἱ φοβούμενος τὸν θεὸν was a technical term or even an embryonic technical term for non-Jewish synagogue adherents, the evidence simply does not allow us to say."[32] Kraabel takes it a step further, introducing his article by saying, "This paper explores one instance in which such a serious misreading of the evidence has taken place."[33] He questions the evidence, the history, and the absence of references outside Acts, calling God-fearers an invention of the Evangelist and suggests that finding one inscription would not be enough to prove the historical credibility of the term.

Ironically, around that same time (1976), archeologists uncovered a nine-foot marble slab at Aphrodisias in Caria, Turkey.[34] The inscription, from the third century CE, contains a list of names carved outside a synagogue.[35] The names on the stone include important people and likely donors to the synagogue, and included in this list are two people labeled as θεοσεβής. "The term appears after the mention of individuals (a goldsmith, a coppersmith, two confectioners, a fowler [?], and possibly a greengrocer) and among separately listed identifiable groups (coppersmiths, fullers, etc.). It certainly seems to designate a group distinct from proselytes and ethnic Jews

---

27. Lifshitz, "Du Nouveau"; Hommel, "Juden"; Romaniuk, "Die 'Gottesfürchtigen'"; Siegert, "Gottesfürchtige."

28. Hertzberg, "Jewish Identity," 55. Kraabel would later call this a "wild exaggeration" (Kraabel, "Greeks," 155).

29. Flusser, "Paganism," 10; Hengel, *Judaism*, 313. Also, see Avi-Yonah, *Palestine*, 37.

30. There are no clear references to God-fearers in the New Testament outside of Acts. There may be a foreshadowed reference in Luke 1:50. More on that in chapter 3.

31. Kraabel, "Disappearance," 114. For a full treatment of the inscriptions, see chapters 4 and 7 in Levinskaya, *Diaspora*.

32. Wilcox, "Reconsideration," 107. Many studies also see the phrase σεβομένη τὸν θεόν as similar and referring to the same group, and thus consider it in this same discussion.

33. Kraabel, "Disappearance," 113. Also, see Kraabel, "Beloved Disciple"; "Immigrants"; MacLennan and Kraabel, "Theological Invention."

34. Williams, "Inscription," 297. Also, see Reynolds and Tannenbaum, *God-Fearers at Aphrodisias*.

35. Williams, "Inscription," 297.

yet enrolled in the synagogue."³⁶ This inscription "tipped the balance and proved both the existence of a category of friendly Gentiles and the application to this category of the term θεοσεβής, which was known from other inscriptions."³⁷ This find would forever change the conversation around God-fearers and their legitimacy in the early centuries, although the timing may still be up for debate: "The picture in Acts may or may not be anachronistic, but it can no longer be thought of as preposterous, or the work of a theologically inspired imagination."³⁸

The combination of Kraabel's article and the Aphrodisias find spurred a number of responses.³⁹ Perhaps the most profound of the critiques comes from Overman, who suggests Kraabel's focus on the term/phrase φοβούμενοί/σεβόμενοι τὸν θεὸν is too narrow. "The specific name or title of a group of Gentile sympathizers is far less important than the question concerning evidence from this period which might indicate that Jewish communities of the Diaspora had included such a group of Gentiles in their life and worship."⁴⁰ As he goes on to show, there is ample evidence from the ancient world to suggest this is so. Josephus, for example, talks of Greeks being attracted to Jewish communities.⁴¹ Overman also mentions Juvenal's *Satire* 14, c.130 mentioning "Sabbath-fearing" fathers, and suggests that although this is satire, "there is no reason to assume this does not reflect a situation familiar to both Juvenal and his audience."⁴² Lastly, Overman cites some of Kraabel's work that suggests there may be sympathetic Gentiles in Jewish communities in those time periods.⁴³ Thus, more than simply a title of reference in the ancient world, the evidence suggests that non-Jews did play a role in synagogue life. Conditions appear to have existed that make the notion of a group of God-fearers as a distinct group plausible.

Gager takes a more middling view. He does take into account the Aphrodisias evidence, saying:

> It is no exaggeration to propose that these inscriptions represent the most important epigraphic evidence from the world of Greco-Roman Judaism. They will be the center of the debate for years to come. Yet even at this point, certain results seem assured. θεοσεβής designates a separate category of persons

---

36. Finn, "Reconsidered," 79–80. Also, see Meeks, *Urban Christians*, 39.

37. Levinskaya, "Diaspora," 51. Although the Aphrodisias inscription "tipped the scales," it is not the only epigraphical evidence we have. Levinskaya, "Diaspora," 51–82, surveys this evidence.

38. Hemer, "Hellenistic History," 447. Also, see Finn, "Reconsidered," 75–84; Mellink, "Archeology."

39. Wilcox, "Reconsideration," 107; Finn, "Reconsidered"; Kraabel, "Greeks,"; Gager, "Synagogues." Also, see Collins. "Otherness," 171; Feldman, "Omnipresence"; Millar, "Gentiles"; Esler, *Community*; Jervell, "Church"; McKnight, *Light*; Sanders, "Who Is a Jew"; Tyson, *Images*; Murphy-O'Connor, "God-Fearers"; Lieu, "Good Christians?"; Reiser, "Hat Paulus"; Boer, "God-Fearers."

40. Overman, "Neglected Features," 259.

41. Josephus, *Ap.* 2.282.39; *J.W.* 7.3.3. Also, see Cohen, "Respect," 409–30; "Crossing"; Kroll, "Greek Inscriptions"; Kraemer, "Meaning."

42. Overman, "Neglected Features," 260. Finn, "Reconsidered," 81, agrees.

43. Overman, "Neglected Features," 260. Kraabel, "Judaism," 201–3, 242.

associated with the synagogue; it is used in a technical fashion as a title; the category itself is distinct from both proselytes and other Jews; it appears to cover Gentiles, whether exclusively or not.[44]

Despite these statements, Gager still distrusts Luke, suggesting he "uses the 'God-fearers' for his own theological purposes" and claims that God-fearers converting to Christianity over Judaism is "Luke's invention" for which, "apart from Acts, there is no support for this claim whatsoever."[45] He is in one accord with Kraabel's own opinion on this matter, whose response does not appear to take into consideration the Aphrodisias evidence, but rather seeks to discredit Luke as a historical source.[46] Needless to say, (dis)trusting Luke historically while pointing out the author's theological purposes are separate issues. What matters for our purposes is Gager's insistence that an empirical group of God-fearers in all likelihood existed in the first century. It is probable, therefore, that Luke's implied audience would have been able to see the narrative's relevance for God-fearers.[47] In the end, the reader is left wondering if Kraabel overlooked the issue of the new epigraphical information.

Then, in 1989, referring to his dissertation (cited above), John Nolland stated:

> Indeed, I thought then, and think now, that the ideal first-century reader for much of the Gospel of Luke (and of Acts) is a God-fearer; one whose birth is not Jewish and whose background culture is Hellenistic, but who had been attracted to Judaism, drawn to the God of Israel and the worship of the synagogue; one who had taken on from his Jewish mentors many of the ethical and religious values of the faith on whose threshold he stood; but one who had not yet taken the final step of circumcision and full incorporation into the national and cultural life of the Jews.
>
> Such a God-fearer would have experienced the ambiguity of his situation in Judaism: welcomed, but at the crucial divide still considered to be an outsider to the promises of God. Luke's God-fearer will have been no stranger to the Christian gospel; perhaps he has been reached in an evangelistic itineration

---

44. Gager, "Synagogues," 98.

45. Gager, "Synagogues," 99. Gager states that Luke's theological purposes for using the God-fearers are "specifically to justify his view that Gentiles have replaced Jews as the chosen people of God." In the rest of this monograph, I will talk about the scope of the people of God expanding through decentralization to include Gentiles and God-fearers (see below and chapter 5). However I am not comfortable describing this as a replacement of Jews, as they continue to remain involved and important to what God is doing throughout the period of the New Testament.

46. Kraabel, "Greeks." For other volumes on the trustworthiness of Luke as a historian, see Keener, *Historical Jesus*; Keener, *Acts* (vol. 1); Cadbury, *Acts*; Robertson; Howard, *Source*. For a fuller list, see Mattill, *Bibliography*.

47. There is a puzzling discrepancy in Gager's argument. One the one hand, he trusts Luke's testimony about God-fearers as a distinct group in the first century. On the other hand, however, he distrusts Luke's report that God-fearers converted to Christianity, and attributes that to "theological purposes." It is unclear why Gager chooses to trust Luke in one area and not trust him in another, or why he feels that Luke's theological aims make him an untrustworthy historian.

like those attributed to Paul in Acts. Luke's God-fearer is also, however, no stranger to Christianity's detractors (whose form he will also recognize in the Acts material). He has not fully found his way into Judaism, and now he stands at the crossroads. On the one hand Christianity is being offered to him as the completion and fulfillment of the Judaism to which he has been drawn, a version of Judaism which can embrace him in his Gentile identity, while itself holding dear all from Judaism that he has come to hold dear. On the other hand, there are his Jewish friends who consider Christianity to be a dangerous perversion of their Jewish heritage, and who urge our God-fearer to make the break and to abandon his Gentile identity once and for all and to come all the way into Judaism, to become a Jew.[48]

Nolland's suggestion of the ideal reader as God-fearer provides a major watershed. It opens up new considerations for Luke's purposes and helps us fully embrace both the Jewish nature of Luke as well as his emphasis on diversity, the latter of which is seen by a full embracing of outsiders (Ethiopian Eunuch, Cornelius, etc.), as well as a movement away from the Twelve. Thus, the empirical research and data about God-fearers helps us with the literary aims.

Over the next decade, Nolland's claim was met with significant agreement by others. Irina Levinskaya devoted four chapters of her work on the diasporic setting of Acts to God-fearers, calling them "central for both [Luke's] historical and theological conception."[49] Later, in 2006, Dietrich-Alex Koch would say, "The picture of the God-fearers in Acts is indeed a literary picture as well, but as it is the case for the proselytes, we can reasonably assume that the picture of the God-fearers has its equivalence in the social and religious world of Luke and his readers."[50]

Lastly, Craig Keener, in his multi-volume work on Acts, reports, "Writing after 70 CE to Diaspora Christians, Luke might deal with Jewish communities on the whole less conservative and more likely to accept God-fearers."[51] And again, "For Luke–Acts, however, I tend to favor a mainstream Greco-Roman audience in Macedonia and Achaia, with Jewish founders (not least Paul), a mixture of Gentile and Jewish members, and considerable Jewish and God-fearing didactic input."[52] More pointedly, contra Kraabel, Keener asks, "since Luke fails to explain the God-fearers, how would his audience know what they were intended to represent if they corresponded to nothing in their world?"[53] Keener calls Kraabel's argument "unconvincing."[54] Nonetheless,

48. Nolland, *Luke*, xxxii.
49. Levinskaya, "Diaspora," 49. See also Levinskaya, "Inscription"; Gilbert, "Disappearance."
50. Koch, "Facts," 80. Also, see Collins, *Athens*; "Symbol"; Stanton, "Dialogue"; Bartlett, *Cities*.
51. Keener, *Acts*, 1:438.
52. Keener, *Acts*, 1:438.
53. Keener, *Acts*, 2:1751. This work is the primary place Keener addresses his thoughts on God-fearers, though he does briefly also in *Background* and *Women*.
54. Keener, *Acts*, 2:1752. Kraabel is not the only one to have questions raised about his case. Cheng, *Characterization*, 232n1, suggests, "However, in arguing that these terms refer not to the membership

some modern thinkers still continue to wonder if "God-fearer" was simply a descriptive term of piety rather than an identity marker.[55]

Thus, with the evidence and a number of reputable authors claiming over the last three decades that God-fearers make up a significant part of the Lukan audience, some going so far as to say that the *ideal* reader is a God-fearer,[56] we can approach the portrayal of God-fearers in Acts with some confidence. I propose to examine specifically the speeches of Acts 7 and 13 to seek to understand how a first-century Gentile God-fearer would have understood his or her place in the salvation history of God, what Luke's purpose was for sharing these stories with this group, and how that affected the way these God-fearers understood their social identity within the context of the early church.

But these scholars, for all of their work on the empirical world that was the world of Acts, have not gone far enough. Reading early Christian literature as identity-forming documents for their intended audiences has not been considered deeply enough, specifically regarding Acts and God-fearers. Luke's transformative illocutionary intent is to create identity among his God-fearing readers. Two keys to this are the utilization of minor characters in the narrative and a focus on decentralization of established power.

Minor Characters and Decentralization

A major part of Luke's identity-forming agenda includes demonstrating for the God-fearing reader his or her place in the kingdom of God. But how do outsiders join a movement that has historically excluded them? There must be change that takes place in the system that allows for the inclusion of the marginalized. This is done in Luke–Acts through decentralization of the Jewish establishment. Decentralization, for the purposes of this investigation, refers to the early Christian movement's directionality away from established Jewish norms, symbols of centralization, and power structures (food laws, power of a few, Sanhedrin, Temple, Jerusalem centric faith, etc.) toward a more inclusive and open faith that welcomes outsiders as participants and owners of

---

of a class but to piety itself, Wilcox, throughout his presentation, fails to provide explicit, forceful, and convincing support for his conclusion."

55. Brink, *Soldiers*, 157. In 2014, Ross Kraemer wrote an article in which she suggested abandoning the title God-fearer, as she calls it a "broad, unparsed category" and "vastly overblown." Her argument is primarily semantic and flows from a survey of how the term is used in both Greek and Latin in the ancient world, noting the diversity of usage, and arguing that this diversity should lead scholars to abandon the term as a "universal, static category." While Kraemer rightly reminds us of the importance of precision when using ancient terms, the phrase is important because Luke crafts a narrative that includes it and is (at least somewhat) targeted at this group. Furthermore, empirical evidence makes it at least plausible that a group like this existed in the ancient world. Put differently, our assumption of a significant existence of God-fearers explains a lot of narrative and contextual evidence, which seems to be a stronger argument than one solely based on semantics. See Kraemer, "Giving."

56. Nolland, *Luke*, xxxii.

the faith.⁵⁷ Whereby centralization typically promotes the exclusive position of ministry and the power differential that favors the elite and the insiders, decentralization minimizes these sociological factors in favor of democratizing social groups. Consequently, more participants are empowered to act formatively with a view to setting the group on a developmental path of radical transformation. To the degree that it can be shown that Luke–Acts focuses on the decentralization of the Jewish power structures and creates space for outsiders, specifically God-fearers, Luke is involved in identity formation for the God-fearing reader. As we established in chapter 1, for two separate groups to come together, a superordinate group identity must be created. Thus, outsiders do not become Jewish, but rather, Jews and Gentiles (including God-fearers) are subsumed under the superordinate group of "the Way."⁵⁸

Additionally, Luke uses "minor characters" regularly in Acts, who end up playing a major role in the narrative and in Luke's agenda. Minor characters are those characters that the reader is surprised play a significant part in the narrative due to certain roadblocks, be they social, racial, gender based, or otherwise. As Rhoads, Dewey, and Michie explain, minor characters are "marginal people with no power—children, women, a beggar, a foreigner, a poor widow. Many are excluded from common life because of their afflictions."⁵⁹ Luke has an agenda to include the marginalized as central to his narrative because it demonstrates God's love for the outcasts. This strategically serves his identity-forming purpose for his God-fearing

---

57. Few, if any, studies of this feature in Acts exist, though some have drawn attention to this need. See Beers, *Servant*, 179, who says, "My project suggests the need for future research in Acts scholarship regarding the decentralization motif. A common scholarly argument is that Luke reserves a distinctive role for the twelve apostles; however, my research, with its focus on those outside the twelve embodying the servant task, suggests exactly the opposite. The lack of activity on the part of the apostles (with the possible exception of Peter and perhaps John) thus implicitly critiques them, though the positive side to their apparent sedentary life is the extension of the Isaianic mission to the larger group of Jesus' followers. It is this latter group in Acts who is truly faithful to Jesus' commission and continues to preach the good news 'with all boldness and without hindrance' (Acts 28:31)." Some do acknowledge this motif without using the word "decentralization." For example, Johnson, *Acts*, 186, says "Luke has shown his reader how the good news spread both geographically and demographically, reaching in the evangelization of the detested Samaritans and the sexually mutilated Ethiopian those who would be considered at best marginally Jewish by the strict standards of the Pharisees." Dillon, *Hymns*, 43, talks of "disengagement between the divine word and human privilege." Others speak on specific issues, such as Green on the Temple. See Green, "Demise."

58. See chapter 1 on Social Identity Theory and footnotes there. "The Way" is a common label for Luke to describe the new Christian movement. Acts 9:2; 19:9, 23; 22:4; 24:14, 22. However, this should not be thought of as a replacement for Judaism along the lines of supersessionism. Rather, this is a renewal of the Jewish story that goes back to the origins of the people (Hebrew Scriptures, Exodus, etc.) and includes outsiders, as Isaiah foresaw. See Turner, *Power*.

59. Rhoads et al., *Mark as Story*, 130. They also suggest that there is an element of minor characters where they "do not play ongoing roles in the story" but "make brief appearances and disappear." Both of these elements are present regarding minor characters in Luke–Acts, though I am focusing more on the element of marginalization. Cornelius is an outsider who because the prototypical God-fearer (see chapter 4) and is only in the narrative for a few chapters. Paul, on the other hand, is a minor character in the sense that he was an enemy to Christianity, but continues through the narrative of Acts.

audience, who are marginalized themselves.[60] As minor characters take a lead role in the narrative, the audience sees itself in these characters and is invited into the story of Jesus and the early church.[61]

When Jesus leaves the disciples, he charges them with being his witnesses, which is what the reader expects to see happen. To some extent, this does happen on a small scale. Peter speaks at Pentecost,[62] Peter and John become "verifiers" of what the Holy Spirit is doing,[63] Peter leads Cornelius to the faith.[64] But more surprising are the many minor characters who enter the narrative and play more important roles than the Twelve. Philip and Stephen are selected in Acts 6:1–5 to oversee food distribution and "wait on tables."[65] Philip leads another minor character (the Ethiopian Eunuch) to the faith in chapter 8. Stephen gives the longest speech in Acts and speaks so ferociously that he is accused of speaking against the law of Moses and is stoned to death as the first martyr in the book.[66] Cornelius, a Roman centurion, is supernaturally visited and converted (and will become the prototypical God-fearer).[67] Barnabas becomes a missionary and a companion of Paul.[68] There are many more examples of this as well.[69]

This decentralization happens in two ways: (1) it is personal, in the sense that there is a movement away from the Twelve apostles. These Twelve apostles started out as minor characters as well, as unassuming fisherman,[70] tax collectors,[71] and zealots.[72] Despite the outward movement that takes place throughout the two-volume work, the disciples shift from being at the cutting edge of the mission to being in the background, if present at all. The decentralization is also (2) geographical, in the sense that it is moving away from the Temple and Jerusalem. These thematic elements are in

---

60. For general treatments of Luke's emphasis on the marginalized, see Johnson, *Function*; Karris, "Poor"; Beavis, "Return"; Pilgrim, *Rich and Poor*. For a look at treatments of specific elements and groups Luke features in his treatment of the marginalized, see Ching, "Incompatibility"; Williamson, "Singing"; Dale, "Dismantling"; Oakman, "Countryside."

61. For more on readers seeing themselves in the characters, see chapter 4, "Luke's Use of Prototypes and Exemplars."

62. Acts 2.

63. Acts 8:14.

64. Acts 10.

65. The apostles' own words in Acts 6:2b. Also, see Pao, "Waiters"; Finger, "Table Fellowship."

66. Acts 7.

67. Acts 10. See chapter 4.

68. Acts 11:30; 12:25.

69. Other minor characters in the narrative could include Ananias and Sapphira (Acts 5:1–11), the other Ananias (Acts 9:10–19), Lydia (16:14, 40), Titus Justus (Acts 18:7), Apollos (Acts 18:24–28), Eutycus (20), Paul's traveling companions (Silas in 15:40, the list of characters in chapter 20), Felix (23:24–24:27), Festus (25:1–12), and many others.

70. Luke 5:1–11.

71. Luke 5:27–28.

72. Luke 6:15.

addition to the blatant statements of decentralization that are made in the book,[73] as well as the words of Jesus in Acts 1:8. There are still some central focuses ("the apostles' teaching . . . the fellowship, the breaking of bread, and . . . prayer"), but they are more decentralized than one might expect. This passage in Acts 2:42–47, for example, is one of the few times the church will be united and centered in Jerusalem. After a thriving ministry in chapter 3, chapters 4 and 5 bring persecution and imprisonment, and by chapters 6 and 7 Stephen has become a central character, who will set the stage for Paul. From chapter 6 through the end of Acts, the outward movement happens in spite of the disciples rather than through them.

The geographical decentralization is a well-recognized feature of the book that can easily be demonstrated. Acts 1:8 states "But you will receive power when the Holy Spirit has come upon you; and you will be my witnesses in Jerusalem, in all Judea and Samaria, and to the ends of the earth." Many commentators have pointed out how this geographical progression happens in the narrative.[74] While Judaism was centered on the Temple, the priesthood, and the synagogue, as well as features like the land, the Torah, and the kosher laws,[75] the new Jesus movement was centered only on the Christ.[76] There is much that should be said about the movement away from these specific elements of Judaism.[77] For now, the decentralization of meeting places is worth some comment. While 2:46 suggests that they met in the Temple courts early on in the movement, Keener understands this as continuing in the pattern of Jesus for practical, special purposes.[78] More commonly they met in small communities, at times not even apostolic communities, in homes and public locations.[79] This trajectory of meeting in homes as opposed to the Temple and the synagogue is seen throughout Acts. Pentecost happens in a house (οἶκος).[80] At the end of chapter 2 they are spending time in the Temple, but they are also meeting and breaking bread in homes.[81] In chapter 5, we learn "every day in the temple and at home they did not cease to teach and proclaim Jesus as the Messiah."[82] Although in the second half of volume two, there is a shift to going first into the synagogue in the new town to proclaim

---

73. Acts 8:4; 11:19–20.

74. Keener, *Acts*, 1:708.

75. See chapters 3 and 5 for discussion on Temple and land, respectively. For the importance of this motif, see Wright, *Victory*, 383–84.

76. While the empirical Jesus movement in Acts seems to remain focused on Jerusalem and the Temple in the first seven chapters, the ideal focus that started with Jesus and is reinforced by the Spirit throughout Acts is the centrality of the Messiah.

77. Specific sections on the Temple and the land will be covered in chapter 5, as well as a discussion about Jesus cleansing the Temple in this chapter below.

78. Keener, *Acts*, 1:1032.

79. Acts 2:46; 3:1; 5:42; 16:15; 18:26; 28:7; 1 Cor 16:19.

80. Acts 2:2.

81. Acts 2:46.

82. Acts 5:42. See Barber, "Temple," who incorporates prophetic expectation into this act.

the gospel,[83] key conversions also happen in people's homes. Peter's encounter with Cornelius takes place in his house.[84] The guard at the jail in chapter 16 apparently invites Paul and Silas to his house, where all are converted.[85] The synagogue and the Temple are being decentralized, perhaps because of the opportunity for hospitality and generosity that comes from meeting in homes.[86]

There is certainly a movement away from Jerusalem in volume two.[87] Stephen is accused of speaking against the Temple and offers a response from Jewish salvation history. His speech is about decentralization—from the Temple and from the land—and that fits Luke's program mentioned in 1:8. It also provides a message to a God-fearing reader that all of God's activity in salvation history has been leading up to this climactic point. Stephen's speech, and subsequent martyrdom, provides a major step forward in the progression of this plan. His death advances the cause and leads to a scattering of Christians and the gospel. The modus operandi from this point on will be the inclusion of God-fearers and Gentiles into the story. God is doing a new thing where the boundaries are extended and those outside the central locus of Jerusalem centered Judaism are welcomed into the story.

The second type of decentralization that runs through Acts is personal in nature. It involves the influence of the Twelve. In a number of ways, power is spread and shared, rather than grasped. Consider the emphasis on the apostles' teaching listed in 2:42.[88] Clearly this assumes some significant involvement of the teaching of Peter, John, and the rest in the early part of Acts. However, so much teaching is done by people other than the Twelve Apostles.[89] Paul, who becomes an apostle, teaches more than anyone else, but is not one of the Twelve, and is not even introduced until 8:1 when he is still an enemy of the church. Other teachers include Stephen,[90] Apollos,[91] Phillip,[92] Priscilla

---

83. In Acts, Paul visits the synagogue in Salamis (13:5), Pisidian Antioch (13:14–15), Iconium (14:1), Thessalonica (17:1), Berea (17:10), Athens (17:17), Corinth (18:7), and Ephesus twice (18:19; 19:8). Priscilla and Aquila (18:4) and Apollos (18:26) are also all said to travel to synagogues.

84. Acts 10:2.

85. Acts 16:32.

86. Banks, *Community*, 56, states, "Given the family character of the Christian community, the homes of its members provided the most conducive atmosphere in which they could give expression to the bond they had in common."

87. Although there is a move away from Jerusalem, there remains a connection to it in the narrative. This connection to Jerusalem is key to Luke's strategy of presenting Paul as a prototypical representation of Judaism, which I talk about in chapter 4.

88. It is listed along with fellowship, breaking of bread, and prayer, which all seem to be central focuses of the new community.

89. See Neyrey, "'Teaching'"; Beck, "Evangelism." Not all agree that there is a personal decentralization, but see a hierarchy forming in the institution of the early church. See Keene, "Early Catholicism."

90. Acts 6–7.

91. Acts 18:24–28. Also, see Wilson, "Apostle."

92. Acts 8:5–40.

and Aquila,[93] Barnabas,[94] and James.[95] Although the expectation early on may be that the centralized apostles will do the majority of the teaching, the reality is quite different. This decentralization helps highlight minor characters and create a way to include other marginalized peoples. As Keener states, "The principle of inversion continues from the Gospel into Acts; as in the entire gospel tradition, those who feel most secure with power, including among God's people, are most susceptible to the blindness that power brings. The marginalized, by contrast, are most ready to depend on Christ the healer, liberator, and savior."[96] Thus, it is no longer about the Twelve,[97] but about "whosoever will" answer the call of the kingdom and declare the message with boldness and obedience.[98] And, in fact, these minor characters, participating in the movement as they do, reinforce this decentralization of power.[99]

This pattern of decentralization in Acts falls right in line with the testimony of the rest of Scripture. God regularly picks unlikely candidates through whom he intends to accomplish his work. He picks Abram and Sarai, who are aging and childless, to start the nation of Israel.[100] He chooses Gideon, the least of his family in the weakest of the clans of Manasseh, to bring victory over the Midianites.[101] He selects David, the youngest son of Jesse, to be his king.[102] As Keener notes above, this focus continues into the Gospels. Jesus chooses unlikely disciples, such as fishermen and tax collectors.[103] Women play a prominent role in Luke, as they travel with him and fund his ministry,[104] they sit at his feet and hear him teach,[105] and they are the first

93. Acts 18:26. Also, see Walker, "Portrayal"; Keller, *Priscilla*.

94. Acts 11:26; 13:7, 42–46; 14:1–3; 15:35.

95. Acts 15:13.

96. Keener, *Acts*, 1:508.

97. It is worth noting the change that happens in the Twelve in Acts 1:15–26 with the replacement of Judas.

98. There is some question about groups like the poor and other marginalized groups (i.e., "sinners") disappearing in Acts, though they were prominent in volume 1. For more on this, see Bergquist, "'Good News'"; Roth, *Blind*; Green, *Conversion*.

99. One might ask whether what I call decentralization is simply the passing of the baton to the next generation in Acts. While there is certainly the recognition of a new generation of Christians in Acts (i.e., Stephen, Timothy, Lydia, even Paul), what is happening appears to be much bigger than a mere passing of the baton to the next generation. The mission is expanded in order to incorporate outsiders, such as Gentiles and God-fearers, into the movement. To see this as simply the next generation stepping into ministry is to miss the larger narrative movement that is depicted both geographically and socially throughout Acts. This development seems to reflect the anticipation of the "New Exodus" in some of Israel's Scriptures, especially the book of Isaiah. See Beers, *Servant*; Pao, *New Exodus*; Watts, *New Exodus*.

100. Gen 12.

101. Judg 6–8.

102. 1 Sam 16.

103. Luke 5:2, 27–32.

104. Luke 8:1–3.

105. Luke 10:38–42.

to witness and report his resurrection.[106] Thus, decentralization and the inclusion of the unexpected is not new in Scripture. Rather, Luke is following a common thread and is working intertextually. What is new in Acts is the scope of the decentralization. It undermines the entire Jewish holiness system, as it was known in the first century, as God's plan of inclusion and decentralization reaches new heights in the ministry of the early church.[107]

So, how would decentralization sound to a God-fearing audience? The narrative of decentralization would be attractive to the marginalized. Acts shows that in this new movement everybody gets to play an active role. If the exotic Gentile has a part to play in this story, how much more the faithful God-fearer? A closer examination of some of these minor characters is in order to demonstrate Luke's use of decentralization.

The Ethiopian Eunuch

We have already briefly noted the irony of Philip taking a prominent role in Acts as a minor character. His encounter with the Ethiopian Eunuch is the climax of his ministry. As mentioned in chapter 1, the Ethiopian Eunuch is key in the identity formation process in Acts.[108] Conversion stories, like speeches, take up a large amount of space in Acts and are important to Luke's program.[109] There is much discussion about the identity of this Ethiopian Eunuch in scholarship and in the early church.[110] Eusebius calls him the first Gentile convert.[111] Others have disagreed, and claimed he could not have been a Gentile. For example, Haenchen holds, "Luke cannot and did not say that the eunuch was a Gentile; otherwise Philip would have forestalled Peter, the legitimate founder of the Gentile mission!"[112] He continues, suggesting that the conversion of the eunuch, since he is not heard of again, not contested, and not made public, is insignificant in the narrative.[113] Haenchen's conclusions seem weak for three reasons. First, as Tannehill states, the encounter with the eunuch was a private event, unlike

---

106. Luke 23:55—24:12. For more on the inclusion of the outcasts and the poor in God's plan in Luke, see York, *Last*.

107. See Borg, *Conflict*, who argues that the major conflict in Jesus' ministry was the conflict between the politics of holiness in the Jewish establishment verses the politics of compassion in Jesus.

108. See chapter 1.

109. Matson, *Household Conversion*, 11.

110. Boismard and Lamouille, "Les Actes"; Spencer, *Portrait*; Watson, *Judaism*; Smith, "Understand"; Gaventa, *Acts*; Felder, *Troubling*; "Ambiguities"; Martin, "Chamberlain's Journey"; Scott, "Horizon"; Schmidt, "Bekehrung."

111. Eusebius, *Ecclesiastical History* 2.1.13.

112. Haenchen, *Acts*, 314.

113. "So much for the significance of the eunuch's conversion, in the context of Luke's history of the mission, as a stepping-stone between those of the Samaritans and the Gentiles" (Haenchen, *Acts*, 314).

the public conversion of Cornelius and his household.[114] As chapter 4 will show, Cornelius is the prototypical God-fearer in Luke's narrative, but that does not force the identity of the eunuch into being a Jew. Second, Haenchen's view depends too much on his assumption that Luke wants to portray the apostles as the pioneers in the early church. The text shows that minor characters are actually the ones who primarily do the work of accomplishing what Jesus wants his followers to accomplish in the Roman Empire. Peter plays his role, but as chapter 4 will show, it is less than the reader expects after reading the Gospel of Luke. This shift from the ministry of the internal circle of the Twelve to the ministry of a multiplicity of minor characters is a major way Luke emphasizes the decentralization of the new movement of Christianity. God is not only working in what is publicly recognized by the establishment, but rather, is embracing those who seek him whether the apostles and Jewish leaders recognize it or not. Third, the conversion of the eunuch is a major part of Luke's agenda of the inclusion of outsiders as prophesied in Isaiah. To this third point we now turn.

The eunuch is a Gentile, but more specifically, he is best described as a God-fearer.[115] This character fits Luke's narratival purpose of decentralization and inclusion of outsiders quite well. As an Ethiopian, he holds a connotation of "a strong representative of foreignness within a Jewish context."[116] Some suggest that ancient people believed that Ethiopia was "the ends of the earth" as predicted in 1:8.[117] Beers, on the other hand, argues that the phrase refers to Gentiles more generally.[118] Either way, the strong foreign connotation is clear. Interestingly, though, Luke does not choose to use the term "God-fearer" for this character, despite what seems to be a clear indication that the label applies to him. This must be because his intention is to use the term God-fearer first in the paradigm-shifting scene that happens with Cornelius and his family. The Eunuch does represent the outward expansion of the kingdom of God and the inclusion of outsiders, but this scene does not lead to the acceptance of God-fearers and Gentiles as the Cornelius scene does. Thus, Luke saves the term for chapter 10. Second, he is a eunuch, and therefore is mutilated in some way and is "forbidden entrance into the assembly (ἐκκλησία) of the Lord. . . . In spite of this, eunuchs are promised a place in God's house in Isa 56:5, overcoming previous exclusion. This passage may well stand in the background of our scene, for Isa 56:3–8 is concerned with two excluded classes: the eunuch and the foreigner. The Ethiopian Eunuch is both."[119]

---

114. Tannehill, *Acts*, 110.

115. Keener, *Acts*, 2:1541. Also, see Bruce, *Acts*, 175; Bock, *Acts*, 45.

116. Tannehill, *Acts*, 108.

117. Unnik, "Der Ausdruck"; Tannehill, *Acts*, 17n26, 109.

118. Beers, *Servant*, 147n123. For more, see Ellis, "End"; Moore, "Earth"; Weissenrieder, "Searching."

119. Tannehill, *Acts*, 109. The extreme outsider identity of the eunuch has led to a number of modern explorations of his "otherness" as it relates to gender and sexuality. See Kartzow and Moxnes, "Complex Identities"; Wilson, "'Neither'"; Solevag, "Disability"; Lev, "Treat." For using the eunuch symbolically in discussions about sexual orientation and gender identity, see Burke, *Queering*; Hester,

There is a connection between the conversion of the eunuch and the account of Jesus cleansing the Temple. First, when Jesus cleanses the Temple, only two verses in Luke's account,[120] he quotes from Isaiah 56:7: "For my house shall be called a house of prayer for all peoples."[121] This quotation by Jesus is only a couple verses away from the passage in Isaiah 56:5, as mentioned by Tannehill above as the potential background for Philip's encounter in Acts. It is a rare example of the Hebrew Scriptures talking about eunuchs in a positive way.[122] Thinking intertextually, Jesus is not just referencing the individual passage he quotes, but the entire section of Isaiah, which moves toward including eunuchs. The phrase "all peoples" covers this, but the fuller context of Isaiah 56 expands the point.

Second, the narrative seems to assume that the cleansing of the Temple happened in the court of the Gentiles.[123] Josephus describes both Solomon's portico and the Royal Stoa, either being a likely location for buying and selling.[124] It was likely the Gentile section that was being turned into a "den of robbers."[125] This reference to Jeremiah 7:11 comes from the Temple Sermon where Israel is doing wicked deeds which are an abomination to God, and then expects safety in God's Temple.[126] The two contexts of Jeremiah and Jesus are similar. Thus, Jesus' actions and words may be a symbol of future Gentile (and eunuch) inclusion.

"Constructions."

120. Luke 19:45–46.

121. Luke 19:46. Jesus only quotes the first part of the verse, but the "all peoples" context is implied.

122. The exclusion placed on eunuchs comes from Deuteronomy 23:1. Other references are simply descriptive in nature, as in Esther 2:15; Daniel 1:3.

123. The debate concerning from where Jesus drove the sellers and moneychangers is an interesting one. Some scholars, like Klausner, suggest that the Pharisees would not allow sellers and moneychangers in the temple area, though perhaps the Sadducees, who controlled the Temple, did. See Klausner, *Jesus*, 314. Abrahams holds that the state of affairs when Jesus cleanses the Temple is more of an exception than the norm, and for this reason understands Jesus' indignation. See Abrahams, *Studies*, 87. Gaston suggests that the idea of "Court of the Gentiles" was unknown in the ancient world, and regarding the idea that noisy selling was prohibiting Gentiles from praying in peace, he calls it laughable. See Gaston, *No Stone*, 87. Sanders, *Judaism*, 365n6, states, "We cannot settle the question of precise location, but we may assume that trade was allowed only in the court of the Gentiles—if anywhere in the temple confines." He also suggests that *Barakoth* 9.5 may be the background for assuming moneychangers and sellers were not allowed inside, but thinks that it is mostly talking about visitors to the Temple (i.e., tourists), not those coming to sacrifice. See Sanders, *Judaism*, 67–68, 367n45. The best defense may be from Davies. See Davies, *Land*, 350–53.

124. Josephus, *Ant.* 15.11.3; *J.W.* 5.5.

125. Josephus writes about the structure of the Temple, and using that information, we are able to infer about some locations in Luke's implied world. I am not moving to an empirical or historical argument; rather, I am giving the accessible empirical evidence a voice to the extent that it helps us understand the implied world of Luke–Acts. For more on my approach to the implied and the empirical, see the Introduction and chapter 1.

126. See Jeremiah 7:8–15.

The connection to Isaiah 56 highlights some important emphases present for Isaiah and for Acts. Pao suggests that this story is understandable only against the context of Isaiah 56:1–8.[127] Verse eight reads:

> Thus says the Lord God,
>   who gathers the outcasts of Israel,
> "I will gather others to them
>   besides those already gathered."

Two elements are present in this verse. First, the focus on the inclusion of outsiders and foreigners is obvious. The mention of "still others" reminds the reader that God's reach is far beyond simply the children of Israel in Isaiah's day. Certainly that moment is realized with the eunuch in Acts. Pao argues that this story is about "completing the account of the restoration of Israel in Acts as the outcasts are now included in the restored people of God."[128] What is more, there is mention here of gathering exiles. "Exile" is closely connected with the New Exodus, and both connect with the mission of Jesus in Luke.[129] The same way that the exiles of Israel return to the land, and "still others" are gathered, Jesus speaks of declaring freedom to the captives (Luke 4) and focuses his ministry on spending time with the outcasts. Thus, we see in Jesus and the movement of the early church the fulfillment of Isaiah's dream from Isaiah 56, and perhaps that dream is never more pointedly realized than in the conversion of the Ethiopian Eunuch.[130]

Secondly, Isaiah 56 emphasizes obedience as the criterion for acceptance over nationality or race. Verses four to seven specifically mention eunuchs and foreigners. Isaiah looks forward to a time when it is the ones who "keep my Sabbath" and "who choose the things that please me and hold fast my covenant" that will be included, as opposed to simply the ones belonging to Israel. The eunuch is an example of obedience and righteousness.[131] He has been to Jerusalem to worship, presumably at the Temple, he is studying Scripture, which he is curious about and asks Philip for help, and ultimately responds by wanting to be baptized. The eunuch models obedience and piety. Pao states, "The reconstituted Israel will not merely be a community that is restored to its previous state of its historic past; this community will be transformed into one in which every member will witness the mighty acts of God."[132] The assumption is that all of God's contingent promises in this section of Isaiah 56—an everlasting name that will endure forever, gathering to his holy mountain and house of prayer, and his

---

127. Pao, *New Exodus*, 142. Also, see Beuken, "Example"; Parsons, "Isaiah 53."
128. Pao, *New Exodus*, 141.
129. The New Exodus will be further explored in chapter 3.
130. Also, see Chrupcala, *Everyone*; Tiemeyer, "Death"; Schuele, "Isaiah 56:1–8"; Hoop, "Interpretation"; Gosse, "Sabbath"; Nihan, "Ethnicity."
131. Cornelius will be an even more remarkable example of obedience and piety in Acts 10.
132. Pao, *New Exodus*, 121.

sacrifices accepted—are offered to the eunuch because of his piety. The statement is that his conversion into the people of God fulfills these promises through inclusion in God's church, redemption, and salvation.[133]

Related to the inclusion of outsiders is Israel's rejection of God. Verses 10–11 bring the chapter to a close with some challenging words for Israel. These harsh words about disobedience fit well with what is seen in Luke–Acts. Acts narrates the systematic rejection of many of the Jews to the message of Jesus, and the inclusion of outsiders instead. Several times Paul starts by proclaiming the gospel in the synagogue,[134] only to have the message rejected, at which time he turns to the Gentiles.[135] This does not eliminate the fact that all of the early Christians before Acts 8 are Jews, and the council of Jerusalem in Acts 15 promotes guidelines so these groups can share a superordinate identity together as children of God. Nonetheless, the rejection of the gospel by the Jewish people is common in the second half of Acts. Likewise, Jesus encounters a similar pattern in his ministry in Luke. Jesus is often at odds with the religious elite,[136] while he intentionally makes room for the poor and the marginalized.[137] Of particular interest is the parable of the banquet in Luke 14:15–24. This is the third story in a row that takes place while Jesus is eating at the house of a prominent Pharisee (who along with the others is said to be closely watching Jesus). The occasion starts with Jesus healing on the Sabbath, followed by Jesus' teaching about choosing seats at a banquet.[138] This third story continues by challenging the assumptions of the Jewish elite he is eating with. When the invited guests do not want to come, but rather make excuses, the banquet is extended to the "poor, the crippled, the blind, and the lame."[139] "This list recalls 14:13 and is similar to 1:51–53; 6:20–23; and 7:22."[140] This resembles Isaiah 29:18–19; 35:5–6; and 61:1–2.[141] Bock suggests that the reference to ἀναπείρους, translated as "crippled" or "maimed" is particularly significant, as they were "banned from full participation in Jewish worship."[142] This parable, then, be-

---

133. This is not to be confused with replacement theology, also known as supersessionism, where the church is thought to replace Israel as God's people. Rather, a new superordinate identity is created that includes Jews, Gentiles, and all people. Israel is redefined in a way, as centered around Christ. The community of God's people now has room for people like this eunuch. For more on supersessionism, see Vlach, *Replacement*; Bloesch, "Supersessionism"; Klawans, *Purity*.

134. Acts 9:20; 13:5, 14–15; 14:1; 15:21; 17:1–2, 10, 17; 18:4, 19; 19:8.

135. Acts 13:46; 17:5–9; 18:6; 19:9–10.

136. Luke 5:21, 30–33; 6:1–11; 7:29–30, 39; 11:37–54; 12:1; 14:1–24; 15:2; 16:14; 18:10–11; 19:39.

137. Luke 5:27, 29–32; 7:34, 39; 15:1; 18:13; 19:2–10.

138. Luke emphasizes decentralization of the Sabbath, as this is the fifth account of Jesus healing on the Sabbath, more than any other gospel. Luke 4:31–37, 38–39; 6:6–11; 13:10–17. Also, see Hartsock, "Healing"; Story, "Banquet"; "Ready."

139. Acts 14:21.

140. Bock, *Luke*, 2:1275. Also, see Tannehill, *Luke*, 64, 127–32; "Discourse."

141. Bock, *Luke*, 2:1275. The illusion to Isaiah 61 would remind readers of Jesus first sermon in Luke 4.

142. Bock, *Luke*, 2:1276. Bock sites Leviticus 21:17–23 (which uses a different Greek word, but

comes another foreshadowing of the eunuch and his inclusion into the kingdom (i.e., banquet) of God. When there is room remaining at the banquet, another round of invitations is extended. "They may picture an additional group that is invited and may suggest for Luke a preview of a Gentile mission."[143] In the end, the invited guests who remain outside resemble the Jewish elite of the day, who are most likely to seek the honored seats, whereas the poor and infirmed are welcomed into the banquet.[144] Once again, this is the realization of the words of Isaiah 56 in the mission of Jesus and of the early church. Thus, if these connections are sound, Luke's versions of Jesus' cleansing of the Temple and the parable of the banquet, as well as the quotation from Isaiah 56 are foreshadowing the conversion of the eunuch in Acts 8.

Sanders rejects the idea that Jesus' clearing in the Gentile court is to promote inclusion of the Gentiles in worship.[145] He claims that Jesus is not directly concerned with the Gentiles.[146] He doubts that the court of the Gentiles is the only place for a possible cleansing (rather than one choice for a demonstration among many), and finds a rebuke of the Saducean priesthood of the Temple more plausible.[147] He considers one possible prophecy that is connected from Zechariah 14:20–21,[148] which is a noteworthy text to consider. The closing words of the book look to a time where all will be declared as "Holy to the Lord" (ἅγιον τῷ κυρίῳ) and all may come to sacrifice in the Temple, as well as the absence of "traders" (Χαναναῖος),[149] the latter part often being connected to Jesus' cleansing. Gaston suggests that Jesus may have been teaching on this passage prior to the cleansing, which led to the event.[150] He also suggests that Jesus is referring to an eschatological Temple, "[ignoring] the empirical temple completely," which undercuts any Gentile inclusion readers may have in mind.[151] Sanders ultimately rejects the Temple cleansing's link to Zechariah and does not consider the quotation from Isaiah 56 at all, nor does he consider the larger narrative mission of any of the specific Gospels. The Temple cleansing in Luke must be considered in the two-volume narrative trajectory of Luke–Acts. It fits with Luke's larger program of decentralization and the inclusion of outsiders. Thus, the Temple cleansing is not an aberration in Luke, but consistent with what Jesus has been doing the whole time.[152]

---

does talk of defects) and some scroll texts (i.e., 1Q28a [= 1QSa = Rule Annex] 2.3–10; CD 13:4–7).

143. Bock, *Luke*, 2:1268.

144. Also, see Longenecker, "Humorous"; Dippenaar, "Table Fellowship"; Krüger, "La Inclusión"; Eck et al., "Feast"; Sullivan, "Great Supper"; Wendland, "Blessed."

145. Sanders, *Judaism*, 67.

146. Sanders, *Judaism*, 68–69.

147. Sanders, *Judaism*, 68–69.

148. Sanders, *Judaism*, 67.

149. The LXX uses the same word as the Hebrew (כְּנַעֲנִי) which can mean "Canaanite" or "trader." See Bauer et al., *Greek-English Lexicon of the New Testament* (BDAG).

150. Gaston, *Stone*, 86.

151. Gaston, *Stone*, 87–88.

152. Perhaps this is why Luke devotes the least amount of space to it of all the Gospels. More will

There is another narrative connection with Ebed-melech, the eunuch who intervenes with the king and saves Jeremiah from death and is later spared when the city is destroyed.[153] Contra the circumcision group in Acts who are said always to "persecute" the prophets of God,[154] this foreigner risks his own life to help one of God's prophets. The reader who recalls this incident while encountering the Ethiopian Eunuch in Acts 8 will be struck by the faithfulness and piety of both characters.[155]

In the end, the Ethiopian Eunuch is spiritually hungry, has some sense of biblical literacy,[156] and is miraculously converted. He models the new criteria for inclusion into the Christ community: spiritual hunger, desire to follow the God of Israel, and confession of Jesus. The physical limitations and ethnic identity hold him back no longer.[157]

Cornelius

Clearly the most prototypical Gentile convert in Acts is the Roman soldier of chapter 10.[158] He is a God-fearer, as he and his family are said to be φοβούμενος τὸν θεόν (v. 2). Cornelius will be discussed more fully in chapter 4, but an introduction to his role as a minor character is appropriate here because of his importance as a God-fearer in Acts.

Luke has already included Roman centurions in his narrative,[159] but those characters are much more peripheral than Cornelius. While they both offered positive commentary about Jesus and received it from him, we know of neither going to the extent of converting to Christianity, as Cornelius does. Roman centurions represented the pagan empire to which Israel is subject. The implied audience would likely have been aware of the intense persecutions that were carried out by the Romans against the Christians. For example, Tacitus describes Nero as having Christians killed as a matter of sport by being "covered in wild beasts' skins and torn to pieces by dogs; or were fastened to crosses and set on fire in order to serve as torches by night when daylight failed."[160] As the Ethiopian Eunuch was exotic because of his occupation as

---

be said on Luke's trajectory of Temple decentralization in chapter 3.

153. Jeremiah 38:7–13; 39:16–18.

154. Acts 7:52.

155. For more on Ebed-Melech, see Ullendorff, *Ethiopia*; Hays, *Every*; Seitz, "Prophet"; Stulman, "Insiders"; Stevenson, "Rise."

156. The Ethiopian Eunuch appears to be more biblically literate than Cornelius. See Keener, *Acts*, 1:541; Smith, "Understand"; Spencer, "Waiter"; Crehan, "Confirmation."

157. Keener, *Acts*, 2:1541, highlights the difference between Cornelius and the eunuch in that the former could have converted to Judaism had he wanted to, where the latter was physically unable.

158. See chapter 4 on prototypical characters.

159. Jesus' encounter with the centurion in Luke 7 and the proclamation of the centurion at the foot of the cross in Luke 23:47. See Gagnon, "Motives"; Karris, "Luke"; Radin, "Promotion."

160. Tacitus, *Annals* 15.44.6.

treasurer of the queen of the Ethiopians, Cornelius is likewise exotic in his conversion because of his occupation.

Luke offers a glowing picture of Cornelius.

- Roman Centurion in the Italian Cohort (10:1)
- Devout and God-fearing (10:2a, 22)
- Gives alms generously to the people (10:2b)
- Prays constantly to God (10:2c)
- Visited by an Angel (10:3, 22c)
- Respected by the Jews (10:22b)
- Shows great respect to Peter (10:25)

A God-fearing reader, or anyone on the fence about Gentile inclusion, will take notice. This is an example of the rhetorical strategy of ethos, where a writer would establish the character of the speaker, showing that he or she is trustworthy.[161] What is more, as Tannehill notes, after the initial encounter with the angel in 10:3–4, we are told of the encounter again in 10:22 and are reminded that Cornelius is "an upright and God-fearing man, who is well spoken of by the whole Jewish nation."[162] Again in 10:30–31 we are reminded of the encounter, and of Cornelius's prayers and gifts to the poor, and then again briefly in 11:13–14. The encounter will be told one more time at the council in Jerusalem in chapter 15. The repetition is present because the Cornelius event represents a clear theological focus for Luke. This is not the first God-fearer, but will be the most prominent in the narrative.

Tannehill emphasizes the integration of Jew and Gentile Christians as a primary focus in the text. "Everything in the narrative conspires against maintaining the barrier between Jews and this Gentile."[163] This is primarily done through examining what the text calls clean and unclean. First, the stage is set by Peter's vision, cuing the reader about clean and unclean foods. Three times Peter calls the animals on the sheet κοινὸν καὶ ἀκάθαρτον ("common and unclean") and is rebuked for it.[164] The present active imperative, as well as the structure of verse 15, emphasizes the rebuke.[165] The food laws are being decentralized. Interestingly, Luke does not mention food laws in the gospel. This is one of several places in his gospel where he appears to omit something from the presumed source material (Mark), quite likely to address it more fully in

---

161. Mack, *Rhetoric*, 36. Much more will be said about Luke's rhetorical strategy and ethos in chapter 5.

162. Tannehill, *Acts*, 130. Also, see Scott, "Cornelius"; Wall, "Peter"; Witherup, "Cornelius"; Brown, "Tuning."

163. Tannehill, *Acts*, 133.

164. Acts 10:12–16.

165. ἃ ὁ θεὸς ἐκαθάρισεν, σὺ μὴ κοίνου. "The use of the explicit fronted subject pronoun makes the statement more emphatic" (Parsons and Culy, *Handbook*, 198).

Acts.¹⁶⁶ For example, Mark 7:1–22 includes an extended section on clean and unclean foods and practices, including a rebuke by Jesus and a statement by the narrator that Jesus was declaring all foods clean (v. 19). Matthew 15:1–20 does something similar. Luke has Jesus mention cleanliness with regard to hand washing rituals only in 11:37–41, and does not mention food laws at all.¹⁶⁷ The author is intentionally subtle here, knowing he will address the issue more fully and dramatically in volume two with Peter and Cornelius. There also appears to be a preference with regard to the implied author to state issues using narrative rather than stating them explicitly. This is actually more powerful, as it engages the imagination of the reader and speaks to the narrative substructure of the human mind. Peter's statement in Acts 10:28 is the culmination of all of Luke's writing up to this point, declaring Cornelius "clean." This declaration goes beyond simply cultural laws about food, but speaks to Cornelius as a representative of the Gentile people as being clean, a vessel for the Holy Spirit, and worthy of acceptance into community.¹⁶⁸

Second, Tannehill points out "the Jewishness of this non-Jew."¹⁶⁹ Associating a presumably unclean God-fearing Gentile with the clean Jewish faith by his character helps to reduce the unclean barrier as well. In addition to his piety rivaling that of a devout Jew, "he is favored with a vision of an angel of God, and the narrator presents the encounter in a form common in the Old Testament and previously used in Luke–Acts to describe divine messages to faithful Jews like Mary (Luke 1:26–38) and Ananias (Acts 9:10–17)."¹⁷⁰

Third, since Cornelius is said to give "alms generously to the people" (ποιῶν ἐλεημοσύνας πολλὰς τῷ λαῷ), the reader is reminded of Jesus' words in Luke 11:37–41. In the scene, where Jesus is invited to the home of a Pharisee, who is surprised (ἐθαύμασεν) at Jesus for not washing, Jesus says,

> Now you Pharisees clean the outside of the cup and of the dish, but inside you are full of greed and wickedness. You fools! Did not the one who made the outside make the inside also? *So give for alms those things that are within; and see, everything will be clean for you.*¹⁷¹

---

166. Other examples of this include Luke's shortening of Jesus' cleansing of the Temple (Luke 19:45–48), the absence of the false accusations of Jesus, and Jesus not commenting on the land in the beatitudes (Luke 6:20–23, though he does mention wealth).

167. For more on food and boundaries in Luke–Acts, see Moritz, "Dinner Talk"; Neale, *None*; Mendez-Moratalla, *Paradigm*. Also, see an engagement with and discussion of Neale in Carter, *Forgiveness*, 156.

168. See Woodington, "Charity"; Valle and Milagros, "Actes"; O'Loughlin, "Sharing"; Perry, "Gentiles."

169. Tannehill, *Acts*, 133.

170. Tannehill, *Acts*, 133.

171. Luke 11:39–41 (emphasis added).

The connection to "clean" and "unclean" could not be clearer.[172] The Pharisees, who supposedly lead lives of ritual purity, are unclean because of their lack of generosity to the poor. Cornelius, by contrast, is viewed as unclean for being a Gentile, but his generous giving makes him clean.

Lastly, the narrative builds to the point of the God-fearing Gentiles being filled with the Spirit in 10:44–47. The infilling of the Holy Spirit is the ultimate display that Cornelius is not unclean, since "the extreme opposite of the unclean is the holy."[173] This infilling of the Holy Spirit causes surprise in the circumcised believers (v. 45), but is also the reason for allowing baptism and conversion (v. 47), as well as for the disciples staying with Cornelius and dining with him (v. 48).[174]

There is more to be said about Peter's speech in Cornelius's house as well, considering the importance of speeches.[175] Although Peter is processing his own awareness of the situation, the mission to God-fearers is clearly stated in 10:34b–35. The Greek participial phrase used here, ὁ φοβούμενος αὐτὸν, reflects the technical term used of God-fearers (φοβούμενος τὸν θεόν).[176] This story is the central conversion narrative of a God-fearer in Luke's two-volume work, one that the God-fearing reader could not have missed.

Thus, in Cornelius, Luke is presenting a person any devout Jew can respect as well as a model of conduct and behavior for a God-fearing reader. The presence of prescribed norms, values, goals, and ideology in the Cornelius story allow Luke to create a model worthy of emulating for his God-fearing readers. In addition, Cornelius and his family participate in boundary crossing rituals of early Christianity, water and Spirit baptism.[177] This demonstrates the identity-forming elements of the Cornelius story.

Scholarship has failed to consider thoroughly the literary character of Cornelius as an identity-forming prototype. As such, a prominent character in Luke's work, and one who shifts paradigms so severely, deserves our continued attention.

The Critic-Response Type-Scene

Decentralization happens in Luke–Acts partly through the criticism of and response by the prototypes in the story. Tannehill suggests that there might be echoes of the critics of Jesus in the protest of Acts 11:3,[178] even suggesting that it might be a kind

172. See Borg, *Conflict*.

173. Tannehill, *Acts*, 135.

174. Although the text does not mention dining here, it is assumed, and is part of the accusation of 11:3. Pelikan, *Acts*, 136, notes that the usage of the "fell" (ἐπέπεσεν) emphasizes the sovereignty of God in that the Holy Spirit blows where it wants. Also, see Tyson, "Dinner"; Ripley "'Those Things."

175. For more on the importance of speeches in Acts and in the ancient world, see Gempf, "Public Speaking"; Soards, *Speeches*; Bruce, *Speeches*; "Thirty Years,"; Cadbury, "Speeches."

176. The only difference is the use of the pronoun in place of θεόν.

177. Acts 10:47–48.

178. "Why did you go to uncircumcised men and eat with them?" (Acts 11:3).

of characteristic type-scene in Lukan literature.[179] Considering the similarities, a look into this type-scene in Luke's two volumes is necessary.

There are three instances in Luke's Gospel where Jesus is criticized for engaging with people on the outskirts of the social spectrum. They are Luke 5:30; 15:2; and 19:7; and many similarities exist between these scenes and Acts 11:2–3.[180] Luke reinforces the decentralizing mission of the kingdom of God using this type-scene method four times. The series of scenes builds through Luke and then ends in Acts in a surprising way, making a strong statement about the early church's inclusion of God-fearers into the community. This is worth examining, lest we miss the brilliant narrative move the implied author is making.

Each type-scene follows the same pattern:

1. A "complaining" verb
2. Subject
3. Attendant circumstance participle λέγοντες
4. Accusation
5. Response

We will examine more deeply each of these elements. Alter suggests that type-scenes are not "imaginative impression of the story," but rather "minute critical attention to the biblical writer's articulations of narrative form."[181] With the flexibility of word order in Greek, the similar form of these elements make a type-scene clear.

"Complaining" Verb

The three occurrences of the type-scene in Luke each use some version of the word γογγύζω (this word used in Luke 5:30, and διαγογγύζω used in Luke 15; 19). These both mean essentially the same thing, which is "to murmur" or "to grumble."[182] The scene in Acts uses a different "complaining" verb, διακρίνω. This has a slightly different meaning, according to BDAG, "to be at variance with," "to take issue with or

---

179. Tannehill, *Acts*, 137. There are a number of other times where Jesus is criticized or opposed and responds, but these do not fit the type-scene pattern in quite the same way. Consider Luke 5:21, 33; 6:2; 7:36–50; 11:37–39, 53–54; 14:1–23; 16:14; 19:39.

180. There is another scene in Luke 7:36–50, where the sinful woman washed Jesus' feet in the home of Simon the Pharisee and he critiques Jesus for letting her do that. This prompts Jesus to tell the parable of the two debtors and pronounce her sins forgiven. While the general outline of this scene (critique and response) fits with this pattern and Jesus' response about forgiveness could be seen as a type of mission statement, many of the verbal cues of the type-scene are missing (i.e., grumbling, attendant circumstance participle λέγοντες, etc.).

181. Alter, *Art*, 12. To be fair, Alter is discussing Hebrew narrative, not ancient Greco-Roman historiography. However, many of his considerations apply here as well. Also, see Frei, *Eclipse*; Fokkelman, *Reading*; Sailhamer, *Pentateuch*.

182. BDAG.

criticize."¹⁸³ Perhaps Luke chooses a different word in Acts to emphasize the division of the early church. This seems to be the key divisive issue in the church, so using the word that highlights this is appropriate. It also may emphasize the judgment of the accusers with the relationship of the word to κρίνω. The word used in 5:30 (γογγύζω) may hearken back to the grumbling in the wilderness.¹⁸⁴ In each case, the "complaining" verb precedes the identification of the subject, with the exception of the Zacchaeus account in Luke 19 where those complaining are "all the people" (πάντες) and the emphasis is on everyone seeing this scene unfold.

Subject

In each case, the subject of the "complaining" verb is clearly spelled out and each scene contains slight variations of who exactly is doing the criticizing of the behavior. Clearly the role of the characters tells us more about the larger narrative context of the story and how it unfolds than a particular type-scene characteristic, but the differences are worth mentioning here. The accounts in Luke 5 and 15 are very similar in this regard, both mentioning Pharisees and scribes: οἵ τε Φαρισαῖοι καὶ οἱ γραμματεῖς. The difference here is with the addition of τε ("both") in Luke 15 and αὐτῶν ("their," i.e., the scribes belonging to the sect of the Pharisees, often translated as such) in Luke 5.¹⁸⁵

The Zacchaeus account in Luke 19 identifies "all the people" (πάντες) as the subject of the "complaining" verb, breaking the semantic pattern created in the three other instances. Perhaps this change is because of the widely known reputation of Zacchaeus and his role as the chief tax collector.¹⁸⁶ The emphasis is on "when all the people saw this" (καὶ ἰδόντες πάντες διεγόγγυζον). The use of πάντες highlights the strong nature of the complaining in this scene against the others and makes Jesus declaration of salvation at his house more noteworthy. This scene also seems to be the most public of the three, lending itself to criticism by more people.

The accusers in Acts 11 are identified as "the circumcised believers" or more literally, "the ones from circumcision" (οἱ ἐκ περιτομῆς).¹⁸⁷ Clearly a faction exists between a certain group that is "more conscientious of the Hebrew Christians" and everybody

---

183. Based on narrative flow, BDAG may be correct. Culy and Parsons, *Handbook*, 217, opt for "started arguing."

184. Bovon, *Luke*, 190. He notes that this verb occurs about fifteen times in the LXX, and particularly at some key wilderness wandering texts (such as Exod 16:7; 17:3; Num 11:1; 14:27–29). Furthermore, Bock, *Luke*, 1:496, suggests that Luke "reserves this word group for complaints about Jesus' relationship to outsiders." Also, see Schweizer, *Good News*.

185. Nolland, *Luke*, 1:245.

186. Lamb, "Stereotyped"; Hays, "'Sell'"; Corbin-Reuschling, "Zacchaeus's"; Sick, "Zacchaeus"; Tannehill, "Story"; Hamm, "Revisited."

187. There has been some debate over the translation of this verse. Marshall, *Acts*, 195, and Bock, *Acts*, are both likely right in suggesting that "circumcision party" is incorrect, as this is referring to the Jewish believers (i.e., Christians).

else within the church.[188] And, as mentioned above, the use of the verb διακρίνω intensifies this division in the reader's mind, as well as the transformation that occurs in the people in verse 18 ("When they heard this, they were silenced. And they praised God, saying, 'Then God has given even to the Gentiles the repentance that leads to life'"). This is a remarkable turn in that the main opponents are won over by Peter's recounting of God's work in the story. "God is now seen as the one who brought this about, so they rejoice."[189] Despite this response, this will be a debate that will persist through chapter 15. "Some old ways die hard in the new era."[190] It is interesting to consider how much this group of critics in chapter 11 relates to the groups of Pharisees and Scribes in two of the other type-scenes. These circumcised believers play a similar role and are stressing issues that scribes and Pharisees would stress. Is Luke associating the critics in Acts 11 with the Pharisees by using these type-scenes? This fits with when the Pharisees speak at the Jerusalem council and say, "It is necessary for them to be circumcised and ordered to keep the law of Moses."[191]

Pharisees are mostly portrayed as opponents of Jesus in the Gospel of Luke.[192] They provide many opportunities for Jesus to communicate his message of decentralization as he interacts with them. Even when they invite him to their houses for dinner, conflict ensues over whom Jesus allows to anoint him or how he washes his hands.[193] However, there are examples in Luke where Pharisees are seen in a more positive light. In Luke 13:31, they warn Jesus that Herod wants to kill him. Then, in Acts 5, Gamaliel (perhaps the most prominent Pharisee) becomes a defender of the New Christian Movement. Paul, the main character of the second half of the book and the prototype for Gentile inclusion[194] is a former Pharisee, and the Pharisees defend Paul in 23:9–10.[195] Despite these exceptions, the Pharisees represent a faction of centralized power and elitism in and around Jerusalem,[196] which includes major badges of national identity, such as Temple, land, Sabbath, and Torah. Jesus' decentralizing kingdom had to clash with this group in order to accomplish its

188. Bock, *Acts*, 406.

189. Bock, *Acts*, 409. Also, see Jiménez, "Spirit"; Skarsaune, *Shadow*.

190. Bock, *Acts*, 406.

191. Acts 15:5.

192. Luke 5:17–26, 21, 30, 33; 6:2, 7; 7:30; 11:42–43, 53; 12:1; 15:2; 16:4; 17:20; 18:10; 19:39. They are portrayed more positively than the other gospels, as Luke–Acts includes a few positive accounts of Pharisees.

193. Luke 7:36–50; 11:37–41; 14:1–23.

194. See chapter 4, "Luke's Use of Prototypes and Exemplars."

195. Acts calls Paul a Pharisee in 23:6; 26:5.

196. While empirically it was likely the Sadducees that controlled the Temple and the Temple tax, the Pharisees remain central to the established power in the Lukan corpus. Marshall, *Portrayal*, 154, holds that the author "presents the Pharisees as a group with a degree of power and influence and enjoying considerable reputation." Also, see Neusner and Chilton, *Quest*; Freyne, *Galilee*; Lührmann, "Paul." Lürmann does other writing on the Pharisees that focuses primarily on other gospels, such as Lürmann, "Die Pharisaer."

mission. Because of Jesus' focus on the outcasts and marginalized of society, conflict with the Pharisees was inevitable.[197]

Attendant Circumstance Participle λέγοντες

In each case, as is common for introductions to quotations of characters in the Greek,[198] the main verb is complimented with a participle, and each occurrence uses λέγοντες. This helps establish the consistency of the type-scene.[199]

Accusation

The accusation differs slightly in each instance. In Luke 5, it is posed as a question, "why do you eat and drink with tax collectors and sinners?" (διὰ τί μετὰ τῶν τελωνῶν καὶ ἁμαρτωλῶν ἐσθίετε καὶ πίνετε;). This occurrence and the Acts 11 scene are the only two times where it is posed directly to the accused. The other times the accusations are spoken among the accusers themselves as asides.[200] We are left to speculate at the impact of the differences in the form here.[201] However, the narrative result of the scene, whether it is spoken directly or muttered amongst themselves, is the same. The emphasis of the accusation is on the eating and drinking, which will come up again in the Luke 15 and Acts 11 occurrences. This is the one time that drinking is mentioned. Furthermore, the characters, tax collectors and sinners (τῶντελωνῶν καὶ ἁμαρτωλῶν), are common in that three of the four type-scenes include the description of "sinner."[202] This occurrence is the one place that tax col-

---

197. Nolland, *Luke*, 1:246: "Pharisaism had strong separatist tendencies, and because of the prominence in Pharisaic piety of food and ritual cleanliness rules, Pharisees would only accept hospitality from one another. By analogy with the avoiding of communicable ritual uncleanliness, the Pharisees considered it necessary also to avoid contamination from contact with the morally suspect elements of Jewish society (and Gentiles)."

198. Because of the influence of the Hebrew language on the Greek of the New Testament, the doubling up of an action (verb plus participle) is common (i.e., "Moses got up and went to Dathan and Abiram" [Num 16:25]). For one example of the gospel writers' regular use of this feature, consider that Luke uses the participle ἀποκριθεὶς ("answering") this way thirty-three times in connection with another verb.

199. Parsons, Culy, and Stigall agree with the attendant circumstance syntax. See Parsons and Culy, *Handbook*, 218; Parsons et al., *Luke*, 590. Wallace, however, seems to have a more narrow definition of this syntactical category, but it is not clear how he would categorize these instances. See Wallace, *Grammar*, 640–45.

200. Luke 15:2; 19:7.

201. Perhaps this accusation is posed as a question directly to Jesus because, given that he is calling his disciples and it is at the beginning of his ministry he is somewhat unknown and his accusers are giving him a chance to speak for and defend himself.

202. Bock, *Luke*, 1:496, suggests that the word "refers to a wide group of people, including the potentially impious, like tax collectors. In other words, it refers to any who need to be healed and not only to the worst sinners in the harshest possible sense. The judgment by the Pharisees is not

lectors are mentioned in the accusation,²⁰³ although they are mentioned in the surrounding narrative in both Luke 15 and 19.²⁰⁴

In the scene in Luke 15 the focus shifts to welcoming and eating (προσδέχεται καὶ συνεσθίει). The narrative shows that tax collectors and sinners are gathering around Jesus to hear him teach. He welcomes them and eats with them, as his accusers tell us. The accusation here is not directed to Jesus, but they mutter, presumably to one another.²⁰⁵ Jesus becomes aware of their protest and responds.²⁰⁶

The Luke 19 scene returns implicitly to the idea of welcoming, as accusation focuses on him having "gone to be the guest of one who is a sinner" (παρὰ ἁμαρτωλῷ ἀνδρὶ εἰσῆλθεν καταλῦσαι). Eating and drinking is not mentioned, but it is implied. "All the people" are muttering to each other and Jesus becomes aware of it and responds.²⁰⁷

Lastly, the accusation in Acts 11 differs in remarkable ways: "You went into the house of an uncircumcised man and ate with them" (εἰσῆλθες πρὸς ἄνδρας ἀκροβυστίαν ἔχοντας καὶ συνέφαγες αὐτοῖς).²⁰⁸ Several things stand out. First, the usual descriptors used previously of sinners and tax collectors are not used here because neither applies to Cornelius. The scene up to this point has been focused on Cornelius's impressive resume as a devout fearer of God.²⁰⁹ The normal Jewish roadblocks—nefarious profession of tax collector and bad reputation—do not apply here. Instead, the label used of Cornelius and his people is "uncircumcised men" (ἄνδρας ἀκροβυστίαν ἔχοντας). This serves to highlight that the only thing keeping Cornelius from participating in the full fellowship of the people of God is a religious conversion ritual, specifically lacking the procedure of circumcision.²¹⁰ The repetition of the accusers being identified as from the circumcised believers and their labeling Cornelius as uncircumcised provides repetition to the issue at hand. The variance of this scene compared to the others makes this point clear. This is not a behavioral problem that needs to change, as we see with Levi, the tax collectors, and Zacchaeus. The emphasis of those stories was missional, that Jesus came to seek out even those people and

---

necessarily harsh. It may accurately describe these people, but for Jesus, recovery is the issue, not quarantine." Also, see Luce, *Gospel*; Fitzmyer, *Luke*, 1:591; Schürmann, *Das Lukasevangelium*; Völkel, "Freund"; Sanders, *Judaism*, 174–211.

203. Luke 5:30.

204. Luke 15:1; 19:2.

205. Luke 15:2.

206. Luke 15:3–32.

207. Luke 19:9–10.

208. The NRSV poses this as a question, but it is not a question in Greek. For that reason, I have altered the translation. However, Bock, *Acts*, 406, suggests that the connotation would carry the force of "Explain yourself!," demanding a response. See Goatley, "Coloring"; Morton, "Between"; Garroway, "Pharisee"; Matson, "Tuning"; Scholz, "Rise."

209. Acts 10:1–3, 22, 25.

210. This is a sign of being an outsider to the Jews but not for Luke.

include them. The emphasis here, however, is that God has already accepted and welcomed Cornelius, the archetypal God-fearer, but the people remain behind the move of God, not yet acknowledging this man as a brother in the Lord. God is ahead of the people in his decentralizing move. This, too, speaks loudly to a God-fearing reader in a similar situation as Cornelius. This is an invitational statement aimed at persuading them to join what God is doing, thereby affirming who they are and their ability to participate in God's kingdom in a significant way.

The accusation combines elements seen in previous type-scenes, mentioning both "going into (the house)" and "eating with" this person ("the house" is implied). The other type-scenes cause the departure in Acts 11 to stand out.[211]

Response

The response is the climax of the type-scene, and it provides the narrative payoff for Luke. Luke 5:31b–32 finds Jesus responding to his accusers with an explanation of his mission: "Those who are well have no need of a physician, but those who are sick; I have come to call not the righteous but sinners to repentance." In chapter 15, we see Jesus respond with three parables, some of the most notable in his teaching ministry, talking of the lost sheep, the lost coin, and the lost son. This becomes the type-scene's longest response at twenty-nine verses and also serves to set up one of the longest teaching sections in Luke, extending into chapter 17. In the teaching section, Jesus argues with and challenges the Pharisees as well as turns to his disciples to instruct them. The parables point to Jesus' mission, seeking what is lost, although they do it in a more dramatic, haggadic fashion.[212] The mission is stated clearly in 15:7 and 15:10 ("Just so, I tell you, there will be more joy in heaven over one sinner who repents than over ninety-nine righteous persons who need no repentance" and "Just so, I tell you, there is joy in the presence of the angels of God over one sinner who repents").[213] Jesus regularly responded to questions or situations with parables.[214] His use of haggadic method here does not soften the statement of his mission, but intensifies it.

The Zacchaeus incident becomes something of an outlier again. Following the accusation of the people, Zacchaeus offers the first defense, this time by declaring to change his behavior ("Zacchaeus stood there and said to the Lord, 'Look, half of my possessions, Lord, I will give to the poor; and if I have defrauded anyone of anything, I

---

211. For other examples and studies of accusation texts, see Elliot, "Criticism," 858, 10; Bredin, "Synagogue"; Elliot, "Parable"; Neyrey, "Bewitched"; Atkins, "Trial."

212. "Three parallel parables portray God's desire to find the lost sinner" (Bock, *Luke*, 2:1294). For more on Haggadah, see Goldin, "Freedom"; Carmichael, "Passover"; Hauptman, "Haggadah?"

213. "God will go to great effort and rejoice with great joy to find and restore a sinner to himself" (Bock, *Luke*, 2:1295).

214. Luke 5:33–39; 7:36–42; 10:25–37; 11:1–13, 14–22; 12:13–21; 14:15–24; 20:1–16.

will pay back four times as much'").²¹⁵ We see again the regular emphasis on generosity as a norm for Luke. This gives Jesus the opportunity to make the purpose statement about himself after commenting on Zacchaeus directly: "Today salvation has come to this house, because he too is a son of Abraham. For the Son of Man came to seek out and to save the lost." In each case, Jesus makes a statement about his mission to outsiders and lost people.²¹⁶ This is clearly intentional by Luke. These type-scene responses build in volume one and reach their climax in volume two.²¹⁷

In Acts 11, Peter responds to his accusers by telling the story: "Then Peter began to explain it to them, step by step, saying" (Ἀρξάμενος δὲ Πέτρος ἐξετίθετο αὐτοῖς καθεξῆς λέγων·).²¹⁸ The story ends with a similar purpose statement as in the ministry of Jesus, although tailored for this context: "If then God gave them the same gift that he gave us when we believed in the Lord Jesus Christ, who was I that I could hinder God?" (εἰ οὖν τὴν ἴσην δωρεὰν ἔδωκεν αὐτοῖς ὁ θεὸς ὡς καὶ ἡμῖν πιστεύσασιν ἐπὶ τὸν κύριον Ἰησοῦν Χριστόν, ἐγὼ τίς ἤμην δυνατὸς κωλῦσαι τὸν θεόν;).²¹⁹ The purpose statement here comes as a rhetorical question: Who was I to hinder God? The surprise comes in their full acceptance of his story and the accusers' restatement of the issue: "When they heard this, they were silenced. And they praised God, saying, 'Then God has given even to the Gentiles the repentance that leads to life.'"²²⁰ A bold statement is made about the inclusion of God-fearers both to the God-fearers themselves, but also to those who would oppose outsider inclusion, as the question (who was I to hinder God?)²²¹ offers a clear challenge, stating that if you oppose what God is doing among the God-fearing Gentiles you are hindering God.²²² The prescribed response of the critics is also offered, as they praise God and offer no more objections. This is perhaps the most impactful addition to the type-scene formula, and likely the entire point of Luke using four related type-scenes that build to a climax: the critics are persuaded to welcome God-fearing Gentile believers. In none of the previous scenes are we given any indication that the accusers have any change of heart in the face of the response of Jesus. In Luke 5, Jesus' defense is met with further challenges about his

---

215. There is a debate about how to understand Zacchaeus's defense, but it is outside the scope of this work. For more on this issue, see Bock, *Luke*, 2:1520; Fitzmyer, *Luke*, 2:1220, 1225; Marshall, *Luke*, 697–98; Nolland, *Luke*, 3:906.

216. Luke 5:31b–32; 15:7, 10; 19:9–10.

217. Luke 5:31b–32; 15:7, 10; 19:9–10; Acts 11:17.

218. Acts 11:4–16 contains a repetition of the story already told, though with slight variations.

219. Acts 11:17.

220. Acts 11:18. For a discussion about the attitudes of Jews toward Gentiles being converts, see Keener, *Acts*, 2:1828; Skarsaune, *Shadow*, 165–66; Wise, "Scrolls"; Sanders, *Judaism*, 213–17; Niehoff, "Circumcision."

221. Acts 11:17. This word, hinder (κωλύω), is common for Luke, who uses the word twelve times in his two volumes compared to eleven in the rest of the NT. Keener, *Acts*, 2:1827, calls it a significant term in Acts (8:26; 28:31).

222. Keener, *Acts*, 2:1827, points out that orators in the ancient world would often times appeal to divine authority. See Black, *Rhetoric*, 128.

disciples' fasting habits. In Luke 15, the first response we see of his accusers is sneering at him in response to his teaching and parables (16:14). Luke 19 contains no comment about the response of the critics.[223] The full acceptance of the critics in Acts 11 is a remarkable climax that stands out as a notable exception to the established pattern.[224] This is arguably the turning point in Acts, as two verses later (Acts 11:20), intentional missionary activity to the Greeks is initiated. The narrative shifts in the second half of Acts to focus on missionary activity to Gentiles, all precipitated on the conversion of Cornelius, which was the climax of the critic-response type-scene.

Cornelius and the Eunuch

While Cornelius is not the first Gentile convert in Acts, there are some important differences that set this scene apart from the conversion of the Ethiopian Eunuch in Acts 8:26–40, chief among which is scope of impact. Tannehill says, "The conversion of the Ethiopian was a private and isolated event that had no effect."[225] While it may seem extreme to say the event had no effect, from the perspective of the transformation of the early church in Judea, Tannehill is right. Philip is transported elsewhere and we never hear of the Ethiopian again. However, the story plays a key role in the narrative. Clearly, Luke's inclusion of it at this point shows its importance, and the missional element should not be missed: an outsider who is deformed in some way and excluded from the community of faith is included, converted and baptized.

By contrast, the Cornelius story becomes the key event in the early church that leads to the acceptance of Gentiles as brothers and sisters in the Lord. Although Cornelius, like so many other minor characters in Luke's writing, essentially fades out of the narrative after this point, he is one of the heroes of the book.[226] He is the prototypical God-fearer.[227]

A second interesting difference comes from the identities of the characters. Despite the exotic nature of this Ethiopian, there is nothing about his ethnicity that would create an enmity between him and the Jews. He is merely an outsider who is unwelcomed into Jewish worship. Cornelius, on the other hand, is a Roman soldier who works for Rome. Keener notes that the Jews had "considerable cause for offense

---

223. Jesus continues teaching (19:11–27) before leaving the area and beginning his entry into Jerusalem for his final week.

224. Peterson, "Pneumatology," 211, suggests that though the text reads that there were no further objections, "there were probably some who remained uneasy about the situation." Also, see Pedersen, "Restoration"; Williams, "Brotherhood"; Lunn, "Allusions."

225. Tannehill, *Acts*, 137.

226. See Green, "Cornelius"; Julius, "Cornelius." Keener, *Acts*, 2:1727, calls Cornelius an exception, "who serves as a harbinger for future exceptions."

227. See more in chapter 4 on prototypical figures in Acts. Also, see Davies, "Cornelius"; Finkel, "Stranger," 2–10, 14.

Timothy

Timothy presents an interesting case in Acts. His mother is Jewish, but his father is Greek (Acts 16:1). He is a disciple in the church without being circumcised until Paul opts to take him along on a missionary journey in chapter 16 and circumcises him because of "the Jews who were in those places, for they all knew that his father was a Greek."[231] Thus, while Timothy is circumcised only two verses after the narrative introduces him, clearly his prior life is depicted as that of one who feared and loved the God of Israel but had not taken the last step of full conversion. Timothy's experience before his entrance into the narrative appears to be that of a God-fearer. It seems that Paul circumcises him only to appease certain audience members on their missionary journey, rather than meeting a theological standard. Furthermore, Timothy does not act as a prototype or the symbol of boundary expansion like many of the other characters we have talked about.

Others

There are other places where God-fearers appear, while not being utilized in the narrative as much as the others. The pattern in Paul's early ministry is to go to the synagogue,[232] where he speaks not only to Jews, but to Gentiles present as well.[233] Gentiles who are attracted to the fellowship of the synagogue and the worship of the God of Israel are God-fearers. In Acts 13, Paul addresses God-fearers directly two different times.[234]

There are other characters in the narrative that may or may not be God-fearers. For example, Theophilus (Θεόφιλος), the addressee of Luke's two volumes has a Greek name meaning "friend of God." Nolland wonders if the name could be a representative

---

228. Keener, *Acts*, 2:1727.
229. Luke 3:12–14.
230. Keener, *Acts*, 2:1727.
231. Acts 16:3. Also, see Meiser, "Timothy"; Cohen, "Timothy"; Samartha, "Daughter," 14.
232. Acts 13:14; 14:1.
233. Acts 13:16, 26, 48; 14:1b.
234. Acts 13:16, 26. Barrett, *Acts* 1:353; Jervell, *Die Apostelgeschichte*, 356. "Seine Anrede macht deutlich, dass es in der Synagoge zwei Gruppen gibt, die voneinander getrennt sind. Es sind die Juden, und die Gottesfürchtigen. Die Auseinandersetzung mit den Juden und die Aufnahme der Heidengeschieht in der Synagoge. Paulus redet beide Gruppen an, wobei er in der Ansprache, die auch Heiden gilt, über Israel redet."

title for a God-fearer.²³⁵ However, Alexander suggests strongly that Theophilus is a real person, saying we can be "reasonably certain" that he is.²³⁶ Thus, considering the central role of Cornelius's conversion (not to mention the Ethiopian Eunuch and others) and the consideration that God-fearers make an appropriate audience for Luke–Acts, it seems quite probable that Theophilus is a God-fearer himself.²³⁷ Whether or not Theophilus is a real person, the point that matters more is that he symbolically represents God-fearers. Rather than speculating on the empirical question of his identity, scholars would do better to focus on this symbolic representation since that is the actual interpretive question.

There is another character to consider. Cornelius in chapter 10 tells everything to his "devout soldier" (στρατιώτην εὐσεβῆ:) and personal attendant and sends him to Joppa. First, do we understand the word εὐσεβῆ as "godly"? Although nearly all render it as "devout," some translations render this as "God-fearing soldier" (BBE) and "soldier who feared the Lord" (Douay). Second, since this is Cornelius's personal attendant and the first person he chooses to tell of his vision, it is most likely that this is also a God-fearer.

Conclusion

In this chapter we have established the importance of God-fearers in Acts and surveyed relevant scholarship over the last one hundred and fifty years. Although not without controversy, the majority view justifiably remains that there existed in the first century Gentiles that were attracted to the synagogue and worshipped the God of Israel that were called God-fearers. We also noted how Luke's narrative contains God-fearers as key characters in the unfolding of the narrative. This group is the ideal audience for Luke–Acts, and also fits with the larger narrative movement of decentralization away from the established Jewish power structures. The narrative is written in such a way that the audience is expected to imagine themselves in the story. This element of imagination is crucial for the God-fearers. When we view the God-fearers as an ideal audience, we notice the emphasis on Gentiles and other outsiders, while acknowledging the strong Jewish focus of both volumes. This Jewishness, which is evidenced by the emphasis on Israel's history, provides the cultural memory as a context for identity formation in the New Christian Movement. In order to understand fully Luke's transformative illocutionary intent, we must consider the Jewishness of his approach, one that reflects a desire to account for both the roots of historical Judaism and the Christologically redefined mission of Christianity. We turn to those issues now.

---

235. Nolland, "Luke's Readers," 3.

236. Alexander, *Preface*, 188. She suggests that if it was a representative title, the correct Greek adjective would be Θεόφιλης rather than Θεόφιλε.

237. For more on the identity of Theophilus, see Creamer et al., "Theophilus"; Nodet, "Théophile"; Heil, "Theophilos."

3

The Gospel and Decentralization in Luke–Acts

THE ARGUMENT OF THIS thesis is that Luke has a transformative illocutionary intent, which is to create social identity in a God-fearing reader. God-fearers are clearly emphasized in Luke's narrative (chapter 2). Additionally, Luke infuses his narrative with minor characters to connect better with his audience. This serves his focus on the decentralization of the centralized power of Judaism, in order to welcome the outsider. We can better understand how Luke does this by employing Social Identity Theory (chapter 1). However, despite Luke's emphasis on including outsiders and welcoming God-fearers, Luke–Acts is very Jewish, clearly rooting the movement of Jesus in the historic faith and history of Israel and her Scriptures. Allowing the reader to connect with this historic faith creates cultural memory (chapter 1), which is central to the formation of social identity.[1] We recall that cultural memory is the process of encapsulating origins and other important memories of the group as stories, making it possible for new members to share in group history. To the degree that Luke utilizes the framing stories of Israel and her Scriptures for his audience, he is utilizing cultural memory and creating social identity. Methodologically, it is important for us to observe how the implied author uses storytelling to connect the past with the implied audience's present. Luke's identity-forming message is rooted in salvation history and intertwined with the gospel.[2] Thus, he builds his narrative around

---

1. Liu and László, "Narrative Theory," 88.

2. By "gospel," I mean a life and identity-forming movement that sees Jesus as the climactic fulfillment of Israel's story that is for all people. I do not mean the evangelical idea of a message to be communicated, such as "justification by faith." Similarly, McKnight, *King*, 37, states, "The story of Jesus as the Messiah and Lord resolves what is yearning for completion in the story of Israel. This Jesus is the one who saves Israel from its sins and the one who rescues humans from their imprisonments.... The story of Jesus, though, is first and foremost a resolution of Israel's story and because the Jesus Story completes Israel's Story, it saves." McKnight also offers a fuller definition of gospel, which includes the story of Israel/the Bible, the story of Jesus, the plan of salvation, and the method of persuasion all as elements considered in the notion of the gospel. I am also aware that "gospel" may be considered an anachronistic term, as Luke's only uses the noun εὐαγγέλιον twice (Acts 15:7; 20:24), although he does use the verb twenty-five times (Luke 1:19; 2:10; 3:18; 4:18, 43; 7:22; 8:1; 9:6; 16:16; 20:1; Acts 5:42; 8:4, 12, 25, 35, 40; 10:36; 11:20; 13:32; 14:7, 15, 21; 15:35; 16:10; 17:18). Paul uses the noun in Acts 15:7, and he speaks of the Gentiles hearing "the message of the good news." So, Luke is familiar with this

communicating transformatively by engaging the imagination of his audience.³ He also invites the audience into Israel's story. This gospel reaches both backward and forward. It reaches backward in that Luke sees the gospel as connected to the ancient faith, that is, the story of Israel and how it relates to all of humanity. He is showing a trajectory that starts with Adam, goes through Israel, the patriarchs, and the prophets, and continues to its climax in Jesus and the early church. The God-fearing reader is invited to join this story that is not new, but is ancient. To the degree that Luke emphasizes the antiquity and the historic dimension of the faith of the early church, he is creating identity for his God-fearing readers.⁴ Naturally, God-fearers are attracted to the God of Israel, not least because of this antiquity. Luke's Gospel is intertextual with Isaiah and he sets up tremendous expectations early in volume one that are not met at the end of Luke. Thus, the gospel also reaches forward. The mission of Jesus and the gospel continues into volume two where the promises are more fully realized. The gospel is about outward expansion and inclusion, and no longer about simply the nationalism of the previous era. The story is not new, but it builds and reaches its climax in Acts by including others.⁵

In the interest of delimitation, this chapter focuses on the canticles and infancy narratives, as well as other key scenes early in Jesus' ministry. These scenes set tremendous expectations for the rest of the two volumes. In chapter 4, we will look at prototypes and exemplars, so our focus will be primarily on characters that show us in the text and how they are presented. Chapter 5 will focus on the two historiographical speeches in Acts 7 and 13 as the key places Luke uses rhetoric in Acts. These texts are central to Luke's social identity forming agenda and also somewhat undervalued in the quest to understand Luke's mission to God-fearers.⁶

---

idea. However, although I use the term "gospel" here, if one preferred "identity-forming movement" instead, little would be lost. The point is not about the word, but about the concept.

3. Stagg, *Acts*, 5–18. Also, see Keener, *Acts*, 1:435–58, who has a chapter on this topic and suggests that competing purpose claims for Luke need not be mutually exclusive.

4. Sharing these stories from the past "makes it possible for new members to share group history." Liu and László, "Narrative Theory," 88; Assmann, *Das kulturelle*.

5. This sentiment is present in the work of Wright, *Challenge*, 35: "First, [Jesus] believed that the creator God had purposed from the beginning to address and deal with the problems within his creation through Israel. Israel was not just to be an "example" of a nation under God; Israel was to be the means through which the world would be saved. Second, Jesus believed, as did many though not all of his contemporaries, that this vocation would be accomplished through Israel's history reaching a great moment of climax, in which Israel herself would be saved from her enemies and through which the creator God, the covenant God, would at last bring his love and justice, his mercy and truth, to bear upon the whole world, bringing renewal and healing to all creation." Wright is speaking of the technical terms of election and eschatology, as he says in the next line. Also, see Richardson, *Pioneer*; Wright, "Acting"; Matera, *Christology*; Nguyen, "Passion"; Newman, *Restoration*.

6. Although much has been written about the canticles, most (e.g., Tannehill, *Luke*; Bock, *Luke*) do not properly evaluate them with regard to Luke's outward mission of inclusion and decentralization that continues through two volumes. And although much has been written about the speeches of Stephen and Paul in Acts 7 and 13, few have approached these with an eye toward social identity formation and rhetoric. Dillon, *Hymns*; Kaut, *Befreier* are notable exceptions to this critique, and for

In order to bring the God-fearing reader into God's saving story, Luke needs to communicate the narrative trajectory of God's activity. This provides the basis and the expectations for Jesus and the ministry of the early church. To the degree that we see Luke rooting his story of all humanity in Jewish salvation history, he is educating his reader on the narrative trajectory that will include outsiders and lead to the climax of human history. Two elements that will help accomplish this in Luke's two-volume work are (1) redemption that starts in the past and continues into the present and (2) promises, which find their climactic fulfillment in the New Testament age.

The reader encounters these ideas right away in Luke, as the extended birth narratives are all about redemption history and fulfilled promises.[7] The characters recite songs of poetry, which beautifully highlight the issues Luke is interested in. These key stories work as anthology scenes, hinting at redemption and climactic fulfillment of Israel's story and reach an interesting moment in Acts 7 and 13 with speeches by Stephen and Paul, respectively. They offer concise versions of the story of redemption history in two speeches. These are Luke's attempt to bring the God-fearing reader into the trajectory of the story. An examination of the canticles, these two speeches, and other key scenes in Luke–Acts is needed. This will give us a sense of how Luke is setting up the narrative for his God-fearing reader.

In addition, Luke seems to foster a hope among his readers in a "New Exodus," of which the people of the New Christian Movement are a part. Luke presents Acts as a form of the exodus story as seen through an Isaianic lens.[8] Thus, we will start by exploring the New Exodus in Luke and its relevancy for his identity-forming goals.

The New Exodus in Luke–Acts

The New Exodus is a key feature in Second Isaiah.[9] Pao, in his significant work on the New Exodus, concludes, "The entire Isaianic New Exodus program provides the structural framework for the narrative of Acts as well as the various emphases developed within this framework."[10] He goes on to say that it is the national story of Israel that forms the identity of the early Christian movement.[11]

---

that reason, we will engage with these sources throughout this chapter.

7. Luke 1:1, 13, 16–17, 30–33, 37–38, 48, 50, 54–55, 68–70, 72–73; 2:10–11, 14, 25–27, 29–32, 38–39.

8. Pao, *New Exodus*.

9. Scholars argue for two or three "Isaiahs." Despite the different views of the divisions of the book, Isaiah 40–66 presents Isaiah's vision of the New Exodus, a vision of restoration and salvation. A look into the historical-critical issues in Isaiah is outside the scope of this project, which is concerned with the narrative dynamic Luke is utilizing. For more, see Blenkinship, 42–43; Dahl, "Interpretations"; Gelston, "Notes"; Kapelrud, "Concern"; Graham, "Rescue."

10. Pao, *New Exodus*, 250.

11. Pao, *New Exodus*, 250.

His argument is that Luke is able to weave the diverse stories from the early church into the tapestry—"a meaningful and coherent 'history'"—built on the paradigm offered by Isaiah's understanding of the New Exodus.[12] Pao sees Luke 4:18–19, quoting Isaiah 40:3–5, as inaugurating both the second half of Isaiah that looks toward restoration, and the public ministry of Jesus.[13] Acts 1:8 is also seen as key for the Lukan New Exodus, as it outlines "the three stages of the Isaianic program: the dawn of the era of salvation upon Jerusalem, the restoration of Israel, and the mission to the Gentiles."[14] Furthermore, Pao claims that by using this schema, the early Christian community is portrayed as the true people of God.

Denova offers an interesting perspective, suggesting that Luke–Acts is an attempt "to continue the story of Israel into the life of Jesus and his followers," particularly seeing this done through the lens of Isaiah. She identifies five major elements from Isaiah around which Luke constructs his narrative: "(1) The prediction of a remnant (Isa 10:20–23; 14:1–2); (2) the release of the captive exiles (Isa 49:22–26; 60:1–17); (3) the inclusion of the nations who would worship the God of Israel as Gentiles (Isa 49:7; 56:5; (4) prophetic condemnation of the unrepentant (Isa 66:24); and (5) the restoration of Zion (Isa 2:2–4; 62:1–17)."[15] Although the result is different, the common starting point for Pao and Denova is Isaiah.

However, not all are convinced. Mallen, for example, is troubled by the shift that happens about halfway through the book of Acts where Gentiles become the primary audience responding to the gospel, whereas Jews hardly have any more positive responses.[16] He sees restoration of Israel as key to Isaiah's New Exodus, whereas that mission seems to wane: "The narrative ends with Paul's ongoing mission at the centre of the Gentile nations (i.e., Rome), rather than with the renewal of Jerusalem's splendor (Isa 52:1–2; 54:11–17), which is the goal of the New Exodus."[17] Furthermore, Mallen ties his conclusion to his dating of Luke, suggesting a time after the destruction of the Temple in 70 CE, and holds that a destroyed Jerusalem Temple "would appear to be the antithesis of New Exodus hopes."[18]

However, Mallen seems to miss the major emphasis on decentralization that begins in the birth announcements of Jesus, continues throughout his ministry, and

---

12. Pao, *New Exodus*, 249.

13. Pao, *New Exodus*, 249.

14. Pao, *New Exodus*, 249–50. Pao goes on to outline four ideas introduced in the prologue of Isaiah 40:1–11 and developed in Luke-Acts: "The restoration of Israel, the word of God, the anti-idol polemic, and the status of the nations/Gentiles."

15. Denova, *Accomplished*, 26.

16. Mallen, *Transformation*, 187. The one example of the faithful response of Israel after Acts 15 is 21:12. For other critiques of Pao, see Tuckett, "Christology"; Beale, "Review."

17. Mallen, *Transformation*, 187. For more on the restoration of Israel in Isaiah, see Bauckham, "Restoration" and literature cited.

18. Mallen, *Transformation*, 187.

is fully realized in the community of the early church.[19] The goal of Luke–Acts and of the Isaianic New Exodus is not Jerusalem's splendor, but the splendor of God and his people, made up of both Jews and Gentiles, Israel and those previously unwelcomed.[20] In fact, the city of Jerusalem and the Temple are both clearly and specifically decentralized in the movement of Jesus' kingdom in favor of God's Spirit that dwells within community, regardless of geographic location. These are key ideas that Luke brings together in his work (see below). In addition, his focus on the date of Luke misses the larger narratival drive regarding God's activity through Jesus of leading people out of their bondage.

Thus, despite being thoughtful, Mallen's critique ultimately fails in that it does not give enough attention to Pao's claims of the shift that occurs in Acts 13:46–47 where the Gentiles become the focus, "emphasized through the Isaianic quotation of Isa 49:6."[21] Pao also notes the transformation of the New Exodus vision that occurs in Luke: "Unlike the Isaianic New Exodus, the New Exodus in Acts provides a striking vision of the soteriological equality of the Jews and the Gentiles."[22] Thus, Mallen misses the major narrative point of decentralization.[23]

In short, the New Exodus has become an important topic in the study of Luke–Acts. Understanding the New Exodus as a salvific restoration centered on the gospel and the New Christian community, containing both Jews and Gentiles, is a helpful way to understand what the author is doing. It seeks to take into account the larger narrative moves of Luke–Acts and note similarities and dependence where they exist.

The Rhetorical Use of Names in Luke–Acts

Names are an important part of a narrative rhetorical strategy that fits Luke's transformative illocution of identity formation. As we will see below, Luke will utilize name meanings in the canticles that fit with his purpose of connecting the story of Jesus to salvation history.

---

19. See chapter 2 on Luke's God-fearers.

20. Pao, *New Exodus*, 81, 93, 105, 107–10, 198, talks about the reversal in Isaiah and in Luke–Acts. Mallen's view of the New Exodus seems too Jerusalem centric and does not take Luke's emphasis on decentralization into account.

21. Pao, *New Exodus*, 250.

22. Pao, *New Exodus*, 250.

23. See Brodie, "Imitation," 79, who sees Luke as an "imitation," a Greco-Roman form where the author uses an ancient text and seeks to "rework and reproduce both the form and content of the model or source text in a variety of ways." Brodie (discussed below) sees the Elijah–Elisha narrative as the ancient text Luke is using and points out a number of similarities, although his case remains only focused on specific events (rather than including linguistics or larger narrative issues) and only accounts for a small amount of material in Luke–Acts. Moessner makes a similar argument regarding the exodus wandering narrative in Deuteronomy. Moessner, *Banquet*. For a fuller critique of Moessner, see Pao, *New Exodus*, 9–10.

Names can be symbols of larger realities.[24] By referencing the name of a hero of the faith, the connotations of that character come into the reader's mind in a way that affects the communication experience. These names call to mind "themes and language already familiar" to the audience.[25] Moreover, nearly every name in Hebrew and Greek literature had a meaning, many of which were significant.[26] Luke carefully leverages the meanings of names. We will explore a few of the ways that the names in these chapters contribute to that strategy and will explore the use of names again in chapter 5 with regard to the speeches in Luke.[27]

An obvious place we observe this phenomenon in Luke is in the genealogy, particularly as we contrast Luke's version with Matthew's.[28] Matthew emphasizes Jesus' royal lineage and his connection with David, although he also includes several women of particular intrigue.[29] Matthew connects his genealogy back to Abraham and the Jewish people for rhetorically strategic reasons. Luke, by contrast, traces his genealogy back to Adam, the father of humanity, because it fits his agenda of universal inclusion among God's people.[30] Luke, other times, will leverage the meanings of names as well, which was common in the Jewish Scriptures. A few examples will help establish the tradition Luke continues.

A famous example of names being important in the Jewish Scriptures is with Melchizedek, a figure who played a role early in the story of Abraham in Genesis, which is then capitalized on by the Psalmist.[31] The character of Melchizedek is a popu-

---

24. Burke, *Philosophy*, 27–28.

25. Cameron, *Rhetoric*, 130.

26. Sometimes this is overt, as with Moses, who was named for being drawn out of the water, he will also draw out his people from Egypt (Exod 2:10). Others include Adam, Eve, Isaac, and Abram/Abraham. Other names have meanings that could be significant, such as David meaning "beloved," but the text never makes a direct connection to the name meaning of the character. For an examination of Old Testament name meanings, see Coote, "Meaning"; Barr, "Symbolism"; Hartman, "Name."

27. For examples of this, see Hendrickson, "Literary"; Kennedy, *Greek Rhetoric*; *New History*; Bass, "Narrative." Billig, "Psychology," 119, makes a reference to modern writers doing this as well. This is not unique to Luke in the New Testament period. Romans 9, for example, Paul utilizes characters like Abraham, Sarah, Isaac, Rebecca, Jacob, and Esau. Later on in the chapter, he speaks of Moses and Pharaoh. These are more than just names, but representations of narrative realities that are shared by his audience. Similarly, in Galatians 3, Paul connects being children of Abraham with having faith. Abraham is obviously a rhetorically strategic character to utilize here, as he represents faith, God's covenant with Israel, and the formation of the Hebrew people. This strategy will continue into chapter 4, where Abraham's two sons by two women are mentioned. Hagar, the slave woman, is mentioned by name, although Sarah is not. His purpose is to emphasize the slavery of the law, which he connects to Hagar. See Elliot, *Rhetoric*; Heil, "Remnant"; Tolmie, "Paulus." Though it is highly questionable whether Luke had access to Paul's writings, this nonetheless shows that other authors in the New Testament period are doing a similar thing.

28. Matt 1:1–17; Luke 3:23–38.

29. Tamar, Rahab, Ruth, and Bahsheba (called Uriah's wife).

30. Also, see Trow, *Geneologies*; Loubser, "Invoking"; Buell, "Producing."

31. The writer of Hebrews utilizes the character of Melchizedek, though it is unlikely that Luke was aware of this.

lar figure in Jewish apocryphal literature as well.[32] His theologically inspired name is the key indicator of his identity, and he becomes something of a mascot for the proto-priesthood for both Old Testament and New Testament writers.

There is precedent for this in the prophets as well. The best example is Hosea who, after God calls him to marry a "wife of whoredom," has three children.[33] His children's names are symbolic for what Israel is experiencing at that time in her history. The first son, Jezreel, was so named because of judgment coming on Israel for the blood of Jezreel, which is to occur in the valley of the same name.[34] Hosea's daughter is named Lo-Ruhamah, meaning "not loved," representing that he will no longer have pity or show love to Israel.[35] His third child, a son, was named Lo-Ammi meaning "not my people," and God says to the people harshly, "for you are not my people and I am not your God."[36] The book of Daniel offers a Babylonian example of this, as Daniel ("God is my judge") and his three friends, Hananiah ("God is gracious"), Mishael ("Who is as God is?"), and Azariah ("Yahweh is a helper"), are renamed Belteshazzar ("Bel protects his life"), Shadrach ("Command of Aku"), Meshach ("Who is as Aku is?"), and Abednego ("Slave of Nabu"), respectively.[37] These are the most overt examples where the giving of names is serving as a rhetorical strategy to communicate something in the narrative.[38] We will observe more of this in the discussion of the canticles below, but an introduction to the promise and fulfillment is necessary first.

Promise and Fulfillment in Luke

Luke emphasizes promise[39] and fulfillment regarding the Messiah, which he roots in the LXX. He uses an "anthological style" early on to connect the life of Jesus to the past saving acts of God. This is descriptive of "the use of terms and themes from the OT as

---

32. See *Targum Yerushalmi* to Genesis 14; *Genesis Rabbah* 46:6, 7; *Nedarim* 32b; *Avodah Zarah* 36a. Melchizedek has been a figure of interest in Rabbinic, Qumranic, and Christian Literature. See McNamara, "Melchizedek"; Davila, "Melchizedek"; "King"; Kobelski, *Melchizedek,* 115–29; Woude, "Melchizedek"; Yadin, "Aspects"; Cockerill, "Melchizedek"; Lane, *Hebrews,* 161; Fitzmyer, "Further Light"; Carmignac, "Le document."

33. Hos 1:1–3.

34. Hos 1:4–5.

35. Hos 1:6–7.

36. Hos 1:8–9.

37. Dan 1:6–7. Also, see Chia, "Naming"; DeBruyn, "Clash."

38. Also, see Viljoen, "Identity"; Butler, "Families"; Moon, "Honor"; Mitchell, "Search"; Schreiber, "Dialectic."

39. We will sometimes use the word "climax" in addition to "promise," referring to the expectations of characters rooted in the promises that reach a new level in the scenes. For more on this motif, see Farris, *Hymns,* 101.

well as more developed typological correspondence,"[40] and fits best with how Luke uses such scenes in parallel to testify to the birth and mission of Jesus.[41]

Promise and fulfillment are part of the agenda from the opening words of the book, which talk about "the events that have been fulfilled among us,"[42] setting the tone for the fulfillment of the gospel. This represents one of five key places that special words for fulfillment are used. The opening line uses a form of the word πληροφορέω,[43] its only occurrence in Luke–Acts.[44] There are four places where forms of the verb τελέω[45] are used. These come at key places in the narrative.[46] Luke is using this word as a way to signal the importance of promise and fulfillment at important scenes in the life of Jesus, including his birth and the crucifixion. This shows the centrality of the cross for the mission of Jesus.[47]

Beyond the semantic level, the issue is present throughout the narrative. The birth announcements in Luke of both John and Jesus resemble similar birth announcements of other heroes of Israel who play a significant role in God's purposes.[48] Litwak states that the birth announcements "tell his audience that God is showing his faithfulness to his people by working once again as he did in the scriptures of Israel to bring deliverance and salvation to his people."[49] Thus, this is another way Luke roots the story of Jesus in Israel's story and the Hebrew Scriptures. Luke is also showing the continuity between the story of Jesus and the church in the New Testament and the people of Israel and their Hebrew Scriptures. "Through Jesus' followers, God is continuing his faithfulness to his covenant with Abraham."[50]

40. Nolland, *Luke*, 1:25.

41. See Devillers, "Infancy."

42. Luke 1:1.

43. "Fill completely"; "fulfill"; "convince fully" (BDAG).

44. It also occurs three times in Paul's undisputed letters (Rom 4:21; 14:5; Col 4:12) and two more times in 2 Timothy (4:5, 17).

45. "To complete an activity or process"; "to carry out an obligation"; "to pay what is due" (BDAG).

46. The four occurrences are when Jesus is presented at the Temple (Luke 2:39) and as foreshadowing or referring to the imminent crucifixion (12:50; 18:31; 22:37). It occurs one time on the lips of Paul, also referring to the crucifixion (Acts 13:29).

47. Similarly, just before his arrest, Jesus says, "Indeed what is written about me is being fulfilled" (Luke 22:37). Thus, with the exception of the first usage that talks about Mary and Joseph fulfilling everything required of them when Jesus was born, the other occurrences either look forward to the death of Jesus or look back to it, suggesting the central importance of the cross as a fulfilling act. In tracing climax and fulfillment through the two volumes, the focus on the crucifixion of Jesus becomes evident.

48. Litwak, *Echoes*, 71. Litwak references the birth announcements of Isaac, Samson, and Samuel.

49. Litwak, *Echoes*, 71. For a robust discussion and comparison of these announcement stories, see Litwak, *Echoes*, 71–115.

50. Litwak, *Echoes*, 89: "Luke's framing in discourse shows that the characters in Luke 1–2 stand in continuity with God's people in the past. Luke, as a historian, uses this continuity to validate and identify these characters in his narrative as the true descendants of Abraham, and implicitly, that it is not the opponents of the Way, or the Jewish religious leaders, or some other group within Second Temple

In short, Luke seeks to contextualize the advent of Jesus the Messiah in a particular way. Specifically, he uses minor characters as a feature in his narrative to emphasize decentralization. We will see how the following characters all play a part in helping frame Jesus in the context of the story of Israel, and in so doing, set out the plan to include the marginalized God-fearer in the movement of Jesus.[51] An examination of the characters early in volume one—Mary, Zechariah, Simeon, Anna, John the Baptist, as well as a few key scenes in Jesus' life—is needed because it will set the tone for all that follows in both volumes, that is, the rootedness of the new move of God in the Jewish story, climax and fulfillment, the inclusion of minor characters, and decentralization. Each of these elements is key to understanding Luke's transformative agenda for God-fearers.

In addition, many of these early scenes are songs or poetry, referred to as the canticles of Luke. That Luke strategically uses poetry here to highlight key elements and set the trajectory early in the story is significant. Dillon suggests that "a narrator's lyrical outbursts break through, of a sudden, the required coordinates of space and time to declare the future outcome and eschatological significance of events being told."[52] Likewise, Lohfink sees an implied response from the audience, saying, "When [the story's] actors, at its high points or conclusion raise their voices in a psalm, they become prophets and unlock its larger context, thus inciting readers to make their own expressions of divine praise."[53] Luke's strategy is to not only highlight elements of promise and fulfillment with these canticles, but to invite the reader to engage with and participate in the songs, thus further creating social identity. To these early birth narrative scenes we now turn.

Mary's Song (Magnificat)

Mary's song (Luke 1:46–55) offers a robust introduction to the notion of climactic fulfillments.[54] She is the first of several characters in Luke who respond to the news of the savior's birth in song or poetic verse form.[55] This scene follows and pulls together the pair of initial scenes in the book that announce the births of John and Jesus to their respective mothers. When Elizabeth hears Mary, John leaps inside his mother's womb, an event that commentators see parallels to in the Old Testament.[56]

Judaism. Through Jesus' followers God is continuing his faithfulness to his covenant with Abraham."

51. I am borrowing this word "frame" from Tannen, "Frame?," 41–42. She also offers a complex history of framing, which has a number of definitions. The most succinct seems to be contextualization within a culture. See Tannen, "Frame?," 14–26.

52. Dillon, *Hymns*, 3.

53. Lohfink, "Die Lieder," 390.

54. Bemile, *Magnificat*, suggests that the Magnificat is programmatic for Luke's presentation of Jesus and the early church.

55. For an engagement with the poetic form of the magnificat, see Tannehill, "Magnificat."

56. Fitzmyer, *Luke*, 1:358; Bock, *Luke*, 1:134–35, connect Luke 1:41a to Genesis 25 when Jacob

The song is introduced by the words of Elizabeth: "Blessed are you among women, and blessed is the child you will bear! But why am I so favored that the mother of my Lord should come to me? As soon as the sound of your greeting reached my ears, the baby in my womb leaped for joy. *Blessed is she who has believed that the Lord would fulfill his promises to her!*"(1:42b–45). As is common throughout Luke, Elizabeth is filled with the Holy Spirit.[57]

Luke's account of Mary's response to God's call places her in a long line of characters in Israel's past who are also called by God and respond. Litwak suggests Deborah, Gideon, Jael, Miriam and Moses are all similar to Mary in that God calls them to carry out his purposes.[58] Similarly, Meagher sees the "continuity in the divine redemptive interventions and links Mary with Isaiah . . . with Jeremiah and Ezekiel, with Gideon and Moses."[59] Litwak also notes the quantity of material on Mary, pointing to her being more than just the mother of Jesus, but being a servant of God in her own right, as well as a key piece of the narrative introduction to Jesus.[60]

The song itself contains considerable messianic language, regarding the humble being lifted up and the hungry being fed. Fitzmyer calls this a "mosaic of OT expressions drawn from the LXX."[61] He also sees a loose connection to the surrounding text.[62] However, the song fits Luke's purposes perfectly by stringing together important elements from the Old Testament and connecting them to the work of Jesus. The Magnificat is one of the ways that Luke bridges the gap between Old Testament expectation and New Testament realization in Jesus. He paves the way for the gospel to be shared not just with Jews, but to Gentiles as well. Since the gospel is rooted in the salvation history of Israel, communicating that story in different ways is key to the bringing in outsiders.

Scholars suggest different poetic parallels for the Magnificat, including Psalms both inside and outside of the Hebrew Canon.[63] However, the most obvious parallels seem to be with Hannah in 1 Samuel.[64] Her song in 1 Samuel 2:1–10 begins,

---

and Esau wrestle for position inside their mother, though Bock notes that Luke's scene is without the tension of the Genesis story.

57. Similar things are also said of Zechariah and Simeon, as well as statements made about John's future (Luke 1:67; 2:25–27; for John, see Luke 1:15, 17, 80; for Mary, see 1:35).

58. Litwak, *Echoes*, 90. Also, see Cook, "Magnificat"; Spencer, "Reversal"; O'Day, "Singing."

59. Meagher, "Prophetic Call," 177.

60. Litwak, *Echoes*, 90. See above 17n23. For the role of women in Luke–Acts, see Forbes and Harrower, *Raised*; Anderson, "Difference"; Corley, *Private Women*; D'Angelo, "Women"; Dewey, "Storytelling"; "Healings"; Reid, *Choosing*; Schaberg, *Illegitimacy*; Schottroff, *Impatient Sisters*; Fiorenza, "Liberation"; Seim, *Double Message*.

61. Fitzmyer, *Luke*, 1:359.

62. Fitzmyer, *Luke*, 1:359. He sees this as evidence that the canticle was added to the narrative at a later time.

63. Such as Psalms 33; 47; 48; 113; 117; 135; 136. Fitzmyer, *Luke*, 1:359. He also associates it with some non-biblical songs, such as those in 1 Maccabees and the Qumran Thanksgiving Psalms.

64. Plummer, *Luke*, 30; Ringgren, "Use"; Marshall, "Magnificat."

Ἐστερεώθη ἡ καρδία μου ἐν κυρίῳ, and Mary's song in Luke 1:46b begins, Μεγαλύνει ἡ ψυχή μου τὸν κύριον.[65] There is a parallel in verse 48 at the end of the first couplet as well. Psalm 25:5 (LXX) contains the line ὁ θεὸς ὁ σωτήρ μου, while verse 47 contains the exact phrase τῷ θεῷ τῷ σωτῆρί μου.[66] This is the first occurrence of "'savior' [σωτήρ] in the [Lukan] writings and introduces the theme of salvation."[67] Luke builds a bridge between the common Old Testament usage describing God[68] and the way he will use it about Jesus.[69] Thus, he utilizes an important Old Testament concept, which will become realized in a new way in his writings.[70]

Verse 48 offers an allusion to the emotionally intense issue of barrenness, as the words closely mirror Hannah.[71] Nolland notes that this need not be a reference to childlessness, "except perhaps in a metaphorical sense according to which childlessness is the lack of that child who is to be the messianic deliverer."[72] Mary is mirroring the emotional intensity of the ancient prayers that many women throughout Scripture have prayed regarding barrenness.[73] Few things create a climate for an emotionally intense prayer in the ancient world like barrenness because of the importance given to biological offspring.[74] Luke is addressing this and offering hope in the era of the Messiah. The coming of Jesus is an answer to the prophetic promise made in Isaiah 54:1: "Sing, barren woman, you who never bore a child; burst into song, shout for joy, you who were never in labor; because more are the children of the desolate woman than of her who has a husband,' says the LORD."[75] The emphasis here is her low status. Mary describes herself as God's handmaiden, τῆς δούλης αὐτοῦ, the same language as used in verse 38 (ἰδοὺ ἡ δούλη κυρίου).[76] The reference here is in contrast to the magnification (Μεγαλύνει) of God two lines above.

---

65. Fitzmyer, *Luke*, 1:356.

66. Fitzmyer, *Luke*, 1:356. The only difference is the case based on the usage in the sentence. Also, see Isa 12:2; Micah 7:7.

67. Fitzmyer, *Luke*, 1:367.

68. See the parallels already mentioned, Ps 25:5; Isa 12:2; Micah 7:7

69. Other occurrences of σωτὴρ and σωτηρία include Luke 2:11, 30; 3:6; Acts 5:31; 13:23; 28:28. Forms of this word do not appear in the other synoptics, except for one occurrence in the extended ending of Mark. For more on the ending of Mark, see below 106n128.

70. There are over one hundred seventy references of these two words in the LXX.

71. Mary makes reference to her humble state, ὅτι ἐπέβλεψεν ἐπὶ τὴν ταπείνωσιν τῆς δούλης αὐτοῦ, which most clearly represents the Prayer of Hannah in 1 Sam 1:11, ἐὰν ἐπιβλέπων ἐπιβλέψῃς ἐπὶ τὴν ταπείνωσιν τῆς δούλης σου.

72. Nolland, *Luke 1*, 69.

73. Also, see Gen 11:30; 20:18; 25:21; 29:31–32; 30:22; Judg 13:2–3; 2 Sam 6:23.

74. In discussion of barrenness associated with Mary here, see Bock, *Luke*, 1:150–51; Fitzmyer, *Luke*, 1:367; Klostermann, *Das Lukasevangelium*, 19; Luce, *Luke*, 92; Danker, *New Age*, 43. For a fuller look at barrenness in the ancient world, see Baden, "Barrenness"; Schipper, "Disabling"; Avalos, *Illness*, 332; Stol, *Birth*; Bergmann, *Childbirth*; Callaway, *Sing*; Trible, *Rhetoric*.

75. Also, see Exod 23:26; Ps 113:9; 128:3.

76. Bock, *Luke*, 1:150.

Mary is responding in praise because of what God has done for her, namely, giving her a special child. Farris rightly notes that in the case of Mary, Zechariah, and Simeon, each canticle is a praise response to a fulfilled promise.[77] Verse 50 is a transition, as it begins to shift the focus from Mary to God's actions for all people.[78] Luke's usage of the phrase "to the ones fearing him" (τοῖς φοβουμένοις αὐτόν) here is interesting. Klauck was something of a pioneer in seeing this as a foreshadowing of the role that God-fearers will play in Acts, suggesting in 1997 that it had hardly been considered.[79] He makes his case with regard to the surrounding text, asking to what degree the themes of inclusion and universalism are present in the Magnificat, the canticles, and the Lukan corpus as a whole, making six points of observation in these similarities.[80] After Klauck, others followed suit.[81] However, not all agree. Marshall sees no embracing of Gentiles in the Magnificat[82] and Oliver notes the absence of universalism throughout the song.[83] Bock merely considers it along with a number of other similar descriptions of one who follows God in the Old Testament.[84] This could simply be another example of the mosaic of LXX quotations appearing in Mary's song. However, considering what a central role the God-fearers will have in Acts,[85] Klauck is right in seeing the reference foreshadowing both the role these God-fearing Gentiles would play as well as the use of that phrase as a technical term.[86] Although not used the same way as in Acts, this foreshadows the involvement of God-fearers in volume two.

Tannehill sees verses 51–53 as the climax of the song.[87] God's mercy to the humble and poor is seen on center stage as God has chosen to work with Mary. "Mary [is] an emblem or paradigm of God's saving work which is now beginning."[88] Another important link to the Old Testament is the statement in 1:51: "He has

77. Farris, *Hymns*, 101. Also, see Fitzmyer, *Luke*, 1:369.

78. Bock, *Luke*, 1:153.

79. Klauck, "Gottesfürchtige," 134.

80. Klauck, "Gottesfürchtige," 136–39. Most notably, with regard to the angels talking to shepherds, he says, "keinen Zweifelleiden, daß die Gottes-fürchtigen, die in jedem Volk Gott angenehm und willkommensind (Apg 10.35), zu dieser Gruppe von Menschen, auf denen sein Wohlgefallen ruht, hinzugehören." ("Leave no doubt that those who fear God—who are pleasant and welcome to God in every people (Acts 10:35)—belong to this group of people on whom his pleasure rests.")

81. Dillon, *Hymns*, 28–29, 35. For engagement with these sources, see Chrupcala, *Everyone*, 57n12; Brink, *Soldiers*, 157.

82. Marshall, *Luke*, 85.

83. Oliver, "Birth Stories," 222.

84. Deut 7:9; Ps 25:12; 103:17; Isa 55:3, 6; 57:15; Song 10:4; 13:12.

85. See chapter 2 on Luke's God-fearers.

86. Chrupcala, *Everyone*, 55–138, for example, traces the themes throughout Luke's two volumes that point to a more universal salvation.

87. Tannehill, *Luke*, 28. Also, see McKay, "Political Reading"; Croy and Connor, "Mantic"; Grams, "Mercy."

88. Tannehill, *Luke*, 29.

performed mighty deeds with his arm; he has scattered those who are proud in their inmost thoughts." Nolland states, "βραχίων αὐτοῦ, 'his arm,' is a frequent [Old Testament] image for the power of God, especially as manifested in the exodus and in the new exodus of eschatological salvation."[89] Thus, Luke uses a common Old Testament image to emphasize the power of God in the birth of Jesus. This further helps the reader connect the faith and story of Israel with the new movement of God in Jesus, which is an identity-forming process. The table below shows the many uses of this phrase βραχίων αὐτοῦ in the LXX.

Book	References to God's Arm
Exodus	6:1, 6; 15:16; 32:11
Deuteronomy	3:24; 4:34; 5:15; 6:21; 7:8, 19; 9:26, 29; 11:12; 26:8; 33:27 (LXX only)
2 Maccabees	15:24
Psalms[90]	44:3 (43:4); 71:18 (70:18); 77:15 (76:16); 79:11 (78:11); 89:10, 13 (88:11, 14); 98:1 (97:1); 136:12 (135:12)
Job	40:9
Wisdom of Solomon	5:16; 11:21; 16:16
Sirach	36:5 (LXX only)
Isaiah	26:11; 30:30; 40:10–11; 51:5, 9; 52:10; 53:1; 59:16; 62:8; 63:12
Jeremiah	21:5; 32:17, 21
Baruch	2:11
Ezekiel	20:33–34
Daniel	9:15

The abundance of occurrences of this phrase are in Deuteronomy. In addition, Psalms, Deuteronomy, and Second Isaiah all have numerous occurrences, which discuss the New Exodus. Mary's use of this phrase in 1:51 reminds the reader of God's strength and provision for his people (cf. Isaiah's New Exodus).[91] It also sets the tone for the following lines of the Magnificat. Luke is setting the stage for the dawning of a new age in salvation history, and he is doing it by alluding to this language used in books like Isaiah and Deuteronomy.[92] As an example, Isaiah 40:10–11 not only talks of ὁ

---

89. Nolland, *Luke*, 1:71.
90. English chapters and verses are given first, followed by the LXX.
91. For example, Isa 40:10–11; 51:5, 9. Also, see Bailey, "Song."
92. Consider also Dillon, *Hymns*, 34–35, who notes the strong hints at the reversal theme, which

βραχίων μετὰ κυριείας but also ὡς ποιμὴν ποιμανεῖ τὸ ποίμνιον αὐτοῦ καὶ τῷ βραχίονι αὐτοῦ συνάξει ἄρνας καὶ ἐν γαστρὶ ἐχούσας παρακαλέσει. Thus we have the language of God's strong arm used by Mary, but also the sense of gathering and comforting the flock, as Jesus does in his ministry.[93]

Mary's song ends with a reference to the promises made to ancestors. "Ancestors" will be addressed again several times in the Lukan corpus. In Acts 24:14–15, Paul says in a speech before Felix,

> However, I admit that I worship the God of our ancestors as a follower of the Way, which they call a sect. I believe everything that is in accordance with the Law and that is written in the Prophets, and I have the same hope in God as these men themselves have, that there will be a resurrection of both the righteous and the wicked.

Pao argues that this language is key to understanding Luke's agenda of promise and fulfillment in Acts, suggesting that the language of "the God of our ancestors" works as a claim by Christians "to be the true people of God and the true continuation of the ancestral traditions."[94] The song of Mary is the first place in the Lukan corpus that the phrase "God of our ancestors" occurs. Once again, this creates continuity between the Christian God and the God of Israelite tradition, as Luke did above with σωτὴρ and the deeds of God in verses 51–54. The last occurrence is when Paul testifies before the unbelieving Jews and Roman authorities in Acts 26, bookending the two volumes with "God of our ancestors" language and further connecting the God-fearing audience with this redemptive history.[95]

Verse 55 likely has two primary allusions: Micah 7:20: "You will be faithful to Jacob, and show love to Abraham, as you pledged on oath to our ancestors in days long ago," and 2 Samuel 22:51: "He gives his king great victories; he shows unfailing kindness to his anointed, to David and his descendants forever."[96] Nolland attributes "eschatological coloring" to the first allusion, and "a messianic note" to the second, although he adds that it "probably only reflects the Jewish application to the nation of [Old Testament] promises to the royal line."[97] However, it seems Luke can utilize the spirit of the fulfilling of promises to Israel's kings, while not needing to delimit

---

will continue through both volumes.

93. Many times this term is used in the LXX, the context is this sense of God's power to redeem, save, and comfort Israel or the marginalized. Nearly every reference in Deuteronomy is referring to the Exodus. Consider also the context of Isa 26:11; 40:10–11; 51:5; 52:10; 53:1; 62:8; Ezek 20:33–34; Dan 9:15. Also, see Wegener, "Arrival"; Wilson, "Between," 80–82; Sanborn, "Babe"; Steuernagel, "Theology"; Reid, "Overture"; Croy and Connor, "Mantic."

94. Pao, *New Exodus*, 65. Also, see Strauss, *Messiah*; Hahn, *Kinship*.

95. Other occurrences if this phrase include Luke 1:72–73; Acts 3:13; 5:30; 7:2, 32; 13:17; 22:14; 24:14. A similar motif is the ancestors of Jesus' opponents persecuting the prophets, as in Luke 6:23, 26; 7:51–52; 11:47–48.

96. Nolland, *Luke*, 1:73.

97. Nolland, *Luke*, 1:73.

the scope quite that much. Luke's scope is inclusive. Second, with the coming of the Spirit in Acts, God's "anointed ones" is a growing group.[98] There are more than 20 references to the Holy Spirit filling people, empowering them for prophetic speech, or coming upon them for some other purpose in Acts.[99] In addition to the disciples, it also includes a number of groups of people who were present with the disciples at various times as well as Cornelius, a God-fearing Gentile.[100] Thus, the reference to God's anointed in 2 Samuel 22 seems to have an apt parallel here. Third, Jesus is the true anointed one (Χριστός) of God, so the promises are due him first, and thus, this allusion can work well.

Mary is one of several women in early Christian writings who play a symbolic role as Israel. The song applies to Mary, but not to her alone.[101] The blurring of individual and collective language hints at this duality. In the next chapter Anna becomes something of a symbol for Israel as well, embodying the desperation the nation feels. Similarly, Valentini calls Mary a spokesperson of the whole community, representing the historic-salvific scope of Luke's writings.[102] Later on Luke will use a widow in a symbolic role, as she is an exemplar for generosity.[103] Outside of Luke, women tend to symbolize Israel. For instance in Galatians 4:21–31, Luke uses Hagar and Sarah as representative examples, Hagar as a slave and Sarah as free. Romans 7:1–3 speaks of the married woman as a representative as well.[104] Likewise with the Magnificat, seeing it as a song only about Mary misses the point. Mary represents all Israel. Her hints at nationalistic fulfillment will be fulfilled in other ways, namely, through the Messiah.

Additionally, Mary's song contains elements of the New Exodus. There is the feel of all of history's hopes have come to rest on the baby Mary is carrying. Although most of the hymn focuses on God and what he is like, she does address this promise: "From now on all generations will call me blessed, for the Mighty One has done great things for me—holy is his name."[105] Nolland calls this hymn "a celebration of eschatological fulfillment."[106] As the first of a number of songs by minor characters in Luke, Mary's song touches on the major categories (New Exodus, promises fulfilled, God's

---

98. Acts 1:5, 8; 2:4, 17–18, 33, 38; 4:8, 31; 6:3; 7:55; 8:15–17; 9:17; 10:44–45, 47; 11:15–16, 24, 28; 13:9, 52; 19:6.

99. Acts 1:2, 5, 8, 16; 2:4, 17–18, 38; 4:8, 25, 31; 5:32; 6:3, 5, 10; 7:55; 8:15–17, 18–19, 29, 39; 9:17, 31; 10:19, 38, 44–45; 11:12, 15–16, 24, 28; 13:2, 4, 9, 52; 15:8; 16:6–7; 19:6; 20:22; 21:4, 11; 28:25.

100. Acts 10:38.

101. Fitzmyer even goes so far to suggest that the song is from an early Christian-Jewish source, which Luke inserts, and adds verse 48 to make it apply to Mary. This need not be the case for the song to apply to both Mary and others at large. Fitzmyer, *Luke*, 1:359.

102. Valentini, *Il Magnificat*, 173–74.

103. Luke 21:1–4. See chapter 4.

104. Perhaps others could be mentioned, like the ten virgins in Matthew 25 or the bride imagery in Revelation. Although clearly authored by different writers whom Luke may or may not have been aware of, these documents constitute extremely relevant primary literature.

105. Luke 1:48b–49.

106. Nolland, *Luke*, 1:64.

delivering work among his people) and serves as an appropriate introduction to the Messiah and the genre of songs Luke uses. The hymn creates "the impression of an earth-shaking event and its rippling, ever-expanding shockwaves, on which the singer and her eschatological community *look back*."[107]

In the end, the Magnificat does four things for the narrative of Luke. First, Mary has set the stage for the Messiah she carries. This includes the fulfilling of promises and the hopes of the ancestors. "The Magnificat has hymned the coming of Jesus as the fulfillment of all eschatological hopes."[108] Second, it highlights what is important in the following story.[109] The most obvious example of this is the emphasis on reversal that is so common in Luke–Acts.[110] Third, the song introduces God as a character: "One of the important functions of the Magnificat is to provide an initial characterization of the God whose purpose shapes the following story."[111] Fourth, Luke has built a clear bridge between the God of the Old Testament (i.e., the God of Israel) and the salvation he is going to talk about in the Messiah Jesus.

Zechariah's Song (Benedictus)

The second anthology scene that roots the birth of Jesus in salvation history involves Zechariah. After the birth of John the Baptist, Zechariah prophesies in song form.[112] Dramatically, these are the first words he has said in months because of his inability to speak after his encounter with the angel.[113] Luke has already begun to present John as a hero of the faith in line with numerous other heroes from Israel's past. For example, the statement made in 1:15 that John must "never drink wine or strong drink" is "characteristic biblical language relating to Nazarites, connecting him to Israel's two most famous Nazarites, Samson and Samuel."[114] John is filled with the Spirit while in his mother's womb. Thus, he is similar to numerous prophets in Israel's past who were spokes people

---

107. Dillon, *Hymns*, 38. Emphasis is original to show not only the connection with the past but also the continuing motif through Luke's corpus.

108. Nolland, *Luke*, 1:91.

109. Tannehill, *Luke*, 29–30.

110. Tannehill, *Luke*, 30. Also, see Dillon, *Hymns*, 37–48, who has a robust discussion of the reversal theme in Luke. Examples of the emphasis on reversal in Luke–Acts include Luke 2:34; 6:20–26; 9:24, 46–48; 10:21; 12:1–3; 13:25–30; 14:7–11, 16–24; 16:15, 19–31; 18:9–14; 22:24–27. Many reversals in the plot could be noted as well, particularly in Acts with the stories of Paul and Cornelius.

111. Tannehill, *Luke*, 29. The song is organized around a statement of praise to God, followed by reasons for praise. For more on the organization and poetic elements of this song, see Tannehill, *Luke*, 26–27.

112. Luke 1:67–79.

113. Luke 1:22.

114. Litwak, *Echoes*, 90. See Judg 13:7; 1 Kgs 1:11; Num 6:3.

for God and were given the Spirit.[115] "Luke's discursive framing tells his audience to expect, in John's story, a narrative about a prophet of Israel."[116]

The meaning of the name Zechariah is of interest here. His name means "Yahweh has remembered," and Bock, although he notes that it fits thematically, claims Luke "makes no effort to exploit the point."[117] However, Bock misses that the name works on multiple levels, as will be true in other scenes.[118] That "God remembers" suggests an obvious link to the situation of Zechariah and Elizabeth, who are barren and unable to conceive in their old age. God remembers them by giving them a child. On a larger scale, God has remembered his promise to send a Messiah to the world, and thus, his promise is being fulfilled.

Zechariah's canticle reinforces the content of Mary's song, and continues in the practice of incorporating Old Testament imagery when talking about the Messiah.[119] It is "built up like a mosaic from numerous phrases drawn from the Greek OT."[120] The NRSV translation of "looked favorably" here for ἐπεσκέψατο may be better rendered as "visited,"[121] and the idea of God visiting his people is common in the Old Testament[122] and in the contemporary Judaism of the day.[123] This emphasizes the coming of the Messiah and once again builds a bridge between the God of the Old Testament and the coming of Jesus.

This is also true with the horn of salvation imagery (from a literal translation of v. 69a),[124] which comes from Deuteronomy 33:17 as a young ox raising up his horns to display his power.[125] Fitzmyer calls this a loose reference to the Messiah: "[the phrase] must be understood here as a title for an agent of God's salvation in David's house."[126] The discussion of "the house of his servant David" is similar to 2 Samuel 7:26, which is in the context of Nathan proclaiming God's promises to David of protection,

---

115. Litwak, *Echoes*, 90, connects this to the Spirit of God on Elijah and Elisha in 4 Kgdms 2:9–16. Also, see Isa 61:1; Ezek 11:5; Joel 3:1.

116. Litwak, *Echoes*, 91. For further discussion on the similarities between John and the prophets of Israel's past, see Litwak, *Echoes*, 91–94.

117. Bock, *Luke*, 1:76. Bock's argument is that since Gentile readers are included in Luke's audience and he offers no translation of the name, they would have missed it. However, if the audience is made up of God-fearers, they likely have some knowledge of the Old Testament narratives and Hebrew name meanings.

118. See the discussion on Simeon and Anna below.

119. See Kaut, *Befreier*, 1, who notes a similarity in the motif of liberation between these two canticles.

120. Fitzmyer, *Luke*, 1:376–77.

121. Fitzmyer, *Luke*, 1:382–83.

122. Gen 50:24–25; Exod 3:16; 4:31; 13:19; 30:12; Isa 23:17; Ps 80:14 [Ps 80:15 MT]; 106:4; Ruth 1:6.

123. Wis 3:7; *Pss. Sol.* 3.11; 10.4; 11.6; 15.12; *T. Levi* 4.4; *T. Asher* 7.3; CD 1.7.

124. καὶ ἤγειρεν κέρας σωτηρίας ἡμῖν.

125. Bock, *Luke*, 1:180. The imagery is used in Ps 18:2; 2 Sam 22:3.

126. Fitzmyer, *Luke*, 1:383.

redemption, and his established royal line. Verse 69b suggests that the promise is "now brought to ultimate fulfillment in the provision of the Messiah."[127] Thus, there is a connection with the royalty of David, much like there was, more subtly, in the Magnificat. The use of "savior" here is a feature that will be repeated throughout the song as well as the rest of the Lukan corpus.[128] Repetition is evidence of "framing," and helps emphasize the force of the story.[129]

Verse 70 uses language that is used again in Acts 3:21 (something being told long ago through the "holy prophets"), which some hold to be a Lukan addition to emphasize promise and fulfillment.[130] It fits Luke's agenda of continuity with Judaism, and more overtly connects the coming of Jesus to the promises. This is a reminder that the gospel requires the full scope of salvation history as it reaches its climax in Jesus.[131]

Fitzmyer suggests that the term "enemies" in verse 71 is referring to "all the forms that hostility to the chosen people took over the ages."[132] In this view, the canticle brings up persecution history as a part of salvation history. This will happen again quite prominently in Stephen's speech.[133] Salvation happens in the context of persecution. Despite this, Fitzmyer does not see this as a political reference, and certainly does not have Rome in view.[134] Dillon also leans toward an eschatological understanding of salvation over enemies rather than "the composer's circumstances."[135] Fitzmyer suggests that from Luke's setting, the enemies would include "all those who resist or refuse to accept the new form of God's salvation history."[136]

---

127. Nolland, *Luke*, 1:86.

128. Tannehill, *Luke*, 33–34, 37. See Luke 1:71, 77; 19:9; Acts 4:12; 7:25; 13:26, 47; 16:17; 27:34. The word occurs ten times in Luke–Acts, compared to one time in the other synoptics (Mark 16:8, in a textual variant that occurs in a few texts starting in the seventh century between the original ending of Mark and the continuation of vv. 9–20) and one time in John (4:22). For more on the ending of Mark, see Metzger, *Textual Commentary*, 103; Kahle, "End."

129. Tannen, "Frame," 41–42. For the way I am using this word, see page 97n51.

130. Nolland, *Luke*, 1:86; Fitzmyer, *Luke*, 1:383–84. Also, see Farris, *Hymns*, 151–60, who emphasizes the promise and fulfillment motif.

131. Fitzmyer suggests that the closest we find to this phrase is not in the Old Testament, but rather from Qumran: "As he commanded through Moses and through all his servants, the prophets" (1QS 1:3). See Fitzmyer, *Luke*, 1:384.

132. Fitzmyer, *Luke*, 1:384.

133. Acts 7:39–42, 51–53.

134. Fitzmyer, *Luke*, 1:384.

135. Dillon, *Hymns*, 54–65, goes on to say in note 59, "The absence of pleas for the enemies' devastation decisively indicates that we should not seek the Sitz-im-Leben of the Benedictus in nationalistic or militantly sectarian circles." Also, see Gnilka, "Der Hymnus"; Winter, "Magnificat"; Kaut, *Befreier*, 236–45; Radl, *Der Ursprung*, 129; Hendriksen, *Luke*, 125. Also, see Luke 10:18; 11:14–23; 13:16. Not all agree. Bock, *Luke*, 1:182, sees the political implications alongside wider spiritual referents. For more on the political implications, see Marshall, *Luke*, 91; Danker, *New Age*, 48; Bovon, *Das Evangelium*, 98.

136. Fitzmyer, *Luke*, 1:384.

The phrase ποιῆσαι ἔλεος ("to do mercy") is a common Old Testament expression and is to be understood as an appositive to salvation.[137] Thus, Luke has repetitions of this idea in verses 69, 71, and now 72, although each is stated in its own poetic way. Moreover, mercy is revealed as God's covenant attribute.[138] God remembers his covenant, and this "should encourage Luke's readers that he will act on the rest of his promises."[139] God's activity now in the sending of Jesus is an extension "of his covenant promises to Israel long ago."[140]

This phrase "the oath that he swore to our ancestor Abraham" in verse 73 is very similar to what was said in Mary's song and it also connects the Christian movement to the people of Israel and Abraham.[141] Remembering an oath made to fathers is common in the Old Testament.[142] This is also connected with political freedom in the form of salvation from "the hands of our enemies." Tannehill points out how this builds in order to "heighten the effect of the tragic turn which will take place when the leaders of Israel reject the king who could fulfill this promise."[143]

The idea from verse 71 (saved from our enemies) is restated in verse 74. The speaker desires a life without oppression so he is free to serve God fearlessly. Both the political and spiritual dimensions of freedom and conflict are likely in view here.[144] More pointedly, Nolland helpfully points out that the wording of verse 75, "in holiness and righteousness before him all our days," reflects Joshua 24:14, and is thus evoking "Promised Land" language, thereby hinting at the continuing decentralization of the concept of the land throughout Luke–Acts.[145] The notion of the land was one of the "key symbols of Jewish identity" in the first century.[146] The strength of using Promised Land imagery with the coming of the Messiah, in a time when the Romans occupied the land and heavily taxed and subverted the Jewish people, reinforces what Luke's point will be regarding land, that is, that the time of land ownership as a key identity marker for God's people has passed, and generosity now marks kingdom participants. Much more will be said on this point in chapter 5, but the hint here is noticeable. Tannehill's suggestion that the image in this passage

---

137. Fitzmyer, *Luke*, 1:384. See Gen 24:12; Judg 1:24; 8:35; Ruth 1:8.

138. Fitzmyer, *Luke*, 1:384.

139. Bock, *Luke*, 1:184.

140. Fitzmyer, *Luke*, 1:384. Dillon, *Hymns*, 66–67, mentions the interesting omission of references to land, progeny, and the blessing of others.

141. The original promise is found in Gen 22:16–17.

142. Ps 105:8–9, 11; Jer 11:5; Exod 2:24; Lev 26:42; 1 Macc 4:10; 2 Macc 1:2; CD 8.18.

143. Tannehill, *Luke*, 34. This motif, which is also in 1:68, occurs other places in Luke–Acts: Luke 2:38; 24:21; Acts 1:6.

144. Bock, *Luke*, 1:187.

145. Nolland, *Luke*, 1:88.

146. Wright, *Victory*, 383–84. Much more will be said of the land in chapter 5.

of freedom to worship is connected to the exodus and the Sinai community is apt, and also suggests a hint at later Lukan emphases.[147]

Verse 76 sees a switch from Jesus to John, set against the backdrop of God coming to Israel in the verses before.[148] Nonetheless, the Messiah is still in full view in this section, as is the emphasis on salvation.[149] There is also a shift in verb tense from aorist to future.[150] Some have suggested that since "prophet of the most high" occurs in *T. Levi* 8.15 that there are some messianic hints toward the character of John here.[151] Others rightly reject this view, noting the overwhelming messianic statements about Jesus in the birth narratives, as well as Luke's writings as a whole.[152] The sentiment of 1:17, where John will go before and prepare the way is repeated here. Scholars see Old Testament allusions from Malachi 3:1 and Isaiah 40:3.[153] The former restates John's connection with Elijah.[154] The latter of these will become a teaching emphasis for John.[155] As I will show below, Isaiah 40 becomes an important text for Luke and his messianic expectations.

The dominant metaphor in the second half of the song is the sun/sunrise, which will shine on death and those living in darkness. Kaut sees "the mercy of our God" in verse 78 as the center of the hymn.[156] Tannehill connects the images of light (and in the song of Simeon) with similar imagery about Paul, who thus has an important role in fulfilling these prophetic words.[157] Despite the seemingly clear reference to light here,[158] there may be another option. The term ἀνατολή can be used messianically to refer to a

---

147. Tannehill, *Luke*, 37. More will be said regarding the connection between Luke's projected events and Sinai in chapter 4.

148. Löning, *Das Geschichtswerk*, 108.

149. Much scholarly discussion has been done on how we should understand verse 77 grammatically. The main point for our purposes, though, is the repeated emphasis on salvation. See Bock, *Luke*, 1:189–90; Plummer, *Luke*, 42; Creed, *Luke*, 26–27; Godet, *Luke* 1.115; Schürmann, *Das Lukasevangelium*, 91; Marshall, *Luke*, 93.

150. Fitzmyer, *Luke*, 1:385.

151. Danker, *New Age*, 49; Leaney, *Luke*, 24. Dillon, *Hymns*, 50–51, goes so far as to argue that both the Magnificat and the Benedictus were originally about John. The source critical arguments go beyond the scope of this monograph, but Dillon wonders about Luke's sources and engages with others who do the same.

152. Fitzmyer, *Luke*, 1:385; Bock, *Luke*, 1:187.

153. Dillon, *Hymns*, 71; Bock, *Luke*, 1:188.

154. Godet, *Luke* 1.114.

155. Luke 3:1–6; also Matt 3:1–6; Mark 1:3; John 1:19–23.

156. Kaut, *Befreier*, 197. Also, see Nolland, *Luke*, 1:89, who calls it the lynchpin, which holds together "the activities of John and the [sunrise]."

157. Tannehill, *Luke*, 38. For example, Acts 13:47; 26:17–18.

158. The imagery of light seems obvious since that imagery continues into verse 79.

branch springing up, as it used in the LXX for the Hebrew for branch or shoot (צמח).[159] There may be a double meaning with messianic undertones.[160]

Zechariah, the righteous priest, seems to include himself with those in darkness who need to be led into peace. "People in the nation of Israel stand in need of repentance, a picture that Luke continues to describe throughout his two volumes."[161] Salvation being connected with peace is common in Luke and in the Old Testament.[162] The angels will announce peace as they proclaim the coming of Jesus,[163] as will Simeon in his prophetic words about the baby in the Temple.[164] Jesus will send a forgiven woman[165] as well as the woman with the issue of blood away in peace.[166] He will charge the disciples to speak peace over a house when doing ministry, and the crowds will declare it to him as he rides to Jerusalem on a donkey.[167] Jesus will hope for peace for Jerusalem as he weeps over the city[168] and will speak peace to his disciples after his resurrection.[169] In Acts, the church will at times experience peace,[170] and people will regularly be sent off in peace.[171] The most obvious connection between salvation and peace in Acts is the description of the good news of peace (εὐαγγελιζόμενος εἰρήνην) in Peter's message to the God-fearers in Cornelius's home.[172] The foundation for these other occurrences of peace in the life of Jesus and the church is laid here.

Thus, as with the song of Mary, Zechariah's song sets the emotional stage for the coming of the Messiah by the elements introduced and repeated. Promise, fulfillment, and climax of the rootedness of the gospel in Israel are present in the Benedictus. The repetition of these elements highlights the importance of these ideas for Luke's presentation of the gospel and helps with his larger goal of connecting the God-fearing reader to the salvation history of God's activity with Israel. Zechariah also gives the reader a prophetic introduction to the eschatological character of John.[173]

---

159. Jer 23:5; Zech 3:8; 6:12. See Fitzmyer, *Luke*, 1:387.

160. Bock, *Proclamation*, 73; Bovon, *Luke*, 109.

161. Bock, *Luke*, 1:193. Luke 24:47; Acts 5:31.

162. Jer 14:13; Isa 48:18; 54:10; Ezek 34:25–29.

163. Luke 2:14.

164. Luke 2:29.

165. Luke 7:50.

166. Luke 8:48.

167. Luke 19:38.

168. Luke 19:42.

169. Luke 24:36.

170. Acts 9:31.

171. Acts 15:33; 16:36.

172. Acts 10:36.

173. For more on the Benedictus, particularly with regard to the long scholarly discussion of the sources of the Psalm and how it fits with Luke's gospel, see Gunkel, "Die Lieder"; Winter, "Magnificat"; Benoit, "L'enfance"; Jones, "Background"; Minnear, "Birth Stories"; Carter, "Zechariah"; Brown, *Birth*.

Simeon in Song (Nunc Dimittis)

The string of characters that speak prophetically about the gospel and the mission of Jesus in the anthology scenes in Luke continues with Simeon. Farris calls this a "climax of the promise-fulfillment-praise progression."[174] Similarly, Berger suggests that Simeon brings "a basic understanding of Jesus' function for Israel and for the Gentiles."[175] The text has no prior narrative of Simeon, so verses 25–27 give the background ethos of the character.[176] He is called righteous (δίκαιος), a term applied to four other characters in the Lukan corpus,[177] and devout (εὐλαβὴς), a term unique to Luke in the New Testament,[178] used specifically of one other character,[179] and which Nolland suggests "belongs to the language of Hellenistic piety."[180] Interestingly too, the verb "waiting for" here (προσδεχόμενος) is also used of Anna (38) and Joseph of Arimathea (23:51).[181] Luke seems to see a connection between righteousness and hopeful expectation. Dillon aptly calls "the expectant people," a descriptor that fits Simeon perfectly, an "all important, oft-neglected character of the infancy accounts."[182] There is a narrative connection between the three characters, Simeon, Anna, and Joseph of Arimathea, which is signaled by that word (προσδεχόμενος). Simeon and Joseph are both called righteous. Anna is not, but the narrative clearly portrays her as righteous, since she spends day and night in the Temple, prophesies, and has a special connection with God. Jesus' life as presented in Luke is bookended by his birth and his death with righteous Jews waiting expectantly for God's kingdom to show up. It is the righteous who look for and wait for the Messiah with hopeful expectation and have eyes to recognize him when he comes. The strategic utilization of these minor characters communicates this message to the readers.[183]

Simeon's name, which means "God has heard," is significant.[184] Bock again sees no role in the name meaning for Luke.[185] However, there seems to be a clear link between

---

174. Farris, *Hymns*, 144.

175. Berger, "Das Canticum Simeonis (Lk 2:29–32)," 37, 39. Also, see Koet, "Simeons."

176. This will happen again with other characters, including Stephen, Cornelius, and Paul. See chapter 5.

177. Zechariah and Elizabeth (Luke 1:6), Joseph of Arimathea (23:50), and Cornelius (10:22).

178. Used only in Acts 2:5; 8:2; 22:12.

179. Used four times, all in Luke–Acts. In Acts 2:5; 8:2 it speaks of the Jews in Jerusalem for Pentecost and the men who buried Stephen, respectively. Acts 22:12 is the other reference that applies the term to a specific person, where Paul calls Ananias devout in the retelling of his conversion.

180. Nolland, *Luke*, 1:118.

181. Nolland, *Luke*, 1:118.

182. Dillon, *Hymns*, 73.

183. The use is strategic in that Luke brings these characters into his narrative at unique times. We obviously see here the abundance of material surrounding the birth narrative, but the death of Jesus is a strategic spot as well.

184. Bock, *Luke*, 1:238.

185. Bock, *Luke*, 1:238.

Israel calling out for a deliverer and the call for God to be faithful to his promise, both common Jewish ideas.[186] As God has remembered (Zechariah), God has also heard. It seems more remarkable that in a scene communicating so much through the setting that a name like Simeon's would be meaningless. Furthermore, "God has heard" fits as a working title for Simeon's canticle. Truly God has heard the cry of his people and has sent them their long-awaited deliverer of all humanity.

Simeon's scene takes place in the Temple. Tannehill notes that this is one of several examples of "significant settings which enhance major scenes" in Luke's narratives.[187] Others include the synagogue scene in Luke 4:16–30; the Temple and chambers of the Sanhedrin in Acts 3–5; Paul in the agora of Athens and before the Areopagus in Acts 17:16–34. What better place than God's Temple to declare the future of his presence and activity through his son and the inclusion of all people?[188] This is near the beginning of a trajectory of decentralization that includes even the Temple.[189]

It is said of Simeon in verse 25 that he was waiting for the "consolation of Israel." This phrase (παράκλησιν τοῦ Ἰσραήλ) is a clear reference to Isaiah 40:1–2.[190]

Comfort, O comfort my people, Says your God.	Παρακαλεῖτε παρακαλεῖτε τὸν λαόν μου, λέγει ὁ θεός.
Speak tenderly to Jerusalem, and cry to her that she has served her term, that her penalty is paid, that she has received from the LORD's hand double for all her sins	ἱερεῖς, λαλήσατε εἰς τὴν καρδίαν Ιερουσαλημ, παρακαλέσατε αὐτήν· ὅτι ἐπλήσθη ἡ ταπείνωσις αὐτῆς, λέλυται αὐτῆς ἡ ἁμαρτία· ὅτι ἐδέξατο ἐκ χειρὸς κυρίου διπλᾶ τὰ ἁμαρτήματα αὐτῆς.

There is the strong connection with the leading words of "comfort" as well as with Jerusalem/Israel (Jerusalem will be mentioned in the Anna scene).[191] The word παράκλησις and its forms appears six times in Luke's writings, twice in the Gospel, and four times in Acts.[192] "Israel's consolation was a key element in many strands of Old Testament and Jewish eschatology, referring to the hope of deliverance for the

---

186. Also both are ideas present in Luke–Acts. See Luke 1:55; 2:38; 25:31; Acts 1:4; 7:17; 26:6–7. Also, see LaGrand, "Simeon"; Reicke, "Jesus"; Upchurch, "Hopeful"; Vaughan, "Incident"; Cutler, "Simeon."

187. Tannehill, *Luke*, 38.

188. Fitzmyer notes Luke's usage of ναός for the most holy place and ἱερόν as here for the Temple area in general, including the outer courts. The reason for this would be that Mary would only be allowed in either the Court of the Gentiles or the Court of Women. See Fitzmyer, *Luke*, 1:427.

189. The Temple is important for Luke's narrative early on, as here, but goes through a major reversal throughout the narrative.

190. Forms of the verb παρακαλέω are also used in Isa 40:11; 41:27; 49:10, 13; 51:3, 12; 57:18; 61:2; 66:12–13. Also, see Snodgrass, "Streams"; Conrad, "Oracles."

191. See Serrano, "Characterization."

192. Luke 2:25; 6:24; Acts 4:36; 9:31; 13:15; 15:31.

nation."¹⁹³ The believers and God-fearers in Luke are characterized by a desire for consolation.¹⁹⁴ Similarly, the Qumran community saw Isaiah 40 as a key eschatological text that was fulfilled in them during the last days.¹⁹⁵ Isaiah 40 is the start of the Babylonian section of the book, which inaugurates the end of exile.¹⁹⁶ The same way that the Jews in exile were looking forward to the end of exile that Isaiah was pronouncing, Simeon is looking forward to the end of the exile of sin. This connects with the New Exodus in a rather remarkable way.

In the dramatic scene, Simeon had been told by the Holy Spirit that he would not die before seeing τὸν χριστὸν κυρίου. This is an example of Israel's consolation, as an old, faithful man experiences interaction with the Messiah, which he has desired.¹⁹⁷ God's word is proven faithful once again in the birth narratives, and further emphasizes to the reader that they can trust in God's promises.¹⁹⁸

Simeon's prophecy may be the most succinct and pointed example of climax and fulfillment.¹⁹⁹ The first word, νῦν, Dillon suggests, is a strong statement of fulfillment, similar to Luke 2:11; 4:21; 9:19; and 23:43.²⁰⁰ The usage of the term δοῦλος also carries with it significance, as it points to "common OT imagery for a faithful and righteous servant."²⁰¹ Luke "elaborately designate[s]" the ethos of Simeon through both descriptions and the characters own words.²⁰² There is also a link between the Messiah and peace (εἰρήνη) in both Luke and the Old Testament.²⁰³ Luke is intertextually building an ethos for the Messiah through the words of these minor characters, and creating expectations that will carry the reader through the rest of volume one and into volume two.²⁰⁴

---

193. Bock, *Luke*, 1:238. See Isa 49:13; 51:3; 57:18; 61:2; 2 Bar 44:7.

194. Bock, *Luke*, 1:239. See Luke 6:23–24; 17:22–37; 21:25–36.

195. Bock, *Luke*, 1:188. 1QS 8.13–14; 9.19–20. Later rabbinic tradition associated the Messiah with the comforter. See Fitzmyer, *Luke*, 1:427, Bock, *Luke*, 1:238. See Schmitz and Stählin, "Menahem."

196. McKenzie, *Second Isaiah*, 13–19.

197. Bock, *Luke*, 1:239.

198. Bock, *Luke*, 1:239.

199. Luke 2:29–32.

200. Dillon, *Hymns*, 128. Bock, *Luke*, 1:241, sees the combination of the first two words, νῦν ἀπολύεις, emphasizing the readiness of the speaker to die. There are other examples of ἀπολύω being used to indicate death. See Gen 15:2; Num 20:29; Tobit 3:6; 2 Macc 7:9.

201. Bock, *Luke*, 1:242. See Ps 27:9 [26:9 LXX]; Luke 1:38; Acts 4:29.

202. Johnson, *Luke*, 56, uses the language of "elaborately designated" to describe Simeon as a reliable prophetic spokesperson. The concept of ethos, referring to the character of the speaker, will be explored more fully in chapter 5.

203. Bock, *Luke*, 1:242. Luke 1:79; 2:14; Zech 8:12 LXX; Ps 71:7 LXX; Ps. Sol. 17.26–42. Fitzmyer connects this idea with a very similar construction in the LXX of Genesis 15:15. Bock prefers to see it as "comfort of knowing that God's work comes to fulfillment." See Fitzmyer, *Luke*, 1:243; Bock, *Luke*, 1:242. σὺ δὲ ἀπελεύσῃ πρὸς τοὺς πατέρας σου μετ' εἰρήνης, ταφεὶς ἐν γήρει καλῷ.

204. Note the work of Grelot, "Le cantique," 505–6, who notes the themes in the Nunc Dimittis that will carry through both volumes.

Although there are many examples in the Old Testament of salvation being "seen,"[205] for Nolland this is a clear reference to Isaiah 52:10:[206]

The Lord has bared his holy arm before the eyes of all the nations; and all the ends of the earth shall see the salvation of our God.	καὶ ἀποκαλύψει κύριος τὸν βραχίονα αὐτοῦ τὸν ἅγιον ἐνώπιον πάντων τῶν ἐθνῶν, καὶ ὄψονται πάντα τὰ ἄκρα τῆς γῆς τὴν σωτηρίαν τὴν παρὰ τοῦ θεοῦ.[207]

If the reference is to Isaiah 52, as Nolland suggests, this connects to the larger trajectory of the New Exodus, which particularly builds on Second Isaiah. There are also hints here of inclusivity regarding the ends of the earth, which foreshadow Acts 1:8, a key verse expressing and foreshadowing decentralization in volume two. Once again, through the use of imagery, LXX references, prophetic speech, and encounters with minor characters, Luke is creating an experience for the reader to encounter the Jewish Messiah as one who consoles his people, brings peace, and seeks to save people in all nations and to the ends of the earth.

Simeon's words do not merely hint at, but declare the future inclusion of the Gentiles.[208] The key ideas are present, setting the stage in Luke's narrative for what will come later in Acts. Klauck sees this as right in line with Luke's unfolding agenda up to this point, saying, "Das Wort vom 'Licht zur Offenbarung für die Völker' bringt nicht einen völlig neuen Gesichtspunkt ein, sondern enthüllt das, was verborgen schon anwesend war, spätestens seit dem Auftreten von Gottesfürchtigen im Magnificat. Es hat also selbst teil an jenem Enthüllungsvorgang, an jenem Prozeß der Durchleuchtung und Erhellung, den es prophetisch ansagt."[209] Verse 31 alludes to Isaiah 52:10 as well. Nolland points out many times that Jews and Gentiles are seen as "parallel beneficiaries of that salvation which is offered in the name of Jesus. . . . The Jews have priority, but salvation is there just as much for the Gentile as for the Jew."[210] This will fit with Paul's pattern of starting ministry in a new town by going to the synagogue.[211] In

---

205. Ps 97:3; Isa 40:5; 52:10; Bar 4:24 LXX.

206. Nolland, *Luke*, 1:120.

207. It is worth noting, though, that Simeon uses σωτήριον, the neuter form of the word. This form is rare, only used four times in the NT (also in Luke 3:6; Acts 28:28; Eph 6:17). The usage in Isaiah 52 is feminine, though the neuter usage is common in the New Exodus section of Isaiah, perhaps highlighted by 40:5. In the end, the case that there is dependence on the New Exodus section of Isaiah in Simeon's words here is strong. See Beers, *Servant*, 96; Tannehill, *Luke*, 40; Mallen, *Transformation*, 3n13.

208. Luke 2:32.

209. Klauck, "Gottesfürchtige," 138–39. See also Dillon, *Hymns*, 130–31. ("The word 'light for revelation for the peoples' does not bring a completely new point of view, but reveals what was already hidden, at the latest since the appearance of godly people in the Magnificat. Consequently, it is itself part of the act of revelation, that process of examination and illumination that it prophesies.")

210. Nolland, *Luke*, 1:120.

211. Acts 13:5–43; 14:1; 17:1, 10, 17; 18:7, 19; 19:8.

addition, the imagery of light (φῶς) and glory (δόξα) paired with salvation also have Isaianic references in the Hebrew Scriptures.[212]

Simeon's clear and bold declaration of the inclusion of Gentiles stands out, as the songs of Mary and Zechariah were quite Israel-centric, with mere hints at a wider inclusion. There is movement toward decentralization in the progression of the songs. Mary and Zechariah laid a foundation for a Davidic, Jewish Messiah. Simeon's short song perfectly brings together Israel's deliverance ("consolation of Israel") and the Lukan mission to the Gentiles ("a light for revelation to the Gentiles"). The narrative moves from merely hinting at Gentile inclusion through intertextual clues, to it being declared in the climax of a character's song. The Gentile(s), ἔθνος, becomes central for Luke, particularly in Acts,[213] but this is the first time the term is used, coming as words of prophecy in the Temple. The Messiah comes through Israel, but he is not for Israel alone.[214] Luke is creating cultural memory in the God-fearing reader through the use of these references that are intended to build social identity.

Anna the Prophetess

On the heels of the young couple's encounter with Simeon, they meet another minor character named Anna. Here, too, we have the balancing of male and female characters, as in chapter 1 with Mary and Zechariah.[215] As the infancy narrative started "with an upright and Law-observant man and woman, Zechariah and Elizabeth, and a Temple scene," Brown notes, it "ends with an upright man and woman, Simeon and Anna, and a Temple scene."[216] This inclusion of female perspectives fits Luke's agenda of promoting women's roles in the life of Jesus and the early church. Women prophesy about Jesus, as here. Also at different times, women wash Jesus' feet with their tears,[217] support his ministry financially,[218] sit at his feet and listen to him teach,[219] are exalted in their sacrificial giving,[220] and testify to the resurrection.[221] This strategy of pairing men

---

212. Fitzmyer, *Luke*, 1:428. Isa 49:9; 46:13, respectively.

213. Forms of ἔθνος occur thirteen times in Luke and forty-three times in Acts.

214. Tannehill, *Luke*, 43, suggests that Simeon's words "provide a clear preview of the resistance which Jesus will encounter during his ministry." It is also said of Mary, "a sword will pierce your own soul too," perhaps an early reference to Jesus' death and her resulting grief. For a robust discussion of the different options of what verse 35b is referring to, see Bock, *Luke*, 1:248–50.

215. Interestingly, Flanigan, "Women," 292–93, suggests there are thirteen man-woman parallel's in the gospel of Luke.

216. Brown, *Birth*, 451.

217. Luke 7:36–50.

218. Luke 8:2–3.

219. Luke 10:38–42.

220. Luke 21:1–4.

221. Luke 24:1–12.

and women continues in Acts, as women are added to the number of those saved,[222] are healed by Peter and Paul,[223] and receive Paul into their home.[224]

While we have no quotations from Anna, we do have a description of her situation: "There was also a prophet, Anna the daughter of Phanuel, of the tribe of Asher. She was of a great age, having lived with her husband seven years after her marriage, then as a widow to the age of eighty-four. She never left the Temple but worshiped there with fasting and prayer night and day."[225] Thus, although there are fewer descriptive details offered than were of Simeon, Luke gives an even more dramatic introduction to her and her situation to establish ethos. "The credibility of Anna's witness to the identity of the child is given a double basis: (i) she is a prophetess; (ii) her Jewish piety is outstanding."[226] Thus, we have Anna presented as an old, pious figure who offers prophetic testimony about and support for the child. She is connecting Jesus with the promises of old and, in that way, supports Luke's agenda of intertextual links.

Some have suggested that there are representative symbols in the character of Anna to notice.[227] First, she descends from a tribe in the northern kingdom. She is speaking of the Messiah who comes from a southern tribe, and is paired with Simeon, representative of a southern tribe, perhaps fulfilling of what was spoken of by Pao that part of the Isaianic and Lukan program is to tell of the reunification of the two kingdoms.[228] Asher is the last of the tribes mentioned in Deuteronomy 33:24–5. Others find the presence of a prophetess from the Tribe of Asher at the Jerusalem Temple puzzling.[229] The names involved are once again instructive. Anna (Ἄννα), as is commonly accepted,[230] derives from the Hebrew *hnn* (חנן), related to the name "Hannah," meaning "favor." Her father's name, Phanuel (Φανουήλ) is mentioned, meaning "face to face with God," and is the place Jacob wrestled with God and gave Jacob the name Israel.[231] Once again, Bock wrongly sees no value in these names.[232] Anna represents someone who has been face to face with God in the Temple and witnesses God's favor in the presence of the Messiah as a baby. As a widow who has chosen service to God over remarriage, "an action that was highly regarded in the first-century religious community,"[233] and because of her piety and expectation for God's redemption of Jerusalem, she sees

---

222. Acts 5:14; 8:12; 17:4.

223. Acts 9:32–43; 16:16–34.

224. Acts 18:1–4. For more on the role of women in Luke's writings, see Parvey, "Theology"; D'Angelo, "Women"; Maly, "Women."

225. Luke 2:36–37.

226. Nolland, *Luke*, 1:123.

227. See Nolland, *Luke*, 1:122; Bock, *Luke*, 1:251; Tannehill, *Luke*, 39; Fitzmyer, *Luke*, 1:431.

228. Pao, *New Exodus*, 112.

229. Fitzmyer, *Luke*, 1:431. Also, see Bauckham, "Anna"; Wilcox, "Anna."

230. For instance, see Fitzmyer, *Luke*, 1:430.

231. Bock, *Luke*, 1:251.

232. Bock, *Luke*, 1:251.

233. Bock, *Luke*, 1:252. Also, see 1 Tim 5:5; Jdt 8:4–8.

God's favor in seeing the Messiah and prophesying about him to those present. She is an example of God's favor on unlikely (minor) characters who live obedient lives, a common occurrence in Luke–Acts.[234] In addition to making the Temple her dwelling place, Anna comes face to face with the Messiah.[235]

There may also be a narrative link to Jacob's wrestling, as Anna's daily fasting and praying in the Temple could be seen as a form of wrestling with God in the Temple, pleading for his redemption to come. Thus, the messianic expectancy is robust in the character of Anna. Anna's age, eighty-four, may have some connection to "seven times twelve," perhaps a reference to completion or fulfillment (seven) of the twelve tribes of Israel.[236] These details paint a picture of Anna as a "vessel for revelation from God."[237]

Anna is introduced: "At that moment she came, and began to praise God and to speak about the child to all who were looking for *the redemption of Jerusalem*."[238] The clause acting as the indirect object of the sentence, πᾶσιν τοῖς προσδεχομένοις λύτρωσιν Ἰερουσαλήμ, fits Luke's agenda of expectation. The imperfect verbs in verse 38 (ἀνθωμολογεῖτο and ἐλάλει) suggest that she began praising God and speaking about the child and did not stop. "It does not mean on that occasion alone, but rather that she spread abroad the word about the child."[239] The "redemption of Jerusalem" is New Exodus language taken from Isaiah.[240] Similar to Simeon's vision of comfort, Anna's hope for redemption is an apt counterpart.[241] The reader sees desperation in Simeon and Anna, and this desperation is brought to joy in this baby presented at the Temple. "They represent the long history of an expectant people, nourished by God's promise."[242] They also represent real examples of cultural memory for God-fearing readers, allowing them to enter into the ancient story through these characters. Something climactic is happening that will fulfill these promises of old, referenced by these

---

234. See Luke 2:25–32, 36–38; 21:2–3; Acts 6:1—7:60; 8:26–40; 10:1–48.

235. There is some scholarly discussion about whether Luke can be associated with "incarnational soteriology" and "God come in the flesh," which is more of a Johannine idea. For support of incarnational soteriology in Luke, see Schneider, *Das Evangelium*, 71–72; Fletcher-Louis, *Luke–Acts*, 49, 249. For arguments against, see Fitzmyer, *Luke*, 1:422; Bock, *Luke*, 1:242n22, though Bock mentions that Luke is close to the idea as Jesus refers to God as his Father, is called Lord, and is treated much like God the Father.

236. Nolland, *Luke*, 1:122. There may be a similar thing happening in chapters 9 and 10 as well, with Jesus sending out the Twelve (9:1–2), followed by the sending of the seventy (or seventy-two) (10:1). If once chooses to see these as intentional, we have two examples of twelve and a form of seven in Luke.

237. Bock, *Luke*, 1:251.

238. Luke 2:38 (emphasis added).

239. Fitzmyer, *Luke*, 1:431.

240. Isa 52:9. Anna uses λύτρωσις, whereas the LXX of Isa 52:9 is ῥύομαι. "However, Anna's language is still a good translation of the MT (cf. 43:1; 44:22–23; 48:20; 51:11; 52:3)." See Beers, *Servant*, 95n54; Mallen, *Transformation*, 65n22.

241. Bock, *Luke*, 1:253. See Isa 40:9; 52:9; 63:4.

242. Tannehill, *Luke*, 39.

characters and others. Despite Anna's close connection with the Temple, her words point forward to a new age under the Messiah when a Temple will be unnecessary. Tannehill notes that since there is a shift from Israel in Simeon's song to Jerusalem here with Anna, there is an inference of the destruction of the Temple. "Anna's expectation is expressed in a way that will make its later negation sharp and clear."[243] This is part of Luke's decentralizing agenda.[244]

John the Baptist

The same elements in the anthology scenes of the birth narratives continue afterward, and are peppered through Luke's gospel. When John the Baptist enters the narrative in Luke 3, Luke quotes Isaiah 40:3–5 as the descriptor of John and his mission. Nolland claims that this is the start of Luke's Gospel proper, with the first two chapters of birth narratives being the introductory preface to the book.[245] However, as we have seen, chapters 1 and 2 are key to Luke's identity-forming agenda and cannot be seen as pedantic additions.[246]

The last line of this famous quotation is the most relevant, saying, "and all flesh shall see the salvation of God." Luke extends the quotation used by Mark and Matthew, adding Luke 3:5–6 and emphasizing the universality of salvation as well the imagery of preparing the way (i.e., mountains and valleys).[247] The Lukan addition makes clear his emphasis on salvation for the Gentiles and God-fearers, utilizing the language and imagery of "all flesh" (πᾶσα σάρξ). Again, the readers get the sense that a climactic event is upon them with the advent of the Messiah. Luke is declaring the time foretold by the prophet has now become fulfilled in John, who is the forerunner of Jesus.[248]

The word of God comes to John in the wilderness, "in line with a broad biblical and Jewish tradition that eschatological renewal would begin in the wilderness."[249] Isaiah 40 sets the stage for John's ministry and Jesus' mission by declaring the inauguration of the

---

243. Tannehill, *Luke*, 35.

244. Other resources on the birth narratives include Brown, *Birth*; Tatum, "Epoch"; Kellermann, "Jesus"; Iglesias, *Los Evangelios*.

245. Nolland, *Luke*, 1:83, 136.

246. Burnett, "Prophet"; Jagger, "Presence"; Downing, "Psalms."

247. There is nearly scholarly consensus that Luke is extending the reference, as opposed to the other synoptics shortening it. See Ernst, *Das Evangelium*, 140; Fitzmyer, *Luke*, 1:461; Marshall, *Luke*, 137. The lone dissenter is Schürmann, *Das Lukasevangelium*, 91.

248. Fitzmyer, *Luke*, 1:450, calls this the "Gospel proper," whereas he sees the previous section as part of the birth narrative. However, to separate the birth narrative section apart from the "Gospel proper," suggesting that the birth narratives are somehow less important to Luke's narrative aims, clearly misses the key function of the birth narrative for the identity-forming agenda in the narrative whole of Luke's corpus.

249. Nolland, *Luke*, 1:145.

era of salvation, emphasizes the universal nature of salvation, and roots the ministries of John and Jesus in the Old Testament through intertextuality.[250]

Furthermore, John is a subversive figure in the face of mainstream Judaism in the first century. He fits Luke's agenda of decentralization of the Jewish establishment that will continue through Jesus and the early church. In the scene where John is introduced to the reader, he undermines Abrahamic ancestry,[251] urges the people to give away wealth,[252] and includes tax collectors (outsiders) as well as soldiers in his movement.[253] What is more, John is calling the Jewish people to repentance and baptism,[254] a radical step that was usually reserved for converts and pagans.[255] All of these are clear examples of decentralization of the expectations of God's people in the first century. Some have called him the last of the OT prophets.[256] Others see John as "a bridge figure in whom the transition from promise to fulfillment is made."[257] This fits with the context early in the book and Luke's agenda of promise and fulfillment.

The character of John plays an important role in Luke's narrative beyond the introduction. Baptism will come to be thought of in Acts as the beginning of the Christian experience.[258] John's summary statements of sermons are intertextual clues that bring forward Old Testament emphases for Luke. He calls the crowd vipers (ἐχιδνῶν), perhaps drawing on an illusion from OT prophets,[259] the most important reference being from Second Isaiah in 59:5.[260] The climax of the passage comes in verse 20: "And he will come to Zion as Redeemer, to those in Jacob who turn from transgression, says

---

250. John is the fifth character in the early part of Luke to declare that the new era of salvation has come.

251. "Do not begin to say to yourselves, 'We have Abraham as our ancestor'; for I tell you, God is able from these stones to raise up children to Abraham." See chapter 2 on decentralization. Isa 40:5; Luke 3:7–9; Acts 2:17; 17:30; 22:15.

252. Luke 3:10–11.

253. Luke 3:12–14.

254. Baptism seems to be rooted in the ritual washings (tevilah) of Judaism (Exod 29:1, 4; 40:12; Lev 14:8; 16:4; Heb 10:22). There is evidence of something closer to conversion baptism that requires repentance that happens at Qumran, as it is mentioned in "The Community Rule" (1QS) 3:4–9; 5:13–14; 6:14–23. See Badia, "Baptism"; Robinson, "Baptism"; Benoit, *Paul*.

255. Webb, *John*, 214–15, offers a good summary of John's baptism and what it was designed to do. For other foundational works on John the Baptist, see Dibelius, *Die urchristliche*; Goguel, *Au seuil*; *Life*; Lohmeyer, *Das Urchristentum*; Kraeling, *John*. Yamasaki, *John*, offers a robust discussion of these works and adds contributions of his own.

256. Conzelmann, *Theology*, 18–27; Ernst, *Das Evangelium*, 965; Schürmann, *Das Lukasevangelium*, 149, 183–84; Fitzmyer, *Luke*, 1:450–51.

257. Bock, *Luke*, 1:279. Also, see Marshall, *Luke*, 132; *Historian*, 145–46; Bovon, *Luke*, 165; Wink, *John*, 42–86.

258. Nolland, *Luke*, 1:144. Also, see Acts 1:5; 10:37; 11:16; 13:24–25; 18:25.

259. Isa 14:29; 59:5; Jer 46:22. See Bock, *Luke*, 1:303. Though the exact word (ἐχιδνῶν) does not show up in the LXX, similar concepts do, and this may be an illusion to those.

260. "They hatch adders' (ἀσπίδων) eggs, and weave the spider's web; whoever eats their eggs dies, and the crushed egg hatches out a viper (βασιλικός)."

the Lord." This source text fits with John's role of pronouncing judgment, followed by a call to repent, which would include confession, and then the response from God to send his redeemer. John is witnessing the ultimate climax of this prophecy, as the redeemer has truly come to his people in Jesus. Thus, John introduces key ideas in the life and ministry of Jesus as well as Acts (Spirit being poured out on all flesh, repentance, God's salvation through a redeemer).[261] Once again, we see Luke's masterful ability to weave key elements from Jewish salvation history into key characters and scenes throughout both volumes. This roots the story of Jesus in the promises and teaches the God-fearing reader about God's activity up to this point.

Jesus at the Synagogue

The example of Luke's strategy of using spoken words to emphasize promise and fulfillment is on the lips of Jesus himself in chapter 4. Indeed, Tiede suggests that this account is best understood in light of chapters 1–2, seeing them as "a promising avenue of approach to the programmatic text of Luke 4."[262] When Jesus comes to Nazareth, he goes to the synagogue and offers his first speech recorded in Luke:

The Spirit of the Lord is upon me, because he has anointed me to bring good news to the poor. He has sent me to proclaim release to the captives and recovery of sight to the blind, to let the oppressed go free,	πνεῦμα κυρίου ἐπ' ἐμὲ οὗ εἵνεκεν ἔχρισέν με εὐαγγελίσασθαι πτωχοῖς, ἀπέσταλκέν με, κηρύξαι αἰχμαλώτοις ἄφεσιν καὶ τυφλοῖς ἀνάβλεψιν, ἀποστεῖλαι τεθραυσμένους ἐν ἀφέσει
to proclaim the year of the Lord's favor.	κηρύξαι ἐνιαυτὸν κυρίου δεκτόν.

For Fitzmyer, "Luke has deliberately put this story at the beginning of the public ministry to encapsulate the entire ministry of Jesus and the reaction to it."[263] Similarly, Bock notes that there are ideas here that Luke will continue to develop and calls this scene a "representative sample" and "a paradigm" for his ministry.[264] But what Fitzmyer, Bock and others are noticing in this scene has been present already in Luke, and is only more pointed here at Jesus' first ministry appearance. Since this is the launch of Jesus' ministry, there does appear to be an extra sense of excitement in Luke's narrative.

The quotation from Isaiah 61 is proclaiming renewal among God's people and the New Exodus is present. Luke is combining quotations in a strategic way.

---

261. See (all flesh/people) Luke 3:6; Acts 2:17; 17:30; 22:15; (repentance) Luke 10:13; 11:32; 13:3, 5; 15:7, 10; 16:30; 17:4; Acts 2:38; 3:19; 8:22; 17:30; 26:20; (salvation/redeemer) Luke 1:68, 71, 77; 2:30; 3:6; 6:9; 7:50; 8:12, 50; 9:19, 24; 13:23; 18:26, 42; 19:10; 23:35, 37, 39; 24:21; Acts 2:21, 40, 47; 4:12; 11:14; 13:26, 47; 15:1, 11; 16:17, 30; 27:20, 31; 28:28, 43. Also, see Lupieri, "Law"; Sheerin, "St John"; Averbeck, "Focus"; Garnet, "Soteriology."

262. Tiede, *Prophecy*, 23. He notes later, "The prologue sets the stage for faithful acceptance" (25).

263. Fitzmyer, *Luke*, 1:529. Hofheinz, "Good News"; Balentine, "Scroll."

264. Bock, *Luke*, 1:394. Also, see Tiede, *Prophecy*; Moon and Punt, "Jesus."

"The quotation from Second Isaiah is actually a conflation of 61:1a, b, d; 58:6d; 61:2a."[265] Isaiah 61 brings a message of God's deliverance to exiles, whereas chapter 58 describes release in Sabbath terms and has Jubilee overtones.[266] Furthermore, the reference to Isaiah 61 immediately reminded the audience of the advent of God's salvation: "The time of deliverance for humankind is present. It is a time when much of what the prophets called for can be realized among those who respond. . . . What is in view is a spiritual and social transformation in a new community."[267] Jesus creates this new community through his selection of disciples, teaching ministry, miracles, and prophetic actions that will start in the gospel and continue in the early church. The text foreshadows the new community that will be formed in Acts that will involve shared possessions, signs and wonders, an equality among members, and an openness to outsiders. Luke continues the vision of the new community implicit here throughout both of his volumes.

The four groups of people mentioned in the quotation are noteworthy. The passage speaks of the poor, the prisoners, the blind and the oppressed. Each of these groups are outsiders in some way, marginalized by the society they are in.[268] "Jesus will meet the needs of those who need God."[269] Thus, an emphasis on inclusion that started with the birth narrative continues here that will ultimately include Gentiles in the family of God as a logical next step.

Nolland suggests, "there is a definite Jewish tradition of using the language of Jubilee to image salvation."[270] This has a connection to the salvation plan in Luke. He is importing the Jubilee connotations from Isaiah into the ministry of Jesus in Luke 4, but he appears to be doing so as a metaphor for salvation, as opposed to the literal calling for Jubilee to be enacted.[271]

Jesus' words follow in 21b: "Today this scripture is fulfilled in your hearing." These verses set in motion a dialogue between the synagogue attendees and Jesus. At first they marvel at Jesus and his words, but quickly become agitated.[272] The

---

265. Fitzmyer, *Luke*, 1:532.

266. Bock, *Luke*, 1:408. Bruno, "Jesus"; Dennison, "Jubilee"; Maloney, "Jubilee"; Rodgers, "Call"; Ringe, "Portrait"; Hertig, "Mission."

267. Bock, *Luke*, 1:407.

268. For a fuller discussion on these groups and their role in Luke's narrative, see Bock, *Luke*, 1:408–10.

269. Bock, *Luke*, 1:410.

270. Nolland, *Luke*, 1:197.

271. Others would disagree, for example, see Yoder, *Politics*, 34–40, 64–77; Trocmé, *Revolution*, 27–40, who both argue that Jesus is calling for Jubilee to be literally enacted as a part of his ministry. Bock mentions the Jubilee parallels, but does not argue for a call to literal enactment. See Bock, *Luke*, 1:406.

272. Though most scholars understand the marveling in verse 22 as a good thing, not all do. Violet and Jeremias argue that αὐτῷ in verse 22 could be a dative of disadvantage (i.e., testified against him) and that the audience is marveling that Jesus would omit the vengeance passage from the quotation. This makes the response of the crowd more consistent. See Violet, "Verständnis"; Jeremias, *Promise*,

shift from the positive reaction from the crowd in verse 22 to the more negative response in verses 28–29 has generally been seen as positivity about his message, but a negative response to his reference to Elijah healing Namaan the Syrian, a foreigner, rather than the Jewish people who need healing. "The idea that Jesus might reach out to outsiders produced anger."[273] This reading emphasizes that, at Jesus' first public ministry setting, he declares God's grace toward and the inclusion of outsiders, ideas that will be focus points throughout Luke–Acts.

However, another way to understand the crowd's response is that they are defensive and agitated about Jesus' words from the start. The crowd's initial response is to "speak well of him" (ἐμαρτύρουν αὐτῷ) and to "marvel at his words of grace" (ἐθαύμαζον ἐπὶ τοῖς λόγοις τῆς χάριτος). However, μαρτυρέω, "testify," does not need to be a positive testifying,[274] but could be understood as testify *against* him, understanding αὐτῷ as a dative of disadvantage.[275] Marvel, θαυμάζω, can also be used with a negative emphasis.[276] This reading emphasizes that the text of Isaiah has been strategically and thematically compressed with the intentional omission of the phrase "the day of the vengeance of our God."[277] Fitzmyer calls this "the deliberate suppression of a negative aspect of the Deutero-Isaian message. The 'today' of verse 21 is not to be identified with a day of divine vengeance."[278] Jesus' use of Isaiah focuses intentionally on the positive elements of the prophecy while suppressing the judgment elements. Perhaps the hearers in the synagogue are amazed at his words of grace because they are indignant at his removal of judgment, an attitude that only intensifies with Jesus' reply about God's grace to foreigners.

In Jesus' rebuttal in verses 24–27, he emulates Elijah. Jesus is like Elijah in three ways. (1) He is a prophet leading a prophetic ministry complete with healing, (2) he is largely rejected by the people in his day, and (3) the rejection of the people leads to others receiving the benefit of his ministry.[279] There is perhaps a more complex comparison in Jesus' similarities to Elijah and Peter's likeness to Elisha in Acts 9:36–42, complete with Elijah giving the Spirit to Elisha on his departure, and Jesus promising the Spirit to Peter at Pentecost.[280] Luke uses allusions to the Elijah narrative regularly, comparing John to Elijah in 1:17 and 7:27 and the disciples in a negative comparison

---

44–46; Fitzmyer, *Luke*, 1:534; Tiede, *Prophecy*, 19–63.

273. Bock, *Luke*, 1:419.

274. For example, Matthew 23:31 speaks of people testifying against themselves (μαρτυρεῖτε ἑαυτοῖς).

275. Bock, *Luke*, 1:413.

276. For example, in Mark 6:6 Jesus is amazed (ἐθαύμαζεν) at the unbelief of the people.

277. Fitzmyer, *Luke*, 1:532. He also notes the omission "to heal the brokenhearted," but calls it of little consequence.

278. Fitzmyer, *Luke*, 1:532. Also, see Hofheinz, "Good News"; Baawobr, "Opening"; O'Day, "'Today'"; Kimball, "Exposition"; Notley, "Method."

279. Nolland, *Luke*, 1:201.

280. Nolland, *Luke*, 1:322.

as they seek to call down fire on a Samaritan village in Luke 9:54–5. The aim here is not fulfillment of prophecy, but "the interpretation of God's present acts in line with those of the past," a feature of Luke's anthological style.[281]

Some see this link between Jesus and Elijah as quite central to the whole narrative. Brodie sees the two-volume work of Luke–Acts as being based on the working outline of the Elijah-Elisha narrative.[282] First Kings 16:29–34, for example, begins the Elijah-Elisha narrative by offering "an increasingly dark picture of Ahab, and of Hiel who rebuilt Jericho at the cost of his sons."[283] Then Elijah is introduced. Brodie compares that with the opening of Luke, in which Zechariah and Elizabeth are introduced as "poles apart" figures compared to the former: "Ahab and Jezebel inaugurate new levels of misconduct and false worship; but Zechariah and Elizabeth are meticulous about commandments and well-founded worship."[284] Then, Jesus is introduced.[285] In sum, each two-volume work sees a new outpouring of God's Spirit in a special way. It is quite possible that Luke seeks to borrow that sentiment from the narrative of Elijah and Elisha.

Likewise, Fitzmyer notes the tradition in the Jewish world of the *Elias redivivus*, suggesting that since Elijah was traditionally believed to not die, people expected him to return.[286] This view sees Jesus presented as the return of Elijah. But Fitzmyer suggests that, while Jesus identifies with Elijah in certain ways, he rejects the association with him in other ways.[287] Brodie and Fitzmyer offer insights into the link between Jesus and Elijah, Brodie more from the viewpoint of narrative structure and Fitzmyer from a perspective of characterization. While there may be an intertextuality between Elijah-Elisha and the ministry of Jesus in certain events, seeing Luke–Acts as following an outline provided by the previous narrative seems unlikely.

The Transfiguration and Moses

Another interesting example of promise and fulfillment comes much later in the book, from the mount of transfiguration in chapter 9.[288] While Jesus is praying on the mountain, Moses and Elijah appear with him. Verse 31 says, "[They] were speaking of his departure, which he was about to accomplish at Jerusalem." The Greek

---

281. Nolland, *Luke*, 1:322.

282. Brodie, "Elijah-Elisha," 6. He points, as an initial example, to both having two balanced halves with an ascension in the middle.

283. Brodie, "Elijah-Elisha," 11.

284. Brodie, "Elijah-Elisha," 11.

285. Brodie goes much deeper in his development of the similarities in the volume cited, complete with responses and conversations with critics. See Kloppenborg and Verheyden, *Narrative*.

286. Fitzmyer, *Luke*, 1:213–15.

287. As in Luke 9:54–55.

288. Luke does not use the word used in Matthew and Mark for "transfigured," μετεμορφώθη, but rather simply says "the appearance of his face changed," or "τὸ εἶδος τοῦ προσώπου αὐτοῦ ἕτερον."

reads, ἔλεγον τὴν ἔξοδον αὐτοῦ, ἣν ἤμελλεν πληροῦν ἐν Ἰερουσαλήμ. The word ἔξοδον (exodus), translated "departure," is perhaps the most overt reference to the New Exodus in the New Testament, as it "recalls the great OT event of salvation and suggests that Jesus is doing something not just equivalent, but even greater."[289] Bock also mentions the refusal by Jesus to enact the feast of booths in 9:33 is a way to show Jesus' superiority over the other characters.[290] The feast of Booths (also called Tabernacles or Sukkot) was a "key festival in Judaism [that] looked back at God's provision in the wilderness and was regarded as anticipating God's ultimate deliverance."[291] The connections to Jesus' New Exodus are obvious.[292] If there is also a connection to the feast of booths, it may be another example of decentralization, of a moving past the traditional Jewish establishment.[293] In the end, as Bock notes, the "key theme" of this verse is fulfillment (πληροῦν).[294]

The two figures, Elijah and Moses, strategically link the New Exodus with Luke's understanding of the gospel as Jesus as the fulfillment of Israel's story. We have noted above Jesus' connection with Elijah.[295] Fitzmyer calls the inclusion of Elijah "puzzling" if the reference is to the Israel's exodus experience, although he notes his connection with Mt. Horeb and its place in the exodus experience.[296] However Bovon holds that these figures are representations of the two major divisions of Scripture, the law and the prophets, which had looked forward to Christ and his suffering.[297] Thus, Jesus as the fulfillment of the hopes of Israel as revealed in her Scriptures is displayed here.

Although there may be some connections to Elijah implicit in the narrative, it appears that Luke downplays them compared to the other synoptics. Matthew and Mark both describe John the Baptist, for example, as coming from the wilderness, wearing camel's hair and a leather belt around his waist.[298] This is a clear reference to 2 Kings 1:8 where Elijah is described also as wearing camel's hair with a leather

289. Bock, *Luke*, 1:869.

290. Bock, *Luke*, 1:869.

291. Bock, *Luke*, 1:870–71.

292. Not all agree that the connection with the Feast of Booths is apt. Michaelis argues instead that the tents would have been for more permanent dwelling and that the typology does not align. See Michaelis, *TDNT* 7:379–80.

293. Note that both Pentecost and Passover will be decentralized and redefined in Luke's writings, so a redefining of the feast of booths would be consistent with that practice.

294. Bock, *Luke*, 1:869. There is debate over what Jesus' ἔξοδον refers to. Marshall, *Luke*, 384–85, presents four options: (1) Jesus' death; (2) Jesus' death and ascension; (3) Repetition of the exodus event; and (4) Jesus' whole life. Bock adds a fifth as his preferred understanding, that is "the entire death-parousia career of Jesus" combined with the repetition of the exodus event. See Bock, *Luke*, 1:869–70. Option four seems most likely.

295. For example, the rejected prophet miracle worker who ministers to others besides his own people, and who leaves a spiritual blessing for his follower.

296. Fitzmyer, *Luke*, 1:794–95. See 1 Kgs 19:4–8; Exod 3:1; Deut 1:2; 5:2.

297. Bovon, *Luke*, 376.

298. Matt 3:1, 4; Mark 1:4–6.

belt.[299] Luke intentionally redacts these comparative elements with Elijah, although he does not downplay John, but rather is the only gospel writer to include a birth narrative about him. Having said that, his primary focus is on Moses, possibly at the expense of focusing on Elijah.

The parallels with the character of Moses are profound. To the degree that Luke presents Jesus as a new Moses, he is making bold claims about who Jesus is, the rootedness of the New Christian Movement in the trajectory of salvation history, and the fulfillment of the promise that God will send a prophet like Moses to redeem his people.[300] Note the following similarities between Moses in the Torah and the narrative of Jesus' life in Luke:[301]

- Both Moses and Jesus have remarkable births. Moses, born under a pagan political regime (Egypt), is hidden and placed in a reed basket to escape the decree to kill the male babies by the pagan rulers.[302] Jesus, born under a pagan political regime (Rome), has angels announce his birth and is born during a census levied on his people from the pagan rulers.[303]

- Both Moses and Jesus did not eat for forty days and forty nights.[304] Furthermore, The Israelites, led by Moses, wondered in the wilderness for forty years as a time of testing.[305] Before Jesus started his ministry, he went to the wilderness to be tempted/tested (πειράζω/ἐκπειράζω) by Satan for forty days,[306] where he quotes the verse "Man does not live on bread alone" from Deuteronomy 8, referring to eating manna in the wilderness.[307]

- Jesus, alluding to the manna story, feeds five thousand people with five loaves and two fish,[308] which leads to people picking up leftovers off of the ground, reminiscent of Israelites picking up manna off of the ground.[309] (There are twelve baskets of leftovers, which is an illusion to twelve tribes).[310]

---

299. Elijah is also connected with the wilderness in texts such as 1 Kgs 19.

300. Deut 18:15–18.

301. Matthew's treatment of these similarities is perhaps most pronounced, with Luke's being second, followed by Mark and John.

302. Exod 2:1–10.

303. Luke 2:1–7. Matthew records Herod's decree to kill the babies two years and under (Matt 2:16).

304. Exod 34:28; Luke 4:2.

305. Exod 16:35; Deut 8:2.

306. Luke 4.

307. Deut 8:3; Luke 4:4.

308. Luke 9:13–17.

309. Exod 16:31.

310. Luke 12:17.

- After Moses has his encounter with God on Mount Sinai, his face shines, so much so that the people create a veil for him to wear because of the glory of God shining off of his face.[311] Similarly, Jesus, toward the end of his ministry, goes up to a mountain and his appearance changed there (transfiguration), when Moses and Elijah appear with him, and his clothes became "dazzling white."[312] The characters talk about Jesus' departure (ἔξοδον).

- Moses takes Joshua, his assistant up to the mountain with him,[313] as Jesus does with three of his disciples.[314]

- The regularity of clouds is noteworthy in each narrative. In the time of Moses, God descends in a cloud,[315] a cloud covers the Tent of Meeting,[316] and God speaks to Moses from a cloud so the people will believe Moses forever.[317] Likewise, a cloud appears at the mount of transfiguration,[318] God speaks from the cloud and tells the disciples to listen to him,[319] Jesus predicts his return on a cloud, and is covered by a cloud during his ascension.[320]

- One of the key events in the book of Exodus is the Passover,[321] which becomes one of the most important feasts in the Jewish tradition, where they tell the story again of the exodus of God's people out of slavery. During the last supper, Jesus is celebrating the Passover meal with his disciples.[322] The next day, he would be crucified.[323] Moses ushers in the Old Covenant sacrificial system in blood. Jesus inaugurates the New Covenant sacrifice with his own blood.[324]

- Jesus is called "Mighty in deed and word," which is said about Moses in Acts 7.[325]

---

311. Exod 34:29–35.

312. Luke 9:28–36. Matthew's account is more pronounced, as he says his face "shone like the sun" (Matt 17:2).

313. Exod 24:12–13.

314. Luke 9:28.

315. Deut 23:1–5; 9:9; 10:1–5, 10.

316. Exod 33:10.

317. Exod 19:9.

318. Luke 9:34.

319. Luke 9:34–35.

320. Luke 21:27. The prediction of return on the cloud has more to do with Daniel 7 than with Moses, but it does fit the cloud imagery of Luke. Acts 1:9.

321. Exod 12.

322. Luke 22.

323. Luke 23.

324. Exod 24:8; Luke 22:20.

325. Luke 24:19; Acts 7:22.

- Moessner connects the journey narrative in Luke[326] to the presentation of Moses in Deuteronomy.[327]
- There is a threefold pattern in the Exodus narrative of deliverance from slavery, journey through the wilderness, and arrival at the Promised Land. Those same three categories (deliverance, journey, and arrival)[328] can be seen in the different sections of Luke as well as an organizing structure of the life of Jesus. Deliverance (Luke 1:1—9:50); Journey to Jerusalem (Luke 9:51—19:27); Arrival in Jerusalem (Luke 19:28—24:53).

Regarding threefold structure, Watts, in his work on Mark, laid the groundwork for seeing the pattern in the synoptic Gospels.[329] Some may suggest that Luke's structure is simply the result of using Mark as source material. However, Luke is more intentional than that. For example, there is a clear emphasis on deliverance and redemption in the first section, 1:1–9:50. The canticles sing of God's deliverance.[330] Jesus pronounces deliverance in the synagogue when reading from Isaiah 61. Of the five episodes in Luke of Jesus casting out demons, four of them fall in this first section about deliverance.[331] The fourth exorcism story concludes the first section in 9:50, and 9:51 brings the transition, introducing the journey section where Jesus "sets his face to go to Jerusalem" (καὶ αὐτὸς τὸ πρόσωπον ἐστήρισεν τοῦ πορεύεσθαι εἰς Ἰερουσαλήμ). The journey section (9:51—19:27) includes Jesus' journey to Jerusalem and a fair amount of teaching. Jesus also sends out the 70 in 10:1, which may correspond to Moses sending out the 70 in the wilderness in Numbers 11:16–17. The section ends with the parable of the ten minas, and then transitions in 19:28 when Jesus goes up to Jerusalem, a clear indicator of the arrival section.[332] This third section begins immediately by the disciples obtaining a colt that is used for the so-called triumphal entry. Other events include weeping over Jerusalem, cleansing the Temple, and celebrating the last supper with his disciples. This threefold organization reminds the reader of the exodus event and reinforces Jesus' likeness to Moses.

These similarities, along with the birth canticles and his supernatural ministry, create an ethos for Jesus, framing him as a significant religious figure who was called by God and who echoes the heroes of Israel's faith.[333] More specifically, Jesus is the new Moses, as prophesied in Deuteronomy 18:15–18. Again, this is evidence

---

326. Luke 9:51–19:44.

327. See Moessner, *Banquet*.

328. These categories are developed by Watts, *New Exodus*, 81, as seen through an Isaianic lens.

329. See Watts, *New Exodus*.

330. For example, λύτρωσις is used twice in the canticles, once by Zechariah (1:68) and once in the Anna narrative (2:38).

331. Luke 4:33–35; 7:33; 8:29; 9:42; 11:14.

332. Dinkler, "Reading"; Blajer, "Limit"; Kinman, "Entry"; Cope et al., "Outline."

333. Litwak, *Echoes*, 57–58.

of Luke framing the story in such a way that his readers understand the significance of this character.

However, not all agree that Luke is presenting Jesus as a new Moses. Fitzmyer calls this "problematic" and says that the link between Jesus and Moses in Luke is "not a strong motif," although he notes the connections in Matthew.[334] He suggests the similarities are inherited from tradition.[335] However, Fitzmyer misses the clear comparisons present and the organizing structure that Luke uses to emphasize these ideas in his three sections. Luke's intentionality is clear. In sum, there is strong evidence for Luke's agenda of showing similarity between Jesus and Moses and cannot be the result of being inherited from tradition. Furthermore, this connection plays an important role in Luke's intertextual agenda. The author seeks to show Jesus as the salvation of God who has come to his people.[336] Just as Moses led his people out of the slavery of Egypt, Jesus came to lead his people out of the slavery of sin.[337] Similarly, Luke ends up creating parallels with other characters. Not only does Jesus resemble Moses, but Peter and Paul both mirror Jesus, as they are playing similar roles in the narrative.[338] Furthermore, Stephen's death resembles that of Jesus to a degree.

The Road to Emmaus

The last of the anthology scenes that emphasize the New Exodus and Jesus as the fulfillment of Israel's story is the encounter on the road to Emmaus.[339] The story communicates the impact of the events of Jesus' death on the towns. The two travelers are walking and processing the events that have happened the last few days.[340] The reader is told that Jesus himself joins them but they are kept from recognizing him.[341] Jesus asks what they are discussing, and Cleopas's response[342] suggests that the events of Jesus' arrest and crucifixion are events that have the whole city in a stir. Despite it being the Passover festival, the events surrounding Jesus have made "these

---

334. Fitzmyer, *Luke*, 1:793.

335. Fitzmyer, *Luke*, 1:793. Whether or not Fitzmyer is correct, Luke has, at the very least, adopted the suggested linkage between Jesus and Moses.

336. Luke 1:68, 71, 77; 2:30; 3:6; 6:9; 7:50; 8:12, 50; 9:19, 24; 13:23; 18:26, 42; 19:10; 23:35, 37, 39; 24:21.

337. Luke 4:18–19.

338. These similarities are discussed more fully in chapter 4 on Prototypes and Exemplars.

339. Luke 24:13–32.

340. "The description suggests a wide ranging conversation in which they rehashed all these events" (Bock, *Luke*, 2:1909).

341. There is scholarly discussion about the manner in which they fail to recognize him, whether it is God's doing, their own blindness, or Satan keeping them from it. Bock argues for the option one. See Bock, *Luke*, 2:1909–10.

342. "Are you the only stranger in Jerusalem who does not know the things that have taken place there in these days?"

days" extra noteworthy.³⁴³ Jesus' crucifixion involved public presentation including much of the town and his subversive mission has left them in wonder.³⁴⁴ Second, there is the hopeful expectation of fulfilled promises that, though they looked unfulfilled at first, are ultimately realized.

The travelers expressed disappointment, "But we had hoped that he was the one to redeem Israel" (ἡμεῖς δὲ ἠλπίζομεν ὅτι αὐτός ἐστιν ὁ μέλλων λυτροῦσθαι τὸν Ἰσραήλ). Luke creates tension here, as the reader knows what the characters do not. Jesus is the new deliverer for Israel.³⁴⁵ There are also links to Moses in that he is called "Mighty in deed and word," which is said about Moses in Acts 7.³⁴⁶ The use of the word λυτρόω here is rare in the New Testament, forms of which are used only nine times.³⁴⁷ Luke uses forms of this word at key moments in the narrative where the plot is moving forward in important ways. Two times in the birth narrative, characters declared the redemption that was imminent in God's move of sending a savior. In the Acts 7 speech by Stephen, Moses is described using a form of this word (i.e., λυτρωτήν, "redeemer"), with undertones of Jesus. This occurs only a few verses before the climax of the story, which results in Stephen's Christlike death.³⁴⁸ Similar to the previous examples, here the word is spoken to Jesus by characters who do not know whom they are talking to. The irony of the hope and disappointment expressed by them shapes Luke's illocution of anticipation for his readers. The hope that has been present throughout is restated here.³⁴⁹ Jesus' response and exposition remains a mystery, although it could be assumed that the speeches in Acts that proclaim Jesus from the Old Testament are of similar content.³⁵⁰ Tannehill suggests that this encounter sets the stage for the mission of the apostles and the missionary sermons there, which will further explain these details.³⁵¹

---

343. Bock, *Luke*, 2:1911–12. Bock suggests the attitude of the walkers is, "How could he have missed these events, which were so public and of such interest?"

344. Luke 23:13 records Jesus being presented before the chief priests, the leaders and the people.

345. Fitzmyer connects this to Jeremiah 14:8 where Yahweh is called the hope of Israel. Fitzmyer, *Luke*, 2:1564.

346. Tannehill, *Luke*, 286, notes how closely the connection between Jesus and Moses will be in Stephen's speech. Luke 24:19; Acts 7:22. Bock, *Luke*, 2:1912, calls this a common title throughout the NT. See Rom 15:18; 2 Cor 10:11; Col 3:17; 2 Thess 2:17; 1 John 3:18; Tannehill, *Luke*, 280. Jesus is also called a prophet, which fits Luke 4:16–30; 13:31–35, as well as "the public judgment about him." See Bock, *Luke*, 2:1912. See Luke 17:16, 39; 9:9, 18–19; Acts 10:38–9.

347. This usage here and Titus 2:14; 1 Peter 1:18. λύτροvin Matt 20:28; Mark 10:45. λύτρωσις in Luke 1:68; 2:38; Heb 9:12. λυτρωτής in Acts 7:35.

348. Acts 7:54–57. For more on Stephen dying like Jesus, see chapter 4.

349. Tannehill, *Luke*, 281.

350. Bock, *Luke*, 2:1916. Bock points to texts such as Deut 18:15; Ps 2:7; 16:8–11; 110:1; 118; Isa 53:8. For the missionary sermons in Acts, see 2:25–28; 4:11, 25–26; 8:32–33; 13:35. Also, see Bock, *Proclamation*.

351. Tannehill, *Luke*, 285. Acts 2:14–39; 3:12–26; 7; 10:28–47; 13:16–41; 14:3–7; 17:22–35; 22:1–21.

Luke's (and Jesus') expectation for the travelers to have understood and expected the crucifixion and resurrection[352] from the Old Testament prophets is an interesting one. "The consensus is that first-century Judaism did not anticipate a suffering Messiah."[353] Thus, this seems to be a way for Luke to claim that the Jews misunderstood the Hebrew Scriptures.[354] More than that, Jesus claims that the Hebrew prophets had that expectation. "Here is where Christian and Jewish messianic expectation and eschatology differed greatly."[355] Luke's ability to root the suffering, death, and resurrection of Jesus in the Hebrew Scriptures yet again emphasizes the concept of promise and fulfillment and intertextuality.

Jesus stays at their urging, and during the meal their eyes are opened and they say, "Were not our hearts burning within us while he was talking to us on the road, while he was opening the scriptures to us?"[356] Tannehill suggests that Jesus' exposition of Scripture was the narrative key for "grasping God's purpose" in Jesus.[357] In sum, Luke establishes, even to the very end of volume one, the rootedness of Jesus and his story in the Scriptures of the Hebrew Bible and the expectations found there, through the rich usage of intertextual clues. To the degree that Luke's readers confess Jesus as the Messiah and choose to interpret the Hebrew Scriptures in a way that points to him, they are connecting with the community of the early church and forming identity. Luke is prescribing a certain way of relating to the Hebrew Scriptures in how he uses the exodus story and Isaiah throughout, and it is seen overtly here. However, it is not simply a rootedness in the past that creates social identity for his audience. Rather, there are promises from these Scriptures that look ahead to the present and future realities of Luke's audience. There is reason to believe that the things that were promised long ago are now being fulfilled in the person of Jesus and the community of the early church. The primary place where Luke connects the past with the present ministry of the early church are the historiographic speeches of Acts 7 and 13. A fuller exploration of these speeches is needed. To this we now turn.

Promise and Fulfillment in Acts

The emphasis in Acts on climax and fulfillment is strongest in the speeches by Stephen and Paul in Acts 7 and 13, respectively. These speeches help place the reader in the context of salvation history and connect God's activity in Israel with the early church

---

352. Luke 24:12, 25–26.

353. Bock, *Luke*, 2:1916. Also, see Fitzmyer, *Luke*, 2:1565–66; Marshall, *Luke*, 896.

354. Note also that the pair on the road fault οἱ ἀρχιερεῖς καὶ οἱ ἄρχοντες ἡμῶν with Jesus' death. These two, plus the rejection of the gospel by Jews in Acts, may be Luke's indication that the traditional Jewish institution is off track as they have missed their redeemer. See Tannehill, *Luke*, 280.

355. Bock, *Luke*, 2:1916.

356. Luke 24:32b.

357. Tannehill, *Luke*, 289. Tannehill also notes Luke's proclivity to combine meals (i.e., "breaking of bread") with instruction about Jesus' "person and mission," as here. See Tannehill, *Luke*, 290–93.

movement. They also exhibit elements of rhetorical persuasion, something we will examine more closely in chapter 5. As part of their uniquely historiographical role in Luke's corpus, they trace the trajectory of salvation history through a number of authors, books, characters, and generations. For that reason, they deserve special attention.[358]

Acts 7 and 13

In Acts, Luke uses two characters, Stephen and Paul, to tell lengthy versions of the salvation history of Israel in separate sections of the book to different audiences. One may be tempted to ask, if Luke is attempting to connect with God-fearers and Gentiles, moving the trajectory of God's saving activity beyond Israel, then why does Luke focus so intensely on the history of the Hebrew people? It is clear that Luke understands the gospel in the sense of Jesus and all he did as the climax and fulfillment of the human story as mediated through Israel's story. This makes the salvation history of Israel central to the gospel and to Luke's agenda. It is key to understanding the new movement that was being created, and it was key to understanding Jesus. This new community will be the embodiment of the words of the prophets that envision the inclusion of the outsiders and the far off.[359] It will embrace the other and serve the poor.[360] It will be heavily rooted in the Old Testament, but also open to new ways in which the Spirit is moving. Thus, these speeches become the two primary places that Luke presents for his readers the salvation history of Israel through the lens of first-century Christianity, that they might fully understand Jesus as the fulfillment of Israel's story.

The history of Israel is also key for creating social identity in the reader for Luke. The God-fearing Gentile who spends time at the synagogue would likely have been familiar with the major stories of the Hebrew Bible.[361] The stories of Abraham, Moses, and David would not be completely new to a God-fearing audience, although these particular speeches in Luke that weave these elements into a historic tapestry that culminates in Jesus are likely new for his intended readers. That the trajectory of Jewish salvation history culminates in Jesus and includes God-fearers and other outsiders in the family of God would have been a new revelation to this audience.

There was a hint at this tapestry in Jesus' post-resurrection appearance to the disciples on the road to Emmaus in Luke's Gospel, as discussed above: "Then he said to them, 'These are my words that I spoke to you while I was still with you—that everything written about me in the law of Moses, the prophets, and the psalms must

358. Despite potential Pentecost connections, the underrepresented material requires us to move straight to examining the speeches. For discussion of Pentecost, see Sloan, "Signs"; Bruce, "Spirit."

359. Isa 56; Luke 19:45–48; Acts 8:26–40.

360. Isa 61; Acts 2:43–47; 4:33–37; 6:1–6; 11:27–29.

361. Lieu, *Constructing*, 53–55, 67n3. Lieu points to Paul's letters as examples of Gentiles having some familiarity with these stories, considering the amount of times Paul quotes the LXX suggesting they were "already well familiar with the Greek scriptures and with their elucidation." Also, see Esler, *Community*; Unnik, "Redemption"; Finn, "Reconsidered," 83.

be fulfilled. Then he opened their minds to understand the scriptures.'"[362] Keener suggests that this is a whetting of the appetite for what is to come in Acts 7 and Acts 13 where "the promise-fulfillment theme in Acts' speeches develops Jesus' role in that larger story more explicitly."[363] Likewise, Johnson calls Stephen's speech "the key Luke provides his readers for the interpretation of his entire two-volume narrative."[364] All of the hints in the canticles and birth narratives were pointing to these climactic moments. These two chapters give the reader an expanded look at how the early Christians understood Jesus in light of the Old Testament.[365]

The speeches of Stephen and Paul will be key areas of interest for this monograph. Chapter 4 will argue that Stephen and Paul, among others, are prototypical characters for social identity formation in Luke's writings.[366] Chapter 5 will look into the rhetoric of both speeches and examine the persuasive features present there. In this chapter, the goal is to introduce these speeches and identify what they are doing narratively, which is to introduce the implied reader to the history of God's activity with humanity and set the stage for creating a place for the reader in that story. The speeches play an important function in the unfolding of the narrative of Acts as well, as key events both lead up to and follow after the speech that are important for Luke's purposes. Key in this endeavor will be to identify promise and fulfillment elements in the speeches. Chapter 5 will examine more closely the rhetorical elements of these two chapters.

Stephen's Speech

Stephen is a remarkable example of a follower of Jesus in the early church.[367] Not long after Stephen is introduced, he is martyred, but not before delivering the longest speech in the book. He begins with the story of Abraham and works his way through the key events of Israel's story. This is a unique early example of a Christian telling the story of Jewish Redemption history—the Story of the Old Testament—in concise speech form.[368] Keener says it well: "This is the longest survey of salvation history

362. Luke 24:44–45.

363. Keener, *Acts*, 2:2060.

364. Johnson, *Acts*, 119.

365. For example, Stephen highlights the patriarchs (7:2–16), the slavery in Egypt and the Exodus, including the importance of Moses (7:17–44), and briefly mentions Joshua, David, and Solomon (7:45–47). The exodus and Moses are important points for Luke in connecting Jesus to the Hebrew Scriptures. Similarly, Paul's speech mentions Moses and the exodus, though briefly (13:17–18), but spends more time on David (13:21–23, 32–37) and highlights the failure of the people to listen to the prophets (13:26–28), echoed by Jesus' weeping over Jerusalem (Luke 19:41). For an alternate view, see Richard, "Character," who takes a harsher stance, suggesting that this is the farewell speech to Judaism.

366. Stephen will be presented as the prototypical martyr and Paul will be the prototypical missionary to the Gentiles. See chapter 5.

367. Chapter 4 will argue that he is the prototypical martyr for Luke. See Krauter, "Martyrdom"; Kalimi, "Murders."

368. Despite Jesus' conversation on the road to Emmaus, we have no content of that conversation.

in Luke–Acts and offers insight into Luke's agenda: Jesus and his experience of the church (7:51–52) continue and climax early biblical experience, a living experience of God's activity in the present."[369]

What is more, the speech plays an extremely important role in the unfolding of the narrative. This is the third of three trials before the Sanhedrin in Acts 4–7, and the punishments get progressively worse.[370] The scene becomes a major turning point in the narrative, as it forces the Christians to scatter, and the gospel spreads because of it.[371] The church moves from "a phase of popularity in Jerusalem (2:47) to one of persecution and scattering (8:4)."[372] And, perhaps most importantly, the end of this scene introduces the reader to "Saul," who as a former enemy of the gospel, will soon become the main character of the second half of volume two. This is the classic Lukan focus on decentralization, where those who were the enemies and outsiders become the proponents of the mission.

Luke falls in a long line of Greco-Roman scholars who value speech giving in narrative texts.[373] Chapter 5 will examine first-century rhetoric, but suffice it to say here that ancient historians focused on speeches as events that changed history.[374] Other Greco-Roman writers, such as Plutarch, have characters giving speeches to soldiers regarding the spoils of war as well as right and wrong conduct.[375] Similarly, Wells discusses the conquered people of Rome in Europe and notes information that comes from texts and archeology that clue us into the values and key identity markers of these societies, including authors who had "considerable verbal

---

The closest we have to this are summary statements, as in Luke 24:44–47; Acts 3:19–21.

369. Keener, *Acts*, 2:1330.

370. Witherington, *Acts*, 252. Acts 4:1–21; 5:21–42.

371. As mentioned in chapter 2 about decentralization, the scattering and leaving Jerusalem likely plays on this idea. The focus on Jerusalem being the central hub of the Jewish faith is shifting to wherever God's people are.

372. Keener, *Acts*, 2:1330. Also consider Pesch, *Die Apostelgeschichte*, 235, who says "Seine dauernde Wirksamkeit unter dem Volk harmoniert freilich, da sie im Wirken von Wundern und Zeichen besteht, nicht mit dem Bild des zum Tischdienst Bestellten, auch nicht mit dem des Wortverkündigers; aber Lukas wird den ersten Märtyrer als apostolischen Mann vorgestellt und den Widerstand gegen ihn in der Linie des Widerstandes gegen die Apostel gesehen haben wollen." ("Its lasting effectiveness among the people, in so far as it consists in the work of miracles and signs, does not, of course, align with the image of those ordered to serve at the table, nor with that of the preacher of the word; but Luke will have wanted to see the first martyr introduced as an apostolic man, as well as resistance against him in the line of resistance against the apostles.")

373. In addition to Plato and Aristotle, and the famous "Attic Orators" and their "Canon of Ten," which included Demosthenes and Isocrates among others, also included here would be orators and historians like Thucydides, Polybius, Cicero, and the military commander Arrian. Each of these works includes history and identity formation through some combination of speeches by characters or instructions by the author on what is right, what is noble, etc. Also, see Kennedy, *Classical*; Carawan, *Orators*; Bury, *Historians*.

374. Gempf, "Public Speaking," 261.

375. Dench, *Barbarians*, 81–102.

ability."[376] Other ancient cultures reflected this as well. Insoll, in his study of the archeology and identity in ancient cultures, references Aztec documents that show speeches being given to expectant mothers about their children, including how to raise them and metaphors for the parenting process.[377] Other speeches are given to older children about the appropriate presentation and dress for their life stage, including the proper haircut prescribed.[378] Luke is consistent with the norms of ancient and Greco-Roman writing in that he is both presenting characters who have the ability to articulate and speak for themselves and that speeches are a key feature of his work. Luke is strategic in his use of speeches in Acts as was common in the ancient world and is representative of a Greco-Roman strategy.

The speech is communicating on multiple levels. First, there is the world projected by the text, where Stephen, the character, is speaking to the Sanhedrin defending the charges against him. Secondly, there is the implied author inherent in the text, for whom Stephen, the character, plays the role of appealing to God-fearing Gentiles.[379] This second level of the speech is what concerns this thesis most centrally. It has too often has been ignored. If Stephen's speech is meant as a defense before the Sanhedrin, it is a bit puzzling.[380] It highlights a history of Jewish hardheartedness and idolatry that incites the Jews to anger,[381] not what one would expect in a defense. Rather, I suggest that this speech serves the primary function of placing the story of Israel in a Christian perspective to fully communicate the gospel story for God-fearing readers, and only secondarily as a defense against Stephen's accusations. This can be seen in three ways.

First, the speech crafted for a God-fearing audience by highlighting outsiders. As with any history, the speaker must be selective in what to include. In this case, Stephen speaks of a number of famous characters in Israel's ancient past. Several of these characters are outsiders at different times in their stories. Abraham, Joseph, Moses, as well as the Israelite nation as a whole were outsiders in their respective contexts. However, they were ultimately included in the work of God and God's people, shown by how they are spoken of by Stephen as insiders. There is certainly overlap here with the God-fearing Gentile reader, who also feels like an outsider, but in Luke–Acts, is included in the family of God.[382] The heroes of the Old Testament are characters whom

---

376. Wells, *Barbarians*, 24–32, 66–134. Also, see Shotter, *Texts*.

377. Insoll, *Archeology*, 79. Also, see Jones, *Ethnicity*.

378. Insoll, *Archeology*, 81–82.

379. Much has been written about the nature of which Luke recorded, crafted, or created Stephen's words. That falls outside of the scope here. For a good summary of the different views, see Padilla, "Speeches." Also, see Gempf, "Public Speaking"; Arnold, "Debates"; Cadbury et al., "Traditions"; Bock, *Acts*, 277–79; Gentili and Cerri, "Communication," 143.

380. See Dibelius, *Studies*, 167.

381. Bock, *Acts*, 276–77; Keener, *Acts*, 2:1328–29. Bock states, "The speech is not as disconnected as Dibelius suggests."

382. Nolland, *Luke*, 1:xxxii.

the God-fearing reader can identify with among a number of other characters that offer this contribution to the reader in the book of Acts.

Second, the speech includes hints at the New Exodus. This speech covers a wide range of time, starting with Abraham and leading up to the time of the kings, Temple, and Exile.[383] He begins with Abraham, the father of the Jewish people, but spends more time on Moses and the events surrounding the exodus than any other topic. This is partly because the exodus is the most important identity-forming event in the history of the Jewish people.[384] However, another reason to highlight Moses's exodus is to connect the reader with the New Exodus in Luke–Acts, discussed previously in this chapter. While the original exodus benefitted specifically the Jewish people, the New Exodus affects all people and connects God-fearers to important emphases in the gospel. What the first exodus started by liberating God's people out of slavery, the New Exodus continued by including outsiders.

Third, the speech highlights the failure of Israel making a way for Gentiles to come into the community of God's people. The discussion of Moses reminds the reader of the New Exodus, but it is also working toward a larger trajectory: "repeated resistance to the Spirit who speaks through the prophets, culminating in the rejection of the 'righteous one.'"[385] This works as a defense of Stephen by accusing his opponents of ignoring the Spirit, which is evident in him, also highlighting the Spirit's activity in the early church and presses the reader not to resist the work of the Spirit. Tannehill argues that the first part of the speech is largely to "contrast the great promise of Israel's beginnings" with its later failure.[386] There is an implicit warning to the reader not to make the same mistakes as these synagogue members. This serves Luke's identity-forming illocutionary intent as he crafts behavior and expectations for his audience. There is an indictment of Israel (and the accusers) present in the speech. This serves, as will the rejection of Paul and the gospel in the synagogues later in the book, as an opportunity for Gentiles to be a part of what God is doing.

The Temple in Stephen's Speech

The accusation against Stephen is that he has spoken against the Temple. There are some important Temple elements in the speech,[387] but Luke's focus on the Temple began much earlier. As discussed previously, the role of the Temple in the narrative goes through a radical decentralization process in the Lukan corpus. What was the center of Jewish life, public worship, and religious social identity gets inverted such that it is the community that gathers in all sorts of places that has the Spirit in its midst that

---

383. Also, see Steyn, "Trajectories"; Laytham, "Witness"; Bassler, "Seasons."
384. Harris, *Exodus and Exile*, 1, calls it "one of the central themes of Jewish existence."
385. Tannehill, *Acts*, 87.
386. Tannehill, *Acts*, 88.
387. Acts 7:44–48. Also, see Jung, "Sacredness"; Schwartz, "Philo"; Taylor, "Stephen."

becomes the new center of religious life and social identity.[388] Where God's presence used to dwell within the holy of holies, it now dwells in the community of his people.[389] Luke's programmatic decentralization of the Temple happens in many ways. At the beginning of the narrative, the Temple is the establishment and the central locus of God's presence. Zechariah ministers in the Temple.[390] Jesus is presented in the Temple as a baby.[391] The boy Jesus is left in Jerusalem and is found at the Temple, suggesting he must be in his "Father's house."[392] It is the location of the climactic moment of Jesus' temptation by Satan.[393] It is also a common location for teaching for Jesus and the disciples.[394] Thus, early on in the book, the Temple remains as the awe-inspiring center of God's presence and activity. However, as Passion Week draws near, things begin to shift. In chapter 18, Jesus tells a story of a tax collector who goes to the Temple confessing that he is a sinner and appeals for mercy, standing at a distance. He is contrasted with a Pharisee who brags about his religious activities and that he is superior to the tax collector, but it is the humble one who is justified at the Temple that day.[395] In this scene, Luke's agenda of showing interpersonal decentralization between Pharisees (insiders) and tax collectors (outsiders) intersects with his geographical decentralization around the Temple.[396] This trajectory continues into chapter 19 as Jesus cleanses the Temple and quotes from Isaiah 56, although dramatically leaving off the final phrase, "for all peoples."[397] In the next verse, the chief

---

388. Strack, *Talmud*, 2. For more on the Temple as the center of Jewish life and its role in Luke–Acts, see Repschinski, "Re-Imagining"; Waal, "Temple"; Johnson, "Framework"; Beale, *Temple*; Weinert, "Meaning"; Brodie, "New Temple"; Clements, *God and Temple*; Bachmann, *Jerusalem*; Reitzel, "Image."

389. Some would suggest that Luke is more negative toward the Temple than the other gospel writers. For example, consider Pesch, *Die Apostelgeschichte*, 238: "Das Wort ist von Lukas als Falschzeugnis ausgelegt, weil Jesus zwar die Zerstörung des Tempels vorhergesagt hat, aber nicht alseigene Aktion, sondern als Strafe für die nicht erkannte Heimsuchung Israels. Auf die Tempelzerstörung zurückblickend nimmt Lukas auch aus Mk 14,58 die positive Hälfte des Tempelwortes nicht auf. Das Wort ist von Lukas auch alsFalschzeugnis ausgelegt, weil Jesus zwar das Gesetz unter dem Anspruch der Frohbotschaft der Gottesherrschaft relativiert, aber nicht geändert hat." ("The word is interpreted by Luke as a false testimony because Jesus predicted the destruction of the temple, but not as a self-contained action, but as a punishment for the unrecognized visitation of Israel. Looking back on the destruction of the temple, Luke does not take up the positive half of the temple word from Mark 14:58 either. Luke also interprets the word as a false testimony because, while relativizing relativized the law in light oof the claim of the good news of the rule of God, Jesus did not change it.")

390. Luke 1:9–22.

391. Luke 2:27–37.

392. Luke 2:46–50.

393. Luke 4:9.

394. Luke 19:47; 20:1; 21:37, 38; 22:53; Acts 5:20–21, 25, 42.

395. Luke 18:10–14.

396. For more on Luke's decentralizing agenda, see chapter 2.

397. Luke 19:45–46. Green, "Demise," 512; Fay, "Narrative Function," suggests that the cleansing is actually creating a new link between God and the Temple through the Messiah. This is an interesting idea, but Fay cites the activity surrounding the Temple early in Acts as evidence when it seems to

priests, scribes, and leaders are looking for Jesus at the Temple to kill him.[398] What started as the center for God's presence and religious activity has become the location for seeking to kill God's anointed one.[399] For Green, "Far from serving as a sacred place for the worship of God by Gentiles (and Samaritans), the temple functions as a segregating force, symbolizing socio-religious demarcations between insider and outsider. The time of the temple is not over. . . . But it is no longer the center around which life is oriented."[400] For God-fearers and other outsiders to be a part of God's plan, this *segregating force* must be decentralized.

Following chapter 19, we encounter a few more references to the Temple. The widow is praised over the rich for giving her nearly worthless coins.[401] Jesus responds to his disciples' praise of the Temple's adornments by predicting it's destruction, followed by a lengthy apocalyptic discourse about coming judgment.[402] Chapter 21 ends with Jesus spending the night on the Mount of Olives and people coming to the Temple early in the morning to hear him teach. Jesus has now become the draw, rather than the Temple itself. Judas plots with the Temple guards to betray Jesus, who come later to arrest him.[403] The penultimate reference to the Temple in Luke is the tearing of the Temple curtain while Jesus hangs on the cross: "It was now about noon, and darkness came over the whole land until three in the afternoon, while the sun's light failed; and the curtain of the Temple was torn in two. Then Jesus, crying with a loud voice, said, 'Father, into your hands I commend my spirit.' Having said this, he breathed his last."[404] As light fails, Christ dies. The tearing of the Temple curtain directly precedes Jesus giving up his spirit. Some rightly suggest that the tearing of the curtain means that the Temple is ceasing to be at the center of God's activity.[405] This is consistent with the trajectory of decentralization around the Temple in Luke. There is also discussion about whether the Greek word καταπέτασμα refers to the curtain of

---

be more or a practical function than a spiritual function. What is more, Fay ignores both Stephen's critique of the Temple (discussed below) and the larger theme of decentralization that runs through two volumes. Also, see Chance, *Jerusalem*; Bohlemann, *Jesus*; Smith, *Fate*; Jung, "Sacredness."

398. Luke 19:47.

399. Not all would agree that the Temple becomes decentralized as the Jesus movement forms and moves away from it and Jerusalem. For example, Freyne, *Galilee*, 234–38, suggests that the Jesus movement had a positive view of the Temple and softens the challenge of its authority. Also, see Freyne, "Relations."

400. Green, "Demise."

401. Luke 21:1–4.

402. Luke 21:5–36.

403. Luke 22:3–6, 52.

404. Luke 23:44–46.

405. Green, "Death." Also, see Green, "Demise"; Sylva, "Curtain."

the Holy of Holies[406] or the outer curtain,[407] for it could refer to either.[408] The curtain to the Holy of Holies would signify the end of the centralization of God's presence in the Temple, an idea that certainly fits with Luke's trajectory and identity-forming illocutionary intent up to this point.[409] However, another option is that Luke is referring to the curtain that separated the outer courts from the Temple area.[410] Thus, the purpose of this curtain would be to keep outsiders out of the Temple. Understanding it this way emphasizes the inclusion of those who were formally unwelcomed. This reading also fits with Luke's identity-forming illocutionary intent and his trajectory of interpersonal decentralization, and perhaps fits better as a public sign, as opposed to the somewhat private nature of the Holy of Holies. In the end, either reading would serve to highlight one of Luke's interests.

The last reference to the Temple in Luke is in the closing sentence, as Jesus had appeared to the eleven and given them a final charge. Volume one ends with: "and they were continually in the temple blessing God."[411] This continues into volume two, as the Temple becomes the central hub for ministry of the disciples in the first seven chapters.[412] The Temple is playing a practical role for the early church as a large open space they are able to utilize for public gatherings. However, Stephen's speech accelerates change in several ways. First, from a practical point of view, Stephen's death causes the church to scatter, leaving Jerusalem and the Temple behind.[413] The involvement of the Temple in the narrative after chapter 7 is limited. The narrative speaks of Christians doing ministry around the temples of other gods (i.e., Zeus and Artemis),[414] and Paul is accused of taking a Gentile into the Temple, and goes to pay the purification expenses in an attempt to clear his name.[415] However, references to the Temple subside after chapter 7. Second, there is a theological shift that happens with the Temple in chapter 7.

The accusation against Stephen is, "This man never stops saying things against this holy place and the law; for we have heard him say that this Jesus of Nazareth will

---

406. Lev 21:23; 24:3; Josephus, *J.W.* 5.5.4–5.

407. Exod 26:37; 38:18; Num 3:26; Josephus, *J.W.* 5.5.4. κάλυμμα can also be used of the outer curtain. See Exod 27:17; Num 3:25.

408. Bock, *Luke*, 2:1860.

409. Plummer, *Luke*, 537–38; Arndt, *Luke*, 473; Ellis, *Luke*, 269.

410. Klosterman, *Das Lukasevangelium*, 227; Marshall, *Luke*, 875; Fitzmyer, *Luke*, 2:1518; Pelletier, "Temple"; "Le Grand Rideau"; Benoit, *Passion*, 201; Driver, "Problems."

411. Luke 24:53.

412. Acts 2:46; 3:1–10; 4:1; 5:20–25, 42. For more on decentralization, see chapter 2.

413. See Nash, "Stephen"; Blair, "Death," 2–3; Simon, "Saint Stephen."

414. Acts 14:13; 19:27–37.

415. Acts 21:26–30; 24:6, 12, 18. Chapter 4 will argue that the reason Paul stays connected with Jerusalem is that he needs to be seen as a Jewish representative who works to create a superordinate identity that unites both Jews and Gentiles.

destroy this place and will change the customs that Moses handed on to us."[416] The only place the Temple is referred to is in the section from verses 44 to 48, which starts by talking about the tabernacle, fitting with Stephen's focus on Moses. The word Temple (ναός) is not used, but it is clearly referred to in verse 48, before Stephen transitions by saying, "However, the Most High does not live in houses made by human hands." This statement, and the quotation from Amos that follows it establishing God's dwelling place as all of creation, reinforces decentralization and universality. The clear message is that God is not limited to the Temple and those who participate in it any longer. As Keener puts it, "With regard to the temple, it emphasizes that God is not localized."[417] This scene works as a theological "last rites" on a Temple that is no longer alive with God's presence. God's Spirit no longer dwells in a building, but in a community of people.[418]

The point of the speech goes beyond the significance of the Temple and strings together the activity of God through human history, culminating in the person of Jesus. Jesus is bigger than the Temple. The final words of the speech offer an accusation against the Jews. Jesus is also the ultimate example and the culmination of the unjust death of a Righteous Jew, and Stephen's frustration boils over at that. The Jewish hearers immediately react and stone him, and Stephen dies seeing Jesus welcoming him into heaven.

In conclusion, the speech serves Luke's agenda in multiple ways: it traces salvation history leading up to the time of fulfillment (i.e., the time of Jesus), it helps create identity among God-fearing readers by selecting Old Testament heroes they can identify with, and it places the current movement of God within the context of God's interaction with humanity. The Temple is merely another stop on the road to the Messiah, Jesus Christ. The activity of God quickly moves beyond the Temple. The schema of a centralized location for God's people to come to commune with him becomes the exact opposite of that as he seeks out his people to commune with them through his Spirit. The Temple becomes harmful as it works against the move of God, what Green calls "a segregating force," politically keeping people out that were central to the next move of God.[419] For these reasons, the Temple, like so many other elements in the Jewish establishment (Passover meal, land, food laws, Jerusalem, etc.), is decentralized.[420]

---

416. Acts 6:13b–14.

417. Keener, *Acts*, 2:1329

418. For more on Stephen's Speech and the Temple, see Sweeney, "Speech," 197. Also, see Hötzinger, "Salomo"; Thompson, "Brothers"; Taylor, "Stephen"; Hutcheon, "Temple."

419. Green, "Demise," 512.

420. Also, see Schwartz, "Philo."

Paul's Speech

Stephen's speech recounted God's activity with humanity through Israel in order to give the implied reader the trajectory of salvation history. Paul does a similar thing at the beginning of his ministry. His speech in Acts 13 is his first recorded in the book and his most developed message in a synagogue.[421] It has some obvious differences from Stephen's account. While the occasion for Stephen is a defense against accusations before the Sanhedrin, made up of all Jews, Paul's setting is in a synagogue with both Jews and God-fearers on hand.[422] He is not facing accusations like Stephen (at least not until after his speech), but rather is invited to speak because of the word that has spread about him, the miracle that took place immediately before this in chapter 13, and likely Paul's reputation as a Jewish teacher.[423] Whereas Stephen's speech incites the anger of his hearers, Paul's is followed by appeals to stay and to continue to minister and ultimately draws an even bigger crowd the following week.[424] However, the jealousy of the Jews after they see the crowds causes the scene to end poorly.[425]

In addition to recounting Jewish salvation history, Paul's speech contains some of the same elements as Stephen's. Paul's is a more truncated version of Israel's history and leaves considerable room to explain Jesus' life and passion narrative. Where Stephen focused largely on the patriarchs and Moses, who is the central figure in Stephen's speech, Paul begins with the exodus, and moves quickly through the events until he gets to his central character, David. Also, whereas for Stephen, Christ was a prophet like Moses, Paul emphasizes the Davidic-king Christology.[426]

Luke's emphasis on David is less conspicuous than the link with Moses throughout the two volumes, but it remains important for Luke's understanding of the Davidic Messiah and for his audience. The Davidic emphasis continues through the sermon climaxing in the quotations of the three Scriptures in verses 33–35, each connected through linking keywords or ideas.[427] The first quotation, from Psalm 2, was originally an enthronement psalm, but had been understood as describing the Messiah by this time.[428] This text and its connection to David is the bridge to the next passage, Isaiah 55:3 in the LXX.[429] The next linkage (to verse 35) comes through the word holy (ὅσια/

---

421. Bock, *Acts*, 448.

422. Acts 13:16, 26, 47–48.

423. Acts 13:11–12, 15.

424. Acts 13:42–44.

425. Acts 13:45, 50.

426. Keener, *Acts*, 2:2060. Keener suggests that Paul covers the entire narrative ground of 7:2–44 in just two verses, 17–18, but zooms in on 7:45–46 in 13:19–22.

427. A process called *gezerah shevah*, one of Hillel's rabbinic rules of interpretation found in *Avot de-Rabbi Natan* 37; *Sifraintrod.* 1:7; *B. San.* 7b. Also, see Keener, *Acts*, 2:2071, and footnote there, Bock, *Acts*, 457.

428. Keener, *Acts*, 2:2070; Bock, *Acts*, 456. υἱός μου εἶ σύ, ἐγὼ σήμερον γεγέννηκά σε.

429. τὰ ὅσια Δαυιδ τὰ πιστά. Also, see Bright, *History*; Harrelson, *Fertility*; Vaux, *Israel*.

ὅσιόν) and connects to Psalm 16:10 (15:10 LXX).[430] "The exegetical link with Psalm 16:10 (15:10 LXX) is essential to connect the promise in Isaiah explicitly to the resurrection hope."[431] Thus, Luke is leveraging the connection to David in order to further his emphases on Jesus as the climax.

Luke continues to emphasize Jesus as the fulfillment of the promises of old to the very end of the speech.[432] Following this (in vv. 38–39) is a call to respond, which was not present in Stephen's speech: "Let it be known to you therefore, my brothers, that through this man forgiveness of sins is proclaimed to you; by this Jesus everyone who believes is set free from all those sins from which you could not be freed by the law of Moses."[433] "The key to everything offered here is Jesus."[434] Thus, Paul's speech shows how, in Luke's mind, the history of Israel naturally climaxes in the person of Jesus. The Abrahamic covenant suggested that the whole world would be blessed because of the Hebrew people.[435] From Luke's perspective, this is finally becoming a reality through Jesus and the early church. The God-fearers and Gentiles turning to God and being welcomed into the community is a beautiful fulfillment of what God had promised generations ago. This climactic moment has to remain central for the God-fearing Gentile reader. In this manner, the reader's social identity as a follower of Jesus, as one who responds to the gospel, is shaped as he or she is able to be a part of the story.

These two speeches by Stephen and Paul represent an early Christian view of Jewish salvation history and the promises of the Messiah in the Old Testament, as hinted at on the road to Emmaus. Although they have some overlap, they complement each other in that they highlight different central focuses of Jesus' Messianic role. Stephen emphasizes his connection with outcasts, Moses and the New Exodus, and the failure of the Jewish people hinting at the inclusion of Gentiles. Paul's speech complements the content of Stephen's and emphasizes Jesus' royal connection with David and prophecy of the resurrection. And although the content of Paul's speech seems to be less focused on outsiders, Gentiles are converted at the conclusion of Paul's speech the following week.[436] These are key elements for Luke to include to advance his agenda of identity formation in God-fearers. Not only do these speeches show the trajectory from Israel's history to God's present work in the followers of the Way, they actually lead to the conversion and inclusion of outsiders in the movements, whether directly

---

430. οὐδὲ δώσεις τὸν ὅσιόν σου ἰδεῖν διαφθοράν.

431. Keener, *Acts*, 2:2072.

432. Also, see Merrill, "Four Hundred Fifty Years"; Tannehill, "Israel."

433. Stephen's audience, the Sanhedrin accusers did not afford him the possibility to offer a traditional call to repent. However, there is a statement at the end about who Jesus is (i.e., "the Righteous one") and perhaps sets the scene for what Paul will do here, a few chapters later. Thus, the reader has a chance to respond.

434. Bock, *Acts*, 458.

435. Gen 12:2; 22:18.

436. Acts 13:47–48.

as in the case of Acts 13, or through the introduction of Paul who will become the missionary to the Gentiles in Acts 7.

Conclusion

As I have shown, there is a thread that begins in verse one, running through the canticles and prophecies in the birth narrative of Jesus, declared at the inauguration of his public ministry, and whispered about among strangers walking along the road after his resurrection that this Jesus is the answer to the yearnings of Israel. Wright says it well: "[Early Christians] *told, and lived, a form of Israel's story which reached its climax in Jesus and which then issued in their spirit-given new life and task.*"[437]

The two speeches, then, reemphasize Jewish salvation history and give the reader a historical perspective as to the nature of the gospel, which is Jesus as the fulfillment of Israel's story, fulfilling the promises made to Israel, and making way for all who would come to him in the New Testament era. This thread presents the gospel of Jesus Christ to the God-fearing audience, allowing them to join with the community of the early church and have their social identity formed, going from someone in between Judaism and paganism, to become full members of the body of Christ. However, because of the emphasis in the Luke–Acts narrative on characters, observing characterization as it relates to identity formation in these volumes is key. We will now look at ways in which characters narratively help build identity in the reader through prototypes.

---

437. Wright, *People*, 456.

4

Luke's Use of Prototypes and Exemplars

LUKE'S TRANSFORMATIVE ILLOCUTIONARY INTENT is to include God-fearers, and therefore, presumed outsiders, in the movement of the Way by shaping the sense of social identity of his (God-fearing) audience. It appears that his tool of choice for doing so is the use of cultural memory that alludes to Israel's salvation history. Having explored God-fearers in Acts and in the first century in chapter 2 and the role of decentralization in the advancement of the gospel in chapter 3, we can now turn to two other specific ways Luke seeks to create social identity in his audience. I seek to test whether some of the key characters in Luke's two volumes are best understood as (1) prototypes or (2) exemplars for emulation by his readers. Following an examination of relevant scholarship, we will address the role of Luke's most important prototype: Cornelius. As far as exemplars are concerned, we will have to cover a wide range of narrated events involving minor characters. Irrespective of Luke's narrative emphases (one key prototype but numerous exemplar stories), it is crucial to keep in mind that both strategies serve to form social identity in the readers by drawing on their empathy with key characters in the story, even and especially where those characters are almost inevitably "minor" in status.

A key part of identity formation, according to Liu and László, is to establish "a surface structure empathy hierarchy that influences how the reader or listener constructs the meaning of the narrated event and opens the way for participatory affective responses."[1] Susumu Kuno coins the phrase "surface structure empathy hierarchy," and he is mostly talking about words in sentence construction.[2] Richard Gerrig is particularly interested in the participatory responses of the readers of narratives.[3] He says, "The traveler [i.e., reader, hearer] returns to their world of origin, somewhat changed by the journey. For the majority of narratives, we would be surprised if some mental structures were not changed as a function of their experience. At a minimum,

---

1. Liu and László, "Narrative Theory," 96; Kuno, "Subject"; Gerrig, *Narrative Worlds*.

2. Kuno, "Subject," 432. For examples in other texts, see Esler, "Prototypes"; *Conflict*; Roitto, *Behaving*.

3. Gerrig, *Narrative Worlds*, 65–96.

we would expect to have created memory representations to encode the actual propositional information in the narrative."[4] In other words, how are the original hearers of Acts connecting with the characters, the stories, the rhetoric, and the message of Luke's second volume? To attend to this question, we need to understand the literary function of prototypes. We will follow that discussion by examining a number of prototypes in Luke–Acts, before moving to exemplars, and discussing a number of those as well. We will also look at the use of angels and visions in Luke's corpus as well as the connections between Sinai and Pentecost.

What is a Prototype?

Hogg, Hohmann, and Rivera state, "According to social identity theory, people cognitively represent social groups as fuzzy sets of attributes that define one group and distinguish it from relevant other groups. Called prototypes, these fuzzy sets not only describe the group's attributes but also, very importantly, prescribe how one should think, feel, and behave as a member of the group."[5] The definition used by Smith and Zarate of a prototype is "a summary representation which captures the central tendency of the category."[6] Thus, we must ask how a particular character in Luke–Acts is representative of the target audience. In the narrative, the author offers prototypical characters that the audience can relate to.[7] This allows them to empathize with the character and have their identity formed through engagement with the prototype. It also allows the author to encourage readers toward certain behaviors using the prototypes' words, behaviors, and interactions with other groups. Behavior formation is an important part of forming social identity, as we saw in chapter 1. To this end, Luke will highlight certain characters as prototypes who represent a group (i.e., prototypical martyr, prototypical God-fearer, etc.). Other characters will act as exemplars, who rather than representing a group, will embody a specific value, as we will discuss below.

Prototype theory started as a critique of the classic view of categorization, suggesting that while viewing groups based on shared categories is not all wrong, it is far too simple.[8] The theory "shows that human categorization is based on principles

---

4. Gerrig, *Narrative Worlds*, 16.

5. Hogg et al., "Groups." Also, see the works of the developer of prototype theory, Rosch, such as "Representation," "Natural Categories," and "Principles."

6. Smith and Zarate, "Exemplar," 245; Wattenmaker et al., "Linear," 159.

7. For the sake of clarity, I will refer to exemplars and prototypes as representatives *of* the audience and *for* the audience. The two prepositions denote the audience's sense of identification with story characters ("of") as well as the benefits derived from that sense of identification ("for"). Some scholars prefer "to" and "for," using them interchangeably. To avoid confusion, I will only use the former when I quote an author that uses that term.

8. Lakoff, *Dangerous Things*, 5.

that extend far beyond those envisioned in the classical theory."[9] But elements of this theory are not without criticism. The definition Smith and Zarate offer, for example, has been criticized for being too static and not accurately representing the diversity that may exist in a group.[10] Naturally, groups are made up of individuals who are varied and unique, and thus, a lone, static prototype is difficult, as it does not perfectly represent everyone. Oakes, Haslam, and Turner suggest that "a category *prototype* [is the] best example of the category" and that "category membership requires a certain level of similarity to the prototype."[11]

Prototypical Figures in Acts

A number of characters in Acts may be seen as prototypes of the new Christian identity, starting with Peter and Paul as prototypes for the purpose of Jew and Gentile inclusion in the early church, as some scholars have suggested.[12] These prototypical figures model for the readers the new identity they are moving into and help facilitate the recategorization process.[13] Typically, prototypes in Luke's writings are characterized by a strong connection between the projected goals of the larger narrative in that they engage the imagination of the audience. The projected readers' imagination is drawn into the narrative in such a way that identification takes place on the psychological level. This connection makes the character a prime candidate for emulation in multiple areas by the reader (as opposed to an exemplar, which models only a single area of emulation). We determine which characters in Luke's writings are prototypes by ascertaining their characterological fit with the projected goals of the larger narrative. Where significant overlap exists, the character is a prime candidate for emulation by the reader. When group members' identities are salient, they relate to the prototype of their group and behave in ways consistent with those expected from group members, thus forming social identity.[14] In this case, the group identity that is salient is connection with the new Christian community over and above the individual or subgroup identities (i.e., Jew, Gentile, Greek, God-fearer,

---

9. Lakoff, *Dangerous Things*, 5.

10. See, for example, Marohl, *Faithfulness*, 113; Oakes et al., "Prototypicality," 75. Prototype theory has a vast scholarship and covers a wide range of categories, including culture, anthropology, language, psychology, and mathematics. See Wittgenstein, *Investigations*; Austin, *Papers*; Zadeh, "Fuzzy Sets"; Lounsbury, *Formal Account*; Berlin and Kay, *Color*; Brown, "Thing"; Ekman, *Universals*; Rosch and Mervis, "Resemblances"; Rosch et al., "Objects."

11. Oakes et al., "Prototypicality," 75. Additionally, Lakoff, *Dangerous Things*, 136–52, discusses some misinterpretations of the theory and how some have chosen to return to the classical view.

12. Baker, *Identity*, xv.

13. Baker, *Identity*, 12. For more on prototypes in Acts and elsewhere in Scripture, see Berends, "Pentecost"; Punt, "Paul"; Esler, "Prototypes"; Groenvold, "Child."

14. Turner et al., *Rediscovering*; "Self and Collective"; Turner, "Social Categorization."

etc.). For example, the Ethiopian Eunuch takes on a new social identity by participating in the boundary crossing ritual of water baptism.[15]

Although scholarly work has been done to show how the use of prototypical characters brings together two different subgroups, those open to Gentile inclusion in the Christian movement and those opposed to Gentile inclusion in the Christian movement, this present work, instead, is focused on a third category of people, God-fearers, and considers how prototypical figures in Acts would have impacted this group and their identity-forming process.[16] The claim that Peter and Paul are prototypical of their respective categories stands, but misses the most important prototype in the book. Cornelius is the prototypical God-fearer, and Luke's narrative purpose with this character cannot be overlooked. In addition, a full picture of Luke's narrative aims must include both volumes. Thus, it is vital to trace the use and development of prototypes through the entire work.

Jesus as Prototype

The most important prototype for the Christ group and the central character of Luke's writings is Jesus. As the unique prototype, he is to be followed and worshipped, not simply emulated. This is shown in multiple ways between the narratives of Luke and Acts. Obviously the major points of the narrative, like the birth story,[17] the passion narrative, the long teaching sections, and the miracle stories all focus on Jesus as the central figure. Although Jesus only appears in the first few verses of the book of Acts,[18] the book stresses the continued work that his followers do in seeking to follow his example as a prototype, leader of the New Christian Movement, and Messiah. Jesus remains a central character in the narrative through appearances, quotations, and flashbacks that feature his prototypicality.[19] In addition, other important characters are seen modeling Jesus. The disciples heal in dramatic ways similar to how Jesus healed,[20] they give long, moving sermons the way Jesus had,[21] and we see them communicate concern for the poor and outcasts, something Jesus incorporates in his first prophetic statement about himself.[22] Thus, we see that Jesus is mirrored by his followers in many ways. He serves as the ultimate prototype in the Christian movement.[23]

---

15. Acts 8:27–38.
16. Baker, *Identity*, xv–xviii.
17. See chapter 3.
18. Acts 1:1–9.
19. Acts 9; 10:11–15/11:7–9; 11:16; 18:9–10; 20:32; 22:6–11; 22:17–21; 23:11; 26:14–18. Also, see DeOrio, "Phenomenology"; Warrington, "Healing"; Gempf, "Apollos"; Schalück, "Disciples."
20. See Luke 5:17–26; Acts 3:1–10.
21. See Luke 6:17–38; Acts 2; 7; 13; etc.
22. See Luke 4:18–19; Acts 9:36; 10:4; 24:17.
23. An entire chapter of this book could be written on Jesus as the prototype of the New Christian

This modeling by other prototypical characters of Jesus draws the reader into similar behavior through the empathy with the characters in the story.

The Prototypicality of Peter

Some suggest that Peter is the new prototypical ingroup member in Jesus' absence, signaled by intertextual links between the characters, and highlighted by Peter's transformation in Luke, who starts as a sinner not worthy of Jesus' presence and becomes the leader of the disciples by the end of volume one and of the church by the first few scenes in Acts.[24] A few of these significant similarities are worth noting here. First, Peter's first words in Acts (1:16–17, 20–22) are reminiscent of the last words of Jesus in Luke 24:44–49. Peter can be seen as an interpreter of scripture in the early scenes in Acts. In addition, this is the first parallel of many between the two figures in the early part of the book of Acts.[25]

A second comparison comes from the Pentecost event. Following the arrival of the Holy Spirit and people speaking as the Spirit enabled them (2:3–4), Peter gives a speech in which he quotes one of Israel's prophets and speaks of one of their famous rulers (2:14–36). Tannehill sees similarities to Jesus' baptism, where the Holy Spirit descends on him as a dove (3:22), and Jesus offers his inaugural speech in Nazareth, where he quotes one of Israel's prophets (4:16–30).[26] The crowd's response is similar as well (τί ποιήσωμεν, ἄνδρες ἀδελφοί; in 2:37 compared with τί οὖν ποιήσωμεν; in Luke 3:10).

A third comparison of Peter in Acts with Jesus in Luke is the scene of Peter healing the crippled beggar in Acts 3. Peter encounters a man "crippled from birth," begging for money. Peter tells him to "Get up and walk" ([ἔγειρε καὶ] περιπάτει). Similarly, Jesus, in Luke 5, encounters a "paralyzed man" as he is teaching. After forgiving the man's sins and causing quite a stir among the Pharisees and teachers of the law present, Jesus asks, "Which is easier: to say 'your sins are forgiven' or to say 'get up and walk'?" ([ἔγειρε καὶ] περιπάτει). Tannehilll notes the "resonance" between these scenes that deepens the reader's "experience of the story."[27] Peter's similarities to Jesus in healing help him be viewed as a prototype for the Christ group identity. In this way, Peter is worthy of emulation by the audience as he re-images Jesus and models the transformation and inclusion common in the Way.

Movement, which extends to his followers today. However, this is out of scope, as the focus is the connection to God-fearers in the narrative. That is the reason for the single paragraph introducing Jesus as a prototype. For more on this topic, see Burridge, *Imitating Jesus*.

24. Baker, *Identity*, 74. Toney, "Paul," offers a rundown of the different events in the lives of Jesus, Paul, and Peter that are in common.

25. For Peter's similarities to these other characters in Luke–Acts, see Moessner, "Suffer"; Bond and Hurtado, *Peter*; Krentz, "Peter"; Berder, *Pierre*.

26. Tannehill, *Acts*, 29.

27. Tannehill, *Acts*, 49–52. Also, see Kamba, "Healing"; Parsons, "Character"; Taylor, "Gate"; Cowton, "Alms"; Butticaz, "Actes."

However, it is possible to view Peter and the Twelve less positively than scholars traditionally have. For example, despite the importance of the Twelve and the expectation the reader has for them at the conclusion of Luke, they play a relatively small role in the book of Acts. Tannehill says, "After Stephen and Philip enter the narrative, the apostles are seldom presented as initiators of new stages of the mission. Rather the apostles and the Jerusalem church respond to what others are doing and affirm it."[28] Tannehill is correct about the secondary nature of the Twelve here, but he understates it. Tannehill seems to overlook perhaps the most glaring surprise in the book of Acts, that is, that the group readers expect to lead in the continuation of Jesus' ministry fizzle out rather quickly. At the end of Luke's Gospel, for example, the reader encounters the eleven gathered in a room (24:33), having an experience with the risen Jesus that inspires joy (24:41). He opens their minds to understand the Scriptures and blesses them (24:45–51), leaving them continually in the Temple blessing God (24:53). The reader expects this group to lead the outward expansion of ministry in Acts.[29] While the eleven are on the scene, and Peter does play a role early (Acts 1:15–22; 2:14–38; 3:1–26; 4:1–23; 8:14–25), it is less than one would expect. Instead, the eleven are outdone by others, such as Philip (8:5–38), Stephen (6:5–15; 7:1—8:2), Apollos (18:24—19:1), Priscilla and Aquila (18:2–26) and Paul (9:1–28; 13:9–50; 14:1–23; 15:2–40), who becomes the main character of the second half of the book. As mentioned in chapter 2, this emergence of minor characters is key to Luke's program of decentralization.[30] The fact that the reader will be surprised to learn that people of disadvantaged status play this role should be taken as further evidence of Luke's program of radical inclusion. Tannehill seems to take every opportunity to praise Peter and the disciples, even emphasizing that the role of "verifying and affirming" as an important one,[31] and fails to critique their surprising absence. Perhaps this is because Tannehill is fairly typical in his claim and seeks to view the disciples as the heroes rather than allowing their actions (and failure to act) to tell the story.[32] In fact, it is difficult to find any scholars who are willing to critique the disciples at this point. Ehrhardt suggests that Peter and John are interested in maintaining apostolic control, but still misses the glaring lack of advancement by Peter and the other disciples.[33] Keener states, "Luke carefully documents how the Jerusalem church recognizes each stage in the church's expansion, showing the

---

28. Tannehill, *Acts*, 143.

29. It could be suggested that whereas the apostles do not play a large role in Acts, they did not play are large role in Luke's gospel either. However, as Twelftree, *Spirit*, 19, argues, "The apostles go on to play a larger part in [Luke's] narrative that any other Gospel." The expectation of that continuing in volume two is apt. The disagreement concerns the importance of the role played by the apostles in Acts and whether or not Luke is decentralizing them in favor of other minor characters.

30. See chapter 2 on Luke's God-fearers.

31. Tannehill, *Acts*, 143.

32. In addition to Tannehill, other examples of scholars who are defensive of the apostles are Keener, *Acts*, 2:1521–22; Haenchen, *Acts*, 314; Tyson, "Dinner"; Johnson, *Acts*, 11; Ehrhardt, *Acts*, 45–46.

33. Ehrhardt, *Acts*, 45–46.

continuity between the original apostolic mission and the Diaspora church of his own day."[34] Thus Keener still misses this point. Some go even further. Clark, for example, says "Peter and John, as representatives of the apostles, preach not only in Jerusalem, but also in Samaria. Peter travels more widely still, and is used to preach to a group of Gentiles. . . . In this respect he exemplifies a wider legitimizing role possessed by all the twelve apostles."[35] Perhaps the traveling of Peter and John outside of Jerusalem would be noteworthy of their missional activity and "widening role" if not for those outside of the Twelve who do much more significant ministry in the early church, such as Stephen, Philip, Paul, Barnabas, and others.

It is important that we do not miss this point, for, although the disciples play a relatively minor role compared to what readers of Luke's two volumes expect, the Holy Spirit raises up people to bring forth the message anyway. The Holy Spirit is not content to wait for the Twelve to gain clarity. Rather, God has no trouble finding people like Philip, Stephen, Cornelius, Paul, Barnabas, Priscilla, Apollos, and other minor characters who will do the work of the ministry in the early church.[36] Luke's intent is not to indict the Twelve disciples, but to follow a strategy of using anyone who is willing to partner with the Holy Spirit to expand the geographical and social dimensions of the gospel. This includes both the partnering with and evangelism of marginalized people, including the reader, in both the subject and the object of the mission.[37] The gospel goes forward despite internal or external opposition. This can be seen as a key focus throughout the book of Acts. At almost every turn, opposition arises, whether externally, as in the Jewish leaders,[38] the Artemis cult,[39] or Roman opposition,[40] or internally, as in Ananias and Sapphira,[41] the debate over the Gentiles,[42] Simon the Sorcerer,[43] and

---

34. Keener, *Acts*, 2:1521–22.

35. Clark, "Role," 173.

36. See chapter 2, which discusses minor characters.

37. It may be suggested that the disciples should be seen as heroes and that the reader would be inclined to draw positive conclusions about them. Yet we cannot escape the reality of largely unmet expectations when it comes to the Twelve. The disciples may not be villains, but their underachievement cannot be ignored, lest they unfairly overshadow characters like Stephen, Paul, Philip, the Ethiopian Eunuch, and Cornelius, who somewhat surprisingly emerge on the scene in Acts. This latter group actually delivers the expectations that the reader originally and reasonably had for the disciples. Scholars may view Peter and the other disciples as heroes if they wish. But the outward narrative move of the Holy Spirit to use all sorts of unexpected characters with a view to reach the marginalized remains at the center of Luke's mission in Acts. It sends a direct message to the reader, who shares in the insecurities of the marginalized missionaries and converts.

38. Acts 4; 7; 20–23.

39. Acts 19.

40. Acts 24–25.

41. Acts 5.

42. Acts 11; 15.

43. Acts 8:9–24.

others.[44] This failure of the disciples to drive the ministry throughout Acts can be seen as internal opposition that the Holy Spirit is once again able to overcome. The fact that only Peter and John become verifiers of the inclusion of outsiders (Samaritans and Cornelius) illustrates the failure of the group as a whole.[45]

Peter is the only disciple who continues to appear in the narrative after chapter 8. Paul, not one of the Twelve, becomes the more prominent figure in the book. As we will see, minor characters do remarkable things one would expect the Twelve to do. Thus, while some see Peter is an important prototype modeling inclusion of Gentile converts, he may more accurately be said to be a somewhat reluctant prototype. Consider the following examples.

Peter's primary role is to facilitate Gentile inclusion as the spokesperson and leader of the Twelve, and he does this quite well. It is important not to underestimate the role of Peter in being a part of the inclusion of Cornelius. However, the scene in Acts 10 does not portray Peter all that positively. Tannehill calls Peter a "reluctant initiator."[46] He must be told three times by the heavenly voice to "kill and eat."[47] When Peter does begin to speak at Cornelius's house, for example, his words sound more like a confession: "Then Peter began to speak to them: I truly understand that God shows no partiality, but in every nation anyone who fears him and does what is right is acceptable to him."[48] The account of the falling of the Spirit here is different than previous accounts for several reasons. For one, this is the first time Gentiles are receiving the Spirit. Additionally, there is no laying on of hands or baptism, as in other instances.[49] Peter continues with his explanation, but does not get very far, because "while Peter was still speaking, the Holy Spirit fell upon all who heard the word."[50] Contra Haenchen, who suggests that the speech is concluded and not interrupted,[51] Keener's suggestion is more apt, who states, "the Spirit interrupts Peter's words."[52] The Spirit moves forward without waiting for him to finish his sermon. Peter's words, apparently, are not needed for this move of the Spirit to happen; he is there only to witness and to testify to the critics in the next chapter. He could be seen as an observer of the work of the Spirit in Cornelius's house rather than a participant. In chapter 11, Peter tells the story to the circumcised believers who criticize him, but accept his testimony

---

44. See Marshall, "Enemy"; Schnabel, "Opposition"; Scholtus, "Problemas"; Gradl, "Alles"; Pervo, "Gates."

45. Acts 8:14–17; 10.

46. Tannehill, *Acts*, 143.

47. Acts 10:13.

48. Acts 10:35–36 NRSV.

49. Acts 2:38; 8:17. See Keener, *Acts*, 2:1809.

50. Acts 10:44 NRSV.

51. Haenchen, *Acts*, 353.

52. Keener, *Acts*, 2:1810. Also, see Plunkett, "Ethnocentricity"; Bovon, "Tradition"; Kilgallen, "Clean"; Garroway, "Irresistibility."

and have no further objections.[53] After his testimony in 15:7, he is not mentioned again. Peter does play an important role in facilitating Gentile inclusion to the circumcised believers in Jerusalem. However, so much of the movement of the narrative is being decentralized away from Jerusalem, away from the circumcised group through the inclusion of outsiders, and away from the Twelve, that this might be seen as Peter's (somewhat muted) "last hurrah" in Acts.

In the end, Peter serves as a prototype representing the circumcision group that models the inclusion of Gentile converts to the Way. If members of the circumcision group are in Luke's readership, Peter models for this group the eventual embracing of Gentiles into the family of God. However, I have used the phrase "reluctant prototype" for Peter because, as a representative of the Twelve, he falls short of the expectations set up by Luke's gospel. However, this does not invalidate him as one to be emulated. Instead, it places Peter as one possible character for emulation among many other minor characters in Luke's corpus.

Stephen: The Prototypical Martyr

A notable omission in scholarly discussion of prototypes is Stephen. He plays a crucial role in the narrative that the author expects the reader to understand. In the narrative of Acts, Stephen comes on the scene quickly, makes a noticeable impact, and departs as the first martyr in the book. Appearing in the narrative only in chapters 6 and 7, his climactic speech comes in chapter 7. He is buried in early chapter 8[54] and then referred back to twice more in the book.[55] Despite this quick trajectory of his story, it can be argued that Stephen serves the role of the prototypical martyr for the early Christian movement. As the first to be executed for his faith, Stephen models the noble way one should give his or her life for Christ. He is not only worthy of emulation because he is willing to die, but, as Luke shows, in the way he embraces death and dies like Jesus. Like other prototypes we have discussed, his worthiness of emulation is tied to his connection to Jesus. In addition, he is an example of decentralization in the narrative, as it is Stephen who is introduced so positively and testifies before the Sanhedrin, not Peter who has emerged as the leader of the early church. Stephen emerges as the first character outside of the Twelve to represent the new Christian movement and to speak authoritatively. Surprisingly, an unexpected voice of authority other than the voice of the Twelve emerges powerfully in the narrative.[56]

---

53. "When they heard this, they were silenced. And they praised God, saying, 'Then God has given even to the Gentiles the repentance that leads to life'" (Acts 11:18).

54. Acts 8:2.

55. Acts 11:19; 22:20.

56. See chapters 2 and 3, which discuss decentralization.

Stephen is introduced as positively as anyone in Luke's corpus.[57] He is said to be "full of God's grace and power" and performs "great wonders and signs among the people."[58] He is full of wisdom and apparently a great orator, as his critics could not "withstand the wisdom and the Spirit with which he spoke."[59] In 6:15 his face was like that of an angel. Much like the prophets in the Old Testament, including and especially Moses, Stephen is divinely affirmed as a man of God to be emulated.[60] Inescapably, the reader is reminded of Jesus on the mount of transfiguration.[61] Stephen is now the primary model and inspiration for proper conduct before critics of the gospel.

Many scholars have pointed out that the portrayal of Stephen's death recalls that of Jesus.[62] We have seen how Peter and Paul were equated with Jesus and his ministry in many ways. But Stephen becomes like Jesus in the circumstances surrounding their deaths.[63] Although it has not been typically recognized, it is important to note that his death is key to him being a prototype in the Lukan text. Here are the most significant similarities between the deaths of Jesus and Stephen:

Jesus in Luke's Passion Narrative[64]	Stephen in Acts
Hearing before Sanhedrin (22:66)	Hearing before Sanhedrin (6:12)
Announces Son of Man at God's right hand (22:69)	Sees Son of Man at God's right hand (7:55–56)

---

57. The other character one thinks of being introduced so positively is Cornelius (Acts 10:1–4). It is noteworthy that the two most positive introductions for Luke are a Jewish Hellenist and the prototypical God-fearer. These are clearly strategic moves of inclusion and ethos by Luke.

58. Acts 6:8.

59. Acts 6:10. Tannehill, *Acts*, 83, notes the special emphasis on wisdom (σωφία) here, a word used only four times in Acts, all of which are in chapters 6 and 7. He also sees this as a fulfillment on Luke 21:15.

60. Exod 34:29–35.

61. Luke 9:28–36.

62. This is a common sentiment throughout history. See Abbott, *Acts*, 93; Foakes-Jackson, *Acts*, 58; Simon, *Stephen*, 21; Goulder, *Type*, 42–43; Stronstad, *Prophethood* 100; Hamm, *Acts*, 40–41; Talbert, *Acts*, 66–67; Pervo, *Acts*, 195; Green, *Acts*, 745–46; Keener, *Acts*, 2:1430.

63. See Pesch, *Die Apostelgeschichte*, 238, who talks about the similar conspiracies surrounding the deaths of Jesus and Stephen: "Auch vor Gerich twird die Verleumdung des Stephanus fortgesetzt, jetzt durch 'falsche Zeugen,' die 'aufgestellt,' also bewuß tungesetzlich imVerfahren eingesetzt werden. Im Prozess Jesu läßt Lukas den Hohen Rat selbst zum Falschzeugen gegen Jesus werden; die Falschzeugen mit dem Tempelwort läßter—angesichts der Tempelverbundenheit der Urgemeinde—erst gegen Stephanus auftreten." ("The defamation of Stephen continues even in court, now by 'false witnesses' who 'are set up' in the sense of deliberately being used illegally in the proceedings. In the trial of Jesus, Luke presents the high council itself as a false witness against Jesus. Given the close connection of the temple with the early church, the false witnesses with the word about the temple are only marshaled later, against Stephen.")

64. Keener, *Acts*, 2:1430.

Jesus in Luke's Passion Narrative[64]	Stephen in Acts
Condemned for blasphemy from his own testimony (22:70–72)	Condemned for blasphemy from his own testimony (7:56–57)
Outside the City (23:26)	Outside the City (7:58)
"Receive my spirit!" (23:46)	"Receive my spirit!" (7:59)
"Forgive them" (23:34)	"Forgive them" (7:60)

Stephen's reference to the "Son of man" is one of only four uses of this term in the New Testament outside of the Gospels.[65] Keener connects this as dependence on Jesus' words before the Sanhedrin "all the more likely."[66] Luke is intentionally drawing parallels between these two characters in the way they are presented. Since Jesus is the ultimate prototype in Luke's writings, here is simply another example of an early Christian being portrayed as similar to the ultimate prototype in the way that he dies.[67]

As Keener also points out, Stephen has similarities to Moses as well. "In Acts 7:30–31, Moses sees God's glory in the bush; here Stephen witnesses Jesus along with God's glory in heaven. That Stephen's face is like that of an angel in 6:15 may also evoke Moses's reflecting God's glory. Far from blaspheming Moses (6:11), Stephen is his true follower."[68] Thus, his prototypicality comes not only from his comparison to Jesus, but in a few hints at being like Moses—a hero of the Old Testament, the leader of the first exodus as Jesus is the leader of the New Exodus, and a feature character in his speech—as well. Tannehill includes Joseph in the comparisons, noting "Stephen shares qualities with God's most important messengers."[69]

Lastly, it might be a testament to Stephen's prototypical significance that he plays such a key role in the unfolding of the narrative of the book of Acts. As with the conversion of Cornelius discussed below, his death is a major turning point in the narrative, as it drives the church out from Jerusalem toward much more expansion and advancement of the gospel (Acts 11:19). It also introduces Saul/Paul, who is giving approval to his death.

So, how precisely is Stephen, the prototypical martyr, helpful for the implied Lukan audience? Persecution is a consistently developed subject in Acts.[70] It stands to reason that the implied audience may be facing some sort of persecution. While we should not

65. Used also in Heb 2:6 as a quotation of Ps 144:3; Rev 1:13; 14:14.

66. Keener, *Acts*, 2:1437.

67. Matthews, "Clemency"; Sayles, "Clemency"; Bash, "Difficult Texts."

68. Keener, *Acts*, 2:1437.

69. Tannehill, *Acts*, 83–84. Also, see Moessner, "Suffer"; Moessner, "Paul"; Hilhorst, "Moses"; Donaldson, "Typology."

70. Luke 6:22–23, 27–29; 9:23; 10:3–16; 11:49–52; 14:27; 21:12–18; 22:35–36; Acts 4:1–31; 5:17–32, 40–41; 8:1 and the references to the persecutions of Paul in Acts 9:16; 13; 14; 21:13.

assume direct connections between empirical evidence and implied referentiality, empirical data exists that make the idea of the church in Acts facing persecution plausible.[71] Thus, it would make sense for Luke to provide a model for suffering, a prototype for the audience to connect to. Stephen serves this role, and does it masterfully.

Paul: The Prototypical Missionary to the Gentiles

Another prominent prototypical figure in Acts is the Apostle Paul.[72] Similar to Peter, Paul is also a prototypical figure of the Christ group identity. The difference is, however, that while Peter is connected with Jerusalem, and in some ways with those who oppose Gentile inclusion, Paul not only supports the mission to Gentiles, but is the primary missionary in service of that viewpoint. Paul emerges partway through Acts and serves as the main character of the second half of volume two and the prototype of Christ group identity. As a Jewish Pharisee whose life is transformed into service for Christ for the purpose of reaching the Gentiles, Paul works as a classic example of the outward trajectory of the move of God and as a challenge and model for emulation by audience members who may not be inclusive of outsiders. Interestingly, despite the radical geographic decentralization in Luke–Acts, Paul continues to be connected with Jerusalem, and the city continues to be a part of the narrative even after it ceases to be the epicenter

---

71. Suggested dates for the book of Acts range from the early sixties to the second century (Keener, *Acts*, 1:384). Keener suggests a date of shortly after 70 CE, and mentions that this view has "by far the most adherents" (Keener, *Acts*, 1:384). I tend to agree, as it appears to be written from the vantage point of someone in the middle of the second half of the first century, which is most important for our purposes. For a good summary of the possible date ranges for Luke–Acts, see Dicken, "Author," 7–26. If around 70 CE is accepted as the date, this places the authorship of Acts shortly after the reign of Nero and after the church had come through the great persecutions that accompanied his reign: Tacitus, *Annals*, 15.44, lists some of the terrible persecutions that Christians had to endure under Nero: "Mockery of every sort was added to their deaths. Covered with the skins of beasts, they were torn by dogs and perished, or were nailed to crosses, or were doomed to the flames and burnt, to serve as a nightly illumination, when daylight had expired. Nero offered his gardens for the spectacle, and was exhibiting a show in the circus, while he mingled with the people in the dress of a charioteer or stood aloft on a car. Hence, even for criminals who deserved extreme and exemplary punishment, there arose a feeling of compassion; for it was not, as it seemed, for the public good, but to glut one man's cruelty, that they were being destroyed." This fits with the implied audience prescribed in the text.

72. The title "apostle" (ἀπόστολος) begins to take on an expanded inclusion throughout the book of Acts. The noun form (as opposed to the verb form, ἀποστέλλω, meaning "I send") occurs six times in Luke and twenty-eight times in Acts. All of the references in Luke and most in Acts seem to be referring to the Twelve. However, in 14:14 Barnabas and Paul are called apostles. This certainly seems to show that the term begins to apply to a wider group beyond the Twelve. Paul will use the term for others outside of the Twelve in his other writings (Rom 16:7; Gal 1:19). This is another example of decentralization in the Christian movement. For more on the use of this term in general, see Nolland, *Luke*, 1:265–69; Kennedy, "Scope"; Munck, "Paul"; Lightfoot, "Name"; Rengstorf, *Apostolate*; Barrett, *Signs*; Agnew, "Origin"; "Apostle"; Kirk, "Apostleship"; Horbury, "Twelve." For a look at the use of this term specifically in Luke–Acts, see Menoud, "Additions"; Schmithals, *Office*; Pfitzner, "'Pneumatic'"; Haacker, "Verwendung"; Sweetland, "Following Jesus." For a focus on this term in Paul's letters, see Dorsey, "Apostolos"; Thorley, "Junia."

of the kingdom of God. This may be to remind the reader of Paul's Judean upbringing and customs, and to validate his superordinate identity.[73]

Luke–Acts has an interesting relationship to Jerusalem. Many of Luke's ninety uses of the term are neutral references to the city. However, a number of times it is clear that the relation to the city is surprisingly antagonistic or decentralizing. The canticles set up very positive expectations about the city of Jerusalem and the Temple, and offer a traditional view of the festivals, which Jesus and his family celebrate.[74] Then, the Lukan travel narrative, which begins in 9:51, shifts the focus primarily on Jerusalem as a destination. It is highly surprising, then, that Jesus says things like, "it is impossible for a prophet to be killed outside of Jerusalem,"[75] and "Daughters of Jerusalem, do not weep for me, but weep for yourselves and for your children."[76] The implied reader is stunned to encounter verses like Luke 13:4, where Jesus asks, "Or those eighteen who were killed when the tower of Siloam fell on them—do you think that they were worse offenders than all the others living in Jerusalem?" Another example is the parable of the good Samaritan in 10:30–36. The prospective helpers (the priest and Levite) are coming down (κατέβαινεν)[77] from Jerusalem, presumably having ministered in the Temple, and thus, representing the city. These characters surprisingly do not help the man, but rather the hero is a Samaritan, Jerusalem's enemy!

Luke also presents a movement away from Jerusalem in volume two. The Pentecost encounter, the early days of the church, and initial persecution all occur in Jerusalem. However, by chapter 8, a stronger persecution has broken out and the church scatters. Acts 1:8 paradigmatically describes the outward move of the gospel, resulting in the decentralization of the kingdom of God. What are the clearest examples of the focus having surprisingly shifted from Jerusalem?

Antagonistic Uses of Ἰερουσαλήμ/Ἱεροσόλυμα in Luke–Acts

Antagonistic Texts	Description
Luke 5:17	Pharisees and teachers of the law (from Jerusalem) react negatively to Jesus forgiving sins.
Luke 13:4	Victims of the tower of Siloam are no worse than others living in Jerusalem.
Luke 13:33 (x3)	Jerusalem kills the prophets and stones those sent to it.

73. Baker, *Identity*, 200.
74. Luke 1:8–17, 32, 69, 71, 74, 79; 2:22, 23–38, 41–49.
75. Luke 13:33.
76. Luke 23:28.
77. κατέβαινεν is used of the priest. The word is not used for the Levite, although he is introduced saying, "Likewise," (ὁμοίως).

Antagonistic Uses of Ἰερουσαλήμ/Ἱεροσόλυμα in Luke–Acts

Antagonistic Texts	Description
Luke 18:31	Jesus and the Twelve going up to Jerusalem where "everything written about the Son of man" will be accomplished.
Luke 21:20, 24	Jerusalem's desolation, trampled by Gentiles.
Luke 23:7, 28	Herod connected with Jerusalem.
Acts 4:5, 16	Rulers, elders, and scribed assembling in Jerusalem and persecuting the church.
Acts 5:28	Harsh reaction to teaching about Jesus in Jerusalem.
Acts 8:1	Saul approves of Stephen's execution, and persecution breaks out against the church in Jerusalem.
Acts 10:39	Reference to Jesus' death in Jerusalem.
Acts 11:2	Peter is criticized by circumcised believers in Jerusalem.
Acts 13:27	Jerusalem residents and their leaders condemn Paul and his words, not understanding the message.
Acts 20:22	Travel to Jerusalem means danger for Paul.
Acts 21:4, 11 (x3), 31	Prophetic word about travel to Jerusalem will result in being bound and handed over to the Gentiles. Paul is arrested and dragged from the Temple.
Acts 25:3, 7, 9, 15, 20, 24	Jerusalem represents charges against Paul and a plot to kill him.
Acts 26:10	Paul's previous life in Jerusalem meant locking up saints and condemning them to death.
Acts 28:17	Paul's account of being arrested in Jerusalem and handed over to the Gentiles.

Decentralizing Uses of Ἰερουσαλήμ/Ἱεροσόλυμα in Luke–Acts

Decentralizing Texts	Description
Luke 9:51, 53	Jesus sets his face toward Jerusalem, starting journey that results in decentralization.
Luke 10:30	Traveler leaving Jerusalem is left for dead. Jerusalem leaders do not help, but Samaritan becomes the model of neighborly love.
Luke 24:47	Repentance and forgiveness of will be preached to all nations, starting in Jerusalem.

Decentralizing Uses of Ἰερουσαλήμ/Ἱεροσόλυμα in Luke–Acts

Decentralizing Texts	Description
Acts 1:4, 8	The disciples will be witnesses in Jerusalem, Judea, Samaria, and the ends of the earth.
Acts 2:5, 14	Jews in Jerusalem are from "every nation under heaven."
Acts 8:25, 26 (x2)	Peter and John share about preaching the word to Samaritans. The Ethiopian Eunuch comes to faith outside of Jerusalem.
Acts 9:2, 21	Paul seeks to drag Christians back to Jerusalem for punishment.
Acts 13:13	Paul's first missionary journey, occurring outside of Jerusalem.
Acts 19:21	Paul's desire to minister in Macedonia and Achaia before returning to Jerusalem.
Acts 22:5, 17 (x2)	Retelling of Paul's story and Jesus' urge to leave Jerusalem.
Acts 23:11	Jesus' urge to testify about Jesus in Rome, as he did in Jerusalem.
Acts 26:20	Ministry to Gentiles in Judean countryside.

The implied readers of Luke–Acts may have also expected God to defend the city of Jerusalem, never allowing its destruction or desolation as in 167 BC.[78] However, none of the ninety references to Jerusalem in two volumes indicate this to be the case, and Jesus himself even seems to predict the destruction of the city.[79] This decentralizing-move of God's activity away from Jerusalem makes Paul's ongoing connection to it all the more surprising. The reader remembers Paul as a Judean partly through his ongoing connection with Jerusalem, and this supports the formation of a superordinate identity made up of both Jews and Gentiles.[80]

We may understand the prototypical relationships as follows: Jesus is the first and central prototype. Peter is connected with Jesus, and serves as a sort of successor, although he leaves the narrative rather quickly after serving his purpose. Paul is introduced much later, but is connected with both Peter and Jesus.[81] Again, while there are numerous ways in which Paul may be connected with these other figures in order to establish his prototypicality, here are the most significant examples for the current work.

First, Acts 13 contains Paul's first major speech. Tannehill notes the similarities between Paul's speech here and the first of Jesus in Luke 4 and Peter's first at Pentecost

---

78. Wright, *People*, 159–61.
79. Luke 21:20, 24.
80. For further discussion, see chapter 1.
81. See examples below.

in Acts 2.[82] "Paul's speech in the Antioch synagogue . . . corresponds to Jesus' announcement in the Nazareth synagogue and Peter's Pentecost speech."[83] Paul's and Jesus' speeches both take place in a synagogue and are followed by considerable resistance. Paul mimics Peter's speech in proclaiming Jesus as the promised future Davidic king. All three of these include quotations from the Old Testament and are followed by the healing of a crippled person (14:8–10; Luke 5:17–26; Acts 3:1–10).[84]

A second example is the healing of a crippled man in Acts 14. This is reminiscent of Jesus' healing in Luke 5 and Peter's in Acts 3, already discussed above. "Both the manner of the telling and its relation to the setting echo the healing of the lame man at the temple gate in 3:1–10."[85] These echoes indicate that Paul is the prototype for Christian identity in second half of volume two, expanding the mission started by Jesus and carried forward by Peter.[86]

Third, Paul is like Jesus in that they are both controversial figures. Both characters have to answer questions about their past. Jesus was questioned because of his family roots; Paul because of his past as a persecutor of Christians.[87] Each one faces rejection in his own way.[88] Both characters face groups that want to kill them. The plot to kill Jesus begins in Luke 13:31 from Herod, and continues with the chief priests, teachers, of the law, and leaders in 19:47. For Paul, it begins only several verses after the account of his conversion, in Acts 9:23, 29.

For Luke, Paul is the main character of the second half of Acts.[89] The reader expects to see the Twelve play a leading role in the advancement of the Christian movement. Instead Paul, an enemy of the church and persecutor of Christians, is converted and does what the Twelve were expected to do. This shift, once again, fits with Luke's focus on decentralization.

The portrayal of Peter and Paul as prototypes for the identity forming process is a helpful start, but it does not go far enough. It is important to note the differences between Peter and Paul. Not only does Paul become the main character in the second half of the book, he embodies the spirit of the outward, decentralizing movement of the early church (Acts 1:8) by embarking on three missionary journeys that stretch the boundaries of the kingdom of God outward.[90] Peter seems to be a reluctant mover of

---

82. Tannehill, *Acts*, 165. For a full-length treatment of the similarities between Peter and Paul, see Clark, "Parallel." Also, see Clark, "Role"; Neagoe, *Trial*, 137–39; Mattill, "Parallels"; Kurz, "Narrative"; Harrison, "Inversion."

83. Tannehill, *Acts*, 165.

84. Tannehill, *Acts*, 159–62.

85. Tannehill, *Acts*, 177–78. Also, see Carroll, "Hermes"; Breytenbach, "Zeus."

86. Baker, *Identity*, 144.

87. Acts 9:21, 23–24.

88. Bock, *Acts*, 363.

89. Kurichianil, "Paul"; Tajra, *Trial*; Knox and Hare, *Chapters*; Bruce, "Paul."

90. It is likely that Luke's credibility for the expansion of the boundaries of the Kingdom of God comes from divinely inspired visions, which are common throughout Luke. Paul, for example,

the gospel who may be perceived as trying to control situations. He and the disciples are quick to add another disciple to replace Judas, and is thus involved in an overseeing role. He and the others decide to have people elected to serve food, rather than taking on the servanthood themselves. He also finds himself preaching at Cornelius's house, when the Spirit apparently just wants to fall upon the crowd. By contrast, Paul freely goes on the missionary journeys and pays a high price for his obedience.

Minor Characters

The key prototype to consider for Luke's identity-forming program in Luke–Acts is Cornelius. However, there are a number of minor characters that run through Luke's two-volume work that set the stage for his role in the story. Luke has a high regard for minor characters as they play an important role in the unfolding of his narrative.[91] In many of these characters we see the actualization of Jesus' statement in Luke 13:30, "Indeed, some are last who will be first, and some are first who will be last."[92]

The Centurion in Luke 7: The Precursor to Cornelius

Cornelius is not the first centurion character in Luke's corpus. Luke 7:1–10 tells of Jesus' encounter with a centurion. The reader is intended to remember this when reading Acts 10 based on parallels between the two stories as part of the experience of engaging with Luke–Acts. Jesus' experience with the centurion foreshadows the paradigm-shifting encounter that the early church has in Acts 10. The reader's imagination is stirred as both volumes include a story with a key outsider, both of who are praised as men of great character.[93]

Jesus encounters a centurion who has a sick slave, whom Jesus heals from afar without direct contact with either. The report from the Jewish elders is, "He is worthy of having you do this for him, for he loves our people, and it is he who built our synagogue for us."[94] Despite the Jewish elders' claims that he is worthy, the centurion himself does not see himself as worthy (7:6): "Lord, do not trouble yourself, for I am

---

experiences a paired vision with Ananias when he is converted (Acts 9:1–19) and receives a call to go to the Gentiles (Acts 9:15). See more on the excursus on Angels and Visions in this chapter below. This is also the fulfillment of the prophecies of Isaiah, particularly chapters 56–66, which are central for Luke.

91. Also, see chapter 2.

92. For the occurrence of last/first reversal in Luke, see York, *Last*. Also, see Howard, "Significance"; Gardner, "Reading"; Hinkle, "People"; Sugawara, "Minor Characters."

93. Also, see Haaslam, "Centurion," 109–10; Kyrychenko, *Roman Army*; Burge, *Centurion*. For discussions of the centurion in the book of Matthew, see Pattarumadathil, "Models"; Jeon, "Portrait"; Jennings and Liew, "Identities"; Sorum, "Centurion."

94. Luke 7:4b–5. For discussion about the synagogue he helped build, see Safrai, "Synagogue," 12–14.

not worthy to have you come under my roof." Jesus is "amazed" (ἐθαύμασεν)[95] at the faith of the centurion, and turns to the onlookers praising the faith of this Gentile against the faith of Israel.

This passage is part of a larger narrative purpose in Luke. Tannehill notes that the two stories in chapter 7 correspond to the two stories that Jesus mentions in Luke 4:25–27: Elisha healing Naaman (2 Kgs 5) in 7:1–10 (healing the centurion's slave) and Elijah healing the widow's son (1 Kgs 17:10) in 7:11–17 (Jesus healing the widow's son at Nain).[96] Following these two miracles is Jesus' response to John the Baptist's query, where he gives a summary of the miracles that have occurred and ends with a warning. Tannehill suggests that Jesus' summary connects him with Isaiah 61 and notes: "The narrator is apparently interested in Jesus as a prophet on the model of Elijah-Elisha both because he is a great miracle-working prophet and because of the ministry to outsiders suggested by the incidents cited in 4:25–27."[97] Despite the positivity of the hearers in response to Jesus' testimony about himself earlier in Luke 4:17–19, the mood quickly turns sour as Jesus cites references of outsiders being healed in the Hebrew Scriptures.[98] In fact, there are a number of ways the narrative hints at the future inclusion of outsiders early on, as here on the lips of Jesus.[99] In addition, Marin discusses similarities and differences between this and Cornelius.[100] He observes "the same spatial distance, separation, and nearness to the order of the spirit."[101] However, he also sees differences, in that Luke's gospel emphasizes the centurion's low position and need (i.e., unworthiness, sick servant, special distance).[102] The Acts account does not present Cornelius this way, but rather praises his good character, another similarity between the two centurions, and removes the special distance by Peter entering his house.[103] Thus, the differences between the characters serve to setup a surprise in Acts 10. There are more than just similarities and differences to be noticed, though, as Luke is intentionally crafting expectations and opening the reader to greater surprises in volume two.[104]

The centurion in Luke 7 helps prepare the reader for inclusion as well. The comparisons between the two centurions who become welcomed outsiders would raise

---

95. Many characters are amazed in Luke's writings and the other gospels (Pilate, the crowds, the disciples, etc.), but this is the only time in the narrative Jesus is ever amazed.

96. Tannehill, *Luke*, 72. Also, see footnote in Tannehill, *Luke*, 88.

97. Tannehill, *Luke*, 72. Also, see the connections made by Brodie, as discussed in chapter 2. Poirier, "Jesus."

98. See chapter 2.

99. See chapter 3.

100. Marin, "Analysis," 159. Also, see Lane, *Gentile*; Hooker, *Beginnings*.

101. Marin, "Analysis," 159. Brink, *Soldiers*, 157, also notes similarities.

102. Marin, "Analysis," 159.

103. Marin, "Analysis," 159.

104. For more on narrative comparisons, see Rhoads et al., *Mark as Story*; Hock, "Lazarus"; Ayayo, "Expectations"; Smith, *Genre*.

interest in the reader's mind. "Jesus' commendation helps to nullify the supposed disqualifications of outsiders like this Gentile. When Jesus declares that the centurion is an outstanding example of faith, it becomes difficult for any of his followers to deny this Gentile's share in the salvation which Jesus brings."[105]

One other centurion is worth mentioning. In Luke 23:47, a centurion declares Jesus righteous (or innocent, δίκαιος) at his dying moment. While other gospels have Jesus being declared "a son of God," Luke focuses on Jesus' righteousness/innocence.[106] Yet again, Luke introduces a character who is an outsider to the things of God, but who speaks well of Jesus and prepares the reader for the inclusion of Cornelius into the church in volume two.[107]

Other Minor Characters in Luke

Two other minor characters expected to prepare the reader for Cornelius's inclusion are the sinful woman in Luke 7:36–50 and the Samaritan leper of Luke 17:11–19. Tannehill deals with these stories together, noticing their similarities. Both show ways in which outsiders respond to Jesus in positive ways.[108] These stories are connected semantically as two of the only four stories in Luke where Jesus uses the phrase "your faith has saved you" (ἡ πίστις σου σέσωκέν σε).[109]

Similar to these two, Tannehill connects the story of Zacchaeus in 19:1–10 and the thief on the cross 23:39–43, contrasted with the Rich Young Ruler in 18:18–23. Each of the first two examples fits with the pattern of those seeking help from Jesus who "have some negative characteristic which might seem to disqualify them."[110] The Rich Young Ruler, on the other hand, had wealth and status in society, yet leaves without receiving what he desired. Both stories demonstrate how outsiders who have not been included are being drawn near. Conversely, the religious and well-to-do class is being passed over for those truly seeking.[111]

---

105. Tannehill, *Luke*, 115. Also, see Brodie, "Elijah"; Haslam, "Centurion"; Alegre, "El centurion."

106. Matt 27:54; Mark 15:39.

107. Easter, "Confession"; Shiner, "Pronouncement."

108. Tannehill, *Luke*, 95.

109. Tannehill, *Luke*, 94–95.

110. Tannehill, *Luke*, 120. Another example is the woman with the issue of blood in Luke 8:43–48.

111. In both Luke and Acts, the former point of inclusion of outsiders is stressed more than the latter point of rejection of the elite, but both are present. Other outsiders are included or exalted in Luke, like the women in Luke's gospel or the woman with the issue of blood in 8:40–47. We will discuss these characters more below in the section on exemplars, starting on page 170.

Cornelius: The Prototypical God-Fearer

The most prominent God-fearer in Acts is Cornelius, and the narrative presents him as a prototype for a God-fearing reader. Jervell states, "To Luke, Cornelius is far more than the first Gentile to become Christian. He is the model, the prototype for every non-Jew who wants to be a member of the church."[112] However, this notion of Cornelius as the prototypical God-fearer but has not yet been developed. We see that Cornelius maintains his God-fearer identity (Roman soldier, Gentile, association with the synagogue) while also participating in the boundary crossing rituals of new Christians (water and Spirit baptism).[113] This facilitates identity formation for other members of the group.

Cornelius is shown to have exemplary behavior. He was "a devout man who feared God with all his household," and he is one who "gave alms generously to the people and prayed constantly to God."[114] Cornelius is one of three characters in the book of Acts to be identified as being gracious to the poor, all modeling Jesus' teaching in Luke 11:41. The others are Paul in chapter 24:17 and a minor character in chapter 9, named Tabitha (Dorcas), who dies and then is resurrected by Peter. She is not mentioned again in the narrative. Luke mentions generosity to the poor for these three characters that cover a wide spectrum in the book of Acts—the main character of the book, the prototypical God-fearer, and a minor female character who is not mentioned again. This is Luke's way of offering a cross section of characters, and suggesting the wide-reaching importance of generosity to the poor by all of the followers of the Way, no matter how prominent or humble.[115]

What is more, Cornelius experiences a vision (see excursus below). He is one of only a handful of characters to see visions in Luke's writings, and the only Gentile (and the only God-fearer) to experience one. This suggests divine activity in his life and further increases his reputation with the reader.[116]

In this vision, the angel's message to him underscores his piety even more: "Your prayers and your alms have ascended as a memorial before God."[117] This is echoed again in Acts 10:31. Cornelius welcomes Peter, showing reverence by bowing down: "Now we are all here in the presence of God to listen to everything the Lord has

---

112. Jervell, "Church," 13. Also, see Finn, "Reconsidered," 76.

113. For a fuller discussion of boundary crossing rituals in Judaism and Christianity, see Lieu, *Christian Identity*, 98–146. For an interesting take on this story, see Macdonald, *Gospels*, who compares this episode with Agamemnon's dream and the portent at Aulis in *Iliad* 2.1–335.

114. Acts 10:2.

115. Possessions play an important role in Acts. For more on this, see chapter 1 and later in chapter 4. Also, see Gillman, *Possessions*; Seccombe, *Possessions*; Kraybill, "Possessions"; Johnson, *Literary Function*; Streltsov, "Character"; McGee, "Sharing."

116. In chapter 5 we will explore the concept of ethos as the character of the reader as presented by the author. Also, see Eisen, "Boundary"; Anderson, "Giving"; Downs, *Alms*.

117. Acts 10:4b.

commanded you to tell us."¹¹⁸ After Peter's speech, they are all filled with the Holy Spirit and baptized with water: Peter asks, "Can anyone withhold the water for baptizing these people who have received the Holy Spirit just as we have?"¹¹⁹ Thus, Cornelius and his family participate in the boundary crossing rituals of the New Christian Movement, a radical step in the early church.¹²⁰

Certainly, Cornelius acts out almost everything that would be expected of a devout God-fearer in the first century: Devout, gives to the poor, prays, is filled with the Spirit and baptized in water, practices hospitality, shows honor to the disciples, and leads gatherings in his home. He is portrayed so positively for a number of reasons. First, as mentioned above, this positivity establishes him as the prototypical God-fearer, one to be emulated by the audience, and to create identity in that group as they empathize with the character. Cornelius is a hero in the story, and it is easy for the reader to see that. Second, the positive description reminds the reader of the centurion in Luke 7, mentioned above, as well as a number of other outsiders who precede the Cornelius episode and are accepted, receive what they seek from Jesus or the early disciples, or do noteworthy things in the narrative. These narrative details about Cornelius and the other outsiders appeal to short-term memory and incite the imagination of the implied audience. The small story components are being co-located to fire the imagination and open the reader up for transformation. As the God-fearing reader, who necessarily identifies with Cornelius, is challenged to develop empathy, it leads to a greater likelihood of emulation.

Third, there may be a sense where Luke presents Cornelius so positively to soften the blow to the circumcision party. This group, mentioned in chapter 11 (οἱ ἐκ περιτομῆς), criticizes Peter upon his report of what happened. Luke's audience, as I have argued, is primarily God-fearing Gentiles, but is also likely diverse and includes Jews opposed to Gentile inclusion.¹²¹ Presenting Cornelius with a godly resume helps him to be received by this group. The Cornelius event becomes the catalyst that leads to the major paradigm shift in the early church, culminating in the Jerusalem council. Peter's opening statement of his sermon toward the end of the encounter is central to this point: "Truly I understand that God shows no partiality, but in every nation anyone who fears him and does what is right is acceptable

---

118. Acts 10:33b.

119. Acts 10:47. Also, see Shellberg, *Cleansed*.

120. Lieu, *Christian Identity*, 126–46. Also, see Varzi, "Boundary"; Tajfel and Turner, "Social Identity," 16–17; Brewer and Brown, "Intergroup Relations"; Bowie, *Anthropology*; Brown, *Processes*; Lamont and Molnár, "Study"; Barth, *Ethnic Groups*; Douglas, *Purity*; Fuller, "Boundaries"; O'Loughlin, "Sharing." Some have also considered the practical missiological implications of this scene. As an example of this, see Nguyen, "Dismantling."

121. Keener, *Acts*, 1:428, sees the audience as made up of "a mixture of Jewish and Gentile members, and considerable Jewish and God-fearing didactic input." Also, see Moxon, "Ethnic Conflict"; Arterbury, "Custom"; Wilson, "Urban legends"; Humphrey, "Collision."

to him."[122] Thus, if God and Peter both accept Cornelius, what right does anyone else have to not accept him into the community of believers? Cornelius's resume does soften the blow, but it also extends the challenge to the circumcision group about the need to accept this brother into the fold.[123]

Luke does not mention Cornelius again after chapter 10, although his story is repeated in Acts 15:6–11, but the effects of his role in the narrative continue to effect the second half of the book particularly as it is a key part of the reason for the decision of the Jerusalem council. The council is what initiates Paul's ongoing missionary activity, which result in the conversion of many Gentiles.[124]

This story is also a great example of these prototypical figures leading the way in recategorization. Peter represents those who are opposed to Gentile inclusion in the Christ group, and yet Acts records him going into Cornelius's home (10:24–25), takes part in a large gathering (v. 27), witnesses the Spirit fall "on all who heard the message" (v. 44), and ordered that they be baptized (v. 48). Peter, himself, makes reference to the law that forbids him to "associate with or visit" a Gentile (v. 28). He also accepts the men from Cornelius and invites them into his house (v. 23). In addition, although it is not narrated here, it is quite clear that Peter ate with Cornelius and his family in their home. The accusation in 11:3 reads, "You went into the house of uncircumcised men and ate with them." He does not refute this. Peter stayed with Cornelius "a few days" as a result of the initial vision involving the order to eat. Thus, the narrative makes clear that Peter, a Jew, ate with Gentiles in their home, an act that facilitates recategorization.[125] The fact that Peter appears to be quite ready to enter into table fellowship must mean that he understood that the Spirit brought Cornelius into the community.

The prohibition against eating with Gentiles does not appear in the Old Testament, but comes from other Jewish traditions of the Old Testament and inter-testamental period. An example of the sort of thinking implied here can be demonstrated with reference to Jubilees 22:16:

> And do also, my son Jacob, remember my words,
>
> and keep the commandments of Abraham, your father.
>
> Separate yourself from the gentiles,
>
> And do not eat with them,
>
> And do not perform deeds like theirs.

---

122. Acts 10:34b–35.

123. A fourth reason for the positive description of Cornelius is the rhetorical function of building ethos, which will be discussed in chapter 5.

124. Paul's first missionary journey is recorded in Acts 13:4—14:26. The Jerusalem council in Acts 15 seemingly initiates the second missionary journey, which is recorded in Acts 15:26—18:22, followed by the third missionary journey in 18:22—21:17. Many Gentiles are converted in these texts and after. For example, see Acts 18:6; 21:19; 26:20–23; 28:28.

125. For more on Peter and Gentiles, see Gibson, *Peter*; Lohse, "Apostleship"; Garroway, "Heresy"; Nguyen, "Point of View."

> And do not become associates of theirs.
>
> Because their deeds are defiled,
>
> And all if their ways are contaminated, and despicable, and abominable.[126]

A similar passage is found in Joseph of the Ascension 7:1: "And Joseph came into Pentephres's house and sat down on a seat and he washed his feet and he placed a table in front of him separately, because he would not eat with the Egyptians, for this was an abomination to him."[127]

Finally, 3 Maccabees 3:4, 6–7 offers a bit more context on this issue:

> But reverencing God and conducting themselves according to his Law, they kept themselves apart in the matter of food, and for this reason they appeared hateful to some. They adorned their community life with the excellent practice of righteousness and so established a good reputation among all men. But of this excellent practice, which was common talk everywhere regarding the Jewish nation, the foreigners took no account whatever. Instead they talked incessantly about how different they were in regard to worship and food, asserting that they did not fulfill their contracted obligations either to the king or the armed forces but were hostile and very unsympathetic to his interests. So it was no small charge against them.[128]

Thus, as these texts and others show,[129] this thinking had worked its way into the Judaism of the first century, which causes Peter to come under scrutiny for his actions and makes this transition all the more remarkable.

This scene represents radical reconciliation between two of the key prototypical characters in the Acts narrative and, in fact, sets the stage for a key event in the book (the council of Jerusalem). In this way, Peter and Cornelius lead the way in recategorization for the groups they represent. This superordinate (i.e., Christian) identity[130] is made salient toward the end of the encounter when Peter says, "Surely *no one* can stand in the way of their being baptized with water. They have received the Holy Spirit *just as we have*" (10:47). Peter observes that the Gentiles have experienced God the way they have, and immediately calls for them to take part in the boundary crossing rituals that constitute creating a new group identity (baptism and community fellowship).[131] But Cornelius does not become Jewish. He is baptized into the Christian faith, but maintains his God-fearing Gentile identity as well. Likewise,

---

126. Jubilees 22:16; Charlesworth, *Pseudopigrapha*, 98.

127. Joseph of the Ascension 7:1; Sparks, *Apocryphal*, 479.

128. 3 Macc 3:4–7; Charlesworth, *Pseudepigrapha*, 520–21.

129. For lists of extra-biblical texts relating to this issue of Jew and Gentile contacts, see Keener, *Acts*, 2:1787–92, 1818–21.

130. A superordinate identity is one that overshadows all other identities a person has, and allows them to connect with another person who shares that same superordinate identity, despite differences.

131. See Calpino, "Opened"; Balch, "Accepting"; Gennep et al., *Rites*; Turner, *Process*.

Peter remains Jewish in his personal identity, but also enters into a new superordinate identity by this realization and encounter with Cornelius. Recall from chapter 1 that the most effective types of common ingroups, according to research, are those in which both the superordinate and sub-group identities both remain salient.[132] This is exactly what is happening with Cornelius and Peter.

Excursus: Angels and Visions in Luke's Writings

While praying, Peter's encounter is initiated by a vision. There is an increase in the appearance of visions in Luke's writings in the New Testament. In fact, it is a marker of importance for him, as we see key and prototypical characters as the main figures to experience visions, and these happen in scenes that expand the scope of the mission in Acts. Thus, because of the important role of visions in Luke's two volumes, and the close tie to his narrative aim of gospel expansion and highlighting prototypical characters, which includes God-fearers, and exploration of this motif is needed.

The notion of "seeing" matters greatly to Luke as is evident from the spread of derivations of ὁράω used in the New Testament:

- ὀπτασία four times in NT, two in Luke, one in Acts, one in 2 Corinthians
- ὅρασις three times in NT, one in Acts, two in Revelation
- ὅραμα twelve times in NT, eleven in Acts, one in Matthew[133]

Only key figures in the narrative experience visions.[134] One important time the semantics for vision are not present, but the character, Stephen, "gazed" (ἀτενίσας) up

---

132. Esler, "Outline," 30.

133. Of the nineteen usages of these words in the NT, fifteen are in Luke–Acts compared to four times in the rest of the New Testament. "Seeing" plays an important role in Luke–Acts. In addition to seeing angels and visions, the shepherds journey to see Jesus (Luke 2:15), Simeon will not see death before he sees salvation (Luke 2:26, 30), all flesh will see salvation (Luke 3:6), Jesus sees the faith of the men bringing the crippled friend (Luke 5:20), John's disciples see the miracles that testify to Jesus as the messiah (Luke 7:22), Jesus promises his followers they will see the kingdom (Luke 9:27), Jesus' followers see his glory (Luke 9:31–32), and see what prophets and kings desired to see (Luke 10:24), Jesus suggests the ability to see with regard to eschatological things (Luke 13:28, 35; 17:22; 21:20, 27, 31); and Jesus' followers see the risen Christ, including his hands and feet (Luke 24:39). In Acts, many of the references to seeing revolve around the vision experiences, but Barnabas sees the grace of God (Acts 11:23), Paul sees faith (Acts 14:9), the people see the Righteous One (Acts 22:14), and the book ends with the hope that people will see with their eyes and turn to God (Acts 28:27). For more on the strategic use of seeing in Luke–Acts, see Prince, "Seeing Visions"; Smith, "Seeing"; Miller, "Seeing"; Culpepper, "Kingdom."

134. Zechariah: Luke 1:22, in the Temple; The women at Jesus' tomb: Luke 24:23, being referenced on the road to Emmaus; Ananias: Acts 9:10, 12, in the conversion of Paul; Cornelius: Acts 10:3, seeing a vision of an Angel giving him information about Peter; Peter: Acts 10:17, the vision of the animal and the sheet; 10:19, 11:5 Telling the story of his vision; 12:9 Peter's escape from prison; Paul: Acts 16:9–10, Man in Macedonia; 18:9, Jesus telling Paul not to be silent; 26:19, Paul referencing back to his Damascus road experience.

to heaven and sees Jesus. Similarly, angels appear quite often in Luke's writings.[135] (Sometimes these experiences with angels are called visions, so there is some overlap.) Rather than simply referring to angels, Luke's narrative has many episodes where angels are literally on the scene as characters.[136] Four times in the Gospel of Luke we see angels appear on the scene, three times early in the book connected with the births of John and Jesus, and one reference toward the end referencing angels at the tomb of Jesus. Luke's Gospel is bookended with angelic activity.[137]

Encounters with Angels in Luke–Acts

Zechariah	Luke 1:8–25, Zechariah encounters an angel foretelling John's birth
Mary	Luke 1:27–38, Angel comes to Mary to foretell Jesus' birth
Shepherds	Luke 2:8–15, Angels come declare Jesus' birth to the shepherds
Women at the tomb	Luke 24:1–8, "two men in clothes that gleamed like lighting" meet the women at Jesus' tomb
Peter's First Escape from prison (the apostles with him)	Acts 5:17–20, Angel comes and sets the apostles free from prison
Cornelius	Acts 10:1–8, Angel tells Cornelius to find Peter
Peter's Second Escape from Prison	Acts 12:1–10, Angel comes and leads Peter out of prison

So, in the four narrative books of the New Testament (the Gospels including Luke–Acts), ten times angels are shown on the scene as characters who speak lines and engage with the other characters (as opposed to simple references). Seven of these occur in Luke–Acts.

Furthermore, prototypical characters experience seven of the ten visions in Luke's writings (or eight of eleven when counting Stephen).[138] The other three vision experiences are remarkable in their own right (i.e., the resurrection of Jesus, the foretelling of the birth of John the Baptist, and Ananias participating in the conversion of Paul). Cornelius is the only non-Jew to experience a vision. This fits

---

135. The word ἄγγελος occurs 171 times in the New Testament, 25 times in Luke and 21 times in Acts, for a total of about 27 percent of the occurrences.

136. See chart below. There are only three other instances in the rest of the Gospels combined where angels are speaking characters: Similar to Luke, Matthew includes angels talking to figures in dreams surrounding Jesus' birth (Matt 1:20; 2:19), and at Jesus' tomb (Matt 28).

137. There is one other place, Luke 22:43, where one could argue that angels make a physical appearance when they strengthen Jesus. But it seemed to me closer to a passing reference than it did a crucial event, and thus, I put it in the reference category as opposed to the encounter category.

138. For more on visions, see Wilson, "Hearing"; Miller, *Convinced*; Johnson, *Prophetic*.

with Luke's highlighting of Cornelius as the prototypical God-fearer and a pioneer among the Gentiles in many ways. In addition, three of the ten vision references in Acts have to do with the recategorization experience that happens between Cornelius and Peter. What is more, two times in the narrative the same event has visions experienced by different people individually: (1) Paul's conversion, where Paul and Ananias both experience visions facilitating their encounter, and (2) Peter and Cornelius's encounter, in which both of these characters experience visions independently. These are the most repeated stories in the book[139] as they relate some of the most crucial events in the narrative.[140] Keener suggests that "paired visions or dreams given to different individuals were recounted as the strongest evidence [in the ancient world]."[141] Consequently, important patterns emerge.

First, Luke uses vision and angel language only in important events. Every event listed above is central to the unfolding narrative. Second, Luke uses visions to verify new mission initiatives, as Twelftree rightly notes.[142] Consider how Luke uses visions to expands the outward mission of Acts: the vision of Ananias and Paul (where the latter is called to the Gentiles),[143] the visions of Peter and Cornelius, and Paul's vision of the man in Macedonia.[144] These help facilitate the geographical and personal decentralization of the narrative. Thus, Luke displays God's direct involvement in the expansion of mission to the outsiders, even if the participants are at times reluctant. Third, Luke's narrative involves multiple people experiencing visions. The implication is that the divine activity is richer during these times as God is orchestrating these events to his own ends. Cornelius finds himself in the middle of heightened divine activity, where he and other characters experience angelic visions and communications. These characters are getting a front row seat to God's activity in accomplishing his purposes. The reader, too, is observing the activity of God in a dynamic way vicariously through the characters. The implied audience is invited to share a perception of reality brought about by the exalted Christ. This is identity-forming. Luke's transformative illocutionary intent is clearly on center stage in the message

---

139. More on this in chapter 5.

140. Other potential visions: The story of Paul and the Damascus road experience is told several times, but the word vision is not used every time (only in 26:19 in Paul referring back to it before Agrippa). Stephen sees heaven opened up and Jesus at the right hand of God, but the term "vision" is not used. Even so, whether one considers these visions or simply heightened divine activity, they would fit the pattern of visions being major events seen by prototypical characters in the narrative.

141. Keener, *Acts*, 2:1644.

142. Twelftree, *Spirit*, 155–57.

143. Acts 9:15.

144. Twelftree also considers Stephen's experience in Acts 7:55 a vision (quite likely, though the word is not used) and connected with the spread of the gospel to Judea and Samaria (Acts 8:1). He also calls Philip's experience with the Ethiopian Eunuch "a long visionary experience." Each of these introduces a new mission initiative.

this narrative sends: God is pursuing his Gentile people who seek him. Cornelius is a perfect prototype of that mutual pursuit.[145]

Sinai and Pentecost: Forming a New Covenant

As briefly mentioned previously,[146] there seem to be connections between the Pentecost event in Acts 2 and the giving of the law at Sinai in Exodus chapters 19–32, as we will see below. If these connections are valid, then Luke is making a larger statement about God's people in one of the most prominent scenes in the narrative that is intertextual with the Exodus narrative and creates identity for his readers. A proper understanding of the connections between Sinai and Pentecost is important to grasp Luke's overall narrative strategy. In the Pentecost scene, Luke is making a bold statement about the reconstitution of God's people. Considering the similar shift in Christian identity happening with Cornelius and the other minor characters we have discussed in this chapter, a fuller exploration of the Sinai-Pentecost connection is warranted.

First, although originally a harvest festival, by the time of the first century Pentecost was seen as an anniversary of the giving of the law.[147] The book of Jubilees also suggests that Pentecost was a covenant renewal ceremony looking back to the Sinai event.[148] Keener states, "Many scholars believe that Luke had this understanding of the gift of Torah, or at least of covenant renewal, in mind."[149] Secondly, many of the symbols present correspond to the Sinai event.[150]

Similarities Between Sinai and Pentecost

Sinai	OT Text	Pentecost	NT Text
Thunder and lightning, a thick cloud, and a loud trumpet.	Exod 19:16	Storm and sound imagery: "A sound like the rush of a violent wind."	Acts 2:2

---

145. Also, see Miller, *Convinced*; Macdonald, *Gospels*; Duba, "Disrupted."

146. See pages 41–42.

147. Dunn, *Baptism*, 480–54; Turner, *Spirit*, 79. See Exod 23:16; Deut 16:9–12.

148. "Therefore, it is ordained and written in the heavenly tablets that they should observe the feast of Shebuot [i.e., "Weeks" or "Pentecost"] in this month, once per year in order to renew the covenant in all (respects), year by year" (Jubilees 6:17; Charlesworth, *Pseudepigrapha*, 67).

149. Keener, *Acts*, 1:786.

150. Johnson, *Acts*, 46, sees the cluster of symbols only present in the LXX description of Sinai and states, "So thoroughly does Luke use the Moses story elsewhere, that it would be surprising if the use of sound of fire and languages here did not allude to the Sinai event." Also, see Turner, *Power*, 282–89.

Similarities Between Sinai and Pentecost

Sinai	OT Text	Pentecost	NT Text
Mountain is "wrapped in smoke, because the Lord had descended upon it in fire."	Exod 19:18	"Divided tongues, as of fire, appeared among them, and a tongue rested on each of them."	Acts 2:3
All of the people tremble.[151]	Exod 19:16	All are amazed and astonished.	Acts 2:7, 12
Three thousand people are killed as judgment for idolatry.	Exod 32:28	Three thousand people are saved through the Spirit's work.	Acts 2:41

There are some important contrasts that arise for the reader in these two scenes, as well. Although divine communication happens in both scenes, it happens in very different ways. The Exodus scene shows a God who appears as fire, making even the mountains tremble, and the people cannot touch the mountain without being killed. And later, in the act of idolatry involving the golden calf, three thousand people are killed, as seen in the table.[152] In Acts, however, God is coming near with fire and some other elements, but in this case the Spirit comes to unify the people through language and three thousand people are saved, not killed.[153] In response to this evidence, Talbert states, "The Sinai theophany and the establishment of the Mosaic covenant were brought to mind as surely as would Elijah by the description of John the Baptist's dress in Mark 1:6. The typology of Acts 2:1–11, then, is that of making a covenant."[154]

However, not all agree. Keener does not put enough stock in these comparisons to see an intentional connection.[155] Likewise, Robert Menzies has refuted this idea, taking issue with the view and calling an intentional parallel highly unlikely.[156] In the end, the narratival connections between the two stories are clearly intentional by Luke and the evidence for seeing Pentecost as a new Sinai is too significant to overlook.[157] What is more, this is a key point in the advancement of Luke's narrative. The

---

151. Also, see the author of Hebrews summary of the Sinai event (Heb 12:18–21).

152. Exod 32:28.

153. Acts 2:41.

154. Talbert, *Reading*, 43. Also, see Fitzmyer, *Acts*.

155. Keener, *Acts*, 1:787, states: "Luke provides few clear indications linking the day of Pentecost with Sinai, fewer than one would expect if Luke recognized and hence wished to make use of such a connection."

156. Menzies, *Empowered*, 190–93; Menzies and Menzies, *Spirit*, 97–98.

157. For other perspectives and discussion on this issue, which goes back nearly one hundred years, see Adler, *Pfingstfest*; Welliver, "Pentecost"; Müller-Abels, "Der Umgang"; Hornik and Parsons,

longed-for presence of God, which was limited and dangerous[158] in the first exodus, is now fully present with his people in the community of the early church. This is the crucial difference in the coming of the Spirit who is not limited by the boundaries of the Old Covenant. Luke's narrative is designed to show how the Spirit will continue to move forward with the kingdom plan of inclusion and decentralization despite internal or external opposition.[159]

The scene shows that God has come near in a new way, in the person of Jesus. Now he was coming near again with the outpouring of Spirit. Sinai was a key event in the exodus of God's people out of slavery and to becoming God's people worshipping him in the dessert. Luke–Acts records the New Exodus, with Pentecost being its own Sinai moment, creating the church. God came at Sinai with trembling fire. God comes at Pentecost as tongues of fire, and as a God of many languages who unifies and saves. When we see these parallel elements as intentional and deliberate by Luke, it better explains the narrative in Acts and shows again Luke's interest in the formation of his audience as a community that includes and experiences unity.

The multicultural representation of Jews "from every nation under heaven" points to the outward moving trajectory of God's mission in Acts, which then allows Luke to use prototypical characters for his inclusive purposes. The scene at Pentecost suggests that Jesus inaugurates a new age of salvation history, the way that Sinai introduced a new age of Israel's history. The values and norms of this new age will be largely communicated through exemplars in the narrative. We now turn to these exemplars in Luke–Acts.

Exemplars and Anti-Exemplars

As mentioned above, a prototype is a representation of a person that embodies the identity of the group.[160] Prototypes work as idealized versions of the group's values and central tendencies and help form cultural memory in the reader, creating social identity.[161] Exemplars, by contrast, are examples of group members who embody a single "item of information" (i.e., one value, belief, etc.) about the group.[162] Whereas

---

"Philological"; Estrada, *Followers*, 200–203.

158. Exod 32:28.

159. See section on the Prototypicality of Peter above, pages 146–50, which discusses the Spirit advancing despite internal or external opposition.

160. Smith and Zarate, "Exemplar," 245–46.

161. Smith and Zarate, "Exemplar," 245–46. In some cases this means that the prototype is not a real thing or real person. For example, Smith and Zarate, "Social Categorization," 246, talk of the prototypical rodent, an imaginary animal that possesses all of the rodent qualities that makes it easier to study the various different kinds of rodents. Thus, the prototype does not exist in reality. This becomes interesting when we begin to think of the historicity of the characters in Acts. Understanding Jesus, Peter, Paul and others as prototypes does not (necessarily) mean that they were not historical figures.

162. Smith and Zarate, "Social Categorization," 246.

idealized leaders (prototypes) embody multiple areas of comparison, exemplars are certain characters modeling an individual value shared by the New Christian Movement, and thus, imaginatively call the value to mind for the reader so it becomes part of their Christian practice. These characters are also important in the formation of cultural memory in the reader. Luke is able to target specific behavior more directly by showing what it means to be a part of the Way. That goes to the heart of how he seeks to create social identity for his reader. In this way, exemplars are central to Luke's transformative agenda. Understanding Luke's use of exemplars in his narrative is important and has too often been overlooked. As Kuecker states, "Prototypical characteristics of the group are ascribed to the exemplar, and the characteristics of the exemplar are both desirable for and ascribed to the other members of the community."[163] People judge categories in various ways, and the use of prototypes and exemplars can both work toward this categorization process.[164] The following pages deal with exemplars in Luke's corpus in order of apparent importance for Luke, rather than following narrative order.

Barnabas: Exemplar of Generosity

An excellent example of an exemplar in the book of Acts is Barnabas. He was discussed in the section of transmission of group values in chapter 1 as the embodiment of the value of shared possessions. For Bock, "Communities are often built on the leading example of an important individual. In our account, this is Barnabas."[165] Although, somewhat surprisingly, Barnabas, as he impacts the reader on multiple levels, is a minor character in the narrative of Acts.[166] He is a minor character in the sense that he is not one of the Twelve, whom the audience expects to play larger roles in the narrative. Instead, Barnabas is one of the many new faces who comes on the scene as a model of the way for the audience. First, he embodies the value of shared possessions, which is informally transmitted through socialization and influence, as opposed to formal prescription. Second, he works as an exemplar for identity formation as the

---

163. Kuecker, *Spirit*, 138–39; Turner, "Redefinition."

164. Medin, Altom, and Murphy, "Given," 333.

165. Bock, *Acts*, 218.

166. Of the minor characters in Luke's writings, Barnabas, like Cornelius, is a rather prominent minor character. He is referred to twenty-three times in the book (Acts 4:36–37; 9:27; 11:22, 29–30; 12:25—13:2; 13:7, 43, 46, 50; 14:11–12, 14–15, 20; 15:2, 12, 22–26, 35–40), but many of these simply mention him as accompanying Paul and other characters, rather than playing a significant role. See Bock, *Acts*, 216. Some may be tempted to call Barnabas the prototype of generosity in the early church. However, as we have established, prototypes function as idealized members of groups with multiple point of comparison and emulation for the audience, whereas exemplars tend to embody a single value for the group. Thus, Barnabas fits in the latter category.

readers are able to identify with an ingroup member of the new Christian community by being like him in his generosity.[167]

Ananias and Sapphira: Anti-Exemplars of Greed

In addition to exemplars modeling a value for the group, some authors speak of anti-exemplars, or villains, that represent a behavior from which the group wants to distance themselves.[168] As Pervo suggests, "What we find in Acts is good guys versus villains."[169] At times, these exemplars and anti-exemplars are paired together to heighten the contrast.[170]

The anti-exemplars to generosity of Barnabas are Ananias and Sapphira, who sell a field, donate the money, but untruthfully keep a portion of the money for themselves in Acts 5:1–11. "They contrast starkly with the role of disciples in forsaking all to follow Jesus."[171] They are struck dead for their greed and dishonesty in this manner. In dramatic fashion, Ananias is encountered first and his wife has a similar experience three hours later. This second time the readers are aware of additional details they did not know before and they anticipate her judgment. This is highlighted when Sapphira enters, "not knowing what had happened."[172] Some have connected this scene with similar ones from the Old Testament, such as the judgment of Achan (Josh 7:1, 19–26) and see implied continuity: "Luke's view is that the God of the Hebrew Scriptures is the same God Jesus and the disciples served, and so one should expect continuity of character and action."[173] Others disagree and draw contrasts between this story and the Old Testament counterparts.[174] Regardless of

---

167. Certainly the effect that a character like Barnabas has on the identity formation of a God-fearer compared to Cornelius is quite small. Nonetheless, Luke's use of minor characters allows a fuller picture to be painted for the readership, one potentially made up of diverse ethnicities and subgroups. However, as Kuecker, *Spirit*, 141n71, aptly notes, "Barnabas's significance for early Christian identity is evident in other ancient writings: *Epistle of Barnabas*; *Gospel of Barnabas*; *Acts of Barnabas by John Mark*; *Acta Batholomaei et Barnabae*; and *LaudatioBarnabae*. Tertullian attributed Hebrews to Barnabas (*De Pudicitia* 20). [Markus Öhler, *Barnabas: die historische Person und ihreRezeption in der Apostelgeschichte* (Tübingen: Mohr Siebeck, 2003)] studies the 'historical Barnabas.'"

168. Allen, *Death*, 124. Also, see Kuecker, *Spirit*, 141.

169. Pervo, *Profit*, 28.

170. In addition to the exemplar comparisons of Barnabas versus Ananias and Sapphira, Philip versus Simon the Sorcerer, and the others discussed in this chapter, consider also the two criminals with Jesus on the cross (Luke 23:39–43), Stephen versus the Sanhedrin (Acts 6–7), and Sergius Paulus versus Elymas (Acts 13:6–12).

171. Keener, *Acts*, 2:1185. Also, see Kienzler, *Holy Spirit*, who looks at this story with respect to judgment in Luke–Acts.

172. Acts 5:7.

173. Witherington, *Acts*, 214. Other stories sometimes connected to this story are Nadab and Abihu (Lev 10:2), Abijah's death (1 Kgs 14:1–18). See Bock, *Acts*, 219–20; Bibb, "Nadab"; Houston, "Tragedy"; Jones, "Abijam."

174. Haenchen, *Acts*, 239–41.

the reference, the shock factor of this scene cements Luke's emphasis on generosity and makes the contrast between Barnabas and Ananias and Sapphira quite stark. Luke tells the reader twice that "great fear" seized the whole church.[175] This scene is made all the more stark in that it is surrounded by positive examples of activities in the church, such as Barnabas's generosity (Acts 4:36–37) and the report of many miracles by the disciples (Acts 5:12–16). In addition, a bold statement is being made about the role of possessing land in the new covenant.[176] Barnabas and the contrast with the couple show how a radical shift has taken place in the early church regarding possessions and a new day of wealth ownership is at hand. The sin is not only that they lied, but that they seem to be rejecting the new way of life prescribed by the community of the early church, a rejection of the self-sacrificial giving that is so fundamental to following Christ. This motif will be explored more strongly in chapter 5 in the section titled "The Rhetorical Function of the Land."

Philip and Simon the Sorcerer

Philip, another exemplar, models the valued future of the group in the spreading of the gospel (see chapter 1). Philip embodies the characteristics of being opportunistic, bold, and empowered by the Spirit for signs and faithful witness. He is among those who are scattered after the death of Stephen and is the first example given of those who "go from place to place, proclaiming the word."[177] He is also the first to proclaim the gospel outside of Jerusalem in the book of Acts, in Samaria (8:5). This was the charge given to the disciples in Acts 1:8, which begins to be actualized in Philip.[178] Philip wins the attention of the crowds (8:6) and does miraculous signs (8:7) resulting in "great joy" (8:8).[179] Keener notes how Luke seems to choose "particularly dramatic examples, not merely random ones."[180] These dramatic examples, such as impure spirits departing with shrieks (8:7), help the exemplar stand out in the text as noteworthy and create transformative urgency for the reader.

---

175. Acts 5:5, 11.

176. See the section titled "The Rhetorical Function of Land" on pages 208–15 in chapter 5 and the subsection on Ananias and Sapphira there, pages 213–14.

177. Acts 8:4: Οἱ μὲν οὖν διασπαρέντες διῆλθον εὐαγγελιζόμενοι τὸν λόγον.

178. This is more evidence of decentralization and the fading influenced of the Twelve, as it is Philip, one of the seven selected in Acts 6:5 to oversee food distribution, but ends up taking the gospel to Samaria before the Twelve.

179. Tannehill, *Acts*, 104, suggests that the signs Philip performs are described in such a way as to recall the ministry of Jesus and the disciples. Bock, *Acts*, 326, agrees and mentions how miracles often draw people to consider the message in Luke. See Luke 4:31–37; 5:1–11, 12–16, 18–26; 6:6–10; 7:2–10, 11–17; 8:26–39, 49–56; 9:10–17, 37–43; 13:11–17; 14:1–6; 17:11–19; 18:35–43.

180. Keener, *Acts*, 2:1494.

There is contrast created here between Philip and Simon the Sorcerer.[181] After this initial description of Philip's fruitful ministry, the reader is told of his obedience to God (8:26–27), which leads him to encounter the Ethiopian Eunuch. In-between these two glowing narratives about Philip, we learn of Simon Magus. He is directly contrasted with Philip in several ways. He had been a sorcerer of magic and was said to have God's power (8:9–10); Philip proclaimed the kingdom of God (8:5, 12). Simon worked magic and amazed the people (8:10: "All of them, from the least to the greatest, listened to him eagerly, saying, 'This man is the power of God that is called Great'"); Philip did signs and amazed the people (8:6: "The crowds with one accord listened eagerly to what was said by Philip, hearing and seeing the signs that he did").[182] Simon claims to be someone great (8:9), but Philip is the one who is believed (8:12).[183] Simon follows Philip for a time (8:13) and eventually, seeing the Spirit fall on people through the ministry of James and John, offers to buy this ability (8:18–19).

Here again we see the subject of money and possessions surface, which is highlighted by Peter's response in verse 20: "May your money perish with you, because you thought you could buy the gift of God with money!" Although there is some precedent in the ancient world for paying for priestly offices or buying magical secrets, these events were "less than honorable" and were contrary to the ministry of the Christian movement.[184] While Philip represents a humble, obedient, and authentic disciple of the New Christian Movement, Simon represents one who, although he is intrigued and responds to the message, does not change from his former way of life, and seems inauthentic.[185] He is an anti-exemplar who represents to Luke's readership the dangers of not making a break with one's former life, a temptation that perhaps many of Luke's God-fearing readers face.

This issue of money being a motivator for evil men comes up again and again in the narrative.[186] For example, chapter 16 tells of when Paul commanded the spirit to leave the fortune telling slave girl. Her owners respond harshly: "But when her owners saw that their hope of making money was gone, they seized Paul and Silas and dragged them into the marketplace before the authorities."[187] We see again and again that Luke

---

181. Tannehill, *Acts*, 105.

182. Bock, *Acts*, 326, notes how half of six uses of this word (προσέχω) in Acts appear in this section (5:34–35; 8:6, 10–11 [two times]; 16:14; 20:28). The word used here for "listened eagerly" is προσεῖχον, used in the exact same tense, form in vv. 6 and 10 (the imperfect tense suggesting it was an ongoing attention).

183. For similar lists of comparisons between Philip and Simon, see Spencer, *Portrait*, 88; Samkutty, *Samaritan*, 161.

184. Bock, *Acts*, 333. For ancient examples, see 2 Macc 4:7–8; 4 Macc 4:17–18.

185. Bock, *Acts*, 333, states that Simon may be "syncretizing" his magician background and his experience with the kingdom of God.

186. Tannehill, *Acts*, 106, calls money a "factor in the human corruption of religion, one that receives special attention in Luke-Acts." See Acts 3:3; 4:34–37; 5:1–11; 16:16–19.

187. Acts 16:16–19.

demonstrates group norms, such as generosity, through prototypes and exemplars. He prescribes behavior for a God-fearing reader, and, in so doing, creates social identity. What may seem a simple comparison and contrast between characters is actually a brilliant narrative move by Luke, which he successfully executes over and over in Acts.

The Rich Young Ruler, Zacchaeus, and the Widow

This issue of shared possessions contrasted with the love of money is not new in Acts, but shows itself throughout Luke's two-volume work.[188] For example, Luke 18:18–23 tells the story of the Rich Young Ruler who is unwilling to sell all he has and give it to the poor in order to follow Jesus. Here, as in other places, wealth is seen as a hindrance to salvation.[189] In Luke–Acts, the decision to build personal wealth is at odds with building community, and is emphasizing the wrong kind of social identity in God's people. This man works as an anti-exemplar as well, who is contrasted with the disciples, with Peter as their spokesman, who, after expressing anguish at the difficulty of what Jesus asked the man to do, say "Look, we have left our homes and followed you."[190]

This story also seems to have a second layer of contrast. At the conclusion of this scene in 18:30, there are two short interjections—Jesus warning the disciples that he is going to be killed in Jerusalem (18:31–34) and the healing of the blind man on the road to Jericho (18:35–43)—before the story of Zacchaeus. Zacchaeus, like the Rich Young Ruler, is seeking Jesus.[191] However, he is a more infamous figure for Luke, as he is a "chief tax collector" (ἀρχιτελώνης). Like the Young Ruler, Zacchaeus is also wealthy.[192] However, while the Young Ruler apparently tried to flatter Jesus,[193] Zacchaeus is content to observe from the tree, but Jesus seeks to dine with him, similar to how he goes to the house of Levi the tax collector in Luke 5:27–32. At the meal, Zacchaeus is moved to declare, "Look, half of my possessions, Lord, I will give to the poor; and if I have defrauded anyone of anything, I will pay back four times as much."[194] Thus, the unwillingness of the Young Ruler to sell his possessions and give the money to the poor is contrasted in

---

188. In addition to these two examples and the references cited above (ch.1n146), money and wealth are mentioned in Luke 3:14; 7:41; 9:3; 12:13–21; 14:28; 15:13; 16:9–14; 19:13–15; 21:4; 22:5. Many of these are parables, a common place for Jesus to address wealth and possessions.

189. Also, see Luke 12:13–31; 16:19–31; 18:24–25.

190. Luke 18:28. For a fuller discussion of this story, including why Jesus asked the man to sell everything, see Bock, *Luke*, 2:1473–92.

191. Luke 19:3–4.

192. Luke 18:23; 19:2.

193. Bock, *Luke*, 2:1477–78, holds that Jesus' rejection of the term "good" likely suggests that the young ruler was trying to flatter Jesus (i.e., God's teacher) to try and perhaps earn his way into heaven.

194. Luke 19:8b.

Zacchaeus who apparently voluntarily seeks to pay back and be generous with his wealth.[195] Zacchaeus is another exemplar of generosity.[196]

Another example of generosity is the widow in 21:1–4 who puts two copper coins, all she has, into the treasury.[197] She is praised and made an exemplar by Jesus, and contrasted somewhat ironically with other generous people, but who are rich and are giving out of their riches.[198] She and the other characters who embrace this generosity seem to understand something fundamental about the movement of Jesus that the other characters, who continue to struggle with greed, do not understand. The generous characters have relativized material things in the light of God coming to earth. This climactic return of God to his people is worth celebrating with openness and generosity. The implication for the readers, then, is that they should do likewise and model the norm of generosity among the early Christian community.

Lydia, Timothy, and the "We" Passages

Lydia is a minor character who appears only in Acts 16. In response to Paul's preaching, "the Lord opened her heart to pay attention to what was said by Paul." She and her household were baptized, and she opened her house to them.[199] Lydia is an exemplar of hospitality to ministers of the word. Paul and Silas visit Lydia when they are released from prison later in the chapter.[200]

Timothy occurs more often in the narrative of Acts, but it could be argued that he does less than Lydia, as he is mostly mentioned accompanying Paul. Thus, it is difficult to label Timothy as the exemplar of a specific value (such as generosity, hospitality, etc.) because he is not often used to prescribe behavior in the narrative. He is, however, a faithful companion of Paul and Silas, traveling with them regularly. Since his father was Greek, he is another example of a disciple who does not fit the perfect image of a Jewish disciple. As such, he serves Luke's purposes. Perhaps he is the exemplar of missionary companionship, though little detail is given about this in Acts.

---

195. Though Luke does not record any dialogue between Jesus and Zacchaeus before Zacchaeus's declaration, certainly some conversation took place. However, in the text, the declaration comes without prompting from Jesus.

196. Zacchaeus also fits with Luke's focus on decentralization. He is an outsider, unwelcome by the people and unable to get to Jesus by conventional means. Thus, he is forced to be resourceful, and it pays off. This is yet another hint at the future inclusion of other outsiders, God-fearers included.

197. For the significance of widows in Luke–Acts, see Puthenkulam, "Significance"; Puthenkulam, "Widow"; Wright, "Widow"; Sugirtharajah, "Revalued," 42–43.

198. Bock, *Luke*, 2:1647, states, "It is important to note that Jesus is not putting down the contributions of others. Rather, he is noting the woman's great contribution, despite the gift's small size, since the size of a gift is not always indicative of the sacrifice."

199. Acts 16:14

200. Acts 16:40.

We also might wonder about the function of the "we" group in Acts. As mentioned in the introduction, there are a series of passages in Acts where the narrator uses the first person plural subject, potentially placing the narrator on the scene.[201] The "we" group in the narrative is involved in converting Lydia, witnessing the death and resurrection of Eutychus, warning Paul not to go to Jerusalem, and experiencing tribulation at sea. Again, it is difficult to clearly label this hypothetical "we" group as exemplars of a specific norm, but it is another interesting example of how Luke uses narrative to include the reader in the action of the story and prescribe approval and cooperation of, and even participation in the missionary activity to his audience. This assumption of ongoing missionary activity by the reader may again tie into the surprise ending of Acts if Luke expects the readers to continue in their own contexts in the spirit of the story.

Judas: Anti-Exemplar of Betrayal

Another anti-exemplar in Luke's writings is Judas. Judas embodies much of what is seen as evil in Luke's corpus. He was an instrument of Satan (22:3), he loves money more than Jesus (22:5), and he betrays Jesus with a kiss (22:48).[202] "Treachery or betrayal was considered one of the most heinous offenses in antiquity, a breach of sacred trust."[203]

Luke takes special care to pronounce judgment on Judas multiple times. Acts 1:18 highlights that the thing Judas did was wicked, and tells of the gruesome death that results. The prayer prayed by the apostles in Acts 1:24–5 mentions that Judas left "to go where he belongs." Luke even has Jesus himself pronounce a warning against Judas in 22:22: "The Son of Man will go as it has been decreed. But woe to that man who betrays him!" "Judas is portrayed as particularly hypocritical, for he betrays Jesus with a kiss."[204] The two references in Acts 1 serve as a haunting fulfillment to Jesus' warning in Luke 22. In addition, Judas is replaced by Matthias at Peter's urging, and although he never appears in the narrative again,[205] the episode cements the casting off of Judas.

Various lessons come from this story of Judas for Luke's readers. It is a warning against opposing God's kingdom, as seen elsewhere with Herod (Acts 12:23) and

---

201. Traditionally the "we" passages are listed as Acts 16:11–17; 20:5–15; 21:1–18; 27:1–29; 28:1–16. Some add 20:16–21 and 27:30–44 as well.

202. Judas is a prominent enough character in the narrative that it might be argued that he is more of an "anti-prototype," though the academic literature does not support such a category. Also, see Meyer, *Marginalized*; Bernas, "Death," 46–47.

203. Keener, *Acts*, 1:757. Consider Cornelius Nepos, *Generals* 14, 11.3–5; Quintus Curtius Rufus, *History of Alexander* 4.1.33; Livy *Ab urbe condita* 2.5.7–8; *Rhetorica ad Alexandrum* 36.

204. Bock, *Luke*, 2:1765.

205. A number of the Twelve disciples do not appear in the narrative again.

Ananias (5:5).[206] It also fits Luke's focus on generosity and the proper place of possessions as it subtly warns against the love of money. Lastly, perhaps it shows that although Judas was one of the Twelve, he is not immune to the temptations that come to all people. "In the context of Luke's entire work, Judas' failure to persevere sounds a warning to other would-be disciples."[207] One disciple's response to Jesus' arrest makes for an opportunity to make him into an anti-exemplar as well. In Luke 22:47–53, the disciples all want to fight the mob led by Judas who come to arrest Jesus. One disciple pulls a sword and cuts off the ear of the high priest's servant.[208] This leads to a rebuke by Jesus, "No more of this!"[209] The disciple is an anti-exemplar in his attempt to use violence, even for the seemingly noble cause of protecting Jesus from arrest. This, too, highlights a major change in the unfolding of history. Contrasted against the violence in the Old Testament, the followers of Jesus are not to fight and kill, as nonviolence and peacemaking is better than war and killing. This climactic time for God's people includes a radical shift in the way they relate to violence. Unfortunately, as seen other places, the Twelve do not seem to understand this.[210]

Parables: Exemplars in Story

The parables of Jesus in Luke are filled with exemplars and anti-exemplars, as the teaching moment all but requires them. Often these characters are paired to contrast one another. Scholars have noted the form and structure, and how many parables contain three main characters who represent God, God's people, and those who reject him.[211] Thus, it is easy to see an exemplar and anti-exemplar built into the parables,

---

206. Keener, *Acts*, 1:760.

207. Keener, *Acts*, 1:759.

208. Luke 22:49–50. John identifies the sword fighter as Peter, but the synoptics all leave him nameless. See Nolland, *Luke*, 3:1088; Bock, *Luke*, 2:1770–71; Marshall, *Luke*, 837; Moessner, "Reading." For a look at Jesus opposing violence in this scene, see Scheffler, "Non-Violence."

209. Luke 22:51. Other versions of this story (Matt 26:47–56; Mark 14:43–52; John 18:2–12) contain other details, including longer statements by Jesus. The most well known may be his statement in Matthew, where he says, "Put your sword back into its place; for all who take the sword will perish by the sword. Do you think that I cannot appeal to my Father, and he will at once send me more than twelve legions of angels? But how then would the scriptures be fulfilled, which say it must happen in this way?" Luke has Jesus' rebuke as shorter and simpler, but makes clear Jesus' opposition to fighting nonetheless.

210. Although it is outside the scope of this project, for a full exploration of non-violence in Luke-Acts, see Scheffler, "Vyandsliefde"; Scheffler, "Lord"; Burris, "Good Samaritan"; Welzen, "Vrede"; Okoronkwo, "Sword."

211. Blomberg, *Parables*, 447. Blomberg sees eleven parables that follow this structure, the most of his categories. Certainly scholars have given much attention to the parables of Jesus in the New Testament, and though a full exploration of these short stories goes beyond the scope of this project, some of the more poignant resources are listed bellow. For example, for more on the analysis and structure of parables, see Kistmaker, *Parables*; Inrig, *Parables*; Capon, *Kingdom*; Hultgren, *Parables*; Schottroff, *Parables*; Donahue, *Gospel*; Leonhard, "Parables"; Rindge, "Subversion"; Stagg, "Theological." For more practical interactions with the parables, see Gowler, *Parables*; Snodgrass, *Stories*; Lischer, *Reading*. For

which are clear examples of Luke's narrative strategy of using characters to prescribe behavior. The Good Samaritan in Luke 10 (an unlikely exemplar) is contrasted with the priest and the Levite (unlikely anti-exemplars, at least from the perspective of the people) in the story. Other times the anti-exemplar stands alone as a contrast against good behavior. Consider the rich fool in Luke 12 as another example of the danger of loving money.[212] The story of the prodigal son in Luke 15, which is one of three parables told in response to the criticism from the Pharisees and scribes of Jesus spending time with outcasts, contains several exemplars.[213] The younger son represents wastefulness and rudeness to his father, but is a positive exemplar of humility and change due to the realization of his situation. The older brother is not to be emulated because of his cold attitude toward his younger brother.[214] These exemplars are perhaps less unique to Luke and his mission in Luke–Acts. Other gospels have parables of Jesus that would seem to employ exemplars and anti-exemplars. However, they do not utilize minor characters the way Luke does as part of a transformational narrative purpose. Since parables essentially require exemplars and anti-exemplars to be transformative, the inclusion of such characters in parables is not particularly noteworthy. They are simply utilized to support the parables' various pedagogical functions in the story, rather than being ongoing characters.[215]

Gamaliel: Exemplar of Withholding Judgment

One final exemplar is worth exploring from Luke–Acts. In chapter 5, while Peter and the apostles are facing trial before the Jewish council for proclaiming Jesus, the council was about to put them to death[216] when Gamaliel spoke up. He is introduced as a Pharisee, a teacher of the law, and one respected by the people. This statement about his trustworthiness sets him up to be an exemplar.[217] His short speech ends by saying, "If this plan or this undertaking is of human origin, it will fail; but if it is of God, you will not be able to overthrow them—in that case you may even be

---

a look at the Jewish tradition of parables and how Jesus fits within that tradition, see Young, *Parables*.

212. See Morrison, "Reflections"; Mugabe, "Parable"; Spencer, "Creator"; Schumacher, "Saving."

213. See the section on the "Critic-Response Type-Scene" in chapter 2.

214. Johnson, *Luke*, 240–42; Crossan, *Polyvalent*; Jeremias, "Tradition." Other examples of parables in Luke that seem to suggest prescribed emulation are The Unjust Judge (Luke 18:1–8) and the Friend at Night (Luke 11:5–8), but suggesting persistence in prayer, and the Two Debtors (Luke 7:41–43), where the woman anointing his feet is portrayed as an exemplar, contrasted against the anti-exemplar of the critical Simon. Other parables attempt to simply describe the kingdom of God for the hearers (for example, Luke 13:18–19, 20–21), and do not offer an exemplar.

215. In this way, characters in parables may have more in common with prototypes, who have more of an idealized presentation to them as opposed to exemplars.

216. Acts 5:33.

217. The short introduction is an example of ethos, discussed in chapter 5.

found fighting against God!"[218] Gamaliel does not believe Jesus is the Messiah, but he has the wisdom to withhold judgment in case the movement is from God. "He is a voice of mature, wise reason among the apostles' opponents."[219] Thus, Gamaliel is an exemplar for Jews who may be unconvinced. Luke's message to them is that they should be patient and evaluate if the Christ movement is from God or not, lest they find themselves fighting against God, as the warning suggests. Perhaps the suggestion to await judgment applies to those unconvinced about Gentile inclusion as well. They would do well to model Gamaliel and withhold judgment, letting God's work in history have the last word.[220]

While Gamaliel has a worthy introduction, it is possible that some of Luke's audience know of him already. In Acts 22:3, Paul reports that he studied with Gamaliel in his youth.[221] If any of Luke's audience knew Paul, they may have known of Gamaliel as well. Although these are the only two occurrences of his name in the New Testament, Gamaliel is the only Rabbi named in Acts,[222] and he is quite well known in later Jewish tradition. Sotah 9:15, for example, describes Gamaliel's death: "When Rabban Gamaliel the Elder died, the glory of the Torah came to an end, and cleanness and separateness perished."[223] He was from the school of Hillel and held the title of "Rabban" (i.e., "our teacher").[224] In a text some date to the third century,[225] a suggestion is made that he became a secret disciple of Jesus,[226] saying, "Gamaliel . . . was secretly our brother in the faith, but by our advice remained among them,"[227] although there is much reason to doubt its credibility.[228] He is mentioned extensively in Josephus (in connection to his son)[229] and the Talmud.[230] With such a prominent place in the literature, it is possible

218. Acts 5:38b–39.

219. Bock, *Acts*, 249.

220. Acts 19:35–41 records the speech of the town clerk in Ephesus, who may be an exemplar for civility in the midst of disagreement. Like Gamaliel, the clerk does not agree with the Paul and the other Christians in Ephesus, as he declares the greatness of Artemis and that the statue fell from heaven. However, he does speak up for peace, and settling disputes in a civil manner.

221. "I am a Jew, born in Tarsus in Cilicia, but brought up in this city at the feet of Gamaliel, educated strictly according to our ancestral law, being zealous for God, just as all of you are today" (Acts 22:3).

222. See Bock, *Acts*, 249.

223. *b. Sotah* 9:15 (Neusner).

224. Neusner, *Traditions*, 341; Douglas, "Gamaliel," 395–96.

225. Smith, *Fathers*, 74.

226. Holladay, *Acts*, 146.

227. *Recognitions of Clement* 1:65 (Smith, *Fathers*, 94).

228. Douglas, "Gamaliel," 396. Also, see Smith, *Fathers*, 73, who states, "The writer of the work appears to have had no intention of presenting his statements as facts."

229. Josephus, *Life* 190–93, 216, 309.

230. *b. 'Erub.* 45a; *b. Ros Has.* 23b, 29b; *b. Yebam.* 90b, 115a, 122a (x3); *b. Mo 'ed Qat.* 27a; *b. Ketub.* 10b; *b. Sotah* 49a; *b. Git.* 32a, 33a, 34b, 35b; *b. 'Abod. Zar.* 11a; *b. Ber.* 38a; *b. Nid.* 6b. For a fuller list, see Bock, *Acts*, 349n4. Of course the Talmud only matters here to the extent that it may reflect

that the influential rabbinic teacher, who was at the peak of his career in the thirties and forties, may have been known to God-fearing Gentiles who had some connection to the synagogue and the Jewish faith only a few decades later.[231]

In the end, the council is swayed by Gamaliel's words and the disciples are flogged (rather than killed) and released.[232] The disciples then rejoice "that they were considered worthy to suffer dishonor for the sake of the name. And every day in the Temple and at home they did not cease to teach and proclaim Jesus as the Messiah."[233] The disciples here are exemplars for their boldness in proclaiming Jesus as the Messiah and in their response to suffering. Unfortunately, despite this opportunity to be bold and inspire the young church, the Twelve do not seize the opportunity, but rather, are bypassed in the work of the Spirit as part of the radical decentralization that happens.[234]

Conclusion

As we have seen, Luke employs a number of characters and tactics to serve his purposes of creating a "surface structure empathy hierarchy" for his readers and his transformative illocutionary intent of identity formation. This is done by presenting prototypical figures who serve as leaders in the recategorization process. In the book of Acts, these are Paul, Peter, and Cornelius.[235] The God-fearing reader of Acts is likely able to identify with the story and trajectory of the life of Cornelius. Perhaps this is the first God-fearing Christian the reader encounters. If the reader is facing pressure from Jewish brothers and sisters to complete the process of converting to Judaism then Cornelius provides another way. The reader can relate to Cornelius and certainly sees him as a character to model. His piety and generosity are worthy of emulating. More than that, he receives the Holy Spirit as the others did and receives Christian water baptism as well, thus taking part in the boundary crossing rituals in early Christianity. He is not a second-class citizen, but an important part of the unfolding of God's plan among the Gentiles. He shows hospitality and brings people into his home. This may plant the seed for future Gentile house churches led by God-fearers within the reach of Luke's letter.

Furthermore, Luke encourages and shapes behavior through employing exemplars, characters who model a single trait that is to be emulated. The author offers

---

first-century traditions.

231. Holladay, *Acts*, 146.

232. Acts 5:39b–40.

233. Acts 5:41b–42.

234. Also, see Crabbe, "Fighting"; Chilton and Neusner, "Gamaliel"; Zlotowitz, "Simeon"; Lyons, "Words"; Trumbower, "Historical."

235. Certainly, the prototypicality of Jesus continues into the book of Acts as well, but these three present the most prominent characters in the narrative.

the reader exemplars to emulate, often paired with anti-exemplars, or villains, who model a misuse of the values of the group. This allows the author not only to prescribe behavior and values, but to speak against certain behaviors as well.

In the end, Luke shows that Jesus' kingdom is open and diverse, including not only the Jewish people, but makes a way for God-fearing Gentiles as well. However, perhaps no impact is stronger than reading and hearing the story of Cornelius. This is central to Luke's transformative aim of creating social identity in his God-fearing reader. Narrative is a powerful force. There is an artistry in the way the narrative is crafted and how characters are used strategically. Through the masterful introduction and utilization of characters giving speeches, Luke shapes a narrative that meets his goals of identity formation. To appreciate fully Luke's use of characterization in Luke–Acts, a sophisticated understanding of rhetoric in the first century is needed. It is to these issues we now turn.

5

Luke's Identity-Forming Rhetoric and the Speeches in Acts

THE GOAL OF THIS monograph is to show that, in communicating primarily with an (implied) God-fearing audience, the author offers a narrative designed to craft social identity for (empirical) God-fearers in the first century. In historiographical writings of this sort, one would expect precisely the use of implications (the implied world projected by the text) to affect the empirical (or real) world. Consequently, we have established Luke's narrative insistence that God-fearers be accepted into the salvation story of Israel. This becomes their story through cultural memory. Their identity as children of God becomes salient[1] and Luke's vision of the disciples reaching the ends of the earth is seen.[2] As I will show, the implied author uses the tools of persuasive rhetoric to accomplish this aim. Of particular importance are the speeches by Luke's characters revealing Luke's rhetorical strategy. While a thorough examination of all of the speeches in Acts might be worthwhile, this work has already been done.[3] Two speeches in particular seem specifically focused on ushering God-fearers into the story of Israel, Acts 7 and Acts 13, and the current project will focus on those texts.

This leaves one significant area to consider: how and to what extent does Luke emulate the rhetorical conventions that we find in the literary world of the first century?[4] As mentioned in chapter 1, this will be an area where historical study will work as a checks and balances to help test arguments made about implied authors and audiences. Historical study provides empirical parameters for establishing the basic possibility of reconstructions of the implied author and audience. To this end, we will introduce the three primary elements of classical rhetoric and demonstrate how they can be seen in Luke's volumes. This will involve an examination of the speeches in Acts by Stephen and Paul in order to draw conclusions about Luke's rhetorical strategy. The reason for delaying the full discussion on rhetoric to this

1. Liu and László, "Narrative Theory," 86.
2. Acts 1:8.
3. Soards, *Speeches*, 1.
4. Lundin et al., "Promise," 71.

point is because of the desire to do so close to the robust discussion and application of the speeches. In addition, it made sense for us to establish Luke's narrative aims for identity formation before fully addressing rhetoric.

Rhetoric is the art form of persuasion, and evidence that it was used in the ancient world by first-century Christians is strong. "From the beginning it was taken for granted that the writings produced by early Christians were to be read as rhetorical compositions."[5] Likewise, Satterthwaite suggests that rhetoric was "a pervasive phenomenon in the Greco-Roman world."[6] Furthermore, rhetoric was an important part of Greek and Roman education.[7] In *Progymnasmata*, Kennedy offers various exercises students would do in order to become well versed in the skills of rhetoric.[8] Thus, there is sufficient scholarly evidence of rhetorical and compositional training in the first century, creating a basis for the rhetorical and persuasive skill of Luke.

However, rhetoric went beyond mere persuasion. Consider the following statement by Botha and Vorster: "Since its inception rhetoric has been recognized not only as promoting or effectively transmitting truth, but as actively creating truth, as actively creating social realities."[9] They go on to say that human beings exist within a world created by language.[10]

There were three types of rhetorical speech in the ancient Greco-Roman world as coined by Aristotle in his work, *On Rhetoric*: judicial, deliberative, and epidactic.[11]

---

5. Mack, *Rhetoric*, 10. Mack offers a concise and helpful discussion of rhetoric in the New Testament and will be a helpful starting point to understand the way in which the rhetorical method was present and utilized in the first century. For other treatments of rhetoric in the ancient world, particularly as it relates to the New Testament and material those writers used in crafting their narratives, see Classen, *Rhetorical Criticism*; Clines et al., *Art*; Corbett and Connors, *Classical Rhetoric*; Gitay, *Prophecy*; Jackson and Kessler, *Rhetorical Criticism*. Another important name in this field is George Kennedy, who specifically focuses on rhetoric in the Bible. See Kennedy, *Interpretation*. More modern authors include Kuypers, *Art*; Meynet, *Analysis*. Likewise, Stanley Porter has contributed to a number of works on the topic. See Porter et al., *Rhetorical Criticism*; Porter and Olbrichts, *Rhetoric*; *Scripture*; *Analysis*.

6. Satterthwaite, "Background," 338.

7. Marrou, *Education*, 84–85. Also, see Cordasco, *History*; Chiappetta, "Historiography."

8. Kennedy, *Progymnasmata*. Also, see Mallen, *Transformation*, 160–61. For more on similarities between Luke and the Progymnasmata, see Robbins, "Narrative"; Parsons, "Progymnasmata."

9. Botha and Vorster, "Introduction," 18.

10. Brotha and Vorster, "Introduction," 19.

11. Judicial rhetoric was specifically used in a trial before a jury or a judge. Onlookers to this sort of speech were thought to judge the performance and ask, "Did he do it or not?" Thus, the two subcategories were accusation and defense. Judicial speeches tended to deal with past events. Deliberative rhetoric primarily included the political debate that took place in an assembly or council. Observers to this sort of speech were sometimes called critics, and the content tended to deal with the future (i.e., "Would it be better to do this or that?"). The subcategories for deliberative rhetoric were persuasion and dissuasion. Epidactic rhetoric can be described as "public occasions of memorial." Onlookers to this sort of speech were thought of as spectators and the content had to do with the grounds for praise or blame, which were also the subcategories of the type. See Mack, *Rhetoric*, 34; Kennedy, *New History*, 4, for more on types of rhetoric.

"These three categories . . . remained fundamental throughout the history of classical rhetoric and are still useful in categorizing forms of discourse today."[12] Mack rightly suggests that the different categories were often mixed and the lines blurred. This point becomes even more important when talking about early Christianity: "Early Christian rhetoric was a distinctively mixed bag in which every form of rhetorical issue and strategy was frequently brought to bear simultaneously in an essentially extravagant persuasion."[13] However, early Christian rhetoric is most like deliberative rhetoric, as "every aspect of the new persuasion had to be approached as a matter of policy that would determine the future of (membership in) the community."[14] And, indeed, we will look primarily at the persuasive elements present in the speeches and rhetoric in Luke–Acts. However, this is not to suggest that other types of rhetoric are not seen or that they are unimportant. Kennedy, for example, points out the broadening of the epidactic category to include poetry and other types of writing "not aim[ed] at a specific action but is intended to influence the values and beliefs of the audience."[15] Of central consideration here are the canticles that dominate the early part of Luke's first volume, setting the stage for what follows.[16] Likewise, Mallen sees Luke as falling in line with the epidactic tradition, with an emphasis on strengthening beliefs already held by the audience.[17]

Gempf notes that, in the ancient world, rhetoric was power: "There are two ways to make a group of people do as you wish. You must either force them, or convince them."[18] Thus, "ancient historians tended to focus on battles *and* speeches as the events that shaped history. Modern socio-linguistics has re-discovered the 'event' character in some types of contemporary utterances, using the titles of 'performative speech acts' and 'performative language' for these related concepts."[19] This can most clearly be seen in the work of speech act theory. The theory, which dates back to J. L. Austin in the 1950s, emphasizes the functional nature of language: "Words do not just say things; they also do things."[20] Some have identified categories of speech acts as observed in Scripture, which include confession, forgiveness, teaching, promise, blessing, pronouncing judgment, and worship.[21] Thus, ancient rhetoric and speech-act theory are connected, but they are distinct as well. Where ancient rhetoric focuses on persuasion,

---

12. Kennedy, *New History*, 4.
13. Mack, *Rhetoric*, 35.
14. Mack, *Rhetoric*, 35.
15. Kennedy, *New History*, 4.
16. See chapter 3 on the Gospel, which discusses these canticles at length.
17. Mallen, *Transformation*, 164. Also, see Perelman and Olbrechts-Tyteca, *Rhetoric*, 54.
18. Gempf, "Public Speaking," 260.
19. Gempf, "Public Speaking," 261.
20. Brown, *Scripture*, 32.
21. Brown, *Scripture*, 34. These categories are dealt with in Briggs, *Words*; Thiselton, *Horizons*. Vanhoozer, *First Theology*, adds a couple more categories, such as "in instructing the believing community, testifying to Christ, and covenanting."

speech-act theory focuses on what words actually do. These two approaches combine to demonstrate how Luke creates social identity for his implied audience through using words to shape realities. Some examples will be helpful.

When Luke praises Cornelius the Roman centurion and God-fearer, he is creating a new social reality where that man is welcomed into the community, and social identity is created. When the character of the Ethiopian Eunuch asks, "Look! Here is water. What is to prevent me from being baptized?"[22] he is altering the social reality of exclusion salient for his audience. The narratively implied answer of the implied audience to this rhetorical question has to be, "*nothing* should prevent *us* from being baptized," and the inclusion of those who were once excluded on the basis of their race and nationality is emphasized. Again, the words are altering reality and creating social identity. Luke does this work of culture creation through the brilliant use of narrative. As Barthes says about the pervasiveness of narrative, "There is not, there has never been anywhere, any people without narrative; all classes, all human groups have their stories."[23]

On this point, Thiselton notes, "Texts can actively shape and transform the perceptions, understanding, and actions of readers and reading communities."[24] As an example, he demonstrates the ability of texts to shape reality by discussing a legal will, which holds power over the transfer of property from one party to another. Even if the will is misplaced, as soon as it is found, the text becomes an "act," and "changes the life of the beneficiary, perhaps giving rise to new hopes, new attitudes, and new actions."[25] Similarly, Briggs suggests that when a text teaches something, it can either (1) teach someone how to do something or (2) teach that something is the case, thus shaping behavior and belief.[26] This second function is the case with the narrative of Acts. Turning again to the example of the Ethiopian Eunuch, the reader's understanding of the categories of who is welcomed (and who is excluded) is altered by the text. If the reader holds beliefs that suggest foreign eunuchs, Gentiles, God-fearers, and other outsiders were not allowed to be a part of God's family—even if the reader thinks of him or herself as an outsider—the material presented and taught in the story clashes with that belief. Likewise, if a community reads the story, the beliefs of the community—whom they allow in and the criteria by which they judge fitness for inclusion and exclusion—must be re-evaluated. The boundary lines must be redrawn. Luke's words have the power to do this. As Brotha and Vorster say, we must acknowledge the power of language, "the power that binds and liberates that which we call 'real.'"[27]

---

22. Acts 8:36b.
23. Barthes, "Introduction," 237.
24. Thiselton, *Horizons*, 31.
25. Thiselton, *Horizons*, 32.
26. Briggs, *Words*, 259–60. Also, see Green, *Activities*, 4–9.
27. Brotha and Vorster, "Introduction," 25.

Briggs suggests that teaching by assertion, that is, teaching content, is often thought of as the lesser discipline as opposed to teaching someone how to do something.[28] However, he also states, "It is important not to downplay the significance of teaching content."[29] Quoting Moran, he continues, "The world remains in need of occasions when someone who knows something stands up and says, 'so and so is the case.'"[30] "This must always be held in balance with the all-pervasive activity of showing people how to live."[31] Luke is doing both of these things through his narrative. He is both asserting important information (i.e., God-fearers are not outsiders) and showing, through the use of characters and plotlines, how people should live (i.e., inclusively and generously).[32] Commonly, "one speech act will operate with a variety of illocutionary points of various strengths."[33] The narrative even walks the reader through the tension of the new inclusion and a model of how to defend oneself against critics.[34] Herein lies the power of narrative to shape the reality of the reader.[35]

Rhetoric in the First Century

By the first century, rhetoric had been influential in Palestine for several centuries. "Classical rhetoric was unquestionably a major contributor to the cultural milieu of Hellenistic Jews and Christians."[36] There is evidence of theaters and gymnasia in the Greek towns in Palestine during the time of Jesus that shows the ubiquity of speech-making venues in the first century.[37] "Hellenististic culture was a culture of rhetoric and rhetoric was clearly a public affair."[38] Although only certain people were specifically trained as rhetoricians in school, the influence had a much wider effect: "All people, whether formally trained or not, were fully schooled in the wily ways of sophists. . . . To be engulfed in the culture of Hellenism meant to have ears trained for the rhetoric of speech."[39] Similarly, for Henri Marrou, the historian of ancient education, "from the time of Isocrates, rhetoric was always, in practice, accepted as the normal means to the highest flights of education."[40] Thus, it is reasonable to conclude

---

28. Briggs, *Words*, 260. He calls this the "most mundane sense" and a "weak illocutionary act."
29. Briggs, *Words*, 261.
30. Moran, *Showing*, 33.
31. Briggs, *Words*, 261.
32. Acts 8:26–40; 10:1–48. Briggs, *Words*, 266, goes on to suggest that it is difficult to observe a speech act where it only asserts (i.e., a speech that that only passes on information).
33. Briggs, *Words*, 99.
34. Acts 11:1–30.
35. Bruce, "Significance," 20–28.
36. Black, "Rhetoric," 17. Also, see Marrou, *History*.
37. Mack, *Rhetoric*, 29.
38. Mack, *Rhetoric*, 29. Also, see Kennedy, *New History*, 8–12.
39. Mack, *Rhetoric*, 31.
40. Marrou, *History*, 196.

that whoever the author of Luke-Acts was, they would have likely had the opportunity to gain rhetorical skill. In Acts, the speeches offered by characters are rhetorically shaped, as will become clear below.

Not all agree what rhetorical study should look like. For example, Perelman and Olbrechts-Tyteca in their work *The New Rhetoric*,[41] based on the previous work of Kenneth Burke,[42] suggest that the modern tools of discourse and the social theory of language are central to the understanding of rhetoric.[43] This has energized rhetoric to rise above "the sphere of mere ornamentation, embellished literary style, and the extravagances of public oratory."[44] Several critiques have arisen from this movement. First, Margaret Mitchell, following the approach of Betz,[45] suggests that while true rhetorical study of the New Testament must be historical and rooted in the first century, the "New Rhetoric" tends to be nonhistorical and anachronistic, concluding, "Appeals to Modern philosophical examinations of the rhetorical force of all texts should not be put at the service of historical arguments."[46] This is key for Mitchell, who sees fundamental differences in the two approaches to rhetoric (i.e., old and new, historical and modern).[47] Fiorenza critiques the work of the new rhetorical school from the other side, suggesting that they have not gone far enough: "[Modern rhetorical criticism] has failed to make the full turn to a political rhetoric of inquiry insofar as it has not developed critical epistemological discourses and a hermeneutic of suspicion but instead has sought to validate its disciplinary practices in and through the logos of positivist or empiricist science that occludes its own rhetoricity."[48]

So where does that leave us? Is the rhetoric of the New Testament solely rooted in the historical speeches and handbooks of the ancient world, or can advances in language and speech theory add to the conversation in meaningful and authentic ways? We must explore ways to embrace this tension. Mack acknowledges the advancements of "new rhetoric,"[49] but seeks connections with ancient rhetoric: "As any scholar with some acquaintance with the classical traditions knows, the new rhetoric is actually a rediscovery of the old. The old rhetoric was also a 'treatise on argumentation' based on the discriminating observance of discourse in the social sphere."[50] Thus, for the current

---

41. Perelman and Olbrechts-Tyteca, *Rhetoric*.
42. See Burke, *Motives*.
43. Mack, *Rhetoric*, 15–16.
44. Mack, *Rhetoric*, 15–16.
45. See Betz, *Galatians*.
46. Mitchell, *Reconciliation*, 6–7.
47. Mitchell, *Paul and Rhetoric*, 7–8, and footnotes there.
48. Fiorenza, *Rhetoric*, 86. Fiorenza offers a feminist critique of rhetoric, both old and new, and claims that new rhetoric has only made a "half turn."
49. Perelman and Olbrechts-Tyteca, *Rhetoric*, 1969.
50. Mack, *Rhetoric*, 16. Mack continues, "The Greeks took a fancy to the game of public debate, noticed the skill required to participate in the public forum, worked out the rules, and called it the art of speaking. They thought that knowing the rules would enhance the practice and hone the

work, in dealing with the New Testament, we will seek to stay rooted in the text, the ancient literature, but we will not hesitate to utilize breakthroughs in communication theory and contributions from the new rhetoric as they help us to understand the ancient literature better (i.e., speech act theory).

Having examined two aspects of Luke's rhetorical strategy (the schema of promise-fulfillment [chapter 3] and the transformative use of prototypical characters [chapter 4]), we now turn to two others: his strategic use of speeches and of names.[51]

I will argue that Stephen and Paul are both carefully presented as worthy speakers, and as such, communicate an important message to the audience through their speeches. This matches the accepted schema of speech giving in the ancient world, and thus, Luke's audience, having some experience with the cultural phenomenon of rhetoric, would have picked up on the force of these speeches.

Kennedy breaks down the organization of ancient rhetoric into five parts.[52] The first of these, invention, is where the art of persuasion primarily dwells, and he presents two forms of persuasion: direct evidence and artistic persuasion.[53] The effectiveness of the persuasion usually came down to the artistic elements. These were ethos, pathos, and logos.[54] These three rhetorical tools are essential for persuasion, and although they remain fairly consistent in rhetorical thought throughout the ancient Greco-Roman world, the conversation does not stop there. For example, Dionysius in *On Imitation* adopts these three elements of persuasion, but adds beauty, magnificence, strength, force, intensity, abundance, a multitude of figures, sweetness, persuasion, grace, and naturalness.[55] Others included at times are sublimity, elegance, solemnity, gravity, and combativeness.[56] For the scope and purpose of this book, ethos, pathos, and logos remain the focus, as they are accepted as being most relevant to the ancient world in modern scholarship.[57]

---

performance of speaking persuasively as well. They produced handbooks for teaching this technology, an archive of practical knowledge, educational syllabi, and models for mimesis (imitation). They also cultivated occasions of playing the game of repartee, developed a satire capable of bringing critique to rhetorical performance, and created a culture thoroughly at ease with its knowledge that all discourse was rhetorical."

51. For other discussion on the rhetorical strategies of Luke, see Mallen, *Transformation*, 164–97; Darr, *Character*; O'Toole, *Unity*; Green, *Theology*; Estes, *Questions*.

52. Kennedy, *New History*, 4–6. Kennedy lists the five parts as invention, arrangement, style, memory, and delivery. Also, see Cicero, *Invention*, 4.

53. Kennedy, *New History*, 4.

54. Kennedy, *New History*, 4–5. By contrast, whereas Kennedy outlines the full scope of ancient Greco-Roman rhetoric, Mack focuses more pointedly on these three elements as central to the rhetorical event and the primary points of discussion when evaluating rhetoric. See Mack, *Rhetoric*, 36.

55. Dionysius of Halicarnassensis, "On Imitation," 197–217. See translation in Kennedy, *New History*, 164.

56. Dionysius of Halicarnassensis, *On Thucydides*, 16. For commentary, see Kennedy, *New History*, 164.

57. Consider, for example, that Mack, Black, and Kennedy, the last of these listing many other options, still give priority to these three persuasive elements as industry standards. Mack and Kennedy

Ethos referred to the personhood and character of the speaker. If a speaker did not have a reputation as trustworthy and knowledgeable, he was not a worthy rhetorician for an audience to listen to. "We believe good men more fully and more readily than others: this is true generally whatever the question is, and absolutely true where exact certainty is impossible and opinions are divided."[58] However, even if the speaker was somewhat unknown to the audience, he or she could still develop an ethos early on in the speech to win the audience's ear.

Secondly, it was important for a speaker to know the audience, "its convictions, native traditions, and moods."[59] This is the element of pathos. For Aristotle, "Persuasion may come through the hearers, when the speech stirs the emotions. Our judgments when we are pleased and friendly are not the same as when we are pained and hostile."[60] How a speaker engages his or her audience and plays to them, including appeals to emotion and affective responses, was a key part of rhetoric. These elements were heightened toward the end of a speech when the response was needed. However, ethos and pathos were important to maintain throughout the entirety of the rhetorical event.[61]

Aristotle spoke of emotions quite frequently in *On Rhetoric*.[62] Some rhetoricians after his time took the performance and demonstration of emotion to a new level.[63] From a persuasive perspective, Aristotle held that the speaker wanted to keep his or her audience content and happy.[64] But, this was not universally agreed upon, and certainly other opinions and practices worked their way into the rhetorical culture. Plutarch, for example, a representative of early Roman rhetoric, consistently displays moral outrage, suggesting that in later rhetoric, pathos was heavily reliant on more extreme forms of emotion, rather than simply keeping the audience happy.[65]

The third element is logos, or the content of the speech. "Logos referred to the ideas, structure, and logic of a speech evaluated in terms of their persuasive force."[66] Similarly, Aristotle says, "Persuasion is effected through the speech itself when we have proved a truth or apparent truth by means of the persuasive arguments suitable

---

are cited above. Also, see, Black, *Gospel*.

58. Aristotle, *Rhetoric*, 8.

59. Kennedy, *New History*, 48. Mack, *Rhetoric*, 36. Also, see Wisse, *Ethos*.

60. Aristotle, *Rhetoric*, 8.

61. Mack, *Rhetoric*, 36.

62. After an introduction in book 1, book 2 is almost entirely devoted to discussion of emotions.

63. For example, Marcus Antonius, who was defending a man on trial, once "ripped the toga from the scarred body of the old soldier to exhibit his wounds and evoked the jury's sympathy by calling upon the name 'of every god and man, citizen and ally.'" Or Quintilian, who when describing cases he has defended, explains, "I have frequently been so stirred that not only have tears overwhelmed me, but pallor and symptoms of grief." See Kennedy, *New History*, 112–13, 184.

64. Aristotle, *Rhetoric*, 8.

65. Kennedy, *New History*, 102–3.

66. Mack, *Rhetoric*, 36. Also, see Brown, *Power*; Cahn, "Rhetoric"; Cameron, *Development*.

to the case in question."⁶⁷ Logos received the most attention in ancient rhetorical handbooks.⁶⁸

The concept of *logos* has a complex history in the ancient world.⁶⁹ It was a key trait of humanity in the Greek world, differentiating them from animals.⁷⁰ For example, Isocrates writes,

> In most of our abilities we differ not at all from the other animals; we are in fact behind many in swiftness and strength and other resources, but because there is inborn in us an instinct to persuade each other and to make clear to each other whatever we wish, we not only have escaped from living as brutes, but also by coming together have founded cities and set up laws and invented arts; and logos has helped us attain practically all of the things we have devised. . . . If I must sum up this power, we shall find that nothing done with intelligence is done without speech, but logos is the marshal of all actions and thoughts, and those must use it who have the greatest wisdom.⁷¹

Similarly discussing the power of logos, in the Encomium of Helen, Gorgias compares the effect of speech upon a hearer to the effect of drugs upon the human body.⁷² Suffice it to say, the logos element of persuasion is seen as central in much of the ancient world. It is key to identify the logos present in the speeches in the book of Acts. More will be said on this below.

These three categories help us evaluate Luke's rhetorical skill. We will use these to assess two of the primary speeches in Acts, the defense of Stephen before the Sanhedrin in Acts 7 and Paul's first public address in Acts 13.⁷³ We considered how these speeches resonated with God-fearers in chapter 2. Here we continue that conversation, but give particular attention to Luke's strategic use of rhetorical conventions as he seeks to decentralize the new Christian movement in the first century and to form social identity among the audience. We also investigated Luke's gospel message of promise and fulfillment in chapter 3, noting the importance of Israel's history in creating identity in the audience's present. These two speeches are crucial for achieving that on behalf of the audience. However, before we turn to the rhetorical elements

---

67. Aristotle, *Rhetoric*, 8.

68. Mack, *Rhetoric*, 36. Also, see Billig, "Psychology"; Schiappa, *Protagoras*.

69. For example, it can mean "word," "phrase," "speech," "logic," and even makes its way into the opening line of John's Gospel. Kennedy, *New History*, 11–12.

70. Kennedy, *New History*, 12.

71. Isocrates, "Nicocles or the Cyprians" 5–6, 9a (Kennedy, *New History*, 12).

72. Gorgias of Leontini, "Encomium of Helen" 15 (Dillon and Gergel, *Sophists*, 81–82). "The effect of speech upon the structure of the soul is as the structure of drugs over the nature of bodies; for just as different drugs dispel different secretions from the body, and some bring an end to disease, and others to life, so also in the case of speeches some distress, other delight, some cause fear, others embolden their hearers, and some drug and bewitch the soul with a kind of evil persuasion."

73. Speeches are an emphasis for Luke, with over one hundred verses in Acts alone. Soards, *Speeches,* 1; Schneider, "Die Reden."

in the speeches specifically, given the preponderance of names in those speeches we first need to explore Luke's strategic use of names.

The Use of Names in the Historiographical Speeches in Acts

Acts 7 and 13, the chapters that will be in primary focus below, involve a robust list of names, which puts them in a rare spot compared to other New Testament literature.[74] The high occurrence of names in these chapters is a natural consequence of the recounting of Jewish salvation history. As with the canticles, these names form a crucial part of Luke's rhetorical strategy that fits Luke's transformative illocution of identity formation.[75] Here are three other names that are central to Luke's rhetorical strategy. Moses and David are central Old Testament characters that make their way throughout the central speeches and Shechem is a strategic geographical reference.

Moses

We will discuss more fully the importance of Moses in the discussion on the speech below, but we have mentioned previously that the God-fearing reader identifies with Moses through being an outsider. Johnson suggests that Moses is the key to understanding the purpose of Stephen's speech.[76] Moses also has clear similarities with Jesus as the rejected deliverer, and represents some of the key scenes in Israel's history (i.e., exodus, wilderness wandering, etc.).[77] Moses is a symbol for New Testament Christianity that represents salvation and the New Exodus. He is of interest for Luke, and in fact, "Luke has selected and shaped the materials of the tradition in order to emphasize Moses as a prophet and as the type of Jesus, the 'prophet whom God would raise up.'"[78] In addition to the twenty-nine references to him in the two volumes, the narrative connections of the rejected prophet and deliverer are obvious.[79] Each time Moses's name is mentioned, the reader calls to mind the narrative realities of the liberating New Exodus that is for all people. A fuller exploration of how this works in the speeches is needed, and will be included in the section below.

---

74. Others include genealogies (Matt 1; Luke 3) and Heb 11.

75. See chapter 3. Also, see Barr, "Symbolism"; Hartman, "Into."

76. Johnson, *Acts*, 135. Johnson sees a two-fold structure in both the life of Moses and the life of Jesus, and connects the slaves in Egypt with the Jews in Jerusalem as portrayed in Acts.

77. See above in this chapter.

78. Johnson, *Acts*, 136.

79. Also, see Ringgren, "Old Testament."

David

Likewise, we will examine the role of David in Paul's speech, including the connection of Jesus as the promised son of David. Although only mentioned briefly in Stephen's speech, the Israelite king plays a role throughout Luke's corpus. Luke is interested in connecting Jesus with the Davidic tradition and rooting Jesus' identity as the Messiah in the line of David. For example, there are six references to David in the birth narratives.[80] Bovon rightly highlights Luke 1:32–33 as centrally focusing on the Davidic Messiah-king imagery,[81] but also sees some of the language selected that was more Hellenistic that would be understood by a wider readership.[82] This is a helpful observation, for, if true, it shows evidence of Luke not only tying the story of Jesus and the Way to Israel's history, as is obvious, but that he was intentionally using language to welcome non-Jews. Although God-fearers would have had some familiarity with the narratives and major figures in Judaism due to their regularity at the synagogue, they would also likely have a working knowledge of Hellenism, and thus, a reference that could include both would be quite strategic in creating a superordinate identity. Particularly in Luke 1:32, the author portrays Jesus as the birth of a hero and king, which has parallels to David's life in 2 Samuel 7 and 1 Chronicles 17:11–14, but was also used messianically at Qumran.[83] We see again the author's use of intertextual cues that refer the mind of the reader back to a shared story of cultural memory. Luke is interested in the rhetorical force and messianic implications that come from Jesus being born as a son of David, in the city of David, and with a kingly lineage.[84]

Shechem

The two references to Shechem in 7:16 are the only usages of that word in the New Testament. As we will see, there is a connection with Samaria and the conversion of the Samarians, which will happen only a chapter later. However, Shechem holds an important place in Jewish salvation history that stretches far beyond simply the burial site of Jacob and other ancestors. In addition, Luke seems to be particularly interested in geography, for as we have seen, his gospel presents Jesus journeying to Jerusalem, before Acts shows a move away from Jerusalem to the ends of the earth. Likewise, as we will explore below, Luke uses the concept of the land, so important to Israel's identity, as an important and surprising element of decentralization. Luke understands

---

80. Luke 1:27, 32, 69; 2:4 (x2), 11.

81. "He will be great, and will be called the Son of the Most High, and the Lord God will give to him the throne of his ancestor David. He will reign over the house of Jacob forever, and of his kingdom there will be no end" (Luke 1:32–33).

82. Bovon, *Luke*, 51.

83. Johnson, *Acts*, 37.

84. Also, see Sargent, *David*; Doble, "Songs"; Strauss, *Messiah*.

both the historical importance of the land for identity, but also the need for the shift away from the land and to the community for identity formation.

With regard to Shechem, Joshua chooses it as the place to reaffirm the law and renews the covenant before he himself is buried there a few verses later.[85] In First-Chronicles, it is declared a city of refuge, where people were not able to take revenge.[86] Lastly, Shechem is the location that Rehoboam is made king.[87] Thus, Stephen's mention of Shechem as the burial place for the family of Jacob in Egypt calls to mind a string of history for the informed reader. This may be part of Luke's rhetorical strategy to emphasize covenant renewal and refuge for outsiders in his communication with his God-fearing readers who are clearly somewhat knowledgeable of Israel's history.[88] This important geographical location in Israel's history locates the kingdom of God in Luke is a place of refuge for the outsider, a sign to God-fearers of inclusion.

Stephen's Identity-Forming Rhetoric

I will show that Stephen's speech in Acts 7 mirrors the three primary persuasion factors that can be identified in Aristotelian rhetoric, ethos, pathos, and logos. These rhetorical elements provide an outline for evaluation of the speeches, and serve Luke's purpose of the formation of social identity.

Stephen's Ethos

Aristotle held that the character of the speaker "may almost be called the most effective means of persuasion he possesses."[89] Furthermore, we might say, as Botha and Vorster have, that "discourse is no longer treated as something distinct and separate from the knower, but is seen as an extension of the person."[90] Thus, Stephen's persuasive force to the implied audience flows out from his established character in the narrative. As we will see below, this ethos, with special attention given to the authority he carries, is clearly demonstrated early on, before the character begins to speak. To the degree that Luke presents Stephen as noteworthy and outstanding among his peers, he is establishing a positive ethos and preparing the reader to place special import on what the character does and says. This is a key part of Luke's identity forming intent, and it

---

85. Josh 24:25, 32.

86. 1 Chr 6:67.

87. 1 Kgs 12:1; 2 Chr 10:1. It is also at Jacob's well in Sychar, near Shechem, that Jesus declares his messianic identity to the Samaritan woman in John 4. See John 4:4–6.

88. For more on Schechem, see Lemche, "Past"; Carlen, "Review"; Goff, "Foolish."

89. Aristotle, *Rhetoric*, 8.

90. Botha and Vorster, "Introduction," 20. Also, see Worthington, *Voice*; Sterling, *Historiography*; Tyson, "History."

works in conjunction with his use of prototypes and exemplars.[91] Kennedy asserts that identifying the speaker with the authority of God is a key means of rhetoric in the Bible, and that "the preacher is thus to be a vehicle through which an authoritative message will be expressed."[92] As mentioned in chapters 2 and 4, Luke includes a number of minor characters in his works, and often introduces them quickly.[93] How does he introduce Stephen and establish him as credible? Stephen's ethos is created through (1) what is said about him in the text and (2) his role in the narrative as a change agent.

Stephen enters the narrative as the headlining character of those selected by the people to oversee food distribution. He is presented as, "a man full of faith and the Holy Spirit." Then, in 6:8, he is described as a man full of God's grace and power, who works miracles. Thus, even as he is introduced, Stephen immediately stands out as remarkable. These elements are demonstrated in three ways.

First, Stephen is shown as a worker of miracles who does great wonders and signs (τέρατα καὶ σημεῖα μεγάλα). This puts him in esteemed company, reminding the reader of Jesus and the disciples who also worked miracles. A chapter before (Acts 5:12–13) the disciples perform "many signs and wonders" (σημεῖα καὶ τέρατα πολλὰ) among the people, which wins them favor. While the disciples do many (πολλὰ) signs, Stephen does great (μεγάλα) signs. Pelikan points out the key nature of the term sign (σημεῖον) in the New Testament and in Acts: "[σημεῖον] explicitly points beyond the deed, howsoever spectacular it might be, to that *stignatum* for which the deed served as *signum*. A miracle was not a stained-glass window to be looked at, but a transparent window to be looked through."[94] Pelikan uses a helpful semantic framework to understand and explain what Luke is doing, that is, use these signs to establish Stephen as a trustworthy spokesperson for Christianity. Bruce states that the mention of the laying on of hands in the story of Stephen (Acts 6:6) is after the recognition of him being "full of the Holy Spirit," and that perhaps he is performing signs and wonders before he is recognized by the disciples.[95] If so, Stephen is truly an example of the Holy Spirit selecting a special agent to use in spite of the work of the disciples, although he is confirmed and recognized by them in time. Stephen is not one of the Twelve, but is the representative of the group chosen to oversee food distribution. In the end, it is all the more reason for Stephen to be considered trustworthy.[96]

---

91. See chapter 4 on prototypes and exemplars, which specifically talks about both Stephen and Paul.

92. Kennedy, *New History*, 139. Also, see Wolfe, "Elements"; Kistemaker, "Speeches."

93. Another comparable example of this is Apollos in Acts 18, whose entire resume is given in only a few verses.

94. Pelikan, *Acts*, 98. Also, see BDAG.

95. Bruce, *Acts*, 124.

96. Pao, "Waiters"; Sell, "Seven"; Thompson, "Diaspora"; Paroschi, "Significance"; Brodie, "Accusing."

Second, Stephen is presented as a man of great wisdom. In Acts 6:9, a diverse group of people stood up to argue with Stephen,[97] "but they could not withstand the wisdom and the Spirit with which he spoke."[98] Interestingly, forms of the word σοφία occur in Acts four times, and each of them is in connection with Stephen. In 6:3 the disciples will select men "full of the Spirit and of wisdom," of which Stephen is the prime example. In ch. 6:10, Stephen's opponents are unable to stand up to his wisdom. In chapter 7, σοφία describes Moses, the central character of the speech.[99] He plays a rhetorical role in the speech as representing the exodus and pointing to the New Exodus. In addition, Moses lived among the Midianites and married a Midianite woman,[100] so perhaps outsiders would connect with him.

Because of this direct semantic connection between Stephen and σοφία, Luke's presentation of Stephen as a man of wisdom is all the more acute. The overt point is that when opposition arises from the elite Jewish leadership in the Sanhedrin, they are not able to stand up to the wisdom the Spirit has given him.[101] Thus, Luke is making a statement not only about Stephen, but about the kind of wisdom that the Spirit gives to his people that will prepare them to stand against formidable enemies. Although Stephen has abruptly come on the scene, the reader has no reason to doubt Stephen's wisdom, as he is outdoing the best the opposition has to offer. Luke could hardly establish Stephen's ethos more effectively.

Third, Stephen is falsely accused, but defends himself. The debate with the opponents turns sour when they conspire to have Stephen arrested for speaking "blasphemous words against Moses and God." Luke makes it clear that Stephen is falsely accused (6:13), securing the ethos of Stephen in the midst of these accusations. More than establishing Stephen as innocent, it also sets up his opponents as false witnesses.

---

97. Much is made in scholarship of the identity and significance of this synagogue called "the synagogue of the Freedmen" and those listed as being a part of it. Bruce interprets this to be a synagogue in Jerusalem attended by "Jews from several lands of the dispersion," potentially even the Theodotus inscribed synagogue discovered on Ophel. See Bruce, *Acts*, 124–25. Regardless of the specific synagogue, the point seems to be the diversity of this group, which is somewhat significant, as it creates a picture of those opposing Stephen, who are diverse.

98. Acts 6:10. Also, see Smith, "Spirit."

99. Acts 7:10, 22.

100. Exod 2:18–21.

101. Schneider, *Die Apostelgeschichte*, 435–36, says, "Auf dem Hintergrund des Wunderwirkens überrascht die Angabeüber die Aktion der hellenistischen Synagogenangehörigen, die mit Stephanus disputieren. Ihre Aktion brachte es nicht zustande, dem Stephanus in der Diskussion standzuhalten, d. h. ihn zuwiderlegen... Die Widersacher des Stephanus werden kaum an seinen Wundertaten Anstoß genommen haben. Es ist wohl vorausgesetzt, dass Stephanus gerade unter ihnen in Jerusalem missionierte. In der Disputation, die Stephanus als 'Pneumatiker' führte, konnten die Gegner ihn nicht überwinden. Ihr Widerstand war zum Scheitern verurteilt." ("Against the background of the miracle work, the reference to the Hellenistic synagogue members arguing with Stephen is surprising. In the discussion, their course of action failed to stand up to Stephen, that is, to refute him... Stephen's adversaries will hardly have taken offense at his miracles. There is an apparent presumption that Stephen was an active missionary precisely among them, in Jerusalem. In the disputation conducted by Stephen, the 'pneumatic,' the opponents could not overcome him. Their resistance was doomed to fail.")

Bearing false witness is a "common act of the wicked" in the Old Testament.[102] The Proverbs warn against false witnesses, asserting that they will not go unpunished.[103] This is the only place in Luke's two volumes that ψευδής occurs. Thus, just as wicked people opposed Jesus and other members of the early church, they oppose Stephen as well. He is a Christian example of how to handle oneself in the face of opposition by the wicked, and in that, part of Luke's transformative rhetorical strategy.

There is a common stream in Scripture of false witnesses and the response of the righteous. In the Psalms, David calls for God to take up his case against those who falsely accuse him,[104] and other times calls out their false accusations against him.[105] Keener helpfully connects this story with two other antecedents in Hebrew Scripture, suggesting that the false accusations leading to the stoning of Stephen recall the corruption of Ahab and Jezebel in 1 Kings 21:8–15 toward Naboth, although he actually sees Stephen more as a miracle worker like Elijah.[106] Similarly, the people wanted to stone Moses at one point as well, further intertwining the two characters.[107]

We find similar connections in Mark and Matthew.[108] Although Luke does not include the details of false accusations against Jesus in his gospel as in Mark 14:55–59, some have suggested that this is an intentional omission since he mentions their parallels here.[109] However, he emphasizes Jesus' innocence more than the other gospels, as Pilate pronounces Jesus innocent three different times,[110] and Luke 23:47 records a final time when the centurion at the foot of the cross does so as well.[111] Thus, the innocence of Jesus in the face of his trial and crucifixion highlights the corruption and false accusation not explicitly stated in Luke. This emphasis on false accusation becomes yet another way that the character of Stephen is presented as a disciple who is very similar to his Lord.

Jesus will also teach his disciples about false accusations in Matthew, when he says, "Blessed are you when people insult you, persecute you and falsely say all kinds

---

102. Bock, *Acts*, 273. Haenchen, *Acts*, 271. For the OT references to the wicked practice of bearing false witness, see Exodus 20:16; Deuteronomy 19:16–18; Psalm 27:12; 35:11; Proverbs 14:5; 24:28. Also, see Brehm, "Vindicating."

103. Prov 3:30; 19:9.

104. Ps 35:21–23.

105. Ps 109:1–5.

106. Keener, *Acts*, 2:1315.

107. Exod 17:4.

108. See Mark 14:55–59. Matthew and Mark both present Pharisees, Chief Prists, and Teachers of the Law scheming and plotting to kill Jesus for his teaching and claims (Matt 12:24; 16:21; 26:3; Mark 3:6; 8:31; 11:18; 14:1).

109. Keener, *Acts*, 2:1311, and footnote there.

110. Luke 23:4, 14–15, 22.

111. The word used in this instance, δίκαιος, can be translated "righteous" or "innocent," and versions are split with how they render the English here. NIV11, KJV, HCS, and ASV, go with the former, whereas ESV, NLT, and NASB opt for the latter. See Mack, "Innocent"; Matera, "Death"; Soards, "Tradition."

of evil against you because of me." The parallel in Luke does not include the part about false witnesses, but does include exclusions, insults, and hate on account of their association with Jesus.[112]

There are examples of false accusations of heroes outside of the biblical canon, including the narrative of 1 Maccabees. Telling the story of the suffering of the Jews under the horrendous acts of Antiochus IV Epiphanes, and the valiant rebellion led by Matthias and his three sons, it reports of some particularly unjust suffering of the Jews, including the desecration of the Temple and holy relics.[113] Similarly, 2 Maccabees tells of some particularly horrible suffering of certain people that highlight their honorability and innocence. Eleazar faces the possibility of death if he does not eat pork, while his opponents try to force his mouth open to eat it.[114] His speech before his death highlights his honor in the face of terrible persecution.[115] Lastly, the story of the Jewish mother and her seven sons[116] provides another troubling example of persecution and torture, but also reinforces the idea of honor of the suffering: "And so the boy died, with absolute trust in the Lord, never unfaithful for a minute."[117]

For a final example, consider Socrates, "who though falsely charged, felt no guilt, in contrast to the false witnesses against him."[118] Despite being far removed from Luke's writings, it is at least possible that the author and audience both have some familiarity with the philosopher's story and that he was falsely accused in his death. At the very least, it shows the textual basis and long-standing tradition both inside and outside of Scripture for heroes being falsely accused. Stephen is a part of the men of "good reputation" in 6:3, contrasted with the false witnesses.[119] His authority to speak and his respectability from the audience are clearly established in Luke's narrative.

Luke goes to great lengths to display the positive ethos of Stephen and present him as a wise and trustworthy character. There are semantic (i.e., σοφία) as well as thematic connections (i.e., false accusations) both imbedded within the larger narrative framework of Luke's two-volume work and the litany of minor characters presented. More space is given to Stephen than nearly any other minor character in Luke.[120] These elements show his skill as a rhetorician and how he was aware of the Aristotelian tool of ethos.

---

112. Luke 6:22. This emphasis on false accusations is present various times in the epistles as well, though it is unlikely Luke had access to these writings. See 1 Peter 3:17–20.

113. 1 Macc 1:57–67.

114. 2 Macc 6:18.

115. 2 Macc 6:23–28.

116. 2 Macc 7:1–42.

117. 2 Macc 7:40.

118. Keener, *Acts*, 2:1315. See *Xen. Apol.* 24.

119. Keener, *Acts*, 2:1312.

120. Cornelius in chapters 10–11 may be close, but Stephen, with the length of his speech, still commands more space in the narrative.

Pathos in Stephen's Speech

The pathos of Stephen's speech leads us to three considerations: (1) What was the response of the audience in the narrative? (2) What would have been the expected response of the authorial audience? (3) What is the intended effect of the emotive events referenced by Stephen? We will address these in turn.[121]

What Was the Emotional Response of His Audience in the Narrative?

The most obvious emotional response is from the contextual audience of the Sanhedrin, who get infuriated following the speech. In the last part of the speech, Stephen turns to harsh accusation (7:51–53). As mentioned above, although Aristotle and early rhetorical tradition attempted to keep the audience happy, diverse opinions and practice existed in the ancient world, and certainly depended on context. Stephen's approach comes closest to moral outrage, as modeled by Marcus Antonius, Quintilian, and others.[122] Stephen's closing section opens with three direct accusations.

1. You stiff-necked people
2. Uncircumcised in heart and ears
3. You are forever resisting the Holy Spirit just like your ancestors used to do

These accusations connect the members of the Sanhedrin with disobedient Israel wandering in the wilderness. God himself calls the Israelites of this period "stiff-necked."[123] That word, σκληροτράχηλος, is used of the wilderness community five times[124] and is used only one other time in the Old Testament.[125] Likewise, the word used for "resist" in verse 51, ἀντιπίπτω, is the same word used to describe the wilderness wandering in Numbers 27:14.[126] Bruce connects the accusation of uncircumcised hearts with "unresponsiveness and resistance to God's revelation," reminiscent of warnings such as Deuteronomy 10:16 and Jeremiah 4:4.[127] Ultimately, the connection with wandering, disobedient Israel is quite clear and makes for a harsh critique by Stephen.

---

121. For other examples, see Gorman, "Persuading"; Stock, "Pathos"; DiCicco, *Ethos*.
122. Kennedy, *New History*, 112–13, 184.
123. Exod 33:5. See Bruce, *Acts*, 151–52.
124. Exod 33:3, 5; 34:9; Deut 9:6, 13.
125. Prov 29:1. The only New Testament usage is here in 7:51.
126. Keener, *Acts*, 2:1423. It only occurs three times in the Old Testament—as technical descriptions of building the tabernacle (Exod 26:5, 17) and this one other time describing the wilderness community.
127. Bruce, *Acts*, 152. For more on OT references of uncircumcised hearts, see Keener, *Acts*, 2:1423–25.

Bock also mentions the use of the loaded term "uncircumcised" (ἀπερίτμητοι), connecting the opponents with disobedient Israel. "They are covenantally unfaithful. Both their hearts and ears are unresponsive."[128] There is a long tradition in the Hebrew Scriptures of calling out the Israelites when they act in an "uncircumcised" manner.[129] Thus, again Luke connects the opponents of Stephen with disobedient Israel of the past, unable to remain faithful to God's covenant and honor the prophets that he sends. The obvious irony here, of course, is that the elite Jewish council, who are circumcised, are acting as if they were "uncircumcised" in their hearts and minds, while characters such as the Ethiopian Eunuch and Cornelius who are not circumcised are more in line with what God desires from his people and are welcomed into the family of God. This narrative irony plays an important rhetorical identity-forming function for the uncircumcised reader of Luke's work.

Connected narratively with these ideas in Luke is Jesus' own wilderness wandering and temptation.[130] Many similarities exist between these two accounts (i.e., forty days/forty years, wilderness, time of testing/temptation, etc.). Jesus' first temptation, to turn the stones into bread, is quite reminiscent of manna. His response from Deuteronomy 8:3 connects not only with the giving of manna, but also with the Israelites and Moses at the end of the wilderness wandering. Thus, what Israel was not able to do, such that they became "stiff-necked," Jesus fulfilled. These connections with Jesus have narrative importance as he is being revealed as the prophet like Moses, the Messiah that Stephen's opponents refuse to accept, and as the ultimate hero and model for the implied audience.

The second phase of the accusation begins with a rhetorical question—"Was there ever a prophet you did not persecute?" "Rhetorical questions were often useful for driving home a polemical or apologetic point."[131] Some see the rhetorical shift from the usage of "our fathers" positively in his speech to "your fathers" here is quite negative.[132] "'*Your* fathers' rhetorically emphasizes moral continuity among those in all generations who break God's covenant, but it does not repudiate Stephen's ethnic continuity with Israel or hope for Israel."[133] Persecution of the prophets in the Hebrew Scriptures was common.[134] Jewish tradition held that both Isaiah and Jeremiah were martyred for their prophecies.[135] This long line of persecution of prophets culminates with the killing of Jesus, which Stephen mentions in verse 52. There is

---

128. Bock, *Acts*, 304.

129. Lev 26:41; Judg 14:3; 1 Sam 14:6; 17:26; 2 Chr 28:3; Isa 52:1; Jer 4:4; 6:10; 9:26; Ezek 44:7, 9; 1QS 5:5, 1QpHab 11:13.

130. Luke 4:1–12.

131. Keener, *Acts*, 2:1425. See Maxwell, "Role"; Penner, "Narrative."

132. Keener, *Acts*, 2:1425.

133. Keener, *Acts*, 2:1425. Also, see Snyder, "Motif."

134. 1 Kgs 18:4, 13; 19:10, 14; Jer 2:30; 26:20–24; 2 Chr 24:20–21.

135. *4 Bar.* 9:22–32.

another semantic connection here in the use of betray, προδότης, which connects this group being accused with Judas.

The final verse in this section includes the statement that the audience has not obeyed the law given by angels. It was a common understanding in Jewish tradition that the old covenant was given and mediated by an angel. Although not recorded in the Old Testament, there are references in numerous extra-biblical sources.[136] This idea occurs earlier in 7:38 and in places like Hebrews 2:2 and Galatians 3:19. The retort here by Stephen is perhaps a *kal va-homer* argument, suggesting that his accusers have not even been able to obey the law given by angels, how much more have they failed the law given by the Son of God? The thematic connection to other stories in Scripture is strong. "The narrator imposes story on story on story, building up mutually interpretive layers of similar events. The rejection of Moses resembles the rejection of Jesus, which resembles the rejection of Stephen."[137]

The last point for consideration by the audience of Stephen's speech is the opponents' gnashing of their teeth (ἔβρυχον τοὺς ὀδόντας) in response. There are a couple of ways to take this reference. The most obvious is to connect it with the use of the same phrase in the poetry and wisdom literature of the Hebrew Scriptures (LXX).[138] Four of five times it is used of enemies who face a protagonist. The fifth time it expresses Job's perception of God in the midst of his suffering. The emotion represented by this phrase is anger and evil intent; the sense that the teeth-gnashers want to do harm to the protagonist. Kotze has noted that this phrase is at times paired with animal imagery and suggests a connection with anger being a dangerous animal.[139] It is thus related to losing control, like a wild animal getting loose.[140] Evil intent to harm is the plain reading of the text here, as Stephen's opponents are about to stone him, and gnashing of teeth is symbolic of that.

There is another option. Keener points out that the only other usage of this phrase in the Lukan corpus is Luke 13:28, the story of those shut out of the kingdom banquet. He suggests the emotion could be anguish. As those shut out of the banquet, Stephen's opponents find themselves shut out of what God is doing.[141] Considering the harsh accusations by Stephen and the violent response of the audience, however, the former theory above seems to fit best in this case.

---

136. *Jub.* 1:27–2:1; Philo, *Somn.* 1.143; Josephus, *Ant.* 15.136; *1 En.* 10:1; *Bah.* 9. Not all would agree that the Old Testament is silent on this issue, and point to Deut 33:2 LXX; Ps 102:20 [103:20 MT]; 103:4 [104:4 MT]. See Moo, *Galatians*, 235; Scott, *Knowing*, 226, and lengthy footnote there; Bruce, *Hebrews*, 67.

137. Tannehill, *Acts*, 87.

138. Ps 34:16 (35:16); 36:12 (37:12); 111:10 (112:10); Job 16:9; Lam 2:16.

139. Kotze, "Conceptualization," 95.

140. Kotze, "Anger," 221.

141. Keener, *Acts*, 2:1435. Other references to gnashing of teeth in the New Testament seem to have a demonic or hellish connection, though that is probably better understood as anguish.

In sum, the images and expressions chosen to characterize the opponents of Stephen could hardly be more harsh. They are the stiff-necked false witnesses who, like their fathers, wandered in the wilderness, persecuted and killed the prophets, betrayed like Judas, and gnash their teeth in rage at the one who brings the message of what God is doing in their day. Thus, through the engagement between Stephen and his accusers and the intertextual cues the author gives us, we see him emerge as the trustworthy communicator of God's message. By contrast, considering what we have seen already of Luke pairing positive and negative examples together, the angry members of the Sanhedrin serve as anti-exemplars in their attitude and blindness to the new move of God's spirit. To see this tension between the characters gives ample force to this scene and urges the reader to trust and listen to Stephen all the more. Those who reject him and his message are clearly not worth emulating in this story, and Luke's portrayal of the pathos here makes that clear. The God-fearing reader would be impressed with the righteous example of Stephen, and would be warned against the harsh resistance the Jewish leaders show. To the degree that Luke is using the tools of rhetoric to establish a positive diagnosis of Stephen and the other early Christian examples, he is creating social identity for his audience.

What Was the Response of the Authorial Audience?

Having discussed the emotional appeal at the end of the speech and how it sounded to the Sanhedrin, we must ask how God-fearing Gentiles might respond to the pathos if they experienced the speech Stephen gave. We briefly considered this question above, but must inquire more deeply now. Humphrey rightly suggests, "Perhaps the appeal is more designed to make its impact on the readers of Luke's narrative."[142] There are three primary emphases that resonate with the God-fearing reader. First, the persuasive power of Stephen's speech is that Jesus is the culmination of God's activity in the world. This is essential to the gospel presentation in Luke–Acts. Everything the prophets looked forward to is happening in the time Stephen is narrating. The result would be great excitement for all who have interest in the God of Israel and want access to him.[143] There is a clear rhetorical aim that God-fearing readers respond to Jesus if they have not already done so.

Second, the speech's emphasis on the failings of Israel, their disobedience, and God making a way in spite of them, highlights the need for obedience in their time. The new identifying factor of the family of God is obedience, which plays itself out in love for God and generosity to one's neighbor, as opposed to an ethnic identity, keeping a kosher table, circumcision, and the other elements that made up a specific Jewish identity. This

---

142. Humphrey, "Turned." Also, see Maxwell, "Role"; Porter, *Audience*; Penner, "Civilizing."

143. A similar sentiment is made in 1 Peter 1:12 where in spite of the persecution the audience is experiencing, the author encourages them that even the angels and prophets long to look at the things they were experiencing, though it is unlikely that Luke had access to this writing.

fits the pattern in Acts where, in the context of the rejection of the message by the Jews, more attention is given to the Gentiles.[144] In this case, it is the Jewish authorities who are rejecting Stephen and his message. "Rejection by the Jerusalem authorities will become part of a pattern of rejection that appears when we note connections between the Stephen episode and the series of scenes in which Paul, in the face of Jewish rejection, turns to the Gentiles."[145] This is part of the transformative and identity-forming illocution that Luke continues to emphasize throughout.

Third, Moses and his story would connect with a God-fearing reader. He becomes a foreigner, an outsider, whom God uses to do great things. The rejected becomes the welcomed. As Stephen says in his speech, "It was this Moses whom they rejected when they said, 'Who made you a ruler and a judge?' and whom God now sent as both ruler and liberator through the angel who appeared to him in the bush."[146] Although Moses is one of the most important characters of Jewish history, his identity as an outsider creates empathy in the God-fearing reader and endears them to him, creating connection between both Israel and the Gentiles.[147]

What Was the Intended Effect of the Emotive Events Listed by Stephen in the Speech?

The deeper emotion in the rhetoric may well come from the mention of the truly painful events of Israel's history. The slavery in Egypt followed by the exodus, the wandering in the desert, and the establishing of the Temple highlight the faithfulness of God, but also the emotional experiences from Israel's past. As we will elaborate below, Israel's story becomes "our story" for Luke and the God-fearers. When he says in verse 19, "He dealt treacherously with our people and oppressed our ancestors by forcing them to throw out their newborn babies so that they would die," the reader gets the sense from the phrases "our people" and "our ancestors" that a wider inclusivity is meant by these statements. They are ancestors of the faith, an idea more emphasized than race in the speech. In fact, the terms "Israel" and "Israelites" are used four times in the speech, twice in regards to Moses returning and killing an Egyptian, once in the prophecy quoted from Amos 5, and one final time in regard to the promise of the Messiah coming from "your people," a confirmation of the Jewishness of the Messiah, and by implication, a subtle affirmation of Jesus. There are, however, nine references to "ancestors." This is because it is a retelling of the history of Israel through the lens of Jesus as the Messiah for all who hear it, both

---

144. Acts 13:46; 18:6; 28:23–28. Also, see Shirock, "Growth"; Donaldson, "'Riches"; Moessner, "Leaven."

145. Tannehill, *Acts*, 96.

146. Acts 7:35.

147. Also, see Thompson, "Brothers"; Njoroge wa Ngugi, "Stephen"; Kilgallen, "Function"; Whitenton, "Rewriting"; Kim, "Quotations."

Jews and Gentiles. The story has a wide reach. Yet there is also the sense that cultural memory is being created by sharing the origins of the group with new members and thus creating social identity in those new members.[148]

Stephen's Rhetorical Logos

It has been rightly noted that Stephen's speech is very Jewish, as it recounts the key events of Jewish history. In fact, Kennedy connects this speech most closely with the dual speeches of God and Joshua (Josh 24:1–15) in the recounting of the events of Israel's history.[149] This may seem antithetical to a God-fearing implied audience, but consider a few points. First, God-fearers were synagogue dwellers who followed the God of Israel in a Jewish context, but who had not fully converted.[150] Regardless of what such conversion and assimilation into Jewish culture looked like, following the God of Israel and having some connection with the synagogue would familiarize the God-fearer with the story of redemption history. Abraham, Moses, the exodus, and Babylonian exile would not have been foreign ideas to the average God-fearer. Second, Luke values continuity of the Christian message with the roots of Israel in his writings. This speech is clearly consonant with this. Furthermore, consider that Luke is a Gentile himself,[151] and thus, we see the first example of a Gentile telling the story of Jewish redemption history, all be it through the mouthpiece of Stephen, a Christian Jew. Thus, the story of Israel's redemption becomes "our story" rather than simply Israel's story. This is identity formation through cultural memory as discussed in chapter 1, where memories become stories and public narratives that allow new members to share in the origins of the group.[152] To put a finer point on it, the message to the audience is, "God is working in history now, with us, the way that he has worked throughout history with his people." Finally, although the story is about Jewish salvation history, the message of decentralization is central to the logos of the speech. God's saving work is no longer centralized within the Israelites, their land (Temple), their law, and their customs. Rather, God is on the move. This does not become fully realized in the narrative of Acts for a number of chapters, but as we will see below, the idea is already well represented in this speech.

Fiorenza reminds us that rhetoric seeks to bring about change in the hearers, engaging the attitudes, motivations, and emotions of people: "The evaluative criterion for

---

148. See chapter 1. Also, see Stock, "Pathos"; Peterson, "Speech"; Evans and Sanders, *Interpretation*; Holtz et al., *Geschichte*.

149. Kennedy, *Classical*, 148.

150. Levinskaya, "Diaspora," 52.

151. See discussion about Luke's identity in the Introduction on pages 7–9.

152. Liu and László, "Narrative Theory," 87–88. See chapter 1.

rhetoric is not aesthetics, but praxis."[153] What is the praxis of Stephen's speech? What is the logic it follows? What goals does it seek to accomplish and does it succeed?

After a brief mention of Isaac, Jacob, and the covenant of circumcision, the focus shifts to Joseph. "By various literary connections, Luke links Joseph with Jesus."[154] As Joseph was handed over (ἀποδίδωμι) to Egypt, so Jesus was handed over (παραδίδωμι) to the Romans for crucifixion by his fellow Jews.[155] Joseph is an example of God's continued care even when his own brothers turned against him. Bock notes the phrase "but God was with him" (καὶ ἦν ὁ θεὸς μετ' αὐτοῦ:) in verse 9: "The contrast is important. God was with the one whom the other eleven sons of Jacob rejected, a note introducing the nation's pattern of failure to recognize the one chosen by God."[156]

The next paragraph about the burial at Shechem provided the narrator a chance to reference an important Samaritan city, which will build on the speech's emphasis of outsiders being a part of God's plan. In chapter 8, Philip will take the gospel to a Samaritan village, so this reference introduces the reader to that idea. The more puzzling element to this section, though, is the way events are telescoped or outright mistaken.[157] Perhaps Luke provides an accepted haggadah of the historic story. Or it is possible he makes an unintentional mistake, stemming from the contemporaneous nature of speech giving in the first century.[158] Either way, the connection to the patriarchs of Israel to Shechem should not be missed.

Verse 17 begins the transition to Moses, who will be the central character for Stephen. The accusations against him were for speaking against the law of Moses, so Stephen naturally focuses on the character. Moreover, Moses is the central connection to Jesus, whom Stephen is representing. Jervell suggests that even though Moses comes in view, the discussion of the promise as well as the multitude keeps Abraham and God's dealings with him in focus: "Das weist—zusammen mit dem ἤγγιζεν ὁ χρόνος τῆς ἐπαγγελίας—auf die Massenbekehrungen der Apg hin. Das Wachstum des Volkes ist an sich Erfüllung der Verheissung an Abraham mit Blick auf Nachkommen."[159]

---

153. Fiorenza, *Rhetoric*, 52–66; Kilgallen, "Lesson"; Calduch-Benages and Liesen, *History*.

154. Keener, *Acts*, 2:1362.

155. Keener, *Acts*, 2:1365. See Luke 9:44; 18:32; 20:20; 24:7, 20; Acts 3:13.

156. Bock, *Acts*, 286; Richard, "Character."

157. For example, it was not Abraham but Jacob who purchased the land from Hamor in Genesis 33:19.

158. For a fuller discussion, see Keener, *Acts*, 2:1370–73. Also, see Phillips, *Tomb*; Scobie, "Speeches."

159. Jervell, *Die Apostelgeschichte*, 236. "This—together with ἤγγιζεν ὁ χρόνος τῆς ἐπαγγελίας—points to the mass conversions in Acts. The growth of the people is in itself the fulfillment of the promise to Abraham with regard to descendants."

Although exposing of infants was somewhat common in the ancient world,[160] the Jews rejected this practice.[161] Thus, the idea of a pagan king forcing the Israelites to observe the heinous practice as a form of genocide is quite disturbing. It must have sounded so to Luke's readers. Even though different groups of Gentiles exposed infants due to economic factors or because of birth defects, the God-fearers' familiarity with Israel and the Jewish Scriptures likely introduced them to the resistance to that practice. This is perhaps the most emotionally gripping section of Stephen's speech, but it also sets the stage for the Moses story.

Moses is described in verse 22 as being powerful in words and his deeds (δυνατὸς ἐν λόγοις καὶ ἔργοις αὐτοῦ). This is reminiscent of what the men on the road to Emmaus testify about Jesus, that he was mighty in deed and word (δυνατὸς ἐν ἔργῳ καὶ λόγῳ). Bock also points to the use of the term regarding Peter's inability to resist God in Acts 11:17.[162]

The word for "visit" in verse 23 (ἐπισκέψασθαι) most expresses "salvation-historical activity."[163] This section describes Moses's return to his own people, where he is misunderstood and rejected. This, too, is a connection with Jesus, one that helps Stephen in his defense. Moses is the beloved leader of the Jewish people and perhaps the most important figure of their historic faith. To the degree that Stephen connects Jesus with Moses in the logos of his speech, he offers a sound defense of Jesus and his own actions in proclaiming Jesus. Likewise, Johnson suggests that Luke's portrayal of Moses here sets him up as a man who seeks to bring peace, also connected with Jesus in Luke.[164]

Moses flees to Midian in response, and Stephen calls him a "resident alien" (πάροικος). This may create empathy in God-fearers who take part in the synagogue practices, though feeling alien as they do so. There is a narrative experience here that a God-fearing reader would likely pick up and relate to. Another important connection comes into play with the mention of Moses's two sons.[165] Since he married a foreign woman, this is an example of intermarriage by a hero of the faith. Keener suggests that Joseph may be implied here as well,[166] though he is not mentioned, and states, "These Diaspora, interethnic marriages by two of Israel's greatest leaders challenged the ethnocentrism and geographic chauvinism of Stephen's accusers."[167]

---

160. Some estimate as many as 10 percent were exposed, Keener, *Acts*, 2:1377. Also, see Wagemakers, "Incest"; Schwartz, "Exposure"; Arbel, *Sparing*; Edwards, "Deformity"; Saller, "Poverty."

161. Keener, *Acts*, 2:1379.

162. Bock, *Acts*, 291.

163. Keener, *Acts*, 2:1391. He points to Luke 1:68, 78; 7:16; Acts 15:14 as the other significant uses of this word. Also, see Marguerat and Butticaz, "La figure"; Donaldson, "Moses."

164. Johnson, *Acts*, 127. For Jesus' connection with peace in Luke–Acts, see Luke 1:79; 2:14, 29; Acts 10:36.

165. Moses's sons are mentioned in Exod 2:22; 18:3–4.

166. Keener, *Acts*, 2:1396.

167. Keener, *Acts*, 2:1396. Also, see Whitenton, "Rewriting"; Zehetbauer, "Stephanus." For a

Thus, even in the details of Stephen's speech, we see embedded clues to a God-fearing reader that emphasize decentralization and create space for outsiders. A similar element of decentralization with regard to Moses is the burning bush scene. This shows the presence of God in the wilderness; there is holy ground outside of the holy land.[168] "Given the debate about the sacredness of the temple, Stephen appears to make a similar point. Holy ground is where God is."[169] In the book of Acts, this is largely connected with the Holy Spirit and the community of believers.[170] The emphasis on decentralization remains present throughout.

"Like a powerful rhetorician, Stephen hammers home his point that the very one whom Israel rejected was the deliverer whom God appointed for them."[171] He does this with the repetition of the demonstrative pronoun οὗτος, forms of which occur five times in four verses here. Perhaps the most important link between Jesus and Moses is the prophecy that is stated in verse 37: "God will raise up a prophet for you from your own people as he raised me up." Keener suggests that the most prominent similarity between Jesus and Moses is "the idea of a deliverer rejected by his own people."[172] Barrett offers helpful parallels between Jesus and Moses: "(1) the man rejected by the people becomes ruler and lord; (2) he becomes deliverer through signs and wonders given by God; (3) he is both prophet and prototype of the Coming One; (4) he is mediator between God and people; (5) he is the receiver and giver of words of life; (6) his people reject him."[173] Stählin suggests verse 35 begins a Moses/Christ hymn, though questions arise about form, usage, and origin.[174] Thus, as we saw in chapter 3 we see again here, there is evidence of clear typological connection between Jesus and Moses.

Sweeney characterizes the logos of the next section of Stephen's speech: "You charge me with speaking against the law of Moses; in fact, it is the law (and the prophets) that speak against the disobedience of the Israelites!"[175] The quotation in vv. 42–43 comes from Amos 5:25–27 where the prophet is commenting about the idolatry in the wilderness. Interestingly, the section that precedes the paraphrase by Stephen depicts God declaring his hatred for the religious festivals and sacrifices of the Israelites in Amos because of the injustice that is rampant among them. It seems Stephen is "telescoping" several historical contexts here by referencing the idolatry

---

specific look at Moses's wives, see Winslow, *Memories*; Holder, "Race."

168. Keener, *Acts*, 2:1395.

169. Bock, *Acts*, 294. Also, see King, "Ground."

170. Johnson, *Acts*, 135–38.

171. Keener, *Acts*, 2:1400.

172. Keener, *Acts*, 2:1403.

173. Barrett, *Acts*, 362–63. Barrett is not the first or the only one to make connections between Jesus and Moses, though his six points are helpful. Also, see Via, "Interpretation."

174. Stählin, *Die Apostelgeschichte*, 109. Pesch has also suggested a hymnic character. See Pesch, *Die Apostelgeschichte*, 253.

175. Sweeney, "Speech," 197.

of the wilderness wandering (i.e., golden calf discussed in vv. 39–41), the idolatry in the time of Amos, and Stephen's own day. Verse 44 turns again to the wilderness and the "tent of testimony." Having just quoted the history of idolatry in Israel, this shift in topic may be quite abrasive to the audience, but making the accusation of Temple idolatry quite clear. "The danger of idolatry in the wilderness, signaled by Amos, has been transferred to the Jerusalem temple."[176]

As our treatment of Stephen's speech draws to a close, there remain two key elements that need exploration, which are important for Luke in his writing. Stephen becomes a mouthpiece in Luke's narrative to address these two climactic issues. These emphases are the treatment of the land and the critique of the Temple. Neither of these elements are new with Stephen, nor in this monograph, but they deserve fuller discussion here.

The Rhetorical Function of the Land

There is a focus in Stephen's speech on God working with all kinds of people, not only Israel. This includes God working outside of the land of Israel, with foreigners, and away from the Temple. This echoes Luke's commitment to decentralization that we have seen. Once again, to the degree that Luke emphasizes the move of God away from Jerusalem, the land of Israel, the Temple, and the centralized Jewish power structures, he is involved in decentralization and is intentionally creating space for outsiders to play a part on God's plan. More specifically, there is a shift in Luke–Acts from the land as an identity marker to the community of God and the Holy Spirit as the new signs of identity, as the survey below will show. The role of the land in Luke–Acts generally, and the speech specifically, is important enough that it deserves its own section here.

The phrase "not even a foot of ground" in verse 5 corresponds to Deuteronomy 2:5 where Esau is given land. "If the illusion is deliberate, it evokes awareness of the God who cares for all peoples and is sovereign over all geography."[177] Likewise, in Acts 7:6–7, "God spoke to him in this way: 'For four hundred years your descendants will be strangers in a country not their own, and they will be enslaved and mistreated. But I will punish the nation they serve as slaves,' God said, 'and afterward they will come out of that country and worship me in this place.'" Luke is amalgamating OT quotations here. He starts with Genesis 15:13–14, but cuts that quotation off early and splices in Exodus 3:12 and others that talk of Israel worshipping "in this place" (ἐν τῷ τόπῳ τούτῳ). Keener states, "It is impossible to doubt the connection with the temple and hence the importance of these words for their context."[178] The usage of the

---

176. Keener, *Acts*, 2:1411. Also, see Sandt, "Amos"; Steyn, "Trajectories"; Stowasser, "Qumranüberlieferung"; Klein, "Wie wird," 139–40; Meek, *Mission*.

177. Keener, *Acts*, 2:1358. Also, see Conzelmann, *Acts*, 52; Phillips, "Creation"; Tapie and Mcclain, *Reading*.

178. Keener, *Acts*, 2:1360.

phrase "this place" is reminiscent of the accusations in Acts 6:13–14, and similar to Acts 21:28. Keener continues, "But if the land's (and temple's) purpose was as a place of worship, the defiled worship (cf. 7:39–50) at least temporarily voided the land of its sacred value and Israel of its promised right. The new 'place' of worship was where God was (7:33), and God was dwelling in the midst of Jesus' community through the Holy Spirit (2:4; 4:31)."[179]

Keener does not go far enough in his discussion of the land, and the related ideas of Temple and city. The land is particularly central for understanding identity among the Jewish people in Second Temple Judaism. A brief survey of the opinions of the time is in order as it is so closely tied to identity. The decentralization of land is another step in the movement toward the inclusion of outsiders.[180]

The Land in the Hebrew Scriptures

As we consider the scholarly conversation about the role of the land in the Hebrew Scriptures, Rad's contribution needs to be highlighted.[181] He distinguishes between the historical and cultic conceptions of the land, which may be thought of as the promise and fulfillment in the former and Yahweh as the land's owner, in the latter.[182] In the scholarly literature over the course of the next seventy years, the importance of the land was not in question.[183] Stated most pointedly, Brueggemann suggests that the land is "a central, if not *the central theme* of biblical faith."[184] Wright summarizes the "cardinal concepts," three points that characterize what can be thought of as a "theology of the land in the Old Testament":

1. The land was given by Yahweh in fulfillment of the promise to the fathers—the historical tradition;

2. Nevertheless, Yahweh was still the ultimate owner of the land, a fact that was to be acknowledged in various legal and cultic ways;

3. Israel and its land were bound together in . . . an "umbilical" relationship, that is, a relationship determined by the nature of Israel's own relationship to God.[185]

---

179. Keener, *Acts*, 2:1360.

180. For other examples in other texts, see Pajunen, *Land*; Decker, "Live"; Crawford, "Taking."

181. Rad, "Land," first published in German in *Zeitschrift des Deutschen Palastinavereins* (1943). Rad's work is considered pioneering and seminal in the field of Hebrew land studies, and thus, is an important starting place for a thorough discussion of the land.

182. Also, see Alt, "God," 48.

183. All have emphasized the importance of the land, despite varying views. For example, Clark argued in his dissertation, "Origin," that the idea of a Promised Land is adopted as part of a patriarchal religion outside of Israel, but does not dispute the importance of the land in the Hebrew Scriptures or the people of Israel. Also, see Rost, "Bezeichnungen"; Alt, "God," 66–67.

184. Brueggemann, *Land*, 3.

185. Wright, *People*, 9. Wright attributes the umbilical language to Davies in Davies, *Gospel*, 365.

Wright's third point makes the identity-forming power of "land" most obvious. Others have held similar opinions. Kaiser, for example, notes the connection of the laws to the land, specifically as they relate to lifestyle and conditions for remaining in it.[186]

Needless to say, discussion of the land pertains also to the Temple. The Temple and the city of Jerusalem were closely connected to land with significant overlap. Walker suggests, "Within a first-century Jewish worldview the temple, the city, and the land were understood as three interconnecting theological *realia*. They were like concentric circles. So a new approach to one aspect of this triad might well signify a new attitude toward the others as well."[187] Collins suggests that the Temple in Jerusalem served as a symbol of "the cosmic mountain, the meeting place of heaven and earth, and it was equated with a primordial paradise, the garden of Eden."[188] At the dawn of the New Testament era, the theology of the land was sizable, inhabiting a central role in the identity-forming nature of the Jewish people.

The Land at Qumran

The approximately contemporaneous Qumran community offers an interesting literary picture of how a group understood the land and their connection to it in the first century. This is not to suggest that this community had any influence on the thoughts about the land by other Jewish groups. Rather, it is an attempt to consider all of the literature to paint the clearest picture. In Qumran, the residents preserved and read in the Temple Scroll specific instructions about the building of an ideal Temple.[189] The land (the city) and Temple are spoken of with the highest level of care and holiness: "Their cities [shall be] pure . . . for ever. The city which I will sanctify, causing my name and [my] sanctuar[y] to abide [in it], shall be holy and pure of all impurity with which they can become impure. Whatever is in it shall be pure."[190]

Additionally, atonement for the land was talked about frequently.[191] Garnet attributes this to Numbers 35:33, but the Qumran residents seem to move beyond that and use it more regularly (i.e., beyond bloodshed).[192] Their critique of the land in its current

---

Originally published by University of California Press (1974), Moessner, *Lord*, 264–65, sees four elements with regard to how the land is talked about in Deuteronomy: (1) the first act is writing the law, (2) the land is envisioned as flowing with milk and honey, (3) it is contrasted with Egypt, and (4) wine has a particular symbolism connected with the land. Also, see Lombaard, "Approaches," 185–89; Burge, *Bible*; Brett, *Decolonizing*.

186. Kaiser, "Land," 308. Also, see Reif, "Issues"; Mendels, "Phases"; Regev, *Hasmoneans*.
187. Walker, "Land," 101.
188. Collins, "Dream," 254. Collins points to texts such as Ps 2; 48:1–2; Ezek 5:5; 38:12; 40–48.
189. Collins, "New Jerusalem," 254.
190. 11Q19 47.4–7. Vermes, *Scrolls*, 206.
191. 1QS 8.6, 10; 9.4; 1QS [1Q28a] 1.3.
192. Garnet, "Atonement," 360.

state shows the diversity of opinions among the differing Jewish sects. However, the importance of the land for religious identity is consistent.

The Land in Josephus

Josephus offers another interesting literary picture of Jewish understanding of land in the first century. Since Josephus is writing for the Romans, it is perhaps not surprising that he downplays the importance of land in the Jewish experience. In fact, Josephus goes as far as to "[delete] the theology of covenanted land because he did not want the land to be a focal point, as it was for Davidic messianism, with all its revolutionary implications in Josephus's day."[193] Thus, Josephus is the exception that proves the rule. He stands out in his day for his radical shift in his understanding of land, which goes to show how ingrained the idea of land is for identity in Judaism at the time. But it is important to note that land theology is not absent from Josephus's *Antiquities*, for he does "[retain] land in his prophecies of the future, even to the possible displeasure of his Roman readers."[194] Thus, we might say that even the most pro-Roman example in the first century, which we would expect to be anti-land, retains an element of land theology for God's people. In the end, Josephus stands as a deviation from the pattern we see in Second Temple Judaism.

Another notable reference regarding land in the works of Josephus is the story of Judas the Galilean.[195] The revolt, which is referred to in Acts 5:37, started over the registration of estates by the Roman senator Cyrenius.[196] Josephus credits Judas with the formation of the fourth sect of the zealots (along with Pharisees, Sadducees, and Essenes).[197] The zealots' "inviolable attachment to liberty"[198] shows the land belief taken to its extreme, and also shows the range of passion over the issue of the land in first-century Judaism.

Jesus and the Land

Despite a rich history in the other collections of text we have covered, the New Testament does not emphasize land as much as one would expect.[199] Davies says, "Jesus, as far as we can gather, paid little attention to the relationship between Yahweh, and Israel

---

193. Amaru, "Land Theology," 229.
194. Amaru, "Land Theology," 229.
195. Josephus, *Ant.* 18. Also called Judas the Gaulonite in 1.1.4.
196. Josephus, *Ant.* 18.1.1–4.
197. Josephus, *Ant.* 18.2–6.
198. Josephus, *Ant.* 18.6.23.
199. Some would disagree. See Burge, *Jesus*; Bartholomew, *Mortals*. For more discussion on the land, see Knoppers and McConville, *Reconsidering*; Davies, *Dimension*; Schürer, *History*; Hoffman, *Land*; Marchadour and Neuhaus, *Land*; Walker, *Jesus*; Wright, "Jerusalem."

and the land."²⁰⁰ When Jesus does comment on the land in Luke, it is not positive, offering instead words of condemnation against Jerusalem.²⁰¹ Walker calls this a "surprising reversal."²⁰² However, the land is not unimportant in Luke's Gospel. For example, Jesus does most of his ministry outside of Jerusalem, before the text begins to focus on the holy city more specifically after chapter 9. But even then we see decentralization, with Jesus refocusing the emphasis on himself and his movement, as Wenell states: "Judaism emphasizes the holiness of the temple, city, and land; Jesus fulfills and replaces these categories as a center of holiness himself."²⁰³

One of the most obvious places where Jesus does comment on the land outside of Luke–Acts is Matthew 5:5: μακάριοι οἱ πραεῖς, ὅτι αὐτοὶ κληρονομήσουσιν τὴν γῆν. ("Blessed are the meek, for they will inherit the land").²⁰⁴ Luke's version of the beatitudes omits this part, but immediately goes into the woes, which open with, Πλὴν οὐαὶ ὑμῖν τοῖς πλουσίοις, ὅτι ἀπέχετε τὴν παράκλησιν ὑμῶν ("But woe to you who are rich, for you have received your consolation").²⁰⁵ Considering the important connection that land had to wealth in the ancient world, perhaps this is a condemnation of owning land, and a statement that Jesus' kingdom is not about that.²⁰⁶ Furthermore, this fits with Luke's continual emphasis on possessions and generosity.²⁰⁷ Wright agrees that land theology resides within the language of possessions and wealth: "For most people in the ancient world, the most basic possession was land; for Jews the land was of course the holy land, promised by YHWH to his people."²⁰⁸ Wenell looks at Jesus' selection of the Twelve, suggesting there is something more symbolic going on. She traces the rich symbolic history of the number twelve in Jewish history and concludes that the Twelve are a symbolic representation of a time of unity and wholeness for the nation and "could imply a deep sense of attachment to land for Jesus."²⁰⁹ This land is

---

200. Davies, *Gospel*, 365.

201. Luke 13:33–35; 19:41–44; 21:6–38; 23:27–31.

202. Walker, "Land," 96.

203. Wenell, *Jesus*, 102.

204. For whatever reason, English translations render the word γῆ here as "earth" instead of "land." The tradition has stuck. However, considering the background of land in Jewish thought, and how it ties to Jesus reversal idea of meekness, land seems the most appropriate translation. Though not all agree. See Walker, "Land," 100–101.

205. Luke 6:20–26.

206. Wright, "Jerusalem," 3. More evidence of this would be the reclamation of land during Jubilee in order to redistribute wealth.

207. This emphasis has been highlighted in chapter 1 on the section about norms, as well as the discussion of Barnabas in chapter 4. See Luke 3:14; 7:41; 9:3; 12:13–21; 14:28; 15:13; 16:9–14; 18:18–23; 19:13–15; 21:4; 22:5; Acts 2:45; 3:1–8; 4:32–35; 4:36—5:11; 10:2.

208. Wright, *Victory*, 403.

209. Wenell, *Jesus*, 136. Similarly, Twelftree see Jesus' selection of the Twelve as the origin of the church. See Twelftree, *Spirit*, 21.

a "symbolic alternative" centered on kingdom values, thus making room for outsiders.[210] Even in this view, decentralization is present.

A striking example of decentralization in the life of Jesus occurs when he carries his cross outside of the city. It was expected that the climax of Israel's covenantal relationship with God would occur inside the city of Jerusalem, not outside.[211] Building up to the iconic scene of the gospel Jesus carries his cross, or rather, is assisted by Simon of Cyrene, a diasporic Jew, leading outside of the city to τὸν τόπον τὸν καλούμενον Κρανίον ("the place called the Skull").[212] This is a powerful departure from Israel's expected theological narrative. It is the beginning of the outward expansion of the gospel, which will continue in Acts throughout the Roman Empire. Here again, Jesus is reviled by those in power,[213] but he has his place among the sinners and the outcasts, hanging between κακοῦργοι ("criminals").[214] One of the κακοῦργοι will find salvation in his encounter with Jesus here. Early in Jesus' ministry, he sought out people of questionable character[215] and prophesied about his ministry to the poor, the captives, and the oppressed.[216] Thus, it seems appropriate that, in a crucial move of decentralization, he would lead a diasporic Jew and two criminals outside of the city for his final act.

Ananias, Sapphira, and the Land

But the most intense scene regarding the decentralization of land in the two-volume work is the story of Ananias and Sapphira, mentioned in Acts 5, and discussed in chapter 4 above. They are anti-exemplars[217] who try to keep money for themselves from selling land, despite the example of Barnabas and their own declaration that they had given all the money to the church, and are struck dead because of it. Wright comments, "[Family and property] both functioned symbolically within the total Jewish worldview. To both, Jesus leveled a direct challenge: to those who followed him, who were loyal to his kingdom-agenda, would have to be prepared to renounce them, God-given though they were."[218] Again, we see that it is the community and the kingdom-agenda of that community that is the new identity marker in Acts.

---

210. Wenell, *Jesus*, 139.
211. See McConville, "Jerusalem"; Wright, "Jerusalem."
212. Luke 23:26, 33.
213. Luke 23:35.
214. Luke 23:33–34. See Bilby, *Bandit*; Lourdu, "Jesus"; Wilson, "Crucifixion"; Green, "Eschatology."
215. Luke 5:27–32.
216. Luke 4:18–19.
217. See chapter 4.
218. Wright, *Victory*, 405.

This troubling story has sent scholars searching for parallels, including the fall of Adam and Eve,[219] the temptation of Jesus and betrayal of Judas in Luke–Acts,[220] the community rules at Qumran,[221] Greco-Roman codes of benefaction,[222] and myths of punitive miracles.[223] Most relevant to the issue at hand is how it calls to mind the role of the land. Chapman finds similarities between the narrative of Acts and the book of Joshua, and relates the story of Ananias and Sapphira to the theft of Achan in Joshua 7: "Thus the story of Ananias and Sapphira and their deception over the sale of their land (Acts 5:1–11) is an exact parallel to the story in Joshua of Achan, whose theft and lying held up the advance of the whole army (Josh 7)."[224] There are certainly similarities between these two stories, most notably the keeping of "devoted things" and the harsh death of each of the offending characters. Crawford sees even more dependence on Joshua beyond this story, stating that Luke alludes to Joshua in "nearly every other major section of Joshua as well."[225] It is hard to imagine a more direct way of demonstrating the movement away from land possession and toward community than this scene in Acts 5. This is, of course, within the context of all the other examples of personal and geographical decentralization in Acts, namely the charge for Jesus' followers to be witnesses in Jerusalem, Judea, Samaria, and the ends of the earth,[226] the ministry to the Samaritans,[227] the conversion of the Ethiopian Eunuch,[228] and the conversion of Cornelius the centurion.[229] The previous pattern within the Jewish world of a right to personal land ownership has passed, and a time of common community possessions and identity is at hand.[230]

Paul and the Land

Another more thematic example of decentralization of the land in Acts is the geographic agenda laid out in Acts 1:8. In addition, Paul's missionary journeys send him all across the Roman Empire, only taking him to Jerusalem a few times,[231] including

219. Marguerat, *Historian*, 172–78; Phillips, *Acts*, 141–43.
220. O'Toole, "'Lie.'" Also, see McCabe, *Kill*.
221. Capper, "Interpretation"; "Hand."
222. Ascough, "Benefaction," 91–110.
223. Havelaar, "Parallels." For an in-depth look at the emotional impact of this event, see Spencer, "Scared."
224. Chapman, *Land*, 163.
225. Crawford, "Taking," 251.
226. Acts 1:8.
227. Acts 8:4–25.
228. Acts 8:26–40.
229. Acts 10:1–48.
230. Ascough offers a good summery of the different views of this story, though notably does not consider the story as a statement about moving on from the land. Ascough, "Benefaction," 91–110.
231. After his conversion (9:26), before the first missionary journey (12:25), for the Jerusalem

a final time in chapters 20–21, which record his desire to travel there for Pentecost, but the people plead with him not to go.[232] This is odd, because all indications are that Jerusalem was Paul's home base before his conversion.[233] This, too, is an example of the decentralizing power of the Jesus movement and the early church. Whereas Paul's Judaism was Jerusalem-centric, his post-conversion Christianity is almost entirely outside of the city. Paul plays a big part—although certainly not the only one—in seeing the programmatic vision of Acts 1:8 realized.

Paul's letters provide useful contemporaneous points of comparison with regard to the decentralization of the land.[234] Davies tackled this topic and noticed the "a-territorial" nature of the promises in Paul's letters.[235] Walker notes how radical this was, flying "directly in the face of the increasing Jewish nationalism of Paul's day."[236] Paul would use terminology applied to the land, and instead apply it to the salvation experience in Christ.[237] This radical departure once again shows the move of decentralization away from the physical tenets of the Jewish faith toward Jesus himself, which simultaneously allows for a more natural exporting of Christianity to other lands and makes room for outsiders to be involved.[238]

Summary of the Land in Luke–Acts

In sum, there is a rich theological history of the land in Jewish thought. Luke acknowledges this history and over the course of two volumes, begins a radical decentralization effort that likely explains the Ananias and Sapphira debacle, is echoed in Stephen's speech, and continues in the missionary journeys of Paul. This major identity marker, which was unique to Palestinian Jews, is replaced by the community of Christ followers and the Holy Spirit that dwells in these communities. This is a major part of Luke's identity forming program in that shifting the identity marker from land to community makes room for God-fearing Gentiles to be part of the superordinate group and share in the social identity the Way offers.

---

council (15:2–4), briefly on the way to Antioch (18:22), briefly in the next chapter (19:21), and finally, for the final time, where he is arrested (20–21).

232. Acts 21:12–13.

233. Acts 9:2, 13, 21.

234. The writings attributed to Paul are considered here, as they are another stream of thought in the New Testament connected to Judaism. The consideration here does not assume dependence of one textual tradition on the other nor agreement between them.

235. Davies, *Gospel*, 179.

236. Walker, "Land," 85.

237. Walker, "Land," 85–86.

238. Also, see Patella, "Paul"; Jankowski, "Dieses."

Stephen's Critique of the Temple

As we discussed in chapter 3, Luke has a decentralizing agenda away from the Temple. The previous discussion was concerned with how the critique of the Temple fits the author's larger narrative strategy of geographic decentralization. Currently we are focused specifically on the rhetoric of the Temple critique in the speech, understanding the nature of the challenge. Stephen's climax may be the critique of the Temple. Scholars differ in how they understand this and how close his accusations come to suggesting idolatry. Bruce holds that Stephen is critiquing "the state of mind to which the temple gave rise" rather than the Temple itself.[239] Elsewhere he suggests it is a "polemic against the Temple order."[240] Similarly, Marshall calls it a "sharp criticism of the actual temple and its worship."[241] Keener is nuanced in the way he understands Stephen's critique, seeing him as coming short of calling the Temple an idol (despite some other ways he characterizes Stephen as being quite harsh), and rather demonstrating the biblical support for it, but also calling the wrong approach of his opponents to the Temple idolatrous.[242] However, he suggests that the reference to exile on account of idolatry can be connected to the current exile under Rome.[243] Most scholars understand Stephen as critiquing the Temple in some direct way.[244] Jervell, on the other hand, notes the descriptions of the early church meeting in the Temple and suggests one must read Stephen's critique in light of all that is said positively about the Temple in Acts.[245] Bock has more balanced view.[246] Sweeney is a notable exception. He reacts strongly against the ideas that Stephen is anti-Temple and that he may be suggesting idolatry and suggests that Stephen's purpose is a salvation-historical aim, rather than an anti-Temple aim.[247] Three points should be made in response to Sweeney.

First, Sweeney talks as if the assertion that Stephen (and Luke) considers salvation history as central in the speech eliminates an anti-Temple agenda from view. It does not. It can be both. Clearly, as the present work has aimed to show, salvation history of Israel is in view in Stephen's speech as a central tenet of the New Testament gospel.[248] However, a key way that Luke does this is through the utilization

---

239. Bruce, *Acts*, 149.

240. Bruce, *History*, 222. Longenecker says something very similar. See Longenecker, *Acts*, 345–46.

241. Marshall, *Acts*, 130.

242. Keener, *Acts*, 2:1417.

243. Keener, *Acts*, 2:1412.

244. Also, see Haenchen, *Acts*, 285, 290; Conzelmann, *Acts*, 56; Dunn, *Partings*, 63–71; Barnett, *Jesus*, 219–21.

245. Jervell, *Die Apostelgeschichte*, 245. Jervell points to Acts 2:46; 3:11; 5:20–21; 21:26; 22:17; 24:18.

246. Bock, *Acts*, 303.

247. Sweeney, "Speech," 185–210. Also, see Trudinger, "St Stephen," 240–42; Plymale, *Prayer*.

248. See chapter 3.

of minor characters and decentralization.²⁴⁹ Stephen is a minor character and his discussion of the Temple promotes decentralization. God's presence is no longer concentrated on a building, namely the Temple. God's family is no longer restricted to Israel alone. Church leadership is no longer restricted to the priesthood. Each of these elements demonstrates Luke's decentralizing aim. Thus, focusing on critique of the Temple, almost calling it an idol, and recounting salvation history are both possible focuses in the same speech because they are so closely intertwined and are part of the same bigger program of Luke.

Second, the emphasis of the Scripture quotations referenced by Stephen seem to clearly point to idolatry, although not explicitly stated and perhaps, as Keener suggests, he pulls up a bit short. Sweeney notes the reference to the golden calf, as well as the clear connection in Amos to exile, but he does not do anything with them.²⁵⁰ He does not connect the disobedience of the Israelites with the Stephen's Sanhedrin audience. It is Stephen's rebuke in verses 51–53, Sweeney says, and the connection with disobedient Israel as it relates to Jesus that causes the mob's response.²⁵¹ While Sweeney is partly right—certainly Stephen's harsh rebuke of his audience and accusations against them became the final straw and provoked them to violence—this should not cause us to miss what Stephen has done narratively up to that point, that is, to associate his audience with Israel deserving exile and idolatrous behavior.

Third, Sweeney's exposition of χειροποιήτοις ("made with human hands") fails to take into account the thematic elements mentioned above as part of the understanding of that word. In fact, verse 48 and following may be the climax of Stephen's defense, bringing home his point about decentralization of God's people and the move of God's presence to all who would seek him, rather than a building and a Jewish traditional religion: ἀλλ' οὐχ ὁ ὕψιστος ἐν χειροποιήτοις κατοικεῖ ("the most high does not dwell in houses made by human hands"). Sweeney rightly acknowledges the "idolatrous connotations" of the word.²⁵² Χειροποιήτοις was a technical term for "idol" in the Greek-speaking Judaism.²⁵³ Sweeney argues against Dunn who asserts boldly, "the Temple itself was an idol!"²⁵⁴ Conversely, he suggests that if Stephen wanted to connect the Temple with idolatry, he would have used a more specific word like εἴδωλον. Kilgallen, however, argues that Stephen uses both this word (χειροποιήτοις) and οἶκος very carefully, suggesting that the latter is needed to connect the Isaiah quotation in verse 49, and the former to contrast with the idea found in verse 50 that God has made it

---

249. See chapter 2.
250. Sweeney, "Speech," 197.
251. Sweeney, "Speech," 207–8.
252. Sweeney, "Speech," 201.
253. Keener, *Acts*, 2:1416. Kilgallen, *Stephen*, 90. See Lev 26:1, 30; Isa 2:18; 10:11; 16:12; 19:1; 21:9; 31:7; 46:6; Dan 5:4, 23; Acts 19:26. Bock calls it a deprecating term in the NT. See Bock, *Acts*, 302.
254. Dunn, *Parting*, 66–67. Sweeney, "Speech," 201.

all: "Indeed, Stephen is choosing his words well to attack his enemy."[255] This fits with the practice of saving the most significant and volatile text for the end of a homily.[256] Keener points out the connection in the last line of the verse, "Did not my hand make all these things?" (οὐχὶ ἡ χείρ μου ἐποίησεν ταῦτα πάντα;), with the previous connection to man making their own gods with their hands in 7:40–41, 43.[257] This quotation also emphasizes decentralization. "Since God created all by his 'hand,' there is no reason to limit God to houses made by human 'hands.'"[258] Thus, εἴδωλον would not have worked as well as χειροποιήτοις to make the point. In the end, it may be best to understand Stephen's critique of the Temple as being quite harsh, although perhaps he stops short of calling it an idol. This does not conflict with Luke's larger agenda of salvation history and decentralization, but rather, augments it nicely.

There is an important connection to God-fearers in Stephen's critique of the Temple. God-fearers would not have been able to participate fully in Temple worship without becoming full converts. Thus, decentralization of the Temple falls inline with the outward move of God's presence, from the Holy of Holies to the court of the Gentiles, out of Jerusalem to Samaria and the ends of the earth. This is great news for God-fearers like the Ethiopian Eunuch and Cornelius. Of course, all Gentiles would benefit from this decentralization, not only God-fearers. However, considering the prominent role that the God-fearers play in Acts, it is logical to assume they are the focus. In addition, the decentralization of the Temple may be good news for many Jews as well. With the diasporic nature of Judaism presented in Acts 2, that the Spirit could be present wherever God's community was is good news. However, the new community is not presented in synagogal terms, as the synagogue, by virtue of representing the Temple, functioned in centralizing ways, to attract people to them. The community, by contrast, is presented as missional, inclusive, and moving outward. So, while the access to the Spirit would be good news to all people, there is clearly a shift away from status quo Judaism in the first century, as Luke demonstrates.

There is no question of Stephen's pathos in verse 51, as this is the beginning of his final rebuke, which incites his opponents to rush at him and kill him. Although he has been connecting his audience with disobedient Israel throughout his speech, his accusations become more direct and accusatory here. It is also noteworthy that Stephen shifts the pronouns from first person (we/our) to second person (you/your). The climax of Israel's disobedience shows itself in the betrayal and crucifixion of the Righteous One. Stephen's logos leads rhetorically to that point, even perhaps with an implied call to repent.[259]

---

255. Kilgallen, *Stephen*, 90.
256. Keener, *Acts*, 2:1418.
257. Keener, *Acts*, 2:1418–19.
258. Keener, *Acts*, 2:1419.
259. Bock, *Acts*, 304.

In concluding the discussion of Stephen's speech and the rhetorical aims of Luke in Acts 6–7, we have seen that Stephen is introduced very positively, both in what is said about him and what he does, creating an overwhelmingly positive ethos. His speech also both contains and provokes intense emotion (pathos), which culminates in his execution. Lastly, the logos of Stephen's speech echoes primary themes for Luke's corpus, not only by strategically using names (Moses, David, Shechem) and references from the Hebrew Scriptures (LXX), but also by serving as a climax for two of Luke's major focuses of decentralization, the land and the Temple.

This speech is particularly poignant for a God-fearing reader. The elements of inclusion and decentralization remain at the forefront as Luke gives his version of salvation history. This begins with Jewish origin stories, but also welcomes the outsider into this movement, not least God-fearers, creating social identity for this group. This may model Paul's pattern for the missionary journeys in Acts, where his ministry starts in the synagogue, before turning to the Gentiles. God-fearers are presumably at the synagogues, and thus provide a ready audience for Paul's message.

Having explored Stephen's speech, it is necessary to examine the other instance of recounting salvation history in Luke's corpus, namely, Paul's historiographical speech in Acts 13.

Rhetorical Method in Paul's Speech

In Acts 7, Stephen offers the first documented account of Jewish salvation history on the lips of a Christian. The second time this happens is only a few chapters later on the lips of Paul.[260] After his introduction at Stephen's death (7:58; 8:1, 3) and conversion in chapter 9, Paul is commissioned along with Barnabas for missionary work. After doing ministry on the island of Cyprus (13:4–12), they travel to Pisidian Antioch and visit the synagogue on the Sabbath.

Although there are some similarities between Stephen's and Paul's speeches in that they both recount salvation history of the Jews through the lens of Jesus the Messiah, there are many differences as well. Paul's is much shorter than Stephen's, and he spends less time recounting the past events of Israel's history.[261] Instead, Paul moves rather quickly through the narrative and quotes several Scriptures at the end that serve his purpose. Whereas Stephen was on trial, Paul is an honored guest in the synagogue. Thus, the *Sitzim Leben* is quite different in each case.[262]

---

260. The analysis of Paul's speech considers that of Paul as a character and speech giver in the narrative of Acts, not the writer of epistles or the empirical Paul. Luke uses the Hebrew name "Saul" up until 13:9, when he changes to "Paul," which is simply the Greek version of the Hebrew name. I will use the name "Paul," except where other authors use "Saul" in quotations or where necessary to comment on the Hebrew name.

261. Presumably this is because the reader has already encountered Stephen's speech and needs only to be reminded of the main points here.

262. Sitz im Leben is a form critical category that usually refers to the empirical realities behind

The Ethos of Paul

With Stephen, the minor character is introduced in chapter 6, he gives a speech in chapter 7, and by the end of that chapter he has been killed. Paul's function in the narrative is quite different, as he will become the main character for the remainder of the book and a prototype for Gentile inclusion.[263] The establishment of Paul's ethos is more drawn out and more dramatic, developed through a lengthy narrative. Multiple bold statements were made about Stephen, his wisdom, and his miracle-working power, as well as elements connecting him with Jesus and others.[264] Once again, we see differences with Paul. At the first mention of Saul/Paul in 7:58, and then again in 8:1, 3, the audience is told almost nothing about him, presumably because the readers of Luke's narrative already know him quite well.[265] He is called a "young man," νεανίου, but nothing is told of his past or pedigree. Acts 8:1 tells of his approval of Stephen's death, and 8:3 talks of his quest to go house to house to put men and women in prison. Then 9:1 states that Paul was "still breathing threats and murder against the disciples of the Lord." As he was traveling with legal documents to arrest Christians, Paul encounters the risen Jesus in dramatic fashion. The two summaries of his future during the encounter (9:15–16) foreshadow the rest of Acts.[266] There may be another implied statement about decentralization here. As the trajectory of God's work is outward, away from Jerusalem (i.e., disciples scattered in 8:1, Samaritans converted in 8:4–25, and the Ethiopian Eunuch conversion in 8:26–40), Paul as a representative of Judaism seeks to bring Christians from Damascus to Jerusalem.[267] He is originally opposing decentralization and working against the outward trajectory of God's movement.

Johnson rightly notes the "narrative architecture" of this story in Luke's narrative.[268] It stands as one of three conversion stories nearly back to back to back of the Ethiopian Eunuch, Paul, and Cornelius.[269] These stories of conversion are almost certainly the three most prominent in the book, being the first Gentile convert (Ethiopian Eunuch),[270] the persecutor of Christians who will be the missionary to the Gentiles

---

the text, whereas I am using it here more as the implied world of the text. For more, see Buss, "Idea"; McKnight, *Form*; Byrskog, "Century"; Byrskog, "Quest."

263. I argued in chapter 4 that Stephen is also a prototype, though he takes up much less space than Paul, who becomes the central focus for the second half of the narrative as he travels and does missions work among the Gentiles.

264. Acts 6:8–15.

265. On the introduction of Paul, see Keener, "Notes"; Czachesz, "Exegesis"; Kurichianil, "Paul"; Meijer, *Paulus*.

266. Keener, *Acts*, 2:1597.

267. Acts 9:2.

268. Johnson, *Acts*, 166.

269. Keener, *Acts*, 2:1598.

270. For fuller discussion of the Ethiopian Eunuch, see section on Social Identity in chapter 1 and Minor Characters and Decentralization in chapter 2.

(Paul), and the prototypical God-fearing Gentile convert (Cornelius),[271] whose experience will change the opinion of church leadership on this key issue. Thus, chapters 8–10 constitute a major turning point in the narrative, following the persecution of Stephen's death. They set the stage for Paul's ministry. The structure communicates the gravity of the situation, which speaks to the ethos of Paul.[272]

Luke establishes the ethos of Paul in his conversion in several ways. First, the account records Jesus communicating two prophecies about Paul's future. Chapter 9:15 calls Paul "an instrument whom I have chosen to bring my name before Gentiles and kings and before the people of Israel." Verse 16 follows up by predicting the suffering he will endure "for the sake of my name." These statements not only foreshadow the rest of Acts, but they establish Paul as the main character for the second half of the book and hint at the scope that God's work through him will take on. Tannehill mentions the risk of narrative fragmentation by shifting the central character, but the similarities of the missions of these characters help unify the story (see below).[273]

Secondly, the story about a persecutor and murderer of Christians who transitions to a powerful missionary in service of Christ is a moving one. This adds a certain level of noteworthiness to Paul and his character. The transformation is so radical that the reader cannot miss it. Luke uses the narrative to add flavor to the story. For example, the young man who has the power and motivation to kill members of the Way, loses his sight in the encounter with Jesus and must be led by the hand to the next town. His blindness is a metaphor for his spiritual state.[274] "Though physically blind, Saul's eyes are being opened spiritually."[275] His eyesight returns, and he can see, both physically and spiritually. From the beginning of his encounter with Jesus he is dependent on others, on the body of Christ. What is more, Ananias is another good example of decentralization, as "a non-apostle is the mediator of the Spirit."[276] Bock also notes that this is the first appearance of the Spirit outside of the land of Israel.[277] Both of these narrative elements are

---

271. For more on Cornelius and his role in the narrative, see the chapter on God-fearers and chapter 4 on prototypes.

272. For more on Saul's conversion, see Meagher, "Experience"; Allison "Acts"; Kuepfer, "Light"; Prince, "Picturing"; Böhler, "Saul";Kelhoffer, "Disclosure." For a specific look at the role of blindness in the encounter, see note 275 below.

273. Tannehill, *Acts*, 115. Johnson, *Acts*, 166, suggests that when Saul emerges in 9:1, after his first mention in 8:1, "we find no difficulty in picking up the story just as Luke intended."

274. It may also be noted that the gospel of Mark has two blindness stories (8:22–26; 10:45–52) as bookends around stories about those who fail to understand spiritually. The Twelve resist Jesus' statement about going to Jerusalem to die (8:31–33), they are unable to drive out the evil spirit from the boy (9:17–29), they argue about who is the greatest (9:33–35), they rebuke someone casting out demons (9:38–41), and they stop children from coming to Jesus (10:13–16); the Pharisees test him about divorce (10:2–12); the Rich Young Ruler values wealth over following Jesus (10:17–27). These are all varying degrees of spiritual blindness, as emphasized by the surrounding stories.

275. Fitzmyer, *Acts,* 397. Also, see Barrett, *Acts*, 1:426; Wilson, "Blinding"; Hamm, "Blindness"; Røsæg, "Blinding."

276. Bock, *Acts*, 362. Also, see Warrington. "Acts."

277. Bock, *Acts*, 362.

fitting for the conversion of Paul: "The spread of the Spirit in faraway locales is a mirror of the worldwide focus of Saul's ministry."[278]

Paul's switch from spectator of Stephen's death to persecutor to disciple is radical enough that some have doubted it. Haenchen, for example, suggests it is merely a literary move of Luke.[279] However, Bock rightly sees this as "too skeptical,"[280] and others defend the historicity here, such as Fitzmyer citing Paul's own comments about his past and conversion.[281]

There are numerous similarities between the conversion and ethos of Paul and those comments made about Stephen in Acts 6. For example, verse 17 talks about Paul being filled with the Holy Spirit. Although Stephen is connected with the Spirit three times in chapter 6,[282] the story of Paul's conversion only mentions it here. However, the dramatic nature of his conversion sets him apart as unique and adds to the experience the reader has in thinking about Paul. Truly, his conversion story is one of the most dramatic in Scripture. Keener states, "Paired visions to Ananias and Saul underline the dramatic nature of Paul's transformation."[283] Once again we see the Spirit mediating mission expansion by the use of visions, in this case, to enemies of the Way.[284] The drama continues as he goes to Jerusalem and the disciples are afraid of him (9:26). This creates humorous and dramatic irony as the Christians are scared he is an imposter, "for they did not believe that he was a disciple."[285]

After his conversion, "immediately he began to proclaim Jesus in the synagogues, saying, 'He is the Son of God.'"[286] The perception of Paul being a skilled orator and preacher is similar to that of Stephen, as he confounds those he debates, apparently because of his wisdom. As mentioned previously, forms of the word wisdom are only found in connection with Stephen in Acts, but 9:22 certainly implies it for Paul. It is here, where Paul is arguing and growing in rhetorical skill, that the term "the Jews" (Ἰουδαίους) is first used as a group separate from the Christians.[287] Later in 9:28–29 he will speak boldly in the name of the Lord and argue with Hellenists who want to kill him. The reader comes away struck at the boldness and authority Paul has as an orator "by Jesus' own initiative and election."[288] This reminds the reader of Stephen. Thus,

---

278. Bock, *Acts*, 362.
279. Haenchen, *Acts*, 294–95. For a survey of views on Paul's conversion, see Corley, "Interpreting."
280. Bock, *Acts*, 319.
281. Fitzmyer, *Acts*, 390. Also, see Barrett, *Acts*, 1:390.
282. Acts 6:3, 5, 10.
283. Keener, *Acts*, 2:1644.
284. See section in chapter 4 titled Angels and Visions in Luke–Acts.
285. Acts 9:16b NRSV.
286. Acts 9:20. See Kern, "Conversion"; Pervo, "Paul"; Gaventa, "Overthrown."
287. Bock, *Acts*, 367.
288. Bock, *Acts*, 367.

despite differences between the setting and circumstances of Stephen and Paul and their larger roles in the narrative of Acts, they have much in common as well.

Paul is also like Stephen in that, quickly after coming on the scene, his opponents plot to kill him.[289] Indeed, he shifts quickly in the narrative from aggressive enemy of Christianity to enemy of aggressive Jews. Although Stephen is captured and stoned as the members of his public hearing rush him at the conclusion of his speech, Paul is able to sneak away and continue his ministry. However, he will continue to fear for his life in Acts.[290]

One other element of ethos is worthy of comment. Hengel and Schwemer, taking a salvation historical view, suggest that Tarsus is in the land of Japheth, and thus, according to Josephus, is where Jonah fled to after refusing to preach to Nineveh.[291] Paul and Jonah make similar journeys, but for very different reasons. "Whereas Jonah wants to escape his commission to preach, Paul remains true to his, since with the compulsion upon him (as it was with Jonah) he knows that he cannot escape it: 'for woe is me if I do not preach.'"[292] Both Jonah and Paul have wayward journeys, the former as a direct rejection of a divine call[293] and the latter as a persecutor of Christians.[294] Each is brought back to proclaim the message God gives him through dramatic means, Jonah through being swallowed by a fish[295] and Paul through a miraculous encounter with Jesus, which results in blindness.[296] Both Jonah's time in the belly of the fish and Paul's time of blindness last three days.[297] Jonah and Paul both preach to outsiders, and in each case the preaching brings about fruit.[298] However, in a clear point of contrast, whereas Jonah despairs because of the repentance of the Ninevites, Paul and the other disciples rejoice.[299] Lastly, Paul will also be shipwrecked, facing turbulence at sea, similar to the way Jonah did.[300] Thus, it is at least possible that Luke, who clearly roots the movement of the Way in the origin stories and prophets of Israel, is drawing a comparison and contrasting connection between Paul and the prophet Jonah. Paul may serve as a type of Jonah, modeling proclamation across ethnic boundaries, only surpassing it as a proto-type of the Christian mission by rejoicing

---

289. Acts 9:23.

290. Acts 17:1–9; 18:9; 20:3.

291. Josephus, *Ant.* 9.208.

292. Hengel and Schwemer, *Paul*, 175–77. Also, see Toit, "Tale"; Shea, "Educating"; O'Mahoney, "Stones"; Powell, "Echoes." There may also be a Jonah connection in the story in Luke 8:22–25 of Jesus falling asleep in the boat when the storm occurs.

293. Jonah 1:1–3.

294. Acts 9:1–2.

295. Jonah 1:17.

296. Acts 9:3–9.

297. Jonah 1:17; Acts 9:9.

298. Jonah 3:10; Acts 16:4–5; 16:34; 28:30.

299. Jonah 4:1–3; Acts 13:48–52.

300. Jonah 1:4–5; Acts 27:13–20.

at the conversion of Gentiles. Having Paul outdo a famous Hebrew prophet serves to increase his ethos all the more.

Paul's Pathos

Some of the same elements of pathos are present for Paul as there were for Stephen. Both speak of the exodus event including the wilderness wandering as being central to Israel's history. Paul offers a truncated version of much of the history that Stephen's speech narrates. For example, what Stephen says about the event of the exodus, including the rise and the aftermath, covers about twenty-five verses.[301] Paul summarizes these same events in about three verses.[302] He moves relatively quickly over these events leading up to the time of Jesus. His account of these events does leave out much of the pathos material that Stephen included, such as the murdering of babies and the harsh slavery. Bruce sees a kerygma here in verses 17–22, summarizing the key events of the people of Israel, as seen in Deuteronomy 26:5–10.[303] Tannehill notes regarding the repetition of Israel's history: "It intends to affirm the community relationship that connects the speaker and the audience and to make present some shared presuppositions that will be important in the following argument."[304] He draws on the work of Perlman and Olbrechts-Tyteca for Paul's tactic of presence, stating, "[Importance should be attributed to] the role of presence, to the displaying of certain elements on which the speaker wishes to center attention in order that they may occupy the foreground of the hearer's consciousness."[305] As I have argued previously, there is a strong narrative connection here between the story of Israel and that of Jesus.[306]

The reference to the seven nations is worth noting. Since it reflects a harsh approach to those outside Israel, it is hard to imagine that this is a strategic reference by Luke. However, it is part of Israel's story of the old covenant and, as such, contrasts starkly with the events of Luke–Acts, where outsiders are welcomed and made part of God's plan, rather than destroyed.

Paul seeks to move quickly through the history of the judges, the kings, David, and even John the Baptist to arrive at the story of the crucifixion. Certainly the execution of Jesus holds powerful emotional connections for the early church community. The story is one of passion and injustice, and it calls for an emotional response of sorts. The pathos continues in the arrival of salvation, with Paul's critique of the Jerusalem residents' failure torecognize the advent of the Messiah. "Because the residents of Jerusalem and their leaders did not recognize him or understand the words of the prophets that are

---

301. Acts 9:18–42.
302. Acts 13:17–19.
303. Bruce, *Acts*, 254. Bock, *Acts*, 451, also mentions Josh 24:2–13, 17–18; Ps 78:67–72; 89:34.
304. Tannehill, *Acts*, 166.
305. Tannehill, *Acts*, 166; Perelman and Olbrechts-Tyteca, *Rhetoric*, 142.
306. See chapter 2.

read every Sabbath, they fulfilled those words by condemning him."[307] Paul emphasizes the unjust death of Jesus: "Even though they found no cause for a sentence of death, they asked Pilate to have him killed."[308] Following the emotion is the message of triumph and resurrection. Paul will return to the element of pathos toward the end of the message when he makes the connection between the promises made to the ancestors being fulfilled among their children in his day.[309]

The final push for pathos comes at the end of the message:

> Let it be known to you therefore, my brothers, that through this man forgiveness of sins is proclaimed to you; by this Jesus everyone who believes is set free from all those sins from which you could not be freed by the law of Moses. Beware, therefore, that what the prophets said does not happen to you:
>
> 'Look, you scoffers!
> Be amazed and perish,
> for in your days I am doing a work,
> a work that you will never believe, even if someone tells you.'[310]

Paul both directly invites his audience to respond to the good news message he has presented.[311] The switch from the first person "we" throughout the speech to the first person "you" happens here, as is did for Stephen.[312] There is an obvious difference in that Stephen turns to accusation, whereas Paul proclaims the gospel.[313] He ends by issuing a warning against missing the work of God in their day, taken from the pages of Habakkuk.

---

307. Acts 13:26.

308. Acts 13:28.

309. Acts 13:32–33. Also, see Porter and Dyer, *Paul*; Duncan, "Peter"; Gendy, "Style."

310. Acts 13:38–41.

311. Acts 13:39.

312. Bock, *Acts*, 458, sees a verbal link to the quotation above in verse 34. Also, see Veltman, "Defense"; Hogan, "Defense"; Smith, *Rhetoric*; Shipp, *Paul*; Plümacher, *Lukas*.

313. There is certainly a force to his proclamation. Schneider, *Die Apostelgeschichte*, 139–40, states, "Mit der Wendung 'So sei euch kund!' und der erneuten Anrede ἄνδρες ἀδελφοί (vgl. v. 26) wird nun der 'Bußruf eingeleitet.' Freilich ist hier von μετάνοια keine Rede, sondern es wird (paulinisch!) von der Rechtfertigung des Glaubenden gesprochen. Doch ist die Formulierung und weitgehend auch die Vorstellung lukanisch. Das gilt einmal von der Formulierung, die den Inhalt der Predigt als deren 'Gegenstand' sieht: καταγγέλλεται ἄφεσις ἁμαρτιῶν. Es gilt zudem vom Gegenstand, nämlich der "Sündenvergebung." Die Verkündigung der Sündenvergebung erfolgt *per Christum* (διὰ τούτου). Vv. 38c.39 lassen dann die "paulinische" Verkündigung in direkter Rede folgen. Es dominiert der Satz: 'In Christo (ἐν τούτῳ) wird jeder Glaubende gerechtgemacht.'" (With the phrase 'So it be known to you!' and the renewed address ἄνδρες ἀδελφοί (cf. v. 26), the 'call for repentance is now initiated.' Of course, there is no question of μετάνοια here. Instead (with Paul!), there is mention of the justification of the believer. However, the wording and largely the idea are Lucan. On the one hand, this applies to the formulation that sees the content of the proclamation as its 'subject': καταγγέλλεται ἄφεσις ἁμαρτιῶν. On the other hand, it applies to the object, namely the 'forgiveness of sins.' The forgiveness of sins is proclaimed by Christ (διὰ τούτου). Vv. 38c. 39 follow up with the "Pauline" proclamation in direct speech. The sentence dominates: 'In Christ (ἐν τούτῳ) every believer is justified.'")

This is the last in a series of four quotations from the LXX.[314] These three earlier quotations all connect with David in some way, as he is a major focus of Paul's speech. The warning from Habakkuk is an interesting one. The context of the original quotation is terrible judgment against Judah inflicted by the Babylonians.[315] Bruce suggests the warning is reminiscent of a number of Scriptures where persecuted people are charged with ignoring prophetic warnings.[316] It encouraged the acceptance of Jesus as the Messiah and accepting the gospel. The tone of judgment, using the emotionally charged cultural memories of Babylonian exile, calls for a response.

Clearly the Babylonian exile was a painful moment from Israel's past. As we have seen previously, there is an implied transformative force behind descriptions of events such as this one to the implied audience, which says, "Don't turn away from God like the Israelites did!" This sort of pathos calls for a response both from Paul's audience in the Sanhedrin as well as the authorial audience.[317]

The people in the synagogue respond positively and "urged them to speak about these things again the next Sabbath."[318] They return the next week to a large crowd, bringing out nearly the whole city. The response from others was not as positive: "But when the Jews saw the crowds, they were filled with jealousy; and blaspheming, they contradicted what was spoken by Paul."[319] Here again, a subset of "the Jews" (οἱ Ἰουδαῖοι) is set up as villains. Their response leads to a shift of mission (see below). A number of people are converted, Paul and Barnabas are driven out, and persecution begins. Thus, the response to the speech is quite mixed, leading to the conversion of some and persecution by others. Despite the conflict with the Jews, the scene ends on a note of joy: "And the disciples were filled with joy and with the Holy Spirit."[320]

Paul's Logos

Kennedy notes the simple structure of Paul's message: "He rehearses Jewish history and the prophecy of the coming of the savior. He proclaims Jesus to be that savior and supports his claim with the prophecy of two Psalms. He ends with a warning to those who do not believe."[321] Thus, we must note that although the character and ethos of Paul is more complex than Stephen, and more space given to introduce the apostle, particularly

---

314. Ps 2:7 in Acts 13:33; Isa 55:3 in Acts 13:34; Ps 16:10 in Acts 13:35.
315. Bock, *Acts*, 460. Acts 13:41.
316. Bruce, *Acts*, 263.
317. For more on Paul's quotation of Habakkuk, see Dionne, "Les Actes"; Sandt, "Quotations"; Cotton, "Gospel."
318. Acts 13:42b.
319. Acts 13:45.
320. Acts 13:52.
321. Kennedy, *Classical*, 148–49.

in narrating his conversion,[322] Paul's speech is simpler in many ways. It is shorter and to the point, more fitting of a sermon than a trial defense.

For our purposes, a few persuasive strategies are important to note. First, there is a connection between the characters Paul and king Saul. Saul is the name of the apostle Saul (Σαῦλος), who is called as such until 13:9, when it is said that he is also called Paul (Παῦλος), simply being the Greek version of his name. Thus, King Saul is undoubtedly the namesake of the Apostle Saul/Paul, as both are from the tribe of Benjamin.[323] Keener asks, "Would historical Paul pass over the negative portrayal of King Saul, presumably having grown up with some pride in the Benjaminite king?"[324] What is more remarkable is that King Saul is mentioned at all. This is the only reference to King Saul in the New Testament. Coming in Paul's first sermon, only a few verses after the narrative states that he would now be called Paul, it seems that there is a thematic connection here. What is more, Saul was not a good king. As much as the people wanted him, it did not turn out well. Instead, God raised up David, "a man after my heart, who will carry out all my wishes."[325] This shift, from Saul, a leader who works against the plan of God, to David, whom God will use, seems quite similar to the story of Paul, who is persecuting Christians and working against God's plan, with the shift to the Apostle Paul, whom God will use to carry out his mission. The bold statement "when he had removed him" is made of Saul, which sounds similar to the bold encounter Paul had with Jesus on the road to Damascus. Thus, Paul, in his pre- and post-conversion state, corresponds to both Saul and David, connecting these characters and these stories.[326] These similarities carry a flavor and rhetorical force to help the reader connect with the characters and the speech more effectively.

Another narrative rhetorical element flows from that section as David becomes the central character in Paul's speech, as opposed to Moses in Stephen's speech. Stephen only mentions David briefly in 7:46, and passes over him quickly, noting that although David wanted to build the Temple, it was actually Solomon. Paul refers to David in his Jewish salvation history narrative, noting that through this man came the Messiah, Jesus. "This speech develops Israel's history in detail, phrase by phrase, until it reaches David. It then leaps over one thousand years of Israel's history to go directly to the promise of a son of David who will deliver the nation. This is Paul's point in the speech."[327] Similarly, as David ἤγειρεν ("was raised up") in verse 22, so Jesus ἤγειρεν ("was raised up") in verse 30. He will emphasize David again at the end

---

322. Paul's conversion is narrated three times in Acts (Acts 9; 22; 26).

323. Rom 11:1, Phil 3:5. Also, see Wenkel, "Saul"; McDonough, "Change."

324. Keener, *Acts*, 2:2061.

325. Acts 13:22b.

326. Not much is said in commentaries regarding this connection. Most commentaries see this reference to Saul as a foil to set up King David as the focus of Paul's narrative. See Keener, *Acts*, 2:2016; Barrett, 635.

327. Bock, *Acts*, 453.

of the speech when he quotes four Hebrew Scriptures, the first three connecting with David in some way. Two of these are from Psalms written by David (Ps 2; 16), and the other (Isa 55:3) refers to him by name.

Why is David the central character of this speech? First, it plays nicely as a tension point with the failure of King Saul and the shift to David, echoed in Paul's story. Second, there is an emphasis here and elsewhere of fulfilled promises. This has been central to Luke from the birth narratives in volume one.[328] The end of verse 23 says it well, "Of this man's posterity God has brought to Israel a Savior, Jesus, as he promised." Again in verse 32, he says, "And we bring you the good news that what God promised to our ancestors," as well as in the quotation of Isaiah 55:3 in verse 43, "I will give you the holy promises made to David." Paul presents Jesus as the fulfillment of these prophecies. Third, Bruce connects David, here, with Peter's speech at Pentecost in chapter 2.[329] The first sermons recorded in Acts of both Peter and Paul, two primary prototypical characters, both emphasize David and the royal lineage of Jesus. The illusions to Pentecost also remind the reader of the growth of the church and the Spirit's work as elements of Pentecost are reenacted time and again through the book.[330]

A third logos element of Paul's speech is the inclusivity. While present in Stephen's speech, it functioned mostly in the realm of character selection and narrative. For Paul, the inclusivity is more overt. He opens the speech by saying, "You Israelites, and others who fear God, listen." And again in verse 26; "My brothers, you descendants of Abraham's family, and others who fear God, to us the message of this salvation has been sent." The use of "the ones who fear God," φοβούμενοι τὸν θεόν, is noteworthy. Paul is speaking in a synagogue, but he is cognizant of others not of "Abraham's family" (v. 26) present and interested in the God of Israel. Twice Paul intentionally includes this group. This is also the first time in the narrative where the Jews in a specific area will reject the message, and Paul will declare that he turns to the Gentiles (v. 46).[331]

Not all agree about the inclusive nature of the speech. Bock, for example, only sees Gentile inclusion coming into play at the conclusion of the speech. For him, Paul's aim is the Jewish people.[332] Additionally, Tannehill states, "Both setting and content make clear that this is a speech by a Jew to Jews, for it concerns God's promise to the Jewish people."[333] While it is true that Paul is preaching in the synagogue to mostly Jews, and that he is recounting a common kerygma of Jewish history which connects with his Jewish audience, four points might be made in response. First, Paul

---

328. See chapter 3. Also, see Kilgallen, "Acts"; "Words"; Ellul, "Antioche."

329. Bruce, *Acts*, 258.

330. Acts 2:4; 4:8–10, 31; 7:55; 8:15–17; 10:44–48; 11:15–16 (retelling of previous chapter); 13:52; 19:6.

331. Also in Acts 18:6; 28:23–28.

332. Bock, *Acts*, 461. Also, see Polhill, *Acts*, 305; Moessner, "Fulfillment."

333. Tannehill, *Acts*, 166.

includes God-fearers in his address two different times.³³⁴ Each time he does this, Paul is quite specific in identifying two groups. Second, Paul's call for repentance at the end is overtly universal in nature: [καὶ] ἀπὸ πάντων ὧν οὐκ ἠδυνήθητε ἐν νόμῳ Μωϋσέως δικαιωθῆναι, ἐν τούτῳ πᾶς ὁ πιστεύων δικαιοῦται ("by this Jesus everyone who believes is set free from all those sins from which you could not be freed by the law of Moses"). While the reference to the law of Moses appeals to Jewish thinkers, the emphasis on "everyone who believes" includes all people. Kilgallen even cites the universal aim of the call including Gentiles as the reason that the Jews resist the message.³³⁵ Third, even if Paul's audience is understood as Jews, there are multiple ways to consider audience. While Paul is portrayed as appealing to his empirical audience in the synagogue, Luke is more concerned with his own implied audience, the intended recipients of the book. From this more universal perspective it is hard to ignore the hints at inclusion present in the speech. Fourth, the presentation of Israel's story in various ways throughout the entirety of Luke's two-volume work is the first outworking of a strategic aim to present the robust picture of Jesus' saving work, which is rooted in Israel's redemptive history. Thus, a sermon in a Jewish context that most commentators see as overtly Jewish can and does play a part in Luke's universal plan of Gentile inclusion, even before the rejection and shift of mission in verse 46.

Inclusion is most clearly seen in the mission shift after the speech. Different groups in Paul's audience respond differently, as "the Jews" stir up persecution, while others respond positively and are converted. At the resistance of the first group and the rejection of the gospel, both Paul and Barnabas report a shift in the mission, and quote Isaiah 49:6: "I have set you to be a light for the Gentiles, so that you may bring salvation to the ends of the earth." Stanley suggests, "The decision to introduce a direct quotation into a piece of discourse is a rhetorical act."³³⁶ Moreover, this verse becomes something of a mission statement for Paul's ministry and "sets the agenda for the second half of the book."³³⁷ This is reminiscent of the type-scene spoken of in chapter 2 where Jesus and Peter have opponents criticize them, which leads to an opportunity to clarify the mission. The Gentiles are glad at the news and a certain number are converted. What is more, this is one of four explicit quotations in Luke–Acts from the "Servant Songs" of Isaiah 40–66.³³⁸ Beers connects this to the New Exodus and sees the embodiment of the servant in Jesus and his followers, including

334. Acts 13:16, 26.
335. Kilgallen, "Hostility."
336. Stanley, "Quotations."
337. Meek, *Mission*, 24. Meek is of the opinion that this verse is possibly reflected in Luke 2:32; Acts 1:8; 26:18, 22–23 as well.
338. Luke 4:18–19; 22:37; Acts 8:32–33; and here. See Beers, *Servant*, 1. Meek, *Mission*, 39, suggests "Scholars have found numerous echoes of the servant songs in Luke–Acts." "Luke did not merely utilize Isaiah as a source for prooftexts to support his own point of view. Rather, Luke had investigated Isaiah extensively and had a deep appreciation for Isaianic themes. His mind was saturated with Isaianic texts and concepts, which shaped his views" (Moore, "Ends," 392).

Paul and Barnabas here, as central to bring the New Exodus to fruition.[339] Thus, while the message of inclusion is explicit in the actions of Paul and the quotation, there are also layers of the New Exodus motif present.

What are the implications of this scene? Tannehill notes that it cannot mean that Paul will forego preaching to the Jews, or that Gentiles only receive the word of God because of Jewish rejection, since "the narrator of Luke–Acts has made clear ever since the birth narrative that the purpose of God that shapes this story intends to work salvation for all peoples."[340]

Moreover, as we have seen, by this point of the story, many non-Jews have been converted already (Ethiopian Eunuch, Samaritans, Cornelius and his family). Tannehill sees this as Paul's evangelism in Acts needing to "follow a prescribed order."[341] For Bock, "This is only proper because it is Israel's history that holds the promise."[342] Paul's regular pattern for the rest of Acts will include starting in the synagogue, as he sees it as necessary to start with the Jewish people.[343] However, another concurrent reason may be that the highest volume of God-fearers may be at the synagogue to hear the new word of Paul as well. Bruce suggests that the original plan would have been for the Jews to accept the message and then to evangelize their Gentile neighbors, but upon their rejection, Paul and Barnabas have to take the mission into their own hands.[344] Meek agrees, seeing the origin (and even the requirement) of the Gentile mission in Isaiah 49:6.[345] Tannehill calls the rejection by the Jews a "tragic turn," and mentions the usage of ἀπωθέω, which is only used here and in Stephen's speech in Acts, both times describing rejection.[346] Johnson notes Luke's "stereotypical pattern of acceptance and rejection" that continues through the narrative.[347]

The implications of this scene are major. Pao points out that this is a turning point in the makeup of the people of God: "For the Lukan community, however, this is not simply another stage of the development of the early Christian movement. It signifies the establishment of the identity of the people of God in contradistinction to the ethnic nation of Israel."[348] Although, as we have mentioned, there are other significant turning points in the mission to those outside Israel in Luke–Acts (the hints in the birth narrative,

---

339. Beers, *Servant*, 1.
340. Tannehill, *Acts*, 173. See chapter 3, which discusses the birth narrative of Jesus.
341. Tannehill, *Acts*, 173.
342. Bock, *Acts*, 463.
343. Acts 14:1; 17:1, 10, 17; 18:4, 19, 26; 19:8. Also, see Korner, "Ekklesia"; Windsor, *Paul*; Eberts, "Plurality"; O'Neill, "Strategy."
344. Bruce, *Acts*, 265–66.
345. Meek, *Mission*, 45.
346. Tannehill, *Acts*, 168.
347. Johnson, *Acts*, 239.
348. Pao, *New Exodus*, 99–100.

the Ethiopian Eunuch, Cornelius, etc.), this is perhaps more programmatic. After this, the Gentiles will become the majority.[349]

In conclusion, the inclusivity of Paul's speech is welcoming to the God-fearing reader into the story directly.[350] It is as if the authorial audience was being directly addressed in these instances, invited by Paul and Luke to "listen" and that "the message of salvation" has been sent to this group. Although the motif of inclusion was present before, now that Cornelius has been welcomed in and Paul takes over as the main character of the book, it takes on a new life.

Conclusion

Luke's use of two historiographical speeches to tell the salvation history of God's people displays the strategic use of rhetoric for his implied audience. The implied author reflects the first-century practice of employing the tools of rhetoric. This leads to response, connection, and identity formation in his God-fearing audience, forming social identity in his readers as they are allowed to share in the story through cultural memory and because they are part of the social movement that is early Christianity. These chapters show Luke utilizing the tools of Greco-Roman rhetoric to his advantage in order to create social identity for his God-fearing reader.

---

349. Pao, *New Exodus*, 98.

350. Park, *Either*; Turner, "Paul"; Sim and Mclaren, *Attitudes*; Fredriksen, "Judaism"; Stanton, Stroumsa, *Tolerance*; Feldkeller, *Identitätssuche*.

Conclusion

My thesis is that Luke–Acts was written primarily for the purpose of creating identity for a God-fearing audience within the New Christian Movement of the first century CE. Social Identity Theory was briefly explained in the introduction as allowing us to explore how social identity is formed, noting that since we are dealing with ancient texts, this is a literary argument, though that will not hinder us from using history as a kind of checks and balances where appropriate. We also noted that this project needs to focus primarily on the first half of Acts due to the strategy of the implied author.

Introduction

The introduction also explored the basic elements of Luke–Acts studies, considering the primary questions. Despite theories that approach Luke–Acts as a novel or epic, or a biography, all having significant arguments in their support, most scholars rightly understand Luke-Acts to be historiography. This allows for the narrative emphasis on identity formation to be central, while still highlighting speeches and rhetoric as key elements. The prefaces (or prologues) of Luke were also worth a note in the introduction, considering how much attention scholars have given to these verses. While some authors seek to make major genre decisions based on the prefaces, the narrative dynamics of both volumes must carry more weight than a simple prologue, which we might say merely gives hints at what that genre might be. The prologues are mostly used to urge readers to use volume one as an interpretive lens for volume two.

We also explored the identity of Luke, who has mostly been understood to be a Gentile (or even a God-fearer), though this view is not unanimous. This is significant considering the content and aims the author seems to espouse in the work. In addition, certain purposes attributed to Luke–Acts such as teaching, evangelism, edification, and an emphasis on the term σωτηρία do not conflict with the stated purpose of creating social identity in God-fearers, but rather support it. Lastly, we examined the work of John Nolland, who is among the first to argue for a primarily God-fearing readership for Luke–Acts.

CONCLUSION

Chapter 1

The opening chapter discusses the theoretical basis of Social Identity Theory. The central assumption is that individuals gain value and identity through inclusion into an ingroup and by contrasting their group with outgroups. We traced the timeline of the theory and the primary scholars who contributed to it, culminating in a study of cultural memory. This goes back to the foundation of the group and the stories told to new group members, who are then able to share in these narratives, thereby building social identity. This process is further delineated by Liu and László, who offer a helpful step by step process on how this is done, which serves as an outline for the rest of the work: "Cultural memory goes back to the supposed origins of the group, objectifies memories that have proven to be important to the group, encodes these memories into stories, preserves them as public narratives, and makes it possible for new members to share group history."[1] We investigated some of the stories and public narratives at work in Israel and the early church, most notably the Passover Haggadah.

We further examined the notion of Social Identity Theory and how two separate groups can come together under a single superordinate identity. A helpful example of this was the story of the Ethiopian Eunuch, who while clearly being an outsider, was made an insider in the narrative of Acts. Next, the chapter considered the first key way that Luke creates social identity for his readers, which is through prescribed group beliefs. Bar-Tal understood those beliefs in using the categories of norms, values, goals, and ideology. Each of these categories is investigated with regard to Acts to see how each of these elements was present in the early Christian community.

The chapter closes by exploring two final elements: narrative and intertextuality. Luke primarily uses narrative storytelling to communicate social identity to his readers. A key example is the Lord's Supper, which is a narrative ritual intended to create social identity through reenactment. Intertextuality was not considered enough by Bar-Tal, but needed to be in the current project. "Every text is written and read in relation to that which is already written and read."[2] Thus, Luke is not writing in a vacuum, but importing meaning from the LXX and the Greco-Roman world to make his points as well as making connections between his two volumes.

Chapter 2

The following chapter was a robust exploration of God-fearers, the presumed implied audience of Luke–Acts, beginning by tracing each occurrence of the phrases that give rise to the term "God-fearer" (οἱ φοβούμενος τὸν θεὸν and οἱ σεβομένοι τὸν θεὸν). This leads to a recounting of the scholarship regarding God-fearers over the last century and a half, and the conclusion that, while there is still disagreement among some, most

---

1. Liu and László, "Narrative Theory," 88.
2. Alkier, "Intertextuality," 4.

have come to see the term "God-fearer" as a technical term that referred to a group of synagogue dwelling Gentiles who had not fully converted to Judaism.

We then introduced two major features: minor characters and decentralization. First, the reader notes with surprise Luke's fascination with minor characters, who, because of cultural and religious limitations (i.e., gender, race, occupation, anatomy, etc.), are marginalized by larger society. Second, decentralization is the movement away from established Jewish norms and symbols of centralization toward a more inclusive and open faith. It leads to the welcoming of these marginalized outsiders, a major feature throughout Luke's narrative. This is a theological corner stone as it facilitates the welcoming of God-fearers into God's family. We then consider the two most important God-fearers for Luke, the Ethiopian Eunuch and Cornelius.

The chapter ends by observing the critic-response type-scene. This occurs when the opponents of a main character, usually Jesus, grumble and complain about the people he is associating with. This leads to a clarification of the mission of the protagonist. Luke builds this type-scene over two volumes to set up a reveal in Acts 11. Lastly, several other characters in Luke–Acts are examined as potential God-fearers (Timothy, Theophilus, the "devout soldier").

Chapter 3

Next, we looked at Luke's understanding of the Gospel in Luke–Acts and how he introduces expectations early in Luke that will carry throughout both volumes. A key feature the author uses is the New Exodus, presenting the work through an Isaianic lens as a second exodus event. Luke strategically uses names (and their meanings) as hints at his message. Although he rarely explicitly explains a name or its meaning, his strategy of incorporating them in the narrative is clearly an important part of how the story unfolds. Arguably, narratively building characters with strategic names is more impactful on the reader than if the names were made overly explicit.

The following section explored the elements of promise and fulfillment, how the past is being brought into the audience's present. The promises had been made to all, not only the Jewish people, and they were beginning to be realized early in Luke. The canticles deserved special attention, as these songs are rich with promise and fulfillment language. Mary, Zechariah, and Simeon all contribute to the wonder of the coming Messiah. Anna represents a faithful female servant who is waiting expectantly for the Messiah, and John the Baptist is a decentralizing figure who prepares the way for Christ in the spirit of Second Isaiah. Then several scenes from Jesus' life, which seem to be particularly important for the promise and fulfillment schema, are examined (at the synagogue, the transfiguration, complete with comparisons to Moses and Elijah, and the road to Emmaus).

Promise and fulfillment continues in the two historeographical speeches by Stephen and Paul in Acts 7 and 13 respectively. These are key places where the

CONCLUSION

God-fearing reader is told the story of salvation history and how Christ and the early church plays into that narrative arc. These speeches are similar, but have their own specific contributions to Acts. Stephen takes care to emphasize Moses, while challenging the status of the Temple. Paul focuses more on David and how Christ is the fulfillment of a promised Messiah in his line.

Chapter 4

Two other major strategies for creating social identity in Luke–Acts are the use of prototypes and exemplars for emulation by his audience. Storytelling and the cultivation of group beliefs are intertwined. Smith and Zarate are leaders in prototype studies, helping us understand them as a representative of a group that captures the central tendencies of the category and distinguishes them from other groups. Luke–Acts has a number of prototypes worth examining. Jesus is the first and most important prototype in Luke–Acts. Others effectively attain that status based on their emulation of Christ, such as Peter, who is seen in scholarship as a prototype who continues on the leadership of Jesus after his departure. However, it is possible to understand the work of Peter (and the rest of the Twelve) less positively than scholars traditionally have as part of Luke's decentralizing agenda for the purpose of inclusion. Instead, the Spirit uses all sorts of people to expand the mission, whether they have privileged status or not (i.e., Stephen, Phillip, Paul, Barnabas, etc.). Stephen and Paul are likewise important prototypes. The former becomes a prototype for suffering and dying like Christ. The latter is portrayed as the Prototypical missionary to the Gentiles.

Following an exploration of other minor characters, specifically the centurion in Luke 7, we then consider Luke's most important prototype, Cornelius. Putting such a major focus on Cornelius the God-fearer underscores the likelihood of the implied audience being God-fearers as well. They are expected to identify greatly with this man. In typical fashion, Luke's retelling of his story involves several visions, a classic maneuver to clarify a characters' prototypical role. We looked further at the use of visions and angelic activity in Luke's writings, before examining the Pentecost scene regarding its similarities to the Sinai event. The core issue is intertextuality between these two scenes and how the account in Acts 2 should be seen as the formation of a New Covenant that welcomes outsiders and forms a new people of God.

Finally, exemplars are characters who do not represent large categories, as prototypes do, but rather, symbolize a single value that is worthy of emulation. These characters are often paired with anti-exemplars to heighten the contrast and to prohibit certain behaviors, as well as prescribe other behaviors. A classic example is Barnabas, the exemplar for generosity, as he is contrasted with Ananias and Sapphira, the anti-exemplars of greed. Similarly, Philip, the exemplary miracle worker of the kingdom, is contrasted with Simon the Sorcerer, who tries to purchase the Holy Spirit. Other exemplars include Zacchaeus and the widow at the Temple contrasted with the Rich Young Ruler, and Judas, the anti-exemplar of betrayal. The parables of Jesus also lend themselves to the use of exemplars and anti-exemplars as a function of the storytelling genre. Gamaliel is considered as the final exemplar of withholding judgment when unsure about the activity of God.

Chapter 5

The final key strategy for the formation of social identity is the use of rhetoric. The first century was situated at a time where writers made intentional use of the tools of rhetorical. Luke appears to be a product of his time and do exactly that, using rhetorical strategically to accomplish his purposes. The key elements of rhetoric are ethos (positive introductions of characters), pathos (appealing to the emotions of the audience), and logos (creating a logical and persuasive flow throughout the speech). The chapter then attends to the rhetoric of the two speeches of Stephen and Paul in Acts 7 and 13, respectively.

Stephen is introduced surprisingly positively, both by his reported actions and narrative descriptions about him. This boosts his credibility as a communicator and encourager of his audience, thereby rendering his participation in salvation history trustworthy. The speech involves pathos to the extent that some truly painful events in Israel's history are recalled. At the same time, he displays rhetorical logos in strategically tying the history of Israel to all people. To this end, he specifically highlights aspects that appeal especially to God-fearers, such as God working through Moses outside of the land of Israel, God's ongoing activity in the Samaritan city of Shechem, and the historic rejection of the holy ones by Israel, which leads to the inclusion of outsiders.

Given Stephen's emphasis on geography, an investigation of the rhetorical function of the land is necessary. We traced the theological concept of the land from the Hebrew Scriptures, through Qumran, Josephus, Jesus, Paul, and the key scene in Acts regarding the land, the Ananias and Sapphira incident. Acts has numerous key scenes that demonstrate a radical decentralization of the land. They show, surprisingly, that the key identity forming element for the new Christian movement will precisely not be the land, which excludes the poor and non-Israelites, but rather, the community and the Holy Spirit. This is followed by a discussion of Stephen's harsh critique of the Temple, tainting it with the brush of idolatry, though stopping just short of calling it an idol. Even the Temple, then, is radically decentralized in Luke–Acts. God's presence is no longer limited to the insiders who have access to that building.

Paul's speech has many similarities to Stephen's, although it has differences as well. Paul's ethos, like Stephen's, is robustly established, this time through the narrative of his miraculous conversion, setting him up as a faithful communicator of salvation history as well. Paul moves quickly through much of the history of Israel. Paul, the character, chooses to spend more time than Stephen on John the Baptist and the passion narrative, primarily focusing on Christ with regard to pathos. Paul's logos focuses more centrally on David, in contrast with Stephen's preoccupation with Moses. He specifically addresses God-fearers in the synagogue twice, and his speech culminates in conversions and the request to stay longer. Luke's strategy to tell redemption history in a way that includes God-fearers in God's plan is very clearly on display in Paul's speech.

Bibliography

Abbott, Lyman. *The Acts of the Apostles: With Notes, Comments, Maps, and Illustrations.* New York: A. S. Barnes, 1876.

Abrahams, Israel. *Studies in Pharisaism and the Gospels.* Cambridge: Cambridge University Press, 1917.

Adams, Sean A. *The Genre of Acts and Collected Biography.* Cambridge: Cambridge University Press, 2013.

———. "The Genre of Luke–Acts: The State of the Question." *Issues in Luke–Acts: Selected Essays*, edited by Sean A. Adams and Michael Pahl, 97–120. Piscataway, NJ: Gorgias, 2012.

———. "Luke's Framing of the Feeding of the Five Thousand and an Evaluation of Possible Old Testament Allusions." *IBS* 29 (2011) 152–69.

———. "Luke's Preface and its Relationship to Greek Historiography: A Response to Loveday Alexander." *Journal of Greco-Roman Christianity and Judaism* 3 (2006) 177–91.

Adler, Nikolaus. *Das erste christliche Pfingstfest. Sinn und Bedeutung des Pfingstberichtes Apg 2, 1–13.* Neutestamentliche Abhandlungen 18.1. Münster: Aschendorff, 1938.

Adorno, Theodor W., et al. *The Authoritarian Personality.* New York: Harper and Row, 1950.

Agnew, Francis H. "On the Origin of the Term Apostolos." *Catholic Biblical Quarterly* 38 (1976) 49–53.

Alegre, Xavier. "El centurión de Cafarnaún (Lc 7, 1–10), modelo de cristiano en Lucas: El emigrante y el extranjero, paradigmas del creyente en la Biblia." *Revista Latinoamericana de Teología* 24.71 (2007) 123–59.

Alexander, Loveday C. A. *Acts in Its Ancient Literary Context: A Classicist Looks at the Acts of the Apostles.* London: T&T Clark, 2005.

———. "Formal Elements and Genre: Which Greco-Roman Prologues Most Closely Parallel the Lukan Prologues?" In *Jesus and the Heritage of Israel: Luke's Narrative Claim upon Israel's Legacy*, edited by David P. Moessner, 9–26. Harrisburg, PA: Trinity, 1999.

———. "Luke's Preface in the Context of Greek Preface-Writing." *NovT* 28.1 (1986) 48–74.

———. *The Preface to Luke's Gospel: Literary Convention and Social Context in Luke 1:1–4 and Acts 1:1.* Cambridge: Cambridge University Press, 1993.

Alkier, Stefan. "Intertextuality and the Semiotics of Biblical Texts." In *Reading the Bible Intertextually*, edited by Richard B. Hays et al., 3–21. Waco, TX: Baylor University Press, 2009.

Allen, O. Wesley, Jr. *The Death of Herod: The Narrative and Theological Function of Retribution in Luke–Acts.* Atlanta: Scholars, 1997.

Allison, Dale C., Jr. "Acts 9:1–9; 22:6–11; 26:12–18: Paul and Ezekiel." *JBL* 135.4 (2016) 807–26.

Alt, Albrecht. "The God of the Fathers." In *Essays on Old Testament History and Religion*, by Albrecht Alt, 1–77. Garden City: Doubleday, 1968.

Alter, Robert. *The Art of Biblical Narrative*. New York: Basic, 2011.

Amaru, Betsy Halpurn. "Land Theology in Josephus' 'Jewish Antiquities.'" *The Jewish Quarterly Review* 71.4 (1981) 201–29.

Anderson, Gary A. "Giving to Be Forgiven: Alms in the Bible." *Christian Century* 130.18 (2013) 26–33.

Anderson, Janice Capel. "Mary's Difference: Gender and Patriarchy in the Birth Narratives." *Journal of Religion* 67 (1987) 183–202.

Arbel, V. Daphna, ed. *Not Sparing the Child: Human Sacrifice in the Ancient World and Beyond*. Studies in Honor of Professor Paul G. Mosca. New York: Bloomsbury, 2015.

Aristotle. *Rhetoric*. Translated by W. Rhys Roberts. Fairhope: Mockingbird Classics, 2015.

Arndt, William F. *The Gospel According to St. Luke*. St. Louis: Concordia, 1956.

Arnold, Paula E. "The Persuasive Style of Debates in Direct Speech in Thucydides." *Hermes* 120 (1992) 44–57.

Arrington, French L. *The Acts of the Apostles: An Introduction and Commentary*. Peabody: Hendrickson, 1988.

Arterbury, Andrew E. "The Ancient Custom of Hospitality: The Greek Novels, and Acts 10:1–11:18." *Perspectives in Religious Studies* 29.1 (2002) 53–72.

Ascough, Richard S. "Benefaction Gone Wrong: The 'Sin' of Ananias and Sapphira in Context." In *Text and Artifact in the Religions of Mediterranean Antiquity: Essays in Honour of Peter Richardson*, edited by S. G. Wilson and M. Desjardins, 91–110. Waterloo: Wilfrid Laurier University Press, 2000.

Assmann, Jan. *Das kulturelle Gedächtnis: Schrift, Erinnerung und politische Identität in frühen Hochkulturen*. München: Beck, 1992.

Atkins, J. D. "The Trial of the People and the Prophet: John 5:30–47 and the True and False Prophet Traditions." *Catholic Biblical Quarterly* 75.2 (2013) 279–96.

Auerbach, Erich, and Edward W. Said. *Mimesis: The Representation of Reality in Western Literature*. New and expanded ed. Translated by Willard R. Trask. Princeton: Princeton University Press, 2003.

Aune, David. *The New Testament in Its Literary Environment*. Philadelphia: Westminster, 1987.

Austin, J. L. *Philosophical Papers*. Oxford: Oxford University Press, 1961.

Avalos, Hector. *Illness and Healthcare in the Ancient Near East: The Role of the Temple in Greece, Mesopotamia, and Israel*. Atlanta: Scholars, 1995.

Averbeck, Richard E. "The Focus of Baptism in the New Testament." *Grace Theological Journal* 2.2 (1981) 265–301.

Avi-Yonah, Michael. *The Jews of Palestine*. New York: Schocken, 1962.

Ayayo, Karelynne G. "Magical Expectations and the Two-Stage Healing of Mark 8." *Bulletin for Biblical Research* 24.3 (2014) 379–91.

Baawobr, Richard K. "Opening a Narrative Programme: Luke 4:16–30 and the Black Bagr Narrative." *JSNT* 30.1 (2007) 29–53.

Bachmann, M. *Jerusalem und der Tempel: die geographisch-theologischen Elemente in der lukanischen Sicht des jüdischen Kultzentrums*. Stuttgart: Kohlhammer, 1980.

Backhaus, Knut. "Im Hörsaal des Tyrannus (Apg 19,9) Von der Langlebigkeit des Evangeliums in kurzatmiger Zeit." *TGl* 91.1 (2001) 4–23.

Baden, Joel S. "The Nature of Barrenness in the Hebrew Bible." In *Disability Studies and Biblical Literature*, edited by Candida R. Moss and Jeremy Schipper, 13–27. Basingstoke, UK: Palgrave Macmillen, 2011.

Badia, Leonard F. "The Qumran Baptism." *Indian Journal of Theology* 33 (1984) 10–23.

Bailey, Kenneth E. "The Song of Mary: Vision of a New Exodus (Luke 1:46–55)." *Theological Review* 2.1 (1979) 29–35.

Baker, Coleman. *Identity, Memory, and Narrative in Early Christianity*. Eugene, OR: Pickwick, 2011.

Balch, David L. "Accepting Others: God's Boundary Crossing According to Isaiah and Luke–Acts." *Currents in Theology and Mission* 36.6 (2009) 414–23.

Balentine, Samuel E. "He Unrolled the Scroll . . . and He Rolled up the Scroll and Gave It Back." *Cross Currents* 59.2 (2009) 154–75.

Banks, Robert J. *Paul's Idea of Community*. Peabody, MA: Hendrickson, 1994.

Barber, Michael P. "The New Temple, the New Priesthood, and the New Cult in Luke–Acts." *Letter and Spirit* 8 (2013) 101–24

Barnett, Paul. *Jesus and the Rise of Early Christianity*. Downers Grove, IL: InterVarsity, 1999.

Barr, David L., and Judith L. Wentling. "The Conventions of Classical Biography and the Genre of Luke–Acts: A Preliminary Study." In *Luke–Acts: New Perspectives from the Society of Biblical Literature Seminar*, edited by Charles H. Talbert, 63–88. New York: Crossroad, 1984.

Barr, James. "The Symbolism of Names in the OT." *BJRL* 52 (1970) 11–29.

Barrett, C. K. *A Critical and Exegetical Commentary on the Acts of the Apostles*. 2 vols. Edinburgh: T&T Clark, 1994, 1998.

———. *The Signs of an Apostle*. Philadelphia: Fortress, 1972.

Bar-Tal, Daniel. *Group Beliefs: A Conception for Analyzing Group Structure, Processes, and Behavior*. New York: Springer-Verlag, 1990.

———. *Shared Beliefs in a Society: Social Psychological Analysis*. Thousand Oaks, CA: Sage, 2000.

Barth, Fredrik, ed. *Ethnic Groups and Boundaries: The Social Organization of Culture Difference*. Boston: Little, Brown, and Company, 1969.

Barthes, Roland. "An Introduction to the Structural Analysis of Narrative." *Communications* 8 (1966) 237–72.

Bartholomew, Craig G. *Where Mortals Dwell: A Christian View of Place for Today*. Grand Rapids: Baker Academic, 2011.

Bartlett, John R. *Jews in the Hellenistic and Roman Cities*. Abingdon: Routledge, 2012.

Bash, Anthony. "Difficult Texts: Luke 23:34 and Acts 7:60: Forgiving the Unrepentant?" *Theology* 119.4 (2016) 276–78.

Bass, Kenneth. "The Narrative and Rhetorical Use of Divine Necessity in Luke–Acts." *Journal of Biblical and Pneumatological Research* 1 (2009) 48–68.

Bassler, Jouette M. "A Man for All Seasons: David in Rabbinic and New Testament Literature." *Interpretation* 40.2 (1986) 156–69.

Bauckham, Richard. "Anna of the Tribe of Asher (Luke 2:36–38)." *Revue Biblique* 104.2 (1997) 161–91.

———. "The Restoration of Israel in Luke–Acts." *JSPSup* 72 (2001) 435–87.

———. *The Theology of the Book of Revelation*. Cambridge: Cambridge University Press, 1993.

Bauer, Walter, et al. *A Greek-English Lexicon of the New Testament and Other Early Christian Literature*. 3rd ed. Chicago: University of Chicago Press, 2000.

Beale, G. K. "Review Article: Acts and the Isaianic New Exodus." *Trinity Journal* 25.1 (2004) 93–101.

———. *The Temple and the Church's Mission: A Biblical Theology of the Dwelling Place of God*. Westmont: InterVarsity, 2004.

Beasley-Murray, G. R. *Baptism in the New Testament*. Grand Rapids: Eerdmans, 1962.

Beck, David R. "Evangelism in Luke–Acts: More Than an Outreach Program." *Faith and Mission* 20.2 (2003) 85–103.

Becker, Jürgen. *Paul: Apostle to the Gentiles*. Louisville: Westminster John Knox, 1993.

Beers, Holly. *The Followers of Jesus as "The Servant": Luke's Model from Isaiah for the Disciples in Luke–Acts*. New York: Bloomsbury T&T Clark, 2015.

Benoit, Pierre. "L'enfance de Jean-Baptiste selon Luc 1." *NTS* 3 (1957) 169–94.

———. *Paul and Qumran: Studies in New Testament Exegesis*. Edited by James Murphy-O'Connor. London: Geoffrey Chapman, 1968.

———. *The Passion and Resurrection of Jesus Christ*. Translated by B. Weatherhead. New York: Herder and Herder, 1969.

Berder, Michel, ed. *Pierre, le premier des apôtres*. Paris: Cerf, 2013.

Berends, Bill. "What Do We Celebrate at Pentecost?" *Vox Reformata* 63 (1998) 42–66.

Berger, Klaus. "Das Canticum Simeonis (Lk 2:29–32)." *NovT* 27 (1985) 27–39.

Bergmann, Claudia D. *Childbirth as a Metaphor for Crisis: Evidence from the Ancient Near East, the Hebrew Bible, and 1QH XI, 1–18*. Berlin: de Gruyter, 2008.

Bergquist, James A. "'Good News to the Poor': Why Does This Lucan Motif Appear to Run Dry in the Book of Acts?" *BangTF* 18 (1986) 1–16.

Berlin, Brent, and Paul Kay. *Basic Color Terms: Their Universality and Evolution*. Berkley: University of California Press, 1969.

Bernas, Casimir. "The Death of Judas: The Characterization of Judas Iscariot in Three Early Christian Accounts of His Death." *Religious Studies Review* 40.1 (2014) 46–47.

Bernays, Jakob. "Die Gottesfürchtigen bei Juvenal." In *Commentationes philologicae in honorem Theodor Mommsen*, 563–69. Berlin: Berlini 1877.

Betz, Hans Dieter. *Galatians: A Commentary on Paul's Letter to the Churches in Galatia*. Minneapolis: Fortress, 1989.

Beuken, W. A. M. "An Example of the Isaianic Legacy of Trito-Isaiah." In *Tradition and Re-Interpretation in Jewish and Early Christian Literature: Essays in Honour of Jürgen C. H. Lebram*, edited by J. W. von Henton, H. J. de Jonge, P. T. van Rooden and J. W. Wesselius, 48–64. Leiden: Brill, 1986.

Bibb, Bryan D. "Nadab and Abihu Attempt to Fill a Gap: Law and Narrative in Leviticus 10:1–7." *JSOT* 26.2 (2001) 83–99.

Bilby, Mark G. *As the Bandit Will I Confess You: Luke 23, 39–43 in Early Christian Interpretation*. Strasbourg: Université de Strasbourg, 2013.

Bilezikian, Gilbert G. *The Liberated Gospel: A Comparison of the Gospel of Mark and Greek Tragedy*. Grand Rapids: Baker, 1977.

Billig, Michael. "Psychology, Rhetoric, and Cognition." In *The Recovery of Rhetoric: Persuasive Discourse and Disciplinary in the Human Sciences*, edited by Richard H. Roberts and J. M. M. Good, 119–36. Charlottesville: University Press of Virginia, 1993.

Black, C. Clifton. "The Rhetoric Form of the Hellenistic Jewish and Early Christian Sermon: A Response to Lawrence Wills." *Harvard Theological Review* 81.1 (1988) 1–18.

———. *The Rhetoric of the Gospel: Theological Artistry in the Gospels and Acts*. 2nd ed. Louisville: Westminster John Knox, 2013.

Blair, P. A. "The Death of Stephen." *Tyndale House Bulletin* 2 (1956) 2–3.

Blajer, Piotr. "The Limit of the Lukan Journey Section Reconsidered." *Liber Annuus* 64 (2014) 255–77.

Blenkinship, Joseph. *Isaiah 40–55: A New Translation with Introduction and Commentary*. New York: Doubleday, 2002.

Blomberg, Craig L. *Interpreting the Parables*. 2nd ed. Westmont: IVP Academic, 2012.

———. *Jesus and the Gospels*. 2nd ed. Nashville: B&H Academic, 2009.

Bock, Darrell L. *Acts*. Grand Rapids: Baker Academic, 2007.

———. *Luke*. 2 vols. Grand Rapids: Baker Academic, 1994, 1996.

———. *Proclamation from Prophecy and Pattern: Lucan Old Testament Christology*. Journal for the Study of the New Testament Supplement 12. Sheffield: JSOT, 1987.

Boer, Martinus C. de. "God-Fearers in Luke–Acts." In *Luke's Literary Achievement: Collected Essays*, edited by Christopher M. Tuckett, 50–71. Sheffield: Sheffield Academic, 1995.

Bohlemann, Peter. *Jesus und der Taufer: Schlüssel zur Theologie und Ethik des Lukas*. Cambridge: Cambridge University Press, 1997.

Böhler, Dieter. "Saul, Saul, warum verfolgst du mich?: Zum alttestamentlichen Hintergrund der Damaskusberichte (Apg 9; 22; 26)." *Biblische Zeitschrift* 61.1 (2017) 137–47.

Boismard, Marie-Émile, and A. Lamouille. "Les Actes des deux apôtres." Paris: Lecoffre, 1990.

Bond, Helen K., and Larry W. Hurtado, eds. *Peter in Early Christianity*. Grand Rapids: Eerdmans, 2015.

Borg, Marcus. *Conflict, Holiness, and Politics in the Teachings of Jesus*. New York: Continuum International, 1998.

Botha, Peter J. J., and Johannes N. Vorster. "Introduction." In *Rhetoric, Scripture, and Theology: Essays from the 1994 Pretoria Conference*, edited by Stanley E. Porter and Thomas H. Olbricht, 17–26. Sheffield: Sheffield Academic, 1996.

Bovon, François. *Acts*. Vol. 1. Edited by Helmut Koester. Translated by Christine M. Thomas. Minneapolis: Fortress, 1984.

———. *Das Evangelium nach Lukas, vol. 1: Lk 1,1–9,50*. Evangelisch-Katholischer Kommentar zum Neuen Testament 3/1. Zürich: Benzinger; Neukirchen-Vluyn: Neukirchener Verlag, 1989.

———. *Luke the Theologian: Thirty-Three Years of Research (1950–1983)*. Translated by Ken McKinney. Allison Park, PA: Pickwick, 1987.

———. "Tradition et Rédaction en Actes 10:1–11,18." *Theologische Zeitschrift* 26.1 (1970) 22–45.

Bowie, Fiona. *The Anthropology of Religion: An Introduction*. Malden, MA: Blackwell, 2000.

Bowman, John. *The Gospel of Mark: The New Christian Jewish Passover Haggadah*. Leiden: Brill, 1965.

Brawley, Robert L. *Luke–Acts and the Jews: Conflict, Apology, and Conciliation*. Atlanta: Scholars, 1987.

———. *Text to Text Pours Forth Speech: Voices of Scripture in Luke–Acts*. Bloomington: Indiana University Press, 1995.

Bredin, M. R. J. "The Synagogue of Satan Accusation in Revelation 2:9." *BTB* 28.1 (1998) 160–64.

Brehm, H. Alan. "Vindicating the Rejected One: Stephen's Speech as a Critique of the Jewish Leaders." In *Early Christian Interpretation of the Scriptures of Israel: Investigations and Proposals*, edited by Craig A. Evans and James A. Sanders, 266–99. Sheffield: Sheffield Academic, 1997.

Brett, Mark G. *Decolonizing God: The Bible in the Tides of Empire*. Sheffield: Sheffield Phoenix, 2008.

Brewer, Marilynn, and Rupert Brown. "Intergroup Relations." In *The Handbook of Social Psychology*, edited by Daniel Todd Gilbert et al., 554–94. Boston: McGraw-Hill, 1998.

Breytenback, Cilliers. "Zeus und der lebendige Gott: Anmerkungen zu Apostelgeschichte 14:11–17." *NTS* 39.3 (1993) 396–413.

Bright, John. *A History of Israel*. 3rd ed. Philadelphia: Westminster, 1981.

Briggs, Richard S. *Words in Action: Speech Act Theory and Biblical Interpretation*. Edinburgh: T&T Clark, 2001.

Brink, Laurie. *Soldiers in Luke–Acts: Engaging, Contradicting, and Transcending the Stereotypes*. Tübingen: Mohr Siebeck, 2014.

Brodie, Louis T. "A New Temple and a New Law: The Unity and Chronicler-based Nature of Luke 1:1–4:22a." *Journal for the Study of the New Testament* 2.5 (1979) 21–45.

Brodie, Thomas L. "The Accusing and Stoning of Naboth (1 Kgs 21:8–13) as one Component of the Stephen Text (Acts 6:9–14, Acts 7:58a)." *The Catholic Biblical Quarterly* 45.3 (1983) 417–32.

———. "Luke–Acts as an Imitation and Emulation of the Elijah-Elisha Narrative." In *New Views on Luke and Acts*, edited by Earl Richard, 78–85. Collegeville, MN: The Liturgical Press, 1990.

———. "Luke's Use of the Elijah-Elisha Narrative." In *The Elijah-Elisha Narrative in the Composition of Luke*, edited by John S. Kloppenborg and Joseph Verheyden, 6–28. London: Bloomsbury, 2014.

———. "Not Q but Elijah: The Saving of the Centurion's Servant (Luke 7:1–10) as an Internalization of the Saving of the Widow and her Child (1 Kgs 17:1–16)." *Irish Biblical Studies* 14.2 (1992) 54–71.

Brosend, William F. "The Means of Absent Ends." In *History, Literature, and Society in the Book of Acts*, edited by Ben Witherington III, 348–62. Cambridge: Cambridge University Press, 1996.

Brown, Jeannine K. *Scripture as Communication*. Grand Rapids: Baker Academic, 2007.

Brown, Peter. *Power and Persuasion in Late Antiquity: Towards a Christian Empire*. Madison: University of Wisconsin Press, 1992.

Brown, Raymond E. *The Birth of the Messiah: A Commentary on the Birth Narratives in the Gospels*. New Haven: Yale University Press, 1999.

———. *The Birth of the Messiah: A Commentary on the Infancy Narratives of Matthew and Luke*. Garden City: Doubleday, 1993.

Brown, Roger. "How Shall a Thing be Called?" *Psychological Review* 65 (1958) 14–21.

Brown, Rupert. *Group Processes: Dynamics within and Between Groups*. Oxford: Blackwell, 2000.

Brown, Schuyler. "The Role of the Prologues in Determining the Purpose of Luke–Acts." In *Perspectives on Luke–Acts*, edited by Charles H. Talbert, 99–111. Edinburgh: T&T Clark, 1978.

Brown, Warren S. "Tuning the Faith: The Cornelius Story in Resonance Perspective." *PRSt* 33.4 (2006) 449–65.

Bruce, F. F. *The Acts of the Apostles: The Greek Text with Introduction and Commentary*. Grand Rapids: Eerdmans, 1990.

———. *The Book of Acts*. Grand Rapids: Eerdmans, 1988.

———. *The Epistle to the Hebrews*. Grand Rapids: Eerdmans, 1990.

———. "The Holy Spirit in the Acts of the Apostles." *Interpretation* 27.2 (1973) 166–83.

———. *New Testament History*. New York: Galilee/Doubleday, 1980.

———. *Paul: The Apostle of the Free Spirit*. Exeter: Paternoster, 1977.

———. "Paul's Apologetic and the Purpose of Acts." *Bulletin of the John Rylands University Library of Manchester* 69.2 (1987) 379–93.

———. "The Significance of the Speeches for Interpreting Acts." *Southwest Journal of Theology* 33.1 (1990) 20–28.

———. *The Speeches in the Acts of the Apostles*. London: Tyndale, 1942.

———. "Speeches Thirty Years After." In *Reconciliation and Hope*, edited by Robert Banks, 53–68. Grand Rapids: Eerdmans, 1974.

Brueggemann, Walter. *The Land: Place as Gift, Promise, and Challenge in Biblical Faith*. 2nd ed. Minneapolis: Augsburg Fortress, 2002.

Brunner, Jerome. *Acts of Meaning: Four Lectures on Mind and Culture*. Cambridge, MA: Harvard University Press, 1990.

———. *Actual Minds, Possible Worlds*. Cambridge, MA: Harvard University Press, 1987.

Bruno, Christopher R. "'Jesus Is Our Jubilee' . . . But How?: The OT Background and Lukan Fulfillment of the Ethics of Jubilee." *JETS* 53.1 (2010) 81–101.

Buell, Denise K. "Producing Descent/Dissent: Clement of Alexandria's Use of Filial Metaphors as Intra-Christian Polemic." *Harvard Theological Review* 90.1 (1997) 89–104.

Burge, Gary M. *The Bible and the Land*. Grand Rapids: Zondervan, 2009.

———. *Jesus and the Land: The New Testament Challenge to "Holy Land" Theology*. Grand Rapids: Baker Academic, 2010.

———. *A Week in the Life of a Roman Centurion*. Downers Grove, IL: IVP Academic, 2015.

Burke, Kenneth. *A Rhetoric of Motives*. Berkley: University of California Press, 1950.

Burke, Peter J., and Jan E. Stets. *Identity Theory*. Oxford: Oxford University Press, 2009.

Burke, Sean D. *Queering the Ethiopian Eunuch: Strategies of Ambiguity in Acts*, Emerging Scholars. Minneapolis: Fortress, 2013.

Burnett, Clint. "Eschatological Prophet of Restoration: Luke's Theological Portrait of John the Baptist in Luke 3:1–6." *Neotestamentica* 47.1 (2013) 1–24.

Burridge, Richard A. "The Genre of Acts—Revisited." In *Reading Acts Today: Essays in Honour of Loveday C. A. Alexander*, edited by Steve Walton, Thomas E. Phillips, Lloyd K. Petersen, F. Scott Spencer, 3–28. London: T&T Clark, 2011.

———. *Imitating Jesus: An Inclusive Approach to New Testament Ethics*. Grand Rapids: Eerdmans, 2007.

———. *What Are the Gospels?: A Comparison with Graeco-Roman Biography*. 2nd ed. Grand Rapids: Eerdmans, 2004.

Burris, Ronald D. "Another Look at the Good Samaritan: Luke 10:25–37." *Review and Expositor* 114.3 (2017) 457–61.

Bury, J. B. *The Ancient Greek Historians*. New York: Barnes and Noble, 2006.

Buss, Martin J. "The Idea of Sitz im Leben—History and Critique." *ZAW* 90.2 (1978) 157–70.

Butler, Trent C. "God and Dysfunctional Families: A Social and Theological Study of the Book of Hosea." *Perspectives in Religious Studies* 43.2 (2016) 187–202.

Butticaz, Simon. "Actes 3, 1–26: Le relèvement de l'infirme comme paradigme de la restauration d'Israël." *Études Théologiques et Religieuses* 84.2 (2009) 177–88.

Byrskog, Samuel. "A Century with the Sitz im Leben: From Form-Critical Setting to Gospel Community and Beyond." *ZNW* 98.1 (2007) 1–27.

———. "A New Quest for the Sitz im Leben: Social Memory, the Jesus Tradition and the Gospel of Matthew." *NTS* 52.3 (2006) 319–36.

Cadbury, Henry. *The Book of Acts in History*. Eugene, OR: Wipf & Stock, 2004.

———. "The Speeches in Acts." In vol. 5 of *The Beginnings of Christianity: The Acts of the Apostles,* edited by F. J. Foakes Jackson and Kirsopp Lake, 402–27. Eugene, OR: Wipf & Stock, 2002.

Cadbury, Henry, et al. "The Greek and Jewish Traditions of Writing History." In vol. 2 of *The Beginnings of Christianity: The Acts of the Apostles,* edited by F. J. Foakes Jackson and Kirsopp Lake, 7–29. Eugene, OR: Wipf & Stock, 2002.

Cahn, Michael. "The Rhetoric of Rhetoric: Six Tropes of Disciplinary Self-Constitution." In *The Recovery of Rhetoric: Persuasive Discourse and Disciplinary in the Human Sciences,* edited by Richard H. Roberts and J. M. M. Good, 61–84. Charlottesville: University Press of Virginia, 1993.

Calduch-Benages, N., and J. Liesen, eds. *History and Identity: How Israel's Later Authors Viewed Its Earlier History*. New York: de Gruyter, 2006.

Callan, Terrance. "The Preface of Luke–Acts and Historiography." *NTS* 31.4 (1985) 576–81.

Callaway, Mary. *Sing, O Barren One: A Study in Comparative Midrash*. Atlanta: Scholars, 1986.

Calpino, Teresa. "'The Lord Opened her Heart': Boundary Crossing in Acts 16,13–15." *Annali di storia dell'esegesi* 28.2 (2011) 81–91.

Cameron, Averil. *Christianity and the Rhetoric of Empire: The Development of Christian Discourse*. Berkeley: University of California Press, 1991.

Campbell, William Sanger. *The "We" Passages in the Acts of the Apostles: The Narrator as Narrative Character*. Atlanta: SBL, 2007.

Capon, Robert Farrar. *Kingdom, Grace, Judgment: Paradox, Outrage, and Vindication in the Parables of Jesus*. Grand Rapids: Eerdmans, 2002.

Capper, B. J. "In der Hand des Ananias . . . ": Erwägungen zu 1 QS VI,20 und der urchristlichen Gütergemeinschaft." *RevQ* 12 (1986) 223–36.

———. "The Interpretation of Acts 5:4." *JSNT* 19 (1983) 117–31.

Carawan, Edwin. *The Attic Orators: Readings in Classical Studies*. Oxford: Oxford University Press, 2007.

Carmichael, Calum. "The Passover Haggadah." In *The Historical Jesus in Context,* edited by Amy-Jill Levine et al., 343–56. Princeton: Princeton University Press, 2006.

Carmignac, Jean. "Le document de Qumrân sur Melkisédeq." *Revue de Qumran* 7 (1970) 343–78.

Carter, Tim. *Forgiveness of Sins*. Cambridge: Clarke and Co., 2016.

Carter, Warren. "Zechariah and the Benedictus (Luke 1:68–79) Practicing What He Preaches." *Biblica* 69.2 (1988) 239–47.

Cartledge, Mark J., ed. *Speaking in Tongues: Multi-Disciplinary Perspectives*. Milton Keynes: Paternoster, 2006.

Chance, J. Bradley. *Acts*. Macon: Smyth & Helwys, 2007.

———. *Jerusalem, the Temple, and the New Age in Luke-Acts*. Macon: Mercer University Press, 1988.

Chapman, Colin. *Whose Promised Land?: The Continuing Crisis Over Israel and Palestine*. Grand Rapids: Baker, 2002.

Cheng, Ling. *The Characterization of God in Acts: The Indirect Portrayal of an Invisible Character*. Eugene, OR: Wipf & Stock, 2015.

Chia, Philip P. "On Naming the Subject: Postcolonial Reading of Daniel 1." In *The Postcolonial Biblical Reader*, edited by R. S. Sugirtharajah, 171–85. Victoria: Blackwell, 2006.

Chiappetta, Michael. "Historiography and Roman Education." *History of Education Journal* 4.4 (1953) 149–56.

Chilton, Bruce, and Jacob Neusner. "Paul and Gamaliel." *Review of Rabbinic Judaism* 8 (2005) 113–62.

Ching, Kapi M. "Incompatibility Between Wealth and Neighborly Love: A Re-reading of the Parable of the Poor at the Gate from the Perspective of the Marginalized." *Theologies and Cultures* 7.2 (2010) 142–51.

Chrupcala, L. Daniel. *Everyone Will See the Salvation of God: Studies in Lukan Theology*. Milan: Edizioni Terra Santa, 2015.

Cicero, Marcus. *On Invention*. Edited by Taylor Anderson. Charleston: CreateSpace, 2017.

Clark, Andrew C. "Parallel Lives: The Relation of Paul to the Apostles in the Lucan Perspective." Carlisle: Paternoster, 2001.

———. "The Role of the Apostles." In *Witness to the Gospel: The Theology of Acts*, edited by I. Howard Marshall, 499–518. Grand Rapids: Eerdmans, 1998.

Clark, W. Malcolm. "The Origin and Development of the Land of Promise Theme in the Old Testament." PhD diss., Yale University, 1964.

Classen, Carl Joachim. *Rhetorical Criticism of the New Testament*. Boston: Brill, 2002.

Clements, Ronald Ernest. *God and Temple*. Oxford: Basil Blackwell, 1965.

Clines, David J. A., et al., eds. *Art and Meaning: Rhetoric in Biblical Literature*. Sheffield: JSOT, 1982.

Cockerill, Gareth L. "Melchizedek or 'King of Righteousness.'" *EvQ* 63.4 (1991) 305–12.

Cohen, K. I. "Paul the Benjaminite: Mystery, Motives and Midrash." *Center for the Hermeneutical Studies Protocol* 60 (1990) 21–28.

Cohen, Shaye J. D. "Crossing the Boundary and Becoming a Jew." *The Harvard Theological Review* 82.1 (1989) 13–33.

———. "Respect for Judaism by Gentiles According to Josephus." *The Harvard Theological Review* 80.4 (1987) 409–30.

———. "Was Timothy Jewish (Acts 16:1–3) Patristic Exegesis, Rabbinic Law, and Matrilineal Descent." *JBL* 105.2 (1986) 251–68.

Cohler, Bert J. "Personal Narrative and Life Course." In *Life Span Development and Behavior*, edited by P. Baltes and O. G. Brim, 205–41. New York: Academic, 1982.

Collins, Adela Yarbro. "The Dream of a New Jerusalem at Qumran." In *The Scrolls and Christian Origins*, edited by James H. Charlesworth, 231–54. Vol. 3 of *The Bible and the Dead Sea Scrolls*. Waco, TX: Baylor University Press, 2006.

Collins, John J. *Between Athens and Jerusalem: Jewish Identity in the Hellenistic Diaspora*. 2nd ed. Grand Rapids: Eerdmans, 1999.

———. "A Symbol of Otherness: Circumcision and Salvation in the First Century." In *To See Ourselves as Others See Us*, edited by Jacob Neusner and Ernest S. Frerichs, 163–86. Chico, CA: Scholars, 1985.

Conrad, Edgar W. "The 'Fear Not' Oracles in Second Isaiah." *Vetus Testamentum* 34.2 (1984) 129–52.

Conzelmann, Hans. *The Theology of St. Luke*. Translated by Geoffrey Buswell. New York: Harper and Row, 1960.

Cook, Joan E. "The Magnificat: Program for a New Era in the Spirit of the Song of Hannah." *Proceedings* 15 (1995) 35–43.

Coote, Robert B. "Meaning of the Name 'Israel.'" *Harvard Theological Review* 65.1 (1972) 137–42.

Cope, Lamar, et al. "Narrative Outline of the Composition of Luke According to the Two-Gospel Hypothesis." *Society of Biblical Literature Seminar Papers* 34 (1995) 636–87.

Corbett, Edward P. J., and Robert J. Connors. *Classical Rhetoric for the Modern Student*. 4th ed. New York: Oxford University Press, 1999.

Corbin-Reuschling, Wyndy. "Zacchaeus's Conversion: To Be or Not to Be a Tax Collector (Luke 19:1–10)." *Ex Auditu* 25 (2009) 67–88.

Cordasco, Francesco. *A Brief History of Education: A Handbook of Information on Greek, Roman, Medieval, Renaissance, and Modern Educational Practice*. Lanham, MD: Rowman and Littlefield, 1976.

Corley, Bruce. "Interpreting Paul's Conversion—Then and Now." In *The Road From Damascus: The Impact of Paul's Conversion on His Life, Thought, and Ministry*, edited by Richard N. Longenecker, 1–17. Grand Rapids: Eerdmans, 1997.

Corley, Kathleen E. *Private Women, Public Meals: Social Conflict in the Synoptic Tradition*. Peabody: Hendrickson, 1993.

Cote, James E., and Charles G. Levine. *Identity, Formation, Agency, and Culture: A Social Psychological Synthesis*. Mahwah, NJ: Lawrence Erlbaum Associates, 2002.

Cotter, Wendy. "Cornelius, the Roman Army and Religion." In *Religious Rivalries and the Struggle for Success in Caesarea Maritima*, edited by Terence Donaldson, 279–301. Waterloo: Wilfrid Laurier, 2000.

Cotton, Roger. "The Gospel in the Old Testament According to Paul in Acts 13." In *Trajectories in the Book of Acts: Essays in Honor of John Wesley Wyckoff*, edited by Paul Alexander et al., 277–89. Eugene, OR: Wipf & Stock, 2010.

Cowton, Christopher J. "The Alms Trade: A Note on Identifying the Beautiful Gate of Acts 3:2." *NTS* 42.3 (1996) 475–76.

Cozolino, Louis. *The Neuroscience of Human Relationships: Attachment and the Developing Social Brain*. 2nd ed. New York: Norton, 2014.

Crabbe, Kylie. "Being Found Fighting Against God: Luke's Gamaliel and Josephus on Human Responses to Divine Providence." *ZNW* 106.1 (2015) 21–39.

Crawford, Timothy G. "Taking the Promised Land, Leaving the Promised Land: Luke's Use of Joshua as a Christian Foundation Story." *RevExp* 95 (1998) 251–61.

Creamer, Jennifer, et al. "Who is Theophilus?: Discovering the Original Reader of Luke-Acts." *In die Skriflig* 48.1 (2014) 1–7.

Creed, J. M. *The Gospel According to St. Luke*. London: Macmillan, 1930.

Crehan, Joseph H. "The Confirmation of the Ethiopian Eunuch (Acts 8:39)." In *The Heritage of the Early Church: Essays in Honor of the Very Reverend Vasilievich Florovsky*, edited by Margaret Neiman, 187–95. Rome: Pontificium Institutum Studiorum Orientalium, 1973.

Crook, Z. "Honor, Shame, and Social Status Revisited." *JBL* 128.3 (2009) 591–611.

Crossan, John Dominic, ed. *Polyvalent Narration*. Missoula, MT: SBL, 1977.

Croy, N. Clayton. "Mantic Mary?: The Virgin Mother as Prophet in Luke 1.26–56 and the Early Church." *JSNT* 34.3 (2012) 254–76.

Cullman, Oscar. *Baptism in the New Testament*. London: SCM, 1950.

Culpepper, R. Alan. "Seeing the Kingdom of God: The Metaphor of Sight in the Gospel of Luke." *Currents in Theology and Mission* 21.6 (1994) 434–43.

Cutler, Allan. "Does the Simeon of Luke 2 Refer to Simeon the Son of Hillel." *Journal of Bible and Religion* 34.1 (1966) 29–35.

Czachesz, István. "Socio-Rhetorical Exegesis of Acts 9:1–30." *Communio Viatorum* 37.1 (1995) 5–32.

Dahl, George. "Some Recent Interpretations of Second Isaiah." *JBL* 48.3 (1929) 362–77.

Dahl, N. A. *Studies in Paul*. Minneapolis: Augsburg, 1977.

Dale, Moyra. "Dismantling Socio-Sacred Hierarchy: Gender and Gentiles in Luke–Acts." *Priscilla Papers* 31.2 (2017) 19–23.

Damasio, Antonio. *The Feeling of What Happens: Body and Emotion in the Making of Consciousness*. Orlando: Harcourt, 1999.

D'Angelo, Mary Rose. "Women in Luke–Acts: A Redactional View." *Journal of Biblical Literature* 109.3 (1990) 441–61.

Danker, Frederick. *Jesus and the New Age: A Commentary on St. Luke's Gospel*. Minneapolis: Fortress, 1988.

Darr, John A. *On Character Building: The Reader and the Rhetoric of Characterization in Luke–Acts*. Louisville: Westminster John Knox, 1992.

Dautenhahn, Kerstin, and Chrystopher L. Nehaniv, eds. *Imitation in Animals and Artifacts*. Cambridge: MIT Press, 2002.

Davies, G. N. "When Was Cornelius Saved?" *RefTheolRev* 46.2 (1987) 43–49.

Davies, John D. "Inclusion in the Acts of the Apostles." *The Expository Times* 124.9 (2013) 425–32.

Davies, W. D. *The Gospel and the Land: Early Christianity and Jewish Territorial Doctrine*. Berkeley, CA: University of California Press, 1974.

———. "Paul and the People of Israel." *NTS* 24 (1978) 4–39.

———. *Paul and Rabbinic Judaism: Some Rabbinic Elements in Pauline Theology*. London: Fortress, 1980.

———. *The Territorial Dimension of Judaism*. Berkley: University of California Press, 1982.

Davila, James R. "Melchizedek: King, Priest, and God." In *The Seductiveness of Jewish Myth: Challenge or Response?*, edited by S. D. Breslauer, 217–34. Albany, NY: State University of New York Press, 1997.

———. "Melchizedek, Michael, and War in Heaven." *SBLSP* 35 (1996) 259–72.

Davis, Stephen J. "Crossed Texts, Crossed Sex: Intertextuality and Gender in Early Christian Legends of Holy Women Disguised as Men." *Journal of Early Christian Studies* 10.1 (2002) 1–36.

DeBruyn, J. J. "A Clash of Gods: Conceptualizing Space in Daniel 1." *Hervormde Teologiese Studies* 70.3 (2014) 1–6.

Decker, Timothy L. "'Live Long in the Land': The Covenantal Character of the Old Testament Allusions in the Message to Laodicea (Revelation 3:14–22)." *Neotestamentica* 48.2 (2014) 417–46.

Dench, Emma. *From Barbarians to New Men: Greek, Roman, and Modern Perceptions of People from the Central Apennines*. Oxford: Clarendon, 1995.

Dennison, James T., Jr. "The Eschatological Jubilee: Luke 4:16–30." *Kerux* 31.1 (2016) 31–36.

Denova, Rebecca. *The Things Accomplished Among Us: Prophetic Tradition in the Structural Pattern of Luke-Acts*. Sheffield: Sheffield Academic, 1997.

DeOrio, Anthony R. "The Phenomenology of Transformation and Healing: The Disciples as Miracle Workers and Other Biblical Examples." In *Miracles: God, Science, and Psychology in the Paranormal*, edited by J. Harold Ellens, 114–33. London: Praeger, 2008.

DeSilva, D. A. "The Noble Contest: Honor, Shame, and the Rhetorical Strategy of 4Maccabees." *Journal for the Study of the Pseudopigrapha* 13 (1995) 31–57.

Devillers, Luc. "The Infancy of Jesus and the Infancy of the Church: From the Canticles (Luke 1–2) to the Summaries (Acts 1–7)." In *Infancy Gospels: Stories and Identities*, edited by Benjamin Bertho and Claire Clivaz, 351–73. Tübingen: Mohr Siebeck, 2011.

Dewey, Joanna. "From Storytelling to Written Text: The Loss of Early Christian Women's Voices." *Biblical Theology Bulletin* 26 (1996) 71–78.

———. "Jesus' Healings of Women: Clues for Historical Reconstruction." *Biblical Theology Bulletin* 24 (1994) 122–31.

Dibelius, Martin. *Aufsätze zur Apostelgeschichte*. Göttingen: Vandenhoeck & Ruprecht, 1951.

———. *Die urchristliche Überlieferung von Johannes dem Täufer*. Göttingen: Vandenhoeck & Ruprecht, 1911.

———. *Studies in the Acts of the Apostles*. London: SCM, 1956.

DiCicco, Mario M. *Paul's Use of Ethos, Pathos, and Logos in 2 Corinthians 10–13*. Lewiston, NY: Mellen, 1995.

Dicken, Frank. "The Author and Date of Luke-Acts: Exploring the Options." In *Issues in Luke-Acts: Selected Essays*, edited by Sean A. Adams and Michael Pahl, 7–26. Piscataway, NJ: Gorgias, 2012.

Dillon, Richard J. *The Hymns of St. Luke: Lyricism and Narrative Strategy in Luke 1–2*. Washington: Catholic Biblical Association, 2013.

Dinkler, Michal Beth. "Reading the Potentials of Jesus' 'Triumphal Entry' (Luke 19:28–40)." *Review & Expositor* 112.4 (2015) 525–41.

Dionne, Christian. "Les Actes Des Apotres et la 'Question Juive' (AC 13,46; 18,6; 28,28) Analyse, mise en contexte et effet rhétorique, Première partie." *Theoforum* 46.2 (2015) 359–83.

Dionysius of Halicarnassensis. "On Imitation." In vol. 6 of *Dionysii Halicarnasei Quae Exstant*, edited by Hermann Usener and Ludwig Radermacher, 197–217. Leipzig: Teubner, 1965.

———. *On Thucydides*. Translated by W. Kendrick Protchett. Berkley: University of California Press, 1975.

Dippenaar, Michaelis C. "Table Fellowship and Lukan Christology: Jesus as Guest of Tax Collectors and Pharisees." *Taiwan Journal of Theology* 35 (2012) 2–43.

Doble, Peter. "Luke 24:26, 44—Songs of God's Servant: David and His Psalms in Luke-Acts." *JSNT* 28.3 (2006) 267–83.

Donahue, John R. *The Gospel in Parable*. Minneapolis: Fortress, 1988.

Donaldson, Terrance L. "Moses Typology and the Sectarian Nature of early Christian anti-Judaism: a study in Acts 7." *JSNT* 12 (1981) 27–52.

———. *Paul and the Gentiles: Remapping the Apostle's Convictional World*. Minneapolis: Fortress, 1997.

———. "'Riches for the Gentiles' (Rom 11:12) Israel's Rejection and Paul's Gentile Mission." *JBL* 112.1 (1993) 81–98.

Donfried, Karl P. "Attempts at Discovering the Purpose of Luke–Acts: Christology and the Salvation of the Gentiles." In *Christological Perspectives: Essays in Honor of Harvey K. McArthur*, edited by R. F. Berkey and S. A. Edwards, 112–22. New York: Pilgrim, 1982.

Doohan, Leonard. *Acts of Apostles: Building Faith Communities*. San Jose, CA: Resource, 1994.

Douglas, J. D. "Gamaliel." In *New Bible Dictionary*, edited by I. Howard Marshall et al., 395–96. 3rd ed. Downers Grove, IL: InterVarsity, 2007.

Douglas, Mary. *Purity and Danger: An Analysis of Concept of Pollution and Taboo*. Abingdon: Routledge, 2002.

Downing, F. Gerald. "Law and Custom: Luke–Acts and Late Hellenism." In *Law and Religion: Essays on the Place of the Law in Israel and Early Christianity by Members of the Ehrhardt Seminar*, edited by Barnabas Lindars, 148–58. Cambridge: James Clark, 1988.

———. "Psalms and the Baptist." *JSNT* 29.2 (2006) 131–37.

Downs, David J. *Alms: Charity, Reward, and Atonement in Early Christianity*. Waco, TX: Baylor University Press, 2016.

Driver, G. R. "Two Problems in the New Testament." *Journal of Theological Studies* 16 (1965) 327–37.

Duba, Arlo. "Disrupted by Luke–Acts." *Theology Today* 68.2 (2011) 116–22.

Dunn, James D. G. *Baptism in the Holy Spirit: A Re-Examination of the New Testament on the Gift of the Spirit*. Louisville: Westminster John Knox, 1977.

———. *The Parting of the Ways*. 2nd ed. Norwich: Hymns Ancient and Modern, 2006.

Duhm, Bernard. *Das Buch Jesaia*. 4th ed. Göttingen: Vandenhoeck & Ruprecht, 1922.

Duncan, John M. "Peter, Paul, and the Progymnasmata: Traces of the Preliminary Exercises in the Mission Speeches of Acts." *Perspectives in Religious Studies* 41.4 (2014) 349–65.

Dupont, Jacques. "La nouvelle Pentecote (Ac 2, 1–11)." *Nouvelles études sur les Actes des apôtres* (1984) 193–98.

———. *The Sources of Acts: The Present Position*. Translated by Kathleen Pond. New York: Herder & Herder, 1964.

Easter, Matthew C. "'Certainly This Man Was Righteous': Highlighting a Messianic Reading of the Centurion's Confession in Luke 23:47." *Tyndale Bulletin* 63.1 (2012) 35–51.

Eberts, Harry W. "Plurality and Ethnicity in Early Christian Mission." *Sociology of Religion* 58.4 (1997) 305–21.

Eck, Earnest van, et al. "The Parable of the Feast (Lk 14:16b–23): Breaking Down Boundaries and Discerning a Theological-Spatial Justice Agenda." *Hervormde Teologiese Studies* 72.1 (2016) 1–8.

Eckey, Wilfried. *Die Apostelgeschichte: Der Weg des Evangeliums von Jerusalem nach Rom*. 2 vols. Neukirchen-Vluyn: Neukirchener Verlag, 2000.

Edwards, M. L. "The Cultural Context of Deformity in the Ancient Greek World." *Ancient History Bulletin* 10.3–4 (1996) 79–92.

Ehrhardt, Arnold. *The Acts of the Apostles: Ten Lectures*. Manchester: Manchester University Press, 1969.

Eisen, Ute E. "Boundary Transgression and the Extreme Point in Acts 10:1–11:18." In *On the Cutting Edge: The Study of Women in Biblical Worlds: Essays in Honor of Elisabeth Schüssler Fiorenza*, edited by Esther Fuchs, 154–70. New York: Continuum, 2004.

Ekman, Paul. *Universals and Cultural Differences in Facial Expressions of Emotions*. Edited by James K. Cole. Lincoln: University of Nebraska Press, 1971.

Elliot, John H. "Matthew 20:1–15: A Parable of Invidious Comparison and Evil Eye Accusation." *BTB* 22.2 (1992) 52–65.

———. "Social-Scientific Criticism: Perspective, Process and Payoff: Evil Eye Accusation at Galatia as Illustration of the Method." *HTS Teologiese Studies/Theological Studies* 1 (2011) 1–10.

Elliot, Neil. *The Rhetoric of Romans: Argumentative Constraint and Strategy and Paul's Dialogue with Judaism.* Sheffield: JSOT, 1990.

Ellis, E. Earle. "'The End of the Earth' (Acts 1:8)." *BBR* 1 (1991) 123–32.

———. *The Gospel of Luke.* Greenwood: Attic, 1974.

Ellis, John M. *The Theory of Literary Criticism: A Logical Analysis.* Berkeley: University of California Press, 1974.

Ellul, Danielle. "Antioche de Pisidie: Une predication . . . trois credos? (Actes 13,13–43)." *Filología Neotestamentaria* 5.5 (1992) 3–14.

Engberg-Pedersen, Troels, ed. *Paul Beyond the Judaism/Hellenism Divide.* Louisville: Westminster John Knox, 2001.

Ernst, Josef von. *Das Evangelium nach Lukas.* Regensburg: Pustet, 1977.

Ervin, Howard M. *Conversion-Initiation and the Baptism in the Holy Spirit.* Peabody: Hendrickson, 1984.

Esler, Philip. *Community and Gospel in Luke–Acts: The Social and Political Motivations of Lucan Theology.* 1987. Reprint, Cambridge University Press, 1996.

———. *Conflict and Identity in Romans: The Social Setting of Paul's Letter.* Minneapolis: Fortress, 2003.

———. "Glossolalia and the Admission of Gentiles into the Early Christian Community." *Biblical Theology Bulletin* 22 (1992) 136–42.

———. "Group Norms and Prototypes in Matthew 5:3–12: A Social Identity Interpretation of the Matthaean Beatitudes." In *T&T Clark Handbook to Social Identity in the New Testament,* edited by J. Brian Tucker and Coleman Caker, 147–72. London: Bloomsbury, 2014.

———. "An Outline of Social Identity Theory." In *T&T Clark Handbook to Social Identity in the New Testament,* edited by J. Brian Tucker and Coleman A. Baker, 13–40. London: Bloomsbury, 2014.

———. "Prototypes, Antitypes, and Social Identity in First Clement: Outlining a New Interpretive Model." *Annali di storia dell' esegesi* 24.1 (2007) 125–46.

Estes, Douglas. *Questions and Rhetoric in the Greek New Testament: An Essential Reference Resource for Exegesis.* Grand Rapids: Zondervan, 2017.

Estrada, Nelson. *From Followers to Leaders: The Apostles in the Ritual of Status Transformation in Acts 1–2.* New York: Bloomsbury Academic, 2004.

Eusebius. *Ecclesiastical History.* Vol. 1. Translated by Kirsopp Lake. LCL 153. Cambridge, MA: Harvard University Press, 1926.

Evans, Craig A. *Mark 8:27–16:20.* Word Biblical Commentary 32B. Edited by Bruce Metzger. Grand Rapids: Zondervan, 2001.

Evans, Craig A., and Jeremiah J. Johnston, eds. *Searching the Scriptures: Studies in Context and Intertextuality.* New York: Bloomsbury, 2015.

Evans, Craig A., and James A. Sanders, eds. *Early Christian Interpretation of the Scriptures of Israel: Investigations and Proposals.* Sheffield: Sheffield Academic, 1997.

Farris, James. "Christ as Prototype." *Toronto Journal of Theology* 8.2 (1992) 288–96.

Farris, Stephen. *The Hymns of Luke's Infancy Narratives: Their Origin, Meaning, and Significance*. New York: Bloomsbury Academic, 2015.

Fay, Ronald C. "The Narrative Function of the Temple in Luke–Acts." *Trinity Journal* 27.2 (2006) 255–70.

Fee, Gordon D. "Baptism in the Holy Spirit: Issues of Separability and Subsequence." *Pneuma* 7 (1985) 8–99.

Felder, Cain Hope. "Racial Ambiguities in the Biblical Narratives." In *The Church and Racism*, edited by Gregory Baum and John Coleman, 17–24. Edinburgh: T&T Clark, 1982.

———. *Troubling Biblical Waters: Race, Class, and Family*. Maryknoll, NY: Orbis, 1989.

Feldkeller, Andreas. *Identitätssuche des syrischen Urchristentums: Mission, Inkulturation und Pluralität im ältesten Heidenchristentum*. Göttingen: Vandenhoeck & Ruprecht, 1993.

Feldman, Louis H. "Jewish 'Sympathizers' in Classical Literature and Inscriptions." *Transactions and Proceedings of the American Psychological Association* 81 (1950) 200–208.

———. "The Omnipresence of the God-Fearers." *Biblical Archeology Review* 12.5 (1986) 46–53.

Festinger, Leon. *A Theory of Cognitive Dissonance*. Evanston: Row, 1957.

———. "A Theory of Social Comparison Processes." *Human Relations* 7 (1954) 117–40.

Fike, Barry. *Mikveh: The Relationship of Jewish Ritual Immersion and Christian Baptism*. Baltimore: Publish America, 2009.

Finger, Reta Halteman. "Table Fellowship: The Spirituality of Eating Together." In *Vital Christianity: Spirituality, Justice, and Christian Practice*, edited by David. L. Weaver-Zercher and William H. Willimon, 188–200. New York: T&T Clark, 2005.

———. *Of Widows and Meals: Communal Meals in the Book of Acts*. Grand Rapids: Eerdmans, 2007.

Finkel, Asher. "The Other and the Stranger in Biblical and Rabbinic Tradition." *SIDIC* 25.3 (1992) 2–10, 14.

Finn, Thomas M. "The God-fearers Reconsidered." *Catholic Biblical Quarterly* 47.1 (1985) 75–84.

Fiorenza, Elisabeth Schüssler. "A Feminist Critical Interpretation for Liberation: Martha and Mary: Luke 10:38–42." *Religion and Intellectual Life* 3 (1986) 21–36.

———. *Rhetoric and Ethic: The Politics of Biblical Studies*. Minneapolis: Fortress, 1999.

Fiske, Susan T., and Shelley E. Taylor. *Social Cognition*. 2nd ed. New York: McGraw-Hill, 1991.

Fitzmyer, Joseph A. *The Acts of the Apostles*. New York: Doubleday, 1998.

———. "Further Light on Melchizedek from Qumran Cave 11." *JBL* 86 (1967) 25–41.

———. *The Gospel According to Luke*. 2 vols. New York: Doubleday, 1981, 1985.

Flanigan, N. M. "The Position of Women in the Writings of St. Luke." *Marianum* 40 (1978) 288–304.

Fletcher-Louis, Crispin H. T. *Luke–Acts: Angels, Christology, and Soteriology*. Tübingen: Mohr Siebeck, 1997.

Flusser, David. "Paganism in Palestine." In *Compendia Rerum Iudaicarum ad Novum Testamentum* 1.2, edited by S. Safrai and M. Stern, 1065–1100. Assen: Van Gorcum, 1976.

Foakes-Jackson, Frederick J. *The Acts of the Apostles*. London: Hodder and Stoughton, 1931.

Fokkelman, J. P. *Reading Biblical Narrative: An Introductory Guide*. Louisville: Westminster John Knox, 2000.

Forbes, Greg W., and Scott D. Harrower. *Raised from Obscurity: A Narritival and Theological Study of the Characterization of Women in Luke–Acts*. Eugene, OR: Pickwick, 2015.

Fredriksen, Paula. "Judaism, the Circumcision of Gentiles, and Apocalyptic Hope: Another Look at Galatians 1 and 2." *JTS* 42.2 (1991) 532–64.

Frei, Hans W. *The Eclipse of Biblical Narrative: A Study in Eighteenth and Nineteenth Century Hermeneutics*. New Haven: Yale University Press, 1980.

Freyne, Sean. *Galilee, Jesus and the Gospels: Literary Approaches and Historical Investigations*. Philadelphia: Fortress, 1988.

———. "Urban-Rural Relations in First-Century Galilee: Some Suggestions from the Literary Sources." In *The Galilee in Late Antiquity*, edited by Lee Levine, 75–91. New York: Jewish Theological Seminary of America, 1992.

Fuller, Sylvia. "Creating and Contesting Boundaries: Exploring the Dynamics of Conflict and Classification." *Sociological Forum* 18 (2003) 3–30.

Gager, John G. "Jews, Gentiles, and Synagogues in the Book of Acts." In *Christians Among Jews and Gentiles*, edited by G. Nickelsburg and G. MacRae, 91–99. Philadelphia: Fortress, 1986.

Gagnon, Robert A. J. "Luke's Motives for Redaction in the Account of the Double Delegation in Luke 7:1–10." *Novum Testamentum* 36 (1994) 122–45.

Gardner, A. E. "Reading between the Texts: Minor Characters Who Prepare the Way for Jesus." *Encounter* 66.1 (2005) 45–66.

Garnet, Paul. "Atonement: Qumran and the New Testament." In *The Scrolls and Christian Origins*, edited by James H. Charlesworth, 357–80. Vol. 3 of *The Bible and the Dead Sea Scrolls*. Waco, TX: Baylor University Press, 2006.

———. "Jesus and the Exilic Soteriology." In *Studia Biblica 1978 II: Papers on the Gospels*, edited by Elizabeth A. Livingstone, 111–14. Sheffield: JSOT, 1980.

Garroway, Joshua. "'Apostolic Irresistibility' and the Interrupted Speeches in Acts." *The Catholic Biblical Quarterly* 74.4 (2012) 738–52.

———. "The Pharisee Heresy: Circumcision for Gentiles in the Acts of the Apostles." *NTS* 60.1 (2014) 20–36.

Gaston, Lloyd. *No Stone on Another: Studies in the Significance of the Fall of Jerusalem in the Synoptic Gospels*. Leiden: Brill, 1970.

Gaventa, Beverly Roberts. *The Acts of the Apostles*. Nashville: Abington, 2003.

———. "The Overthrown Enemy: Luke's Portrait of Paul." *Society of Biblical Literature Seminar Papers* 24 (1985) 439–49.

Gebauer, Gunter, and Christoph Wulf. *Mimesis: Culture, Art, Society*. Translated by Don Reneau. Berkeley: University of California Press, 1995.

Gehring, Roger W. *House Church and Mission: The Importance of Household Structures in Early Christianity*. Grand Rapids: Baker Academic, 2009.

Gelston, A. "Some Notes on Second Isaiah." *Vetus Testamentum* 21 (1971) 517–27.

Gempf, Conrad. "Apollos and the Ephesian Disciples: Befores and Afters (Acts 18:24–19:7)." In *The Spirit and Christ in the New Testament and Christian Theology: Essays in Honor of Max Turner*, edited by I. Howard Marshall and Cornelius Bennema, 119–37. Grand Rapids: William B. Eerdmans, 2012.

———. "The God-Fearers." In *The Book of Acts in the Setting of Hellenistic History*, edited by Colin Hemer, 444–47. Wissenschaftliche Untersuchungen zum Neuen Testament 49. Philadelphia: Coronet, 1989.

———. "Public Speaking and Published Accounts." In *The Book of Acts in its Ancient Literary Setting*, edited by Bruce Winter and Andrew Clarke, 259–304. Vol. 1 of *The Book of Acts in its First Century Setting*. Grand Rapids: Eerdmans, 1993.

Gendy, Atef Mehanny. "Style, Content, and Culture: Distinctive Characteristics in the Missionary Speeches in Acts." *Svensk Missionstidskrift* 99.3 (2011) 247–65.

Gennep, Arnold van, et al. *The Rites of Passage*. Chicago: University of Chicago Press, 1961.

Gentili, B., and G. Cerri. "Written and Oral Communication in Greek Historiographical Thought." In *Communication Arts in the Ancient World*, edited by E. A. Havestock and J. P. Hershbel, 137–55. New York: Hastings, 1978.

Georges, Jayson. "From Shame to Honor: A Theological Reading of Romans for Honor-Shame Contexts." *Missiology* 38.3 (2010) 295–307.

Gerhardsson, Birger. *Memory and Manuscript with Tradition and Transmission in Early Christianity*. Grand Rapids: Eerdmans, 1998.

Gerrig, Richard J. *Experiencing Narrative Worlds: On the Psychological Activities of Reading*. New Haven: Yale University Press, 1993.

Gibson, Jack J. *Peter Between Jerusalem and Antioch: Peter, James, and the Gentiles*. Tübingen: Mohr Siebeck, 2013.

Giddens, Anthony. *Modernity and Self Identity: Self and Society in the Late Modern Age*. Stanford: Stanford University Press, 1991.

Gilbert, Gary. "The Disappearance of the Gentiles: God-Fearers and the Image of the Jews in Luke–Acts." In *Putting Body and Soul Together: Essays in Honor of Robin Scroggs*, edited by Virginia Wiles et al., 172–84. Valley Forge, PA: Trinity, 1997.

———. "The List of Nations in Acts 2: Roman Propaganda and the Lukan Response." *JBL* 121.3 (2002) 497–529.

Gilchrist, Mike. "The 'We' Sections as Eyewitness Reporting: Some New Arguments." Paper presented to the Book of Acts Seminar, British New Testament Society, University of Aberdeen, September 3–5, 2009.

Gillis, John. "Memory and Identity: The History of a Relationship." In *Commemorations: The Politics of National Identity*, by John Gillis, 3–24. Princeton: Princeton University Press, 1994.

Gillman, John. *Possessions and the Life of Faith: A Reading of Luke–Acts*. Collegeville, MN: Liturgical, 1991.

Gitay, Yehoshua. *Prophecy and Persuasion: A Study of Isaiah 40–48*. Bonn: Linguistica Biblica, 1981.

Gnilka, Joachim. "Der Hymnus des Zacharias." *BZ* 6 (1962) 215–38.

Goatley, David Emmanuel. "Coloring Outside the Lines: Acts 11:1–18." *Review and Expositor* 108.4 (2011) 579–84.

Godet, Frédérick L. *A Commentary on the Gospel of St. Luke*. Translated by E. W. Shalders and M. D. Cusin. Edinburgh: Clark, 1875.

Goff, Matthew. "The Foolish Nation that Dwells in Schechem: Ben Sira on Schechem and Other Peoples in Palestine." In *The "Other" in Second Temple Judaism: Essays in Honor of John J. Collins*, edited by D. C. Harlow, 173–88. Grand Rapids: Eerdmans, 2010.

Goguel, Maurice. *Au seuil de l'Evangile: Jean-Baptiste*. Paris: Payot, 1928.

———. *The Life of Jesus*. Translated by Olive Wyon. New York: Macmillan, 1933.

Goldin, J. "The Freedom and Restraint of Haggadah." In *Midrash and Literature*, edited by Geoffrey H. Hartman and Sanford Budick, 57–76. New Haven: Yale University Press, 1986.

Goppelt, Leonhard. *Apostolic and Post-Apostolic Times*. Translated by Robert Guelich. Grand Rapids: Baker, 1980.

Gorgias of Leontini. "Encomium of Helen." In *The Greek Sophists*, edited by John M. Dillon and Tania Gergel, 76–84. London: Penguin, 2003.

Gorman, Heather. "Persuading through Pathos: Appeals to the Emotions in Hebrews." *Restoration Quarterly* 54.2 (2012) 77–90.

Gosse, Bernard. "Sabbath, Identity, and Universalism Go Together after the Return from Exile." *JSOT* 29.3 (2005) 359–70.

Goulder, Michael D. *Type and History in Acts*. London: SPCK, 1964.

Gowler, David B. *The Parables after Jesus: Their Imaginative Receptions across Two Millennia*. Grand Rapids: Baker Academic, 2017.

Gradl, H. G. "Alles liegt in deiner Hand: Ein Gebet der ersten Christen." *Erbe und Auftrag* 82.4 (2006) 436–39.

Graham, William Creighton. "The Second Rescue of the Second Isaiah." *The Journal of Religion* 9.1 (1929) 66–84.

Grams, Rollin Gene. "God's Mercy from Generation to Generation: Luke's Use of Psalms 105–108 in His Infancy Narrative Songs to Provide a Salvation Historical Understanding for His Two-Volume History." *Baptistic Theologies* 1.2 (2009) 93–108.

Green, Joel B. *Acts*. Edited by Beverly Roberts Gaventa and David Peterson. Nashville: Abingdon, 2010.

———. *Conversion in Luke–Acts: Divine Action, Human Cognition, and the People of God*. Grand Rapids: Baker Academic, 2015.

———. "Cornelius." In *Dictionary of the Later New Testament and Its Developments*, edited by Ralph P. Martin and Peter Davids, 234–45. Downers Grove, IL: InterVarsity, 1997.

———. "The Death of Jesus and the Rending of the Temple Veil (Luke 23:44–49): A Window into Luke's Understanding of Jesus and the Temple." In *Society of Biblical Literature 1991 Seminar Papers*, edited by Eugene H. Lovering Jr., 543–57. Atlanta: Scholars, 1991.

———. "The Demise of the Temple as 'Culture Center' in Luke–Acts: An Exploration of the Rending of the Temple Veil (Luke 23:44–49)." *Revue Biblique* 101.4 (1994) 495–515.

———. "Eschatology and the Nature of Humans: A Reconsideration of Pertinent Biblical Evidence." *Science and Christian Belief* 14.1 (2002) 33–50.

———. "Luke–Acts, or Luke and Acts?: A Reaffirmation of Narrative Unity." In *Reading Acts Today: Essays in Honour of Loveday C. A. Alexander*, edited by Steve Walton et al., 101–19. London: T&T Clark, 2011.

———. "The Problem of a Beginning: Israel's Scriptures in Luke 1–2." *BBR* 4 (1994) 61–86.

———. *The Theology of the Gospel of Luke*. Cambridge: Cambridge University Press, 1995.

Green, Thomas F. *The Activities of Teaching*. New York: McGraw-Hill, 1971.

Grelot, Pierre. "Le cantique de Siméon (Luc, ii, 29–32)." *RB* 93 (1986) 481–509.

Groenvold, P. C. "The Child Jesus as a Model for the Disciples as 'the Little Ones': A Reconsideration of the Literary and Theological Function of Matthew 2:1–23." *Theology and Life* 36 (2013) 61–70.

Gunkel, Hermann. "Die Lieder in der Kindheitsgeschichte Jesu bei Lukas." In *Festgabe*, edited by A. von Harnack, 43–60. Tübingen, 1921.

Haaslam, J. A. G. "The Centurion at Capernaum: Luke 7:1–10." *Expository Times* 96.4 (1985) 109–10.

Hacham, N. "Third Maccabees and Esther: Parallels, Intertextuality, and Diasporic Identity." *JBL* 126.4 (2007) 765–85.

Haenchen, Ernst. *The Acts of the Apostles: A Commentary*. Louisville: Westminster John Knox, 1971.

Hahn, Scott W. *Kinship by Covenant: A Canonical Approach to the Fulfillment of God's Saving Promises*. New Haven: Yale University Press, 2009.

Hakola, Raimo. "Friendly Pharisees and Social Identity in Acts." In *Contemporary Studies in Acts*, edited by Thomas E. Phillips, 181–200. Macon, GA: Mercer University Press, 2009.

Halliwell, Stephen. *The Aesthetics of Mimesis: Ancient Texts, Modern Problems*. Princeton: Princeton University Press, 2002.

———. "Comic Satire and Freedom of Speech in Classical Athens." *Journal of Hellenistic Studies* 101 (1991) 48–70.

Hamm, M. Dennis. *The Acts of the Apostles*. Collegeville, MN: Liturgical, 2005.

———. "Paul's Blindness and Its Healing: Clues to Symbolic Intent (Acts 9; 22 and 26)." *Biblica* 71.1 (1990) 63–72.

———. "Zacchaeus Revisited Once More: A Story of Vindication or Conversion?" *Biblica* 72.2 (1991) 248–52.

Harrelson, Walter. *From Fertility Cult to Worship*. Garden City, NY: Doubleday, 1969.

Harris, Monford. *Exodus and Exile: The Structure of the Jewish Holidays*. Minneapolis: Fortress, 1992.

Harrison, James R. "Paul's Inversion of a Cultural Icon." In *Christian Origins and Greco-Roman Culture: Social and Literary Contexts for the New Testament*, edited by Stanley E. Porter and Andrew W. Pitts, 213–54. Leiden: Brill, 2012.

Hartman, Lars. "Into the Name of Jesus." *NTS* 20 (1974) 432–40.

Hartsock, Chad. "The Healing of the Man with Dropsy (Luke 14:1–6) and the Lukan Landscape." *Biblical Interpretation* 21.3 (2013) 341–54.

Haslam, J. A. G. "The Centurion at Capernaum: Luke 7:1–10." *Expository Times* 96.4 (1985) 109–10.

Hauptman, Judith. "How Old Is the Haggadah?" *Judaism* 51.1 (2002) 5–18.

Havelaar, Henriette. "Hellenistic Parallels to Acts 5:1–11 and the Problem of Conflicting Interpretations." *JSNT* 67 (1997) 63–82.

Hays, J. Daniel. *From Every People and Nation: A Biblical Theology of Race*. London: InterVarsity, 2003.

———. "'Sell Everything You Have and Give to the Poor': The Old Testament Prophetic Theme of Justice as the Connecting Motif of Luke 18:1–19:10." *JETS* 55.1 (2012) 43–63.

Hays, Richard B. *Echoes of Scripture in the Letters of Paul*. New Haven: Yale University Press, 1989.

———. "The Liberation of Israel in Luke–Acts." In *Reading the Bible Intertextually*, edited by Richard B. Hays et al., 101–17. Waco, TX: Baylor University Press, 2009.

Heil, Christoph. "Theophilos (Lk 1,3; Apg 1,1)." In *"Licht zur Erleuchtung der Heiden und Herrlichkeit für dein Volk Israel": Studien zum lukanischen Doppelwerk*, edited by Christoph G. Müller, 7–28. Hamburg: Philo, 2005.

Heil, John Paul. "From Remnant to Seed of Hope for Israel: Romans 9:27–29." *Catholic Biblical Quarterly* 64.4 (2002) 703–20.

———. *The Meal Scenes in Luke–Acts: An Audience-Oriented Approach*. Atlanta: SBL, 1999.

Hemer, Colin J. *The Book of Acts in the Setting of Hellenistic History*. Edited by Conrad H. Gempf. Tübingen: Mohr Siebeck, 1989.

Hendriksen, William. *New Testament Commentary: Exposition of the Gospel of Luke*. Grand Rapids: Baker Academic, 1980.

Hendrickson, G. L. "Literary Sources in Cicero's *Brutus* and the Technique of Citation in Dialogue." *American Journal of Philology* 27 (1906) 184–99.

Hengel, Martin. *Acts and the History of Earliest Christianity*. Translated by John Bowden. Philadelphia: Fortress, 1981.

———. *Judaism and Hellenism: Studies in their Encounter in Palestine During the Early Hellenistic Period*. Eugene, OR: Wipf & Stock, 2003.

Hengel, Martin, and Anna Maria Schwemer. *Paul Between Damascus and Antioch: The Unknown Years*. Louisville: Westminster John Knox, 1997.

Hertig, Paul. "The Jubilee Mission of Jesus in the Gospel of Luke: Reversals of Fortunes." *Missiology* 26.2 (1998) 167–79.

Hertzberg, Arthur. "Jewish Identity." In vol. 10 of *Encyclopedia Judaica*, edited by Cecil Roth and Geoffrey Wigoder, 53–65. Jerusalem: Keter, 1971.

Hester, J. David. "Queers on Account of the Kingdom of Heaven: Rhetorical Constructions of the Eunuch Body." *Scriptura* 90 (2005) 809–23.

Higgins, A. J. B. "The Preface to Luke and the Kerygma in Acts." In *Apostolic History and the Gospel: Biblical and Historical Essays Presented to F. F. Bruce on His Sixtieth Birthday*, edited by W. Ward Gasque and Ralph P. Martin, 78–91. Grand Rapids: Eerdmans, 1970.

Hilhorst, Anthony. "'And Moses Was Instructed in All the Wisdom of the Egyptians' (Acts 7:22)." In *The Wisdom of Egypt: Jewish, Early Christian, and Gnostic Essays in Honour of Gerard P. Luttikhuizen*, edited by Anthony Hilhorst and George H. Van Kooten, 153–76. Leiden: Brill, 2005.

Hinkle, Mary E. "People Like Us: Minor Characters in Matthew's Passion." *Word & World* 25.1 (2005) 76–83.

Hobbs, E. C. "The Gospel of Mark and the Exodus." PhD diss., University of Chicago, 1958.

Hock, R. F. "Lazarus and Micyllus: Greco-Roman Backgrounds to Luke 16:19–31." *JBL* 106.3 (1987) 447–63.

Hoffman, Lawrence A., ed. *The Land of Israel: Jewish Perspectives*. Notre Dame: University of Notre Dame Press, 1986.

Hofheinz, Marco. "Good News to the Poor: The Message of the Kingdom and Jesus' Announcement of his Ministry according to Luke." *Lexington Theological Quarterly* 47.1–2 (2017) 41–55.

Hogan, Derek. "Paul's Defense: A Comparison of the Forensic Speeches in Acts, *Callirhoe*, and *Leucippe and Clitophon*." *PRSt* 29 (2002) 73–87.

Hogg, Michael A., et al. "Religion in the Face of Uncertainty: An Uncertainty-Identity Theory Account of Religiousness." *Personality and Social Psychology Review* 14.1 (2010) 72–83.

Hogg, Michael A., et al. "Why Do People Join Groups? Three Motivational Accounts From Social Psychology." In *Social and Personality Psychology Compass* 2.3 (2008) 1269–80.

Holder, John. "The Issue of Race: A Search for a Biblical/Theological Perspective." *Journal of Religious Thought* 49.2 (1992) 44–59.

Holladay, Carl R. *Acts: A Commentary*. Louisville: Westminster John Knox, 2016.

Holtz, T., et al., eds. *Geschichte und Theologie des Urchristentums: Gesammelte Aufsätze*. Tübingen: Mohr-Siebeck, 1991.

Hommel, Hildebrecht. "Juden und Christen im kaiserzeitlichen Milet; Überlegungen zur Theaterinschrift." *Istanb. Mitt.* 25 (1975) 167–95.

Hooker, Morna D. *Beginnings: Keys that Open the Gospels*. Harrisburg: Trinity, 1998.

Hoop, Raymond de. "The Interpretation of Isaiah 56:1–9: Comfort or Criticism?" *JBL* 127.4 (2008) 671–95.

Horbury, William. "The Twelve and the Phylarchs." *New Testament Studies* 32 (1986) 503–27.

Hornik, Heidi J., and Mikeal C. Parsons. "Philological and Performative Perspectives on Pentecost." In *Reading Acts Today: Essays in Honour of Loveday C.A. Alexander*, edited by Steve Walton et al., 137–53. London: T&T Clark, 2011.

Hotze, G., "Christi Zeugen bis an die Grenzen der Erde—Die Apostelsgeschichte (Teil 1)." *Bibel und Liturgie* 72.1 (1999) 29–35.

Hötzinger, Heike. "'Und Salomo hat ihm ein Haus gebaut' (Apg 7,47) Konzepte vom Wohnen Gottes im lukanischen Doppelwerk." *Sacra Scripta, Journal of the Centre for Biblical Studies* 13.1 (2015) 74–100.

Houston, Walter J. "Tragedy in the Courts of the Lord: A Socio-Literary Reading of the Death of Nadab and Abihu." *JSOT* 25.90 (2000) 31–39.

Howard, George S. *A Tale of Two Stories: Excursions into a Narrative Psychology*. Notre Dame: University of Notre Dame Press, 1989.

Howard, James M. "The Significance of Minor Characters in the Gospel of John." *Biblioteca Sacra* 163.649 (2006) 63–78.

Howard, Paul E. "The Book of Acts as a Source for the Study of the Life of Paul." PhD diss., University of Southern California, 1959.

Huizenga, Leroy A. "The Old Testament in the New, Intertextuality and Allegory." *JSNT* 38.1 (2015) 17–35.

Hultgren, Arland J. *The Parables of Jesus: A Commentary*. Grand Rapids: Eerdmans, 2000.

Humphrey, Edith M. *And I Turned to See the Voice: The Rhetoric of Vision in the New Testament*. Studies in Theological Interpretation. Grand Rapids: Baker Academic, 2007.

———. "Collision of Modes? Vision and Determining Argument in Acts 10:1–11:18." *Semeia* 71 (1995) 65–84.

Hutcheon, C. R. "'God is with Us': The Temple in Luke–Acts." *St. Vladimir's Theological Quarterly* 44.1 (2000) 3–33.

Iglesias, S. Muñoz. *Los Evangelios de la Infancia 1: Los Cânticos del Evangelio de la Infancia segûn San Lucas*. Madrid: Biblioteca Autores Cristianos, 1990.

Inrig, Gary. *The Parables: Understanding what Jesus Meant*. Grand Rapids: Discovery, 1991.

Insoll, Timothy. *The Archeology of Identities: A Reader*. New York: Routledge, 2007.

Iser, Wolfgang. *The Acts of Reading: A Theory of Aesthetic Response*. Baltimore: John Hopkins University Press, 1978.

Isocrates. "Against the Sophists." In *A New History of Classical Rhetoric*, edited by George A. Kennedy 44–45. Princeton: Princeton University Press, 1994.

———. "Nicocles or the Cyprians." In *A New History of Classical Rhetoric*, edited by George A. Kennedy, 12. Princeton: Princeton University Press, 1994.

Iverson, Kelly R. "A Centurion's 'Confession': A Performance-Critical Analysis of Mark 15:39." *JBL* 130.2 (2011) 329–50.

Jackson, Jared J., and Martin Kessler, eds. *Rhetorical Criticism: Essays in Honor of James Muilenburg*. Pittsburgh: Pickwick, 1974.

Jagger, Keith. "God's Presence on Earth and Christian Holiness: A Reading of Luke's Temple Theology in Luke 3:1–4:13." *Wesleyan Theological Journal* 51.1 (2016) 117–32.

Jankowski, G. "Dieses Land: Die Verheissung des Landes in den Evangelien und den apostolischen Schriften." *Texte & Kontexte* 21.80 (1998) 51–58.

Jennings, T. W., and T. S. B. Liew. "Mistaken Identities but Model Faith: Rereading the Centurion, the Chap, and the Christ in Matthew 8:5–13." *JBL* 123.2 (2004) 467–94.

Jeon, B. H. "Matthew's Portrait of the Centurion and the Double Confrontation." *Korean New Testament Studies* 18.1 (2011) 95–130.

Jeremias, Joachim. *Infant Baptism in the First Four Centuries*. London: SCM, 1960.

———. *Jesus' Promise to the Nations*. Naperville: Allenson, 1958.

———. "Tradition und Redaktion in Lukas 15." *ZNW* 62 (1971) 172–89.

Jervell, Jacob. *Apostelgeschichte*. 17th ed. Göttingen: Vandenhoech & Ruprecht, 1998.

———. "The Church of Jews and Godfearers." In *Luke-Acts and the Jewish People: Eight Critical Perspectives*, edited by J. Tyson, 11–20. Minneapolis: Augsburg, 1988.

———. "Das gespaltene Israel und die Heidenvölken: Zur Motivierung der Heidenmission in der Apostelgeschichte." *ST* 19.1–2 (1965) 68–96.

———. *Luke and the People of God: A New Look at Luke-Acts*. Minneapolis: Augsburg, 1972.

———. *The Theology of the Acts of the Apostles*. Cambridge: Cambridge University Press, 1996.

Jewett, Robert. "Major Impulses in the Theological Interpretation of Romans Since Barth." *Int.* 34 (1980) 17–31.

Jiménez, Pablo A. "The Spirit Told Me to Go: A Hispanic Homiletic Reading of Acts 11:12." *Apuntes* 23.1 (2003) 28–34.

Johnson, Adam J. "A Temple Framework of the Atonement." *Journal of the Evangelical Theological Society* 54.2 (2011) 225–37.

Johnson, Luke T. *The Acts of the Apostles*. Collegeville, MN: Liturgical, 1992.

———. *The Gospel of Luke*. Collegeville, MN: Liturgical, 1992.

———. *The Literary Function of Possessions in Luke-Acts*. Missoula: Scholars, 1977.

———. *Prophetic Jesus, Prophetic Church: The Challenge of Luke-Acts to Contemporary Christians*. Grand Rapids: Eerdmans, 2011.

Jones, Douglas R. "The Background and Character of the Lukan Psalms." *JTS* 19 (1968) 19–50.

Jones, Gwilym H. "From Abijam to Abijah." *ZAW* 106.3 (1994) 420–34.

Jones, Siân. *The Archeology of Ethnicity: Constructing Identities in the Past and Present*. New York: Routledge, 1997.

Josephus. "Against Apion." In *Josephus: The Complete Works*, edited by William Whiston, 926–73. Nashville: Thomas Nelson, 1998.

———. "The War of the Jews." In *Josephus: The Complete Works*, edited by William Whiston, 655–925. Nashville: Thomas Nelson, 1998.

Julius, J. Scott, Jr. "The Cornelius Incident in the Light of Its Jewish Setting." *JETS* 34.4 (1991) 475–84.

Jung, Deok Hee. "Fluid Sacredness from a Newly Built Temple in Luke-Acts." *The Expository Times* 128.11 (2017) 529–37.

Just, Arthur A. *The Ongoing Feast: Table Fellowship and Eschatology at Emmaus*. Collegeville, MN: Liturgical, 1993.

Kahle, P. E. "The End of St. Mark's Gospel: The Witness of the Coptic Versions." *Journal of Theological Studies* 2.1 (1951) 49–57.

Kaiser, Walter C., Jr. "The Promised Land: A Biblical-Historical View." *Bibliotheca Sacra* 138 (1981) 302–12.

Kalimi, Isaac. "The Day of Atonement in the Late Second Temple Period: Sadducees' High Priests, Pharisees' Norms, and Qumranites' Calendar(s)." In *The Day of Atonement: Its Interpretations in Early Jewish and Christian Traditions*, edited by Thomas Hieke, 75–96. Leiden: Brill, 2012.

———. "The Murders of the Messengers: Stephen versus Zechariah and the Ethical Values of 'New' versus 'Old' Testament." *Australian Biblical Review* 56 (2008) 69–73.

Kamba, Micheline. "Holistic Healing in Acts 3:1–10: A Transformative Church for All People." *International Review of Mission* 105.403 (2016) 268–79.

Kapelrud, Arvid S. "The Main Concern of Second Isaiah." *Vetus Testamentum* 32 (1982) 50–58.

Karris, Robert J. *Invitation to Acts: A Commentary on the Acts of the Apostles with Complete Text from the Jerusalem Bible*. Garden City: Image, 1978.

———. "Luke 23:47 and the Lucan view of Jesus' Death." *JBL* 105.1 (1986) 65–74.

———. "Poor and Rich: The Lukan Sitz im Leben." In *Perspectives on Luke–Acts*, edited by C. H. Talbert, 112–25. Danville: Association of Baptist Professors of Religion, 1978.

Kartzow, M. B., and H. Moxnes. "Complex Identities: Ethnicity, Gender and Religion in the Story of the Ethiopian Eunuch (Acts 8:26–40)." *Religion and Theology* 17.3–4 (2010) 184–204.

Kaut, Thomas. *Befreier und befreites Volk: Traditions-und redaktionsgeschichtliche Untersuchung zu Magnifikat und Benediktus im Kontext der vorlukanischen Kindheitsgeschichte*. Frankfurt: Anton Hain, 1990.

Keene, Thomas. "Luke–Acts and 'Early Catholicism': Eschatological and Ecclesiological Trajectories in the Early Church." In *Issues in Luke–Acts: Selected Essays*, edited by Sean A. Adams and Michael Pahl, 287–310. Piscataway, NJ: Gorgias, 2012.

Keener, Craig S. "Acts 10: Were Troops Stationed in Caesarea During Agrippa's Rule?" *Journal of Greco-Roman Christianity and Judaism* 7 (2010) 164–76.

———. *Acts: An Exegetical Commentary*. 4 vols. Grand Rapids: Baker Academic, 2012–2015.

———. *The Historical Jesus of the Gospels*. Grand Rapids: Eerdmans, 2009.

———. *The IVP Bible Background Commentary: New Testament*. 2nd ed. Grand Rapids: InterVarsity, 2014.

———. *Paul, Women, and Wives: Marriage and Women's Ministry in the Letters of Paul*. Grand Rapids: Baker Academic, 1992.

———. "Three Notes on Figurative Language: Inverted Guilt in Acts 7:55–60, Paul's Figurative Vote in Acts 26:10, Figurative Eyes in Galatians 4:15." *Journal of Greco-Roman Christianity and Judaism* 5 (2008) 41–49.

Kelhoffer, James A. "The Gradual Disclosure of Paul's Violence Against Christians in the Acts of the Apostles as an Apology for the Standing of the Lukan Paul." *Biblical Research* 54 (2009) 25–35.

Keller, Marie N. *Priscilla* and *Aquila: Paul's Coworkers in Christ Jesus*. Collegeville, MN: Liturgical, 2010.

Kellermann, U. "Jesus—das Licht der Völker: Lk 2.25–33 und die Christologie im Gespräch mit Israel." *Kul* 7 (1992) 10–27.

Kennedy, George A. *Classical Rhetoric and Its Christian and Secular Tradition: From Ancient to Modern Times*. 2nd ed. Chapel Hill: University of North Carolina Press, 1999.

———. *Greek Rhetoric Under Christian Emperors: A History of Rhetoric*. Eugene, OR: Wipf & Stock, 2008.

———. *A New History of Classical Rhetoric*. Princeton: Princeton University Press, 1994.

———. *A New Testament Interpretation Through Rhetorical Criticism*. Chapel Hill: University of North Carolina Press, 1984.

———. *Progymnasmata: Greek Textbooks of Prose, Composition, and Rhetoric*. Atlanta: SBL, 2003.

Kennedy, H. A. A. "The Scope and Function of the Apostolate in the New Testament." *The Biblical World* 33.3 (1909) 160–70.

Kent, Homer A. *Jerusalem to Rome: Studies in the Book of Acts.* Grand Rapids: Baker, 1972.

Kern, Philip H. "Paul's Conversion and Luke's Portrayal of Character in Acts 8–10." *Tyndale Bulletin* 54.2 (2003) 63–80.

Kienzler, Jonathan. *The Fiery Holy Spirit: The Spirit's Relationship with Judgment in Luke-Acts.* Blandford Forum, UK: Deo, 2015.

Kilgallen, John J. "Acts 13:38–39: Culmination of Paul's Speech in Pisidia." *Biblica* 69.4 (1988) 480–506.

———. "Clean, Acceptable, Saved: Acts 10." *The Expository Times* 109.10 (1998) 301–2.

———. "The Function of Stephen's Speech (Acts 7,2–53)." *Biblica* 70.2 (1989) 173–93.

———. "Hostility to Paul in Pisidian Antioch (Acts 13,45)—Why?" *Biblica* 84.1 (2003) 1–15.

———. *The Stephen Speech: A Literary and Redactional Study of Acts 7,2–53.* Rome: Biblical Institute, 1976.

———. "Stephen's Lesson." *Bible Today* 43.6 (2005) 371–76.

———. "With Many Other Words (Acts 2,40) Theological Assumptions in Peter's Pentecost." *Biblica* 83.1 (2002) 71–87.

Kim, J. W. "Explicit Quotations from Genesis within the Context of Stephen's Speech in Acts." *Neotestamentica* 41.2 (2007) 341–60.

Kimball, Charles. "Jesus' Exposition of Scripture in Luke 4:16–30: An Inquiry in Light of Jewish Hermeneutics." *Perspectives in Religious Studies* 21.3 (1994) 179–202.

King, Nicholas. "The New Testament as Holy Ground." *Way* 44.2 (2005) 57–69.

Kinman, Brent Rogers. "The 'A-Triumphal' Entry (Luke 19:28–48) Historical Backgrounds, Theological Motifs and the Purpose of Luke." *Tyndale Bulletin* 45.1 (1994) 189–93.

Kirk, John Andrew. "Apostleship Since Rengstorf: Towards a Synthesis." *New Testament Studies* 21 (1975) 249–64.

Kistmaker, Simon J. *The Parables: Understanding the Stories Jesus Told.* Grand Rapids: Baker, 2002.

———. "The Speeches in Acts." *Criswell Theological Review* 5.1 (1990) 31–41.

Klauck, Hans-Josef. "Gottesfürchtige im Magnificat?" *NTS* 43 (1997) 134–39.

Klausner, Joseph. *Jesus of Nazareth.* Jacksonville: Bloch, 1997.

Klein, Hans. "Wie wird aus Kaiwan ein Romfan? Eine textkritische Miszelle zu Apg 7,42f." *ZNW* 97.1 (2006) 139–40.

Klostermann, Erich. *Das Lukasevangelium.* Tübingen: Mohr, 1929.

Knoppers, Gary N., and J. Gordon McConville, eds. *Reconsidering Israel and Judah: Recent Studies on the Deuteronomistic History.* Warsaw, IN: Eisenbrauns, 2000.

Knox, John, and Douglas R. A. Hare. *Chapters in a Life of Paul.* Macon, GA: Mercer University Press, 1987.

Kobelski, Paul. *Melchizedek and Malchirea.* Edited by B. Vawter. Washington, DC: Catholic Biblical Association of America, 1981.

Koch, Dietrich-Alex. "The God-Fearers between Facts and Fiction: Two Theosebeis-Inscriptions from Aphrodisias and Their Bearing for the New Testament." *ST* 60 (2006) 62–90.

Koet, B. J. "Simeons Worte (Lk 2,29–32. 34c–35) und Israels Geschick." In *The Four Gospels 1992*, edited by F. van Segbroeck, 1549–69. Leuven: University Press, 1992.

Korner, Ralph J. "Ekklesia as a Jewish Synagogue Term: Some Implications for Paul's Socio-Religious Location." *Journal of the Jesus Movement in its Jewish Setting* 2 (2015) 53–78.

Kotze, Zacharias. "The Conceptualization of Anger in the Hebrew Bible." PhD diss., University of Stellenbosch, 2004.

Kraabel, A. Thomas. "The Disappearance of the 'God-Fearers." *Numen* 48 (1981) 113–26.

———. "The God-Fearers Meet the Beloved Disciple." In *The Future of Early Christianity: Essays in Honor of Helmut Koester*, edited by B. A. Pearson et al., 276–84. Minneapolis: Fortress, 1991.

———. "Greeks, Jews, and Lutherans in the Middle Half of Acts." In *Christians Among Jews and Gentiles*, edited by G. Nickelsburg and G. MacRae, 147–57. Philadelphia: Fortress, 1986.

———. "Immigrants, Exiles, Expatriates, and Missionaries." In *Religious Propaganda and Missionary Competition in the New Testament World: Essays Honoring Dieter Georgi*, edited by Lukas Bormann et al., 71–88. Leiden: Brill, 1994.

———. "Judaism in Western Asia Minor under the Roman Empire." PhD diss., Harvard University, 1968.

Kraeling, Carl H. *John the Baptist*. New York: Scribner's Sons, 1951.

Kraemer, Ross S. "Giving up the Godfearers." *Journal of Ancient Judaism* 5 (2014), 61-87.

———. "On the Meaning of the Term 'Jew' in Greco-Roman Inscriptions." *The Harvard Theological Review* 82.1 (1989) 35–53.

Krauter, Stefan. "The Martyrdom of Stephen." In *Contextualizing Early Christian Martyrdom*, edited by Jakob Engberg et al., 45–74. New York: Frankfurt am Main, 2011.

Kraybill, Donald B. "Possessions in Luke-Acts: A Sociological Perspective." *Perspectives in Religious Studies* 10.3 (1983) 215–39.

Krentz, Edgar. "Peter: Confessor, Denier, Proclaimer, Validator of Proclamation—A Study in Diversity." *Currents in Theology and Mission* 37.4 (2010) 320–33.

Kristeva, Julia. *Revolution in Poetic Language*. Translated by M. Waller. New York: Columbia University Press, 1984.

Kroll, John H. "The Greek Inscriptions of the Sardis Synagogue." *The Harvard Theological Review* 94.1 (2001) 5–55.

Krüger, René. "La Inclusión de Las Personas Excluidas: La Propuesta Contracultural de Lucas 14:12–14." *Cuadernos de Teología* 24 (2005) 67–88.

Kuecker, Aaron. *The Spirit and the "Other": Social Identity, Ethnicity, and Intergroup Reconciliation in Luke-Acts*. London: Bloomsbury T&T Clark, 2011.

Kuepfer, Tim. "'I Saw the Light': The Significance of the Apostle Paul's Conversion Testimony." *Vision* 10.2 (2009) 13–19.

Kuno, Susumu. "Subject, Theme, and the Speaker's Empathy." In *Subject and Topic*, edited by Charles N. Li, 417–44. New York: Academic, 1976.

Kurichianil, John. "Paul in the Acts of the Apostles." *Indian Theological Studies* 45.3 (2008) 255–93.

Kurz, William S. "Narrative Models for Imitation in Luke-Acts." In *Greeks, Romans, and Christians: Essays in Honor of Abraham J. Malherbe*, edited by David L. Bach et al., 171–81. Minneapolis: Fortress, 1990.

Kuypers, Jim A. *The Art of Rhetorical Criticism*. Boston: Pearson and Allyn & Bacon, 2005.

Kwong, Ivan Shing Chung. "Having Everything in Common: The Distribution of Resources in the Book of Acts." *Jian Dao* 41 (2014) 235–53.

Kyrychenko, Alexander. *The Roman Army and the Expansion of the Gospel: The Role of the Centurion in Luke-Acts*. Berlin: de Gruyter, 2014.

Lacoue-Labarthe, Philippe. *Typography: Mimesis, Philosophy, Politics*. Translated by Christopher Fynsk et al. Stanford: Stanford University Press, 1998.

LaGrand, James. "Luke's Portrait of Simeon (Luke 2:25–35) Aged Saint or Hesitant Terrorist?" In *Common Life in the Early Church: Essays Honoring Graydon F. Snyder*, edited by Graydon F. Snyder et al., 175–85. Harrisburg, PA: Trinity, 1998.

Lake, Kirsopp. "Proselytes and God-Fearers." In vol. 1 of *The Beginnings of Christianity: The Acts of the Apostles*, edited by Frederick Foakes-Jackson and Kirsopp Lake, 74–96. Grand Rapids: Baker, 1933.

Lake, Kirsopp, and Henry J. Cadbury. "English Translation and Commentary." In vol. 4 of *The Beginnings of Christianity: The Acts of the Apostles*, edited by Frederick Foakes-Jackson, and Kirsopp Lake. Grand Rapids: Baker, 1979.

Lakoff, George. *Women, Fire, and Dangerous Things: What Categories Reveal about the Mind*. Chicago: University of Chicago Press, 1990.

Lamb, Gregory E. "Sinfully Stereotyped: Jesus' Desire to Correct Ancient Physiognomic Assumptions in the Gospel according to Luke." *Word and World* 37.2 (2017) 177–85.

Lamont, Michèle, and Virág Molnár. "The Study of Boundaries in the Social Sciences." *Annual Review of Sociology* 28 (2002) 167–95.

Lane, Thomas J. *Luke and the Gentile Mission: Gospel Anticipates Acts*. Berlin: Lang, 1996.

Lane, William L. *Hebrews 1–8*. Dallas: Word, 1991.

Larere, Philippe. *Baptism in Water and Baptism in the Spirit: A Biblical, Liturgical, and Theological Exposition*. Collegeville, MN: Liturgical, 1993.

Larkin, William J. "The Recovery of Luke–Acts as 'Grand Narrative' for the Church's Evangelistic and Edification Tasks in a Postmodern Age." *JETS* 43.3 (2000) 405–15.

Laytham, D. Brent. "Stephen's Storied Witness to Jesus." In *Courage to Bear Witness: Essays in Honor of Gene L. Davenport*, edited by L. Edward Phillips and Billy Vaughan, 1–13. Eugene, OR: Pickwick, 2009.

Leaney, A. R. C. *New Testament Commentaries: The Gospel According to St. Luke*. 2nd ed. New York: Continuum International, 1966.

Lee, J. Magness. *Sense and Absence: Structure and Suspension in the Ending of Mark's Gospel*. Atlanta: SBL, 1986.

Leim, Joshua E. "In the Glory of His Father: Intertextuality and the Apocalyptic Son of Man in the Gospel of Mark." *Journal of Theological Interpretation* 7.2 (2013) 213–32.

Lemche, Niels P. "When the Past Becomes the Present." *Scandinavian Journal of the Old Testament* 27.1 (2013) 96–106.

Leonhard, Barbara. "The Parables of Jesus." *St. Anthony Messenger* 122.11 (2015) 14–19.

Lev, S. L. "They Treat Him as a Man and See Him as a Woman: The Tannaitic Understanding of the Congenital Eunuch." *Jewish Studies Quarterly* 17.3 (2010) 213–43.

Levinskaya, Irina. *The Book of Acts in Its Diaspora Setting*. Vol. 5 of *The Book of Acts in Its First Century Setting*. Edited by Bruce W. Winter. Grand Rapids: Eerdmans, 1996.

———. "The Inscription from Aphrodisias and the Problem of God-fearers." *Tyndale Bulletin* 41.2 (1990) 312–18.

Liefeld, Walter Lewis. *Interpreting the Book of Acts*. Grand Rapids: Baker, 1995.

Lieu, Judith M. *Christian Identity in the Jewish and Graeco-Roman World*. New York: Oxford University Press, 2004.

———. "Do God-Fearers Make Good Christians?" In *Crossing the Boundaries: Essays in Biblical Interpretation in Honour of Michael D. Goulder*, edited by S. E. Porter et al., 329–45. Leiden: Brill, 1994.

———. *Neither Jew nor Greek?: Constructing Early Christianity*. New York: Bloomsbury T&T Clark, 2016.

Lifshitz, Baruch. "Du Nouveau Sur Les 'Sympathisants.'" *Journal for the Study of Judaism* 1.1 (1970) 77–84.

Lightfoot, Joseph B. "The Name and Office of an Apostle." In *St. Paul's Epistle to the Galatians*, by Joseph B. Lightfoot, 92–100. Grand Rapids: Zondervan, 1957.

Linde, Charlotte. *Life Stories: The Creation of Coherence*. Palo Alto, CA: Institute for Research on Learning, 1990.

Lischer, Richard. *Reading the Parables*. Louisville: Westminster John Knox, 2014.

Litwak, Kenneth Duncan. *Echoes of Scripture in Luke-Acts: Telling the History of God's People Intertextually*. London: T&T Clark, 2005.

Liu, James H., and Janos Lazlo. "A Narrative Theory of History and Identity." In *Social Representations and Identity: Content, Process, and Power*, edited by Gail Moloney and Iain Walker, 85–107. New York: Palgrave McMillan, 2007.

Lohfink, Norbert. "Die Lieder in der Kindheitsgeschichte bei Lukas." In *Nach den Anfängen fragen*, edited by Cornelius Meyer et al., 383–404. Giessen: Katholische Fakultät der Uni Giessen, 1994.

Lohmeyer, Ernst. *Das Urchristentum. 1. Buch: Johannes der Täufer*. Göttingen: Vandenhoeck & Ruprecht, 1932.

Lohse, Eduard. "St. Peter's Apostleship in the Judgment of St. Paul, the Apostle to the Gentiles: An Exegetical Contribution to an Ecumenical Debate." *Gregorianum* 72.3 (1991) 419–35.

Lombaard, C. "Two Approaches to Life in the Second Temple Period: Deuteronomy and Qohelet." *HTS Teologiese Studies/Theological Studies* 65 (2009) 185–89.

Longenecker, Richard. *Acts*. Grand Rapids: Zondervan, 1996.

———. "A Humorous Jesus?: Orality, Structure and Characteristics in Luke 14:15–24, and Beyond." *Biblical Interpretation* 16.2 (2008) 179–204.

Löning, Karl. *Das Geschichtswerk des Lukas: Israels Hoffnung und Gottes Geheimnisse*. Stuttgart/Berlin/Köln: Kohlhammer, 1997.

Loubser, J. A. "Invoking the Ancestors: Some Socio-Rhetorical Aspects in the Genealogies of the Gospels of Matthew and Luke." *Neotestamentica* 39.1 (2015) 127–40.

Lounsbury, Floyd G. *A Formal Account of the Crow- and Omah-Type Kinship Terminologies*. Indianapolis: Bobbs-Merrill, 1964.

Lourdu, Augustine. "Jesus: A Strategist for Social Inclusion." *Vidyajyoti* 78.11 (2014) 811–23.

Luce, H. K. *The Gospel According to St. Luke*. Cambridge: Cambridge University Press, 1933.

Lührmann, Dieter. "Die Pharisäer und die Schriftgelehrten im Markusevangelium." *ZNW* 78 (1987) 169–85.

———. "Paul and the Pharisaic Tradition." *JSNT* 36 (1989) 75–94.

Lunn, Nicholas P. "Allusions to the Joseph Narrative in the Synoptic Gospels and Acts: Foundations of a Biblical Type." *JETS* 55.1 (2012) 27–41.

Lupieri, Edmondo. "'The Law and the Prophets Were Until John': John the Baptist Between Jewish Halakhot and Christian History of Salvation." *Neotestamentica* 35.1–2 (2001) 49–56.

Lyons, Willliam J. "The Words of Gamaliel (Acts 5:38–39) and the Irony of Indeterminacy." *JSNT* 68 (1997) 23–49.

MacDonald, Dennis R. *Does the New Testament Imitate Homer? Four Cases from the Acts of the Apostles*. New Haven: Yale University Press, 2003.

———. *The Gospels and Homer: Imitations of Greek Epic in Mark and Luke–Acts.* London: Rowan and Littlefield, 2015.

MacIntyre, Alasdair. *After Virtue.* Notre Dame: University of Notre Dame Press, 1984.

Mack, Burton L. "The Innocent Transgressor: Jesus in Early Christian Myth and History." *Semeia* 33 (1985) 135–65.

———. *Rhetoric and the New Testament.* Edited by Dan O. Via Jr. Minneapolis: Fortress, 1990.

MacLennan, Robert S., and A. Thomas Kraabel. "The God-Fearers: A Literary and Theological Invention." In *Diaspora Jews and Judaism: Essays in Honor of, and in Dialogue with, A. Thomas Kraabel,* edited by J. Andrew Overman and Robert S. MacLennan, 131–43. Atlanta: Scholars, 1992.

Maddox, Robert. *The Purpose of Luke–Acts.* Göttingen: Vandenhoeck & Ruprecht, 1982.

Malina, Bruce J., and John J. Pilch. *Social-Science Commentary on the Book of Acts.* Minneapolis: Fortress, 2008.

Mallen, Peter. *The Reading and Transformation of Isaiah in Luke–Acts.* London: T&T Clark, 2008.

Maloney, Francis J. "The Scriptural Basis of Jubilee." *Irish Theological Quarterly* 65.3 (2000) 231–44.

Maly, Eugene H. "Women and the Gospel of Luke." *Biblical Theology Bulletin: Journal of Bible and Culture* 10.3 (1980) 99–104.

March, James, and Herbert Simon. *Organizations.* New York: Wiley and Sons, 1958.

Marchadour, Alain, and David Neuhaus. *The Land, the Bible, and History: Toward the Land That I Will Show You.* New York: Fordham University Press, 2007.

Marguerat, Daniel. "The Enigma of the Silent Closing of Acts (28:16–31)." In *Jesus and the Heritage of Israel: Luke's Narrative Claim upon Israel's Legacy,* edited by David P. Moessner, 284–304. Harrisburg, PA: Trinity, 1999.

———. "'Et quand nous sommes entrés dans Rome': L'énigme de la fin du livre des Actes (28,16–31)." *RHPR* 73.1 (1993) 1–21.

———. *The First Christian Historian: Writing the "Acts of the Apostles."* Translated by Ken McKinney et al. Cambridge: Cambridge University Press, 2002.

———. *La première histoire du christianisme (les Actes des apôtres).* Paris: Cerf, 1999.

———. *Les Actes des Apôtres (1–12).* Geneva: Labor et Fides, 2007.

Marguerat, Daniel, and Simon D. Butticaz. "La figure de Moïse en Actes 7: Entre la christologie et l'exil." In *La Construction de la Figure de Moïse,* edited by T. Römer, 223–47. Paris: Gabalda, 2007.

Marin, Louis. "A Structural Analysis Essay of Acts 10:1–11:18." In *Structuralism and Biblical Hermeneutics: A Collection of Essays,* edited by Alfred M. Johnson Jr., 145–77. Translated by Alfred M. Johnson Jr. Pittsburgh: Pickwick, 1979.

Marohl, Matthew J. *Faithfulness and the Purpose of Hebrews: A Social Identity Approach.* Eugene: Pickwick, 2008.

Marrou, Henri-Irenée. *A History of Education in Antiquity.* Translated by George Lamb. New York: Sheed and Ward, 1956.

Marshall, I. Howard. *Acts.* Downers Grove, IL: InterVarsity, 2008.

———. *The Acts of the Apostles: An Introduction and Commentary.* Grand Rapids: Eerdmans, 1980.

———. *The Gospel of Luke: A Commentary on the Greek Text.* Grand Rapids: Eerdamns, 1978.

———. "The Interpretation of the Magnificat: Luke 1:46–55." In *Der Treue Gottes trauen: Beiträge zum Werk des Lukas. Für Gerhard Schneider*, edited by C. Bussmann and W. Radle, 185–96. Freiburg: Herder, 1991.

———. "The Religious Enemy: The Response of the Early Church to Religious Pressure in Acts." *Anvil* 21.3 (2004) 179–87.

Marshall, Mary. *The Portrayal of the Pharisees in the Gospels and Acts*. Bristol: Vandenhoeck & Ruprecht, 2015.

Martin, Clarice J. "A Chamberlain's Journey and the Challenge of Interpretation for Liberation." *Semeia* 47 (1989) 105–35.

Martin, Oren R. *Bound for the Promised Land: The Land Promise in God's Redemptive Plan*. Downers Grove, IL: InterVarsity, 2015.

Matera, Frank J. "The Death of Jesus According to Luke: A Question of Sources." *The Catholic Biblical Quarterly* 47.3 (1985) 469–85.

———. *New Testament Christology*. Louisville: Westminster John Knox, 1999.

Matson, David Lertis. *Household Conversion Narratives in Acts: Pattern and Interpretation*. Sheffield: Sheffield Academic, 1996.

———. "Tuning the Faith: The Cornelius Story in Resonance Perspective." *Perspectives in Religious Studies* 33.4 (2006) 449–465.

Matthews, Shelly. "Clemency as Cruelty: Forgiveness and Force in the Dying Prayers of Jesus and Stephen." *Biblical Interpretation* 17.1–2 (2009) 118–46.

Mattill, A. J. *A Classified Bibliography of Literature on the Acts of the Apostles*. Leiden: Brill, 1966.

———. "The Jesus–Paul Parallels and the Purpose of Luke–Acts: H. H. Evans Reconsidered." *Novum Testamentum* 17.1 (1975) 15–46.

Maxwell, Kathy R. "The Role of the Audience in Ancient Narrative: Acts as a Case Study." *Restoration Quarterly* 48.3 (2006) 171–80.

McAdams, Dan P. "Narrative Identity." In *Handbook of Identity Theory and Research*, edited by Seth J. Schwartz et al., 99–115. New York: Springer, 2011.

———. *The Person: A New Introduction to Personal Psychology*. 4th ed. Hoboken: Wiley and Sons, 2006.

———. *The Stories We Live By: Personal Myths and the Making of the Self*. New York: Guilford, 1993.

McCabe, David R. *How to Kill Things with Words: Ananias and Sapphira under the Prophetic Speech-Act of Divine Judgment (Acts 4:32–5:11)*. London: Bloomsbury, 2011.

McConville, Gordon. "Jerusalem in the Old Testament." In *Jerusalem Past and Present in the Purposes of God*, edited by P. W. L. Walker, 21–51. Cambridge: Tyndale, 1992.

McDonough, Sean M. "Small Change: Saul to Paul, Again." *JBL* 125.2 (2006) 390–91.

McGee, Daniel B. "Sharing Possessions: A Study in Biblical Ethics." In *With Steadfast Purpose: Essays on Acts in Honor of Henry Jackson Flanders Jr.*, edited by Naymond H. Keathley, 163–78. Waco, TX: Baylor University Press, 1990.

McGiffert, Arthur Cushman. *A History of Christianity in the Apostolic Age*. New York: Scribner, 1900.

McKay, Niall. "A Political Reading of Luke 1:51–52 and 3:8–9 in the Light of Ezekiel 17—Inspired by John Howard Yoder and a Poststructural Intertextuality." *Neotestamentica* 47.1 (2013) 25–45.

———. "Status Update: The Many Faces of Intertextuality in the New Testament." *Religion and Theology* 20.1–2 (2013) 84–106.

McKenzie, John L. *Second Isaiah*. Garden City, NY: Doubleday, 1968.

McKnight, Edgar V. *What Is Form Criticism?* Eugene, OR: Wipf & Stock, 1997.

McKnight, Scot. *The King Jesus Gospel*. Grand Rapids: Zondervan, 2011.

———. *A Light among the Gentiles: Jewish Missionary Activity in the Second Temple Period*. Minneapolis: Fortress, 1991.

McKnight, Scot, and Joseph B. Modica, eds. *Jesus Is Lord, Caesar Is Not: Evaluating Empire in New Testament Studies*. Downers Grove, IL: IVP Academic, 2013.

McNamara Martin. "Melchizedek Gen 14, 17–20 in the Targums, in Rabbinic and Early Christian Literature." *Bib* 81 (2000) 1–31.

McVann, Mark. "Reading Mark Ritually: Honor-Shame and the Ritual of Baptism." *Semeia* 67 (1994) 179–98.

Mead, George Herbert. *Mind, Self, and Society from the Standpoint of a Social Behaviorist*. Chicago: University of Chicago Press, 1934.

———. "The Nature of the Past." In *Essays in Honor of John Dewey*, edited by John Coss, 235–42. New York: Holt, 1929.

Meagher, Gerard. "The Prophetic Call Narrative." *ITQ* 39 (1972) 164–77.

Meagher, P. M. "Paul's Experience of the Risen Lord: Reflections on Mission, Persecution and Religio-Cultural Loyalty." *Jeevadhara* 34.200 (2004) 146–61.

Medin, Douglas L., et al. "Given Versus Induced Category Representations: Use of Prototype and Exemplar Information in Classification." *Journal of Experimental Psychology: Learning, Memory, and Cognition* 10.3 (1984) 333.

Meek, James A. *The Gentile Mission in Old Testament Citations in Acts: Text, Hermeneutic, and Purpose*. New York: T&T Clark, 2008.

Meek, Russell L. "Intertextuality, Inner-Biblical Exegesis, and Inner Biblical Allusion: The Ethics of a Methodology." *Biblica* 95.2 (2014) 280–91.

Meeks, Wayne A. *The First Urban Christians: The Social World of the Apostle Paul*. New Haven: Yale University Press, 1983.

Meijer, Fik. *Paulus: Der letzte Apostel*. Darmstadt: Philipp von Zabern, 2015.

Meiser, Martin. "Timothy in Acts: Patristic Reception." *Annali di Storia Dell'esegesi* 32.2 (2015) 325–32.

Mellink, Machteld J. "Archeology in Asia Minor." *American Journal of Archeology* 81.3 (1977) 289–321.

Mellor, Ronald. *Tacitus*. New York: Routledge, 1993.

Mendels, Doron. "Phases of Inscribed Memory Concerning the Land of Israel in Palestinian Judaism of the Second Century BCE." *Theologische Literaturzeitung* 138.2 (2013) 151–64.

Mendez-Moratalla, Fernando. *The Paradigm of Conversion in Luke*. New York: Bloomsbury, 1999.

Menoud, Philippe H. "The Additions to the Twelve Apostles According to the Book of Acts." In *Jesus Christ and the Faith: A Collection of Studies*, by Philippe H. Menoud, 149–66. Translated by Eunice M. Paul. Pittsburgh: Pickwick, 1978.

Menzies, Robert P. *The Development of Early Christian Pneumatology with Special Reference to Luke-Acts*. Sheffield: Sheffield Academic, 1991.

———. *Empowered for Witness*. New York: Bloomsbury T&T Clark, 2005.

Menzies, William W., and Robert P. Menzies. *Spirit and Power: Foundations of Pentecostal Experience*. Grand Rapids: Zondervan, 2000.

Merrill, Eugene H. "Paul's Use of 'About 450 Years' in Acts 13–20." *Bibliotheca Sacra* 138.551 (1981) 246–57.

Metzger, Bruce M. *A Textual Commentary on the Greek New Testament*. 2nd ed. Stuttgart: Deutsche Bibelgesellschaft, 1994.

Meyer, Marvin W. *The Gospels of the Marginalized: The Redemption of Doubting Thomas, Mary Magdalene, and Judas Iscariot in Early Christian Literature*. Eugene, OR: Cascade, 2012.

Meynet, Roland. *Rhetorical Analysis: An Introduction to Biblical Rhetoric*. Sheffield: Sheffield Academic, 2002.

Michaelis, W. "Feast of Booths." In vol. 7 of *Theological Dictionary of the New Testament*, edited by Gerhard Kittel and Gerhard Friedrich, 379–80. Translated by Geoffrey W. Bromiley. Grand Rapids: Eerdmans.

Michener, H. Andrew, et al., eds. *Social Psychology*. 5th ed. Belmont: Wadsworth, 2004.

Millar, Fergus. "Gentiles and Judaism: 'God-Fearers' and Proselytes." In vol. 3 of *The History of the Jewish People in the Age of Jesus Christ*, edited by Gaza Vermes et al., 150–76. Edinburgh: T&T Clark, 1986.

Miller, David Marvin. "Seeing the Glory, Hearing the Son: The Function of the Wilderness Theophany Narratives in Luke 9:28–36." *Catholic Biblical Quarterly* 72.3 (2010) 498–517.

Miller, Denzil R. *Empowered for Global Mission: A Missionary Look at the Book of Acts*. Springfield: Life Publishers International, 2005.

Miller, John B. F. *Convinced that God Had Called Us: Dreams, Visions, and the Perception of God's Will in Luke–Acts*. Leiden: Brill, 2007.

Mink, Louis O. "Narrative Form as a Cognitive Instrument." In *Literary Form and Historical Understanding*, edited by R. H. Canary and H. Kozicki, 129–49. Madison: University of Wisconsin Press, 1978.

Minnear, Paul S. "Luke's Use of the Birth Stories." *Studies in Luke–Acts*, edited by L. E. Keck, J. L. Martyn, 111–30. London: 1968.

———. *The Obedience of Faith: The Purposes of Paul in the Epistle to the Romans*. Eugene, OR: Wipf & Stock, 2003.

Mirhady, David C. "The Oath-Challenge in Athens." *Classical Quarterly* 41 (1991) 78–83.

Mitchell, Margaret M. *Paul and the Rhetoric of Reconciliation: An Exegetical Investigation of the Language and Composition of 1 Corinthians*. Louisville: Westminster John Knox, 1991.

Mitchell, Matthew W. "Hosea 1–2 and the Search for Identity." *JSOT* 29.1 (2004) 115–27.

Mittelstadt, Martin W. "Eat, Drink, and Be Merry: A Theology of Hospitality in Luke–Acts." *Word and World* 34.2 (2014) 131–39.

Moessner, David P. "'The Christ Must Suffer': New Light on the Jesus-Peter, Stephen, Paul Parallels in Luke–Acts." *Novum Testamentum* 28.3 (1986) 220–56.

———. "The Ironic Fulfillment of Israel's Glory." In *Luke–Acts and the Jewish People: Eight Critical Perspectives*, edited by J. Tyson, 35–50. Minneapolis: Augsburg, 1988.

———. "The 'Leaven of the Pharisees' and 'This Generation': Israel's Rejection of Jesus according to Luke." *JSNT* 34 (1988) 21–46.

———. *Lord of the Banquet: The Literary and Theological Significance of the Lukan Travel Narrative*. Minneapolis: Fortress, 1989.

———. "The Lukan Prologues in the Light of Ancient Narrative Hermeneutics: Παρηκολουθηκότι and the Credentialed Author." In *The Unity of Luke–Acts*, edited by Joseph Verheyden, 399–417. Leuven: Leuven University Press, 1999.

———. "Paul and the Pattern of the Prophet like Moses in Acts." *SBL Seminar Papers* 22 (1983) 203–12.

———. "Reading Luke's Gospel as Ancient Hellenistic Narrative: Luke's Narrative Plan of Israel's Suffering Messiah as God's Saving 'Plan' for the World." In *Reading Luke: Interpretation, Reflection, and Formation*, edited by Craig Bartholomew and Joel B. Green, 125–54. Grand Rapids: Zondervan, 2005.

Molthagen, Joachim. "Geschichtsschreibung und Geschichtsverständnis in der Apostelgeschichte im Vergleich mit Herodot, Thukydides und Polybios." In *Die Apostelgeschichte im Kontext antiker und frühchristlicher Historiograhie*, edited by Jörg Frey et al., 159–81. Berlin: de Guyter, 2009.

Moo, Douglas. *Galatians*. Grand Rapids: Baker Academic, 2013.

Moon, Joshua. "Honor and Shame in Hosea's Marriages." *JSOT* 39.3 (2015) 335–51.

Moon, Sewon, and Jeremy Punt. "Jesus and His Apostles as Apostles Par Excellence in Luke-Acts." *Scriptura* 112 (2013) 1–10.

Moore, Thomas S. "To the Ends of the Earth: The Geographical and Ethnic Universalism of Acts 1:8 in Light of Isaianic Influence on Luke." *JETS* 40 (1997) 389–99.

Moran, Gabriel. "Critical But Real: Reflecting on N. T. Wright's *Tools for the Task*." In *Renewing Biblical Interpretation*, edited by Karl Möller et al., 172–97. Grand Rapids: Zondervan, 2000.

———. *Showing How: The Act of Teaching*. Valley Forge, PA: Trinity, 1997.

Moritz, Thorsten. "Dinner Talk and Ideology in Luke: The Role of the Sinners." *European Journal of Theology* 5.1 (1996) 47–70.

Morrison, Angus. "'More Than the Sum of Our Possessions': Reflections on the Parable of the Rich Fool (Luke 12:13–21)." *Scottish Bulletin of Evangelical Theology* 35.1 (2017) 19–40.

Morton, Russell. "Between Text and Sermon: Acts 11:1–18." *Interpretation* 66.3 (2012) 309–11.

Moxnes, Halvor. "Meals and the New Community in Luke." *Svensk Exegetisk Årsbok* 51 (1986) 158–67.

Moxon, John R. L. "Ethnic Conflict—Some NT Insights from the 'Affective Turn.'" *Practical Theology* 11.1 (2018) 42–53.

Moyise, Steve. "Intertextuality and Historical Approaches to the Use of Scripture in the New Testament." In *Reading the Bible Intertextually*, edited by Richard B. Hays et al., 23–32. Waco, TX: Baylor University Press, 2009.

Mugabe, Henry Johannes. "Parable of the Rich Fool: Luke 12:13–21." *Review and Expositor* 111.1 (2014) 67–73.

Müller-Abels, Susanne. "Der Umgang Mit 'Schwierigen' Texten der Apostelgeschichte in der Alten Kirche." In *The Book of Acts as Church History*, edited by T. Nicklas and M. Tilly, 347–71. Berlin: de Gruyter, 2003.

Munck, Johannes. *The Acts of the Apostles*. Garden City: Doubleday, 1967.

———. "Paul, the Apostles, and the Twelve." *Studia Theologica* 3 (1949) 96–110.

Murphy-O'Connor, J. "Lots of God-Fearers: Theosebeis in the Aphrodisias Inscription." *Revue Biblique* 99.2 (1992) 418–24.

Nash, Charles Harris. "Stephen, the Model Layman: The Unique, Transcendent Image of Jesus in Life and Death, 'Filled With All the Fullness of God.' Acts 6–7." *Review & Expositor* 23.4 (1926) 452–75.

Neagoe, Alexandru. *The Trial of the Gospel: An Apologetic Reading of Luke's Trial Narratives*. Cambridge: Cambridge University Press, 2002.

Neale, David. *None But the Sinners: Religious Categories in the Gospel of Luke.* Sheffield: Sheffield Academic, 1997.

Neil, William. *The Acts of the Apostles.* London: Marshall, 1973.

Neusner, Jacob. *The Rabbinic Traditions About the Pharisees Before 70, Part 1: The Masters.* Eugene, OR: Wipf & Stock, 2005.

Neusner, Jacob, and Bruce Chilton, eds. *In Quest of the Historical Pharisees.* Waco, TX: Baylor University Press, 2007.

Newman, Carey C. *Jesus and the Restoration of Israel: A Critical Assessment of N. T. Wright's Jesus and the Victory of God.* Downers Grove, IL: InterVarsity, 1999.

Neyrey, J. H. "Bewitched in Galatia: Paul and Cultural Anthropology." *Catholic Biblical Quarterly* 50.1 (1988) 72–100.

———. "'Teaching You in Public and from House to House' (Acts 20:20): Unpacking a Cultural Stereotype." *JSNT* 26.1 (2003) 69–102.

Nguyen, VanThan. "Dismantling Cultural Boundaries: Missiological Implications of Acts 10:1–11:18." *Missiology* 40.4 (2012) 455–66.

———. "Luke's Passion as Story of Good News." *Bible Today* 48.2 (2010) 61–67.

———. "Luke's Point of View of the Gentile Mission: The Test Case of Acts 11:1–18." *Journal of Biblical and Pneumatological Research* 3 (2011) 85–98.

Nicholson, Nigel. "Cultural Studies, Oral Tradition, and the Promise of Intertextuality." *American Journal of Philology* 134.1 (2013) 9–21.

Niehoff, Maren R. "Circumcision as a Marker of Identity: Philo, Origen, and the Rabbis on Genesis 17:1–14." *JSQ* 10.2 (2003) 89–123.

Nihan, Christophe. "Ethnicity and Identity in Isaiah 56–66." In *Judah and the Judeans in the Achaemenid Period: Negotiating Identity in an International Context*, edited by Gary N. Knoppers et al., 67–104. Winona Lake: Eisenbrauns, 2011.

Njoroge wa Ngugi, J. "Stephen's Speech as Catechetical Discourse." *Living Light* 33.4 (1997) 64–71.

Nodet, Étienne. "Théophile (Lc 1,1–4; Ac 1,1)." *Revue Biblique* 119.4 (2012) 585–95.

Nolland, John Leslie. *Luke.* Word Biblical Commentary 35A–C. Edited by Bruce M. Metzger. 3 vols. Grand Rapids: Zondervan, 2015–2016.

———. "Luke's Readers: A Study of Luke 4:22–8; Acts 13:46; 18:6; 28:28 and Luke 21:5–36." PhD diss., Clare College, 1977.

Notley, R. Steven. "Jesus' Jewish Hermeneutical Method in the Nazareth Synagogue." In *Early Christian Literature and Intertextuality*, edited by Craig A. Evans and H. Daniel Zacharias, 46–59. London: T&T Clark, 2009.

Oakes, Penelope, et al. "The Role of Prototypicality in Group Influence and Cohesion: Contextual Variation in the Graded Structure of Social Categories." In *Social Identity: International Perspectives*, edited by Stephen Worchel et al., 75–92. London: SAGE, 1998.

Oakman, Douglas E. "The Countryside in Luke-Acts." In *The Social World of Luke-Acts: Models for Interpretation*, edited by Jerome H. Neyrey, 151–79. Peabody, MA: Hendrickson, 1991.

O'Day, Gail R. "Singing Woman's Song: A Hermeneutic of Liberation." *Currents in Theology and Mission* 12.4 (1985) 203–10.

———. "'Today This Word Is Fulfilled in Your Hearing': A Scriptural Hermeneutic of Biblical Authority." *Word and World* 26.4 (2006) 357–64.

Okoronkwo, Michael Enyinwa. "Of What Use Is the Sword for the Disciples of Jesus?: A Discourse Analysis of Luke 22:35–38 in the Light of New Testament Ethics on Non-Violence." *Scriptura* 113 (2014) 1–16.

Oliver, H. H. "The Lucan Birth Stories and the Purpose of Luke–Acts." *NTS* 10 (1963) 202–26.

O'Loughlin, Thomas. "Sharing Food and Breaking Boundaries: Reading of Acts 10–11:18 as a Key to Luke's Ecumenical Agenda in Acts." *Transformation* 32.1 (2015) 27–37.

O'Mahoney, K. J. "Stones That Speak: St Paul and Archaeology." *Milltown Studies* 63 (2009) 85–106.

O'Neill, J. C. "Paul's Missionary Strategy." *Irish Biblical Studies* 19.4 (1997) 174–90.

O'Toole, Robert F. *The Unity of Luke's Theology: An Analysis of Luke–Acts*. Wilmington, DE: Michael Glazer, 1984.

———. "'You Did Not Lie to Us (Human Beings) but to God' (Acts 5,4c)." *Bib* 76 (1995) 182–209.

Overman, J. Andrew. "The God-Fearers: Some Neglected Features." In *New Testament Backgrounds: A Sheffield Reader*, edited by Craig Evans and Stanley Porter, 253–62. New York: Bloomsbury T&T Clark, 1997.

Padilla, Osvaldo. "The Speeches in Acts: Historicity, Theology, and Genre." In *Issues in Luke–Acts: Selected Essays*, edited by Sean A. Adams and Michael Pahl, 171–93. Piscataway, NJ: Gorgias, 2012.

Pajunen, Mika S. *The Land to the Elect and Justice for All: Reading the Psalms in the Dead Sea Scrolls in Light of 4Q381*. Göttingen: Vandenhoeck & Ruprecht, 2013.

Palmer, Daryl W. "Acts and the Ancient Historical Monograph." In *The Book of Acts in Its Ancient Literary Setting*, edited by Bruce W. Winter and Andrew D. Clarke, 1–29. Vol. 1 of *The Book of Acts in Its First Century Setting*. Grand Rapids: Eerdmans, 1993.

———. "Acts and the Historical Monograph." *TynBul* 43.2 (1992) 373–88.

Pao, David W. *Acts and the Isaianic New Exodus*. Grand Rapids: Baker Academic, 2000.

———. "Waiters or Preachers: Acts 6:1–7 and the Lukan table fellowship motif." *JBL* 130.1 (2011) 127–44.

Park, Eung C. *Either Jew or Gentile: Paul's Unfolding Theology of Inclusivity*. Louisville: Westminster John Knox, 2003.

Paroschi, Wilson. "The Prophetic Significance of Stephen." *Journal of the Adventist Theological Society* 9.1–2 (1998) 343–61.

Parsons, Mikeal C. "The Character of the Lame Man in Acts 3–4." *JBL* 124.2 (2005) 295–312.

———. *The Departure of Jesus in Luke–Acts: The Ascension Narratives in Context*. Sheffield: JSOT, 1987.

———. "Isaiah 53 in Acts 8: A Reply to Professor Morna Hooker." In *Jesus and the Suffering Servant: Isaiah 53 and Christian Origins*, edited by William H. Bellinger Jr. and William R. Farmer, 104–19. Harrisburg, PA: Trinity, 1998.

———. "Luke and the Progymnasmata: A Preliminary Investigation into the Preliminary Exercises." In *Contextualizing Acts: Narrative and Greco-Roman Discourse*, edited by T. Penner and C. Vander Stichele, 43–63. Leiden: Brill, 2003.

Parsons, Mikeal C., and Martin M. Culy. *Acts: A Handbook on the Greek Text*. Waco, TX: Baylor University Press, 2003.

Parsons, Mikeal C., et al. *Luke: A Handbook on the Greek Text*. Waco, TX: Baylor University Press, 2010.

Parvey, Constance E. "The Theology and Leadership of Women in the New Testament." In *Religion and Sexism: Images of Women in the Jewish and Christian Traditions*, edited by Rosemary Radford Ruether, 117–49. New York: Simon & Schuster, 1974.

Patella, Michael. "Paul in the Holy Land." *Bible Today* 42.4 (2004) 225–29.

Pattarumadathil, Henry. "Two Great Models of Faith in Matthew: The Centurion and the Canaanite Woman." *Bible Bhashyam* 39.2 (2013) 75–92.

Pedersen, Vicki L. "Restoration and Celebration: A Call for Inclusion in Luke 15:1–10." *Currents in Theology and Mission* 41.2 (2014) 110–18.

Pelikan, Jaroslav. *Acts*. Grand Rapids: Brazos, 2005.

Pelletier, André. "Le Grand Rideau du Vestibule du Temple de Jérusalem." *Syria* 35 (1958) 218–26.

———. "Le 'Voile' du Temple de Jéresalem est-il Devenu la 'Portière' du Temple d'Olympie?" *Syria* 32 (1955) 289–307.

Penner, Todd. "Civilizing Discourse: Acts, Declamation, and the Rhetoric of the Polis." In *Contextualizing Acts: Lukan Narrative and Greco-Roman Discourse*, edited by T. Penner and C. Vander Stichele, 65–104. Leiden: Brill, 2003.

———. "Narrative as Persuasion: Epideictic Rhetoric and Scribal Amplification in the Stephen Episode in Acts." *Society of Biblical Literature Seminar Papers* 35 (1996) 352–67.

Perdue, Leo G., and Warren Carter. *Israel and Empire: A Postcolonial History of Israel and Early Judaism*. Edited by Coleman Baker. New York: Bloomsbury, 2015.

Perelman, Chaim, and Lucie Olbrechts-Tyteca. *The New Rhetoric: A Treatise on Argumentation*. Translated by John Wilkinson and Purcell Weaver. Notre Dame: University of Notre Dame Press, 1969.

Perry, John. "Gentiles and Homosexuals: A Brief History of an Analogy." *Journal of Religious Ethics* 38.2 (2010) 321–47.

Pervo, Richard I. *Acts: A Commentary*. Philadelphia: Fortress, 2009.

———. "Dating Acts." *Forum* 5.1 (2002) 53–72.

———. *Dating Acts: Between the Evangelists and the Apostles*. Santa Rosa: Polebridge, 2006.

———. "The Gates Have Been Closed." *Journal of Higher Criticism* 11.2 (2005) 128–49.

———. "Must Luke and Acts Belong to the Same Genre?" *SBLSP* (1989) 309–16.

———. "The Paul of Acts and the Paul of the letters: Aspects of Luke as an interpreter of the corpus Paulinum." In *Reception of Paulinism in Acts*, edited by D. Marguerat, 141–55. Walpole, MA: Peeters, 2009.

———. *Profit with Delight: The Literary Genre of the Acts of the Apostles*. Philadelphia: Fortress, 1987.

———. *Rethinking the Unity of Luke and Acts*. Minneapolis: Fortress, 1993.

Pesch, Rudolf. *Die Apostelgeschichte, Apg 1–12*. Cincinnati: Benzinger, 1995.

Peterson, Brian. "Stephen's Speech as a Modified Prophetic Rî Formula." *JETS* 57.2 (2014) 351–69.

Peterson, David G. "The Pneumatology of Luke–Acts: The Spirit of Prophecy Unleashed." In *Issues in Luke–Acts: Selected Essays*, edited by Sean A. Adams and Michael Pahl, 195–216. Piscataway, NJ: Gorgias, 2012.

Pfitzner, Victor C. "'Pneumatic' Apostleship? Apostle and Spirit in the Acts of the Apostles." In *Wort in der Zeit: Neutestamentliche Studien*, edited by W. Haubeck and M. Bachmann, 210–35. Leiden: Brill, 1980.

Phillips, Elaine A. *'The Tomb That Abraham Had Purchased' (Acts 7:16)*. Grand Rapids: Eerdmans, 2010.

Phillips, Thomas E. *Acts Within Diverse Frames of Reference.* Macon: Mercer University Press, 2009.

———. "Creation, Sin and Its Curse, and the People of God: An Intertextual Reading of Genesis 1–12 and Acts 1–7." *Horizons in Biblical Theology* 25.2 (2003) 146–60.

Pilgrim, Walter. *Rich and Poor in Luke's Gospel: Wealth and Poverty in Luke–Acts.* Minneapolis: Augsburg, 1981.

Piper, Otto. "Unchanging Promises: Exodus in the New Testament." *Int.* 11.1 (1957) 3–22.

Plümacher, Eckhard. *Geschichte und Geschichten: Aufsätze zur Apostelgeschichte und zu den Johannesakten.* Edited by Jens Schröter and Ralph Brucker. Tübingen: Mohr Siebeck, 2004.

———. *Lukas als hellenistischer Schriftsteller.* Göttingen: Vandenhoeck & Ruprecht, 1972.

———. "Luke as Historian." In *Anchor Bible Dictionary*, edited by David Noel Friedman, 397–420. Translated by Dennis Martin. New York: Doubleday, 1992.

———. "Stichwort: Lukas, Historiker." *ZNT* 9.18 (2006) 2–8.

Plummer, Alfred. *A Critical and Exegetical Commentary on the Gospel According to St. Luke.* Edinburgh: Clark, 1896.

Plunkett, Mark A. "Ethnocentricity and Salvation History in the Cornelius Episode (Acts 10:1–11:18)." *Society of Biblical Literature Seminar Papers* 24 (1985) 465–79.

Plymale, Steven F. *The Prayer Texts of Luke–Acts.* New York: Lang, 1991.

Poirier, John C. "Jesus as an Elijianic Figure in Luke 4:16–30." *The Catholic Biblical Quarterly* 71.2 (2009) 349–63.

Polhill, John B. *Acts: An Exegetical and Theological Exposition of Holy Scripture.* Nashville: Broadman, 1992.

Polkinghorne, Donald E. *Narrative Knowing and the Human Sciences.* Albany: State University of New York Press, 1988.

Porter, James. *Audience and Rhetoric: An Archeological Composition of the Discourse Community.* Upper Saddle River, NJ: Prentice Hall, 1992.

Porter, Stanley E. "Excursus: The 'We' Passages." In *The Book of Acts in Its Graeco-Roman Setting*, edited by David W. J. Gill and Conrad Gempf, 545–74. Grand Rapids: Eerdmans, 1994.

———. *Paul in Acts: Essays in Literary Criticism.* Tübingen: Mohr Siebeck, 1999.

———. "Thucydides 1.22.1 and Speeches in Acts: Is There a Thucydidean View?" *NovT* 32 (1990) 121–42.

Porter, Stanley E., and Anthony R. Cross, eds. *Baptism, the New Testament and the Church: Historical and Contemporary Studies in Honour of R. E. O. White.* Sheffield: Sheffield Academic, 1999.

———. *Dimensions of Baptism: Biblical and Theological Studies.* Sheffield: Sheffield Academic, 1999.

Porter, Stanley E., and Bryan R. Dyer, eds. *Paul and Ancient Rhetoric: Theory and Practice in the Hellenistic Context.* Cambridge: Cambridge University Press, 2016.

Porter, Stanley E., and Thomas H. Olbrichts, eds. *Rhetoric and the New Testament: Essays from the 1992 Heidelberg Conference.* Sheffield: JSOT, 1993.

———. *Rhetoric, Scripture, and Theology: Essays from the 1994 Pretoria Conference.* Sheffield: JSOT, 1996.

———. *The Rhetorical Analysis of Scripture: Essays from the 1995 London Conference.* Sheffield: JSOT, 1997.

Porter, Stanley E., et al., eds. *Rhetorical Criticism and the Bible*. London: Sheffield Academic, 2002.

Potolsky, Matthew. *Mimesis*. New York: Routledge, 2006.

Powell, Mark Allan. "Echoes of Jonah in the New Testament." *Word and World* 27.2 (2007) 157–64.

———. *What Are They Saying About Acts?* New York: Paulist, 1991.

Prince, Deborah Thompson. "Picturing Saul's Vision on the Road to Damascus: A Question of Authority." *Biblical Interpretation* 25.3 (2017) 364–98.

———. "Seeing Visions: The Pervasive Power of Sight in the Acts of the Apostles." *JSNT* 40.3 (2018) 337–59.

Punt, Jeremy. "Paul and the Scriptures of Israel: How Much Hermeneutical Awareness Did He Display?" *Neotestamentica* 34.2 (2000) 311–27.

Puskas, Charles B., and David Crump. *An Introduction to the Gospels and Acts*. Grand Rapids: Eerdmans, 2008.

Puthenkulam, Joseph. "The Significance of 'Widow' in Luke–Acts: The Widows of Joppa (Acts 9,36–42)—An Exegetical Study." *Bible Bhashyam* 40.2 (2014) 85–100.

———. "The Widow of Nain (Luke 7:11–17) The Significance of Widows in Luke–Acts—An Exegetical Study." *Vidyajyoti* 78.7 (2014) 503–12.

Rackham, Richard Belward. *The Acts of the Apostles*. 14th ed. London: Methuen, 1951.

———. *The Acts of the Apostles: An Exposition*. Eugene, OR: Wipf & Stock, 2003.

Rad, Gerhard von. "The Promised Land and Yahweh's Land in the Hexateuch." In *The Problem of the Hexateuch and Other Essays*, by Gerhard von Rad, 79–93. Philadelphia: Fortress, 1966. Previously published in German as "Verheißenes Land und Jahwes Land im Hexateuch." *Zeitschrift des Deutschen Palastinavereins* 66 (1943) 191–204.

Radin, Max. "The Promotion of Centurions in Caesar's Army." *The Classical Journal* 10.7 (1915) 300–311.

Radl, Walter. *Der Urspung Jesu: Traditionsgeschichtliche Untersuchangen zu Lukas 1–2*. Freiburg/Basel/Vienna: Herder, 1996.

Ramsay, William M. *St. Paul the Traveler and the Roman Citizen*. Grand Rapids: Christian Classics Ethereal Library, 1895.

Ray, Jerry Lynn. *Narrative Irony in Luke–Acts: The Paradoxical Interaction of Prophetic Fulfillment and Jewish Rejection*. Lewiston: Mellen Biblical, 1996.

Regev, Eyal. *The Hasmoneans. Ideology, Archaeology, Identity*. Göttingen: Vandenhoeck & Ruprecht, 2013.

———. *The Sadducees and Their Halakhah: Religion and Society in the Second Temple Period*. Jerusalem: Yad Ben-Zvi, 2005.

Reicke, Bo Iver. "Jesus, Simeon and Anna (Luke 2:21–40)." In *Saved by Hope: Essays in Honor of Richard C. Oudersluys*, edited by James I. Cook, 96–108. Grand Rapids: Eerdmans, 1978.

Reid, Barbara E. *Choosing the Better Part? Women in the Gospel of Luke*. Collegeville, MN: Liturgical, 1996.

———. "An Overture to the Gospel of Luke." *Currents in Theology and Mission* 39.6 (2012) 428–34.

Reif, Stefan C. "On Some Issues of Identity Facing the Early Rabbis." *Biblische Notizen* 164 (2015) 115–30.

Reiser, Marius. "Hat Paulus Heiden bekehrt?" *BZ* 39 (1995) 76–91.

Reitzel, Frank X. "St. Luke's Use of the Temple Image." *Review for Religious* 38 (1979) 520–539.

Rengstorf, Karl Heinrich. *Apostolate and Ministry: The New Testament Doctrine of the Office of the Ministry.* London: Concordia, 1969.

Repschinski, Boris. "Re-Imagining the Presence of God: The Temple and the Messiah in the Gospel of Matthew." *Australian Biblical Review* 54 (2006) 37–49.

Reynolds, Joyce, and Robert F. Tannenbaum. *Jews and God-Fearers at Aphrodisias: Greek Inscriptions with Commentary.* Cambridge: Cambridge Philological Society, 1987.

Rhoads, David, et al. *Mark as Story: An Introduction to the Narrative of A Gospel.* 3rd ed. Minneapolis: Fortress, 2012.

Richard, Earl J. "The Polemical Character of the Joseph Episode in Acts 7." *JBL* 98.2 (1979) 255–67.

Richards, E. R. "An Honor/Shame Argument for Two Temple Clearings." *Trinity Journal* 29.1 (2008) 19–43.

Richardson, Christopher A. *Pioneer and Perfecter of Faith: Jesus' Faith as the Climax of Israel's History in the Epistle to the Hebrews.* Tübingen: Mohr Siebeck, 2012.

Ricoeur, Paul. *Time and Narrative.* 3 vols. Chicago: University of Chicago Press, 1990.

Riesenfeld, Harald. *The Gospel Tradition.* Minneapolis: Fortress, 1970.

Riesner, Rainer. *Jesus als Lehrer: Eine Untersuchung zum Ursprung der Evangelien-Überlieferung.* Tübingen: Mohr-Siebeck, 1981.

Riffaterre, Michael. *Semiotics of Poetry.* Bloomington: Indiana University Press, 1978.

Rindge, Matthew S. "Luke's Artistic Parables: Narratives of Subversion, Imagination, and Transformation." *Interpretation* 68.4 (2014) 403–15.

Ringe, Sharon H. "Luke 4:16–44: A Portrait of Jesus as a Herald of God's Jubilee." *Proceedings* 1 (1981) 73–84.

Ringgren, Helmer. "Luke's Use of the Old Testament." *Harvard Theological Review* 79.1–3 (1986) 227–35.

Ripley, J. J. "'Those Things That Jesus Had Begun to Do and Teach': Narrative Christology and Incarnational Ecclesiology in Acts." *Biblical Theology Bulletin* 44.2 (2014) 87–99.

Robbins, Vernon K. "By Land and by Sea: The We-Passages and Ancient Sea-Voyages." In *Perspectives on Luke–Acts*, edited by Charles H. Talbert, 215–42. Edinburgh: T&T Clark, 1978.

———. "The Claims of the Prologues and Greco-Roman Rhetoric: The Prefaces to Luke and Acts in Light of Greco-Roman Rhetorical Strategies." In *Jesus and the Heritage of Israel: Luke's Narrative Claim upon Israel's Legacy*, edited by David P. Moessner, 63–83. Harrisburg, PA: Trinity, 1999.

———. "Narrative in Ancient Rhetoric and Rhetoric in Ancient Narrative." In *SBL Seminar Papers 1996*, 368–84. Atlanta: Scholars, 1996.

———. "Prefaces in Greco-Roman Biography and Luke–Acts." In *SBL Seminar Papers 1978*, edited by P. J. Achtemeier, 198–207. Missoula: Scholars, 1978.

Robertson, Archibald T. *Luke the Historian in Light of Research.* New York: Scribner's Sons, 1920.

Robinson, John A. T. "The Baptism of John and the Qumran Community: Testing a Hypothesis." *The Harvard Theological Review* 50.3 (1957) 175–91.

Rodgers, Margaret. "Luke 4:16–30: A Call for a Jubilee Year." *The Reformed Theological Review* 40.3 (1981) 72–82.

Roitto, Rikard. *Behaving as a Christ-Believer: A Cognitive Perspective on Identity and Behavior Norms in Ephesians*. Winona Lake, IN: Eisenbrauns, 2011.

Rokeach, Milton. *The Nature of Human Values*. New York: Free Press, 1973.

Romaniuk, Kazimierz. "Die 'Gottesfürchtigen' im Neuen Testament." *Aegyptus* 44 (1964) 66–91.

Røsæg, Nils Askel. "The Blinding of Paul: Observations to a Theme." *Svensk Exegetisk Årsbok* 71 (2006) 159–85.

Rosch, Eleanor. "Cognitive Representation of Semantic Categories." *Journal of Experimental Psychology* 104 (1975) 192–233.

———. "Natural Categories." *Journal of Experimental Psychology* 4 (1973) 328–50.

———. "Principles of Categorization." In *Cognition and Categorization*, edited by Eleanor Rosch and B. B. Lloyd, 27–48. Hillsdale, NJ: Erlbaum, 1978.

Rosch, Eleanor, et al. "Basic Objects in Natural Categories." *Cognitive Psychology* 8 (1976) 382–429.

Roser, Matthew, and Michael S. Gazzaniga. "Automatic Brains, Interpretive Minds." *Current Directions in Psychological Science* 13 (2004) 56–59.

Rosner, Brian S. "The Progress of the Word." In *Witness to the Gospel: The Theology of Acts*, edited by I. Howard Marshall and David Peterson, 215–34. Grand Rapids: Eerdmans, 1998.

Rost, Leonhard. "Bezeichnungen für Land und Volk im Alten Testament." In *Das kleine Credo und andere Studien zum Alten Testament*, by Leonhard Rost, 76–101. Heidelberg: Quelle & Meyer, 1965.

Roth, John. *The Blind, the Lame, and the Poor: Character Types in Luke–Acts*. Sheffield: Sheffield Academic, 1997.

Rothschild, Clare K. *Luke–Acts and the Rhetoric of History: An Investigation of Early Christian Historiography*. Tübingen: Mohr Siebeck, 2004.

Safrai, Shmuel. "The Synagogue the Centurion Built." *Jerusalem Perspective* 55 (1999) 12–14.

Sailhamer, John H. *The Pentateuch as Narrative*. Grand Rapids: Zondervan, 1995.

Saller, Richard. "Poverty, Honor and Obligation in Imperial Rome." *Criterion* 37.2 (1998) 12–20.

Samartha, Stanley J. "Pharoah's Daughter (Ex. 2:10), The Prodigal Son's Mother (Lk 15:11), Timothy's Father." *One World* 130 (1987) 14.

Samkutty, V. J. *The Samaritan Mission in Acts*. London: Bloomsbury T&T Clark, 2006.

Sanborn, Scott F. "The Babe in the Manger Anticipates Resurrection Life: Luke 1:46–55, 67–79." *Kerux* 31.2 (2016) 21–29.

Sanders, E. P. *Jesus and Judaism*. Philadelphia: Fortress, 1985.

———. *Paul and the Palestinian Judaism: A Comparison of Patterns of Religion*. London: Fortress, 1985.

Sanders, Jack T. "Who Is a Jew and Who Is a Gentile in the Book of Acts?" *NTS* 37 (1991) 434–55.

Sandt, Hubertus Waltherus Maria van de. "The Quotations in Acts 13:32–52 as a Reflection of Luke's LXX Interpretation." *Biblica* 75.1 (1994) 26–58.

———. "Why is Amos 5,25–27 Quoted in Acts 7,42f." *Zeitschrift für die neutestamentliche Wissenschaft und die Kunde der älteren Kirche* 82.1–2 (1991) 67–87.

Sarbin, T. R. "The Narrative as a Root Metaphor for Psychology." In *Narrative Psychology: The Storied Nature of Human Conduct*, edited by T. R. Sarbin, 3–21. New York: Praeger, 1986.

Sargent, Benjamin. *David Being a Prophet: The Contingency of Scripture upon History in the New Testament*. Berlin: de Gruyter, 2014.

Satterthwaite, Phillip E. "Acts in the Background of Classical Rhetoric." In *The Book of Acts in its Ancient Literary Setting*, edited by Bruce Winter and Andrew Clarke, 337–79. Vol. 1 of *The Book of Acts in its First Century Setting*. Grand Rapids: Eerdmans, 1993.

Sayles, Guy. "Clemency as Cruelty: Forgiveness and Force in the Dying Prayers of Jesus and Stephen." *Review & Expositor* 103.1 (2006) 213–22.

Schaberg, Jane. *The Illegitimacy of Jesus: A Feminist Theological Interpretation of the Infancy Narratives*. San Francisco, CA: Harper and Row, 1987.

Schalück, Hermann. "Disciples of Jesus: Bearers of Compassion, Peace and Hope in our World." *SEDOS Bulletin* 38.7 (2006) 203–13.

Scheffler, Eben. "Jesus' Non-Violence at His Arrest: The Synoptics and John's Gospel Compared." *Acta Patristica et Byzantina* 17 (2006) 312–26.

———. "'Lord, Shall We Strike With the Sword?': Of (Non-)Violence in Luke's Gospel." *Acta Patristica et Byzantina* 17 (2006) 295–311.

———. "Vyandsliefde of Geweld: Oor Die Politiek Van Die Historiese Jesus." *Acta Theologia* 36.2 (2016) 92–124.

Scheib, Karen D. *Pastoral Care: Telling the Stories of Our Lives*. Nashville: Abingdon, 2016.

Schiappa, Edward. *Protagoras and Logos*. Columbia: University of South Carolina Press, 1991.

Schipper, Jeremy. "Disabling Israelite Leadership: 2 Samuel 6:23 and Other Images of Disability in the Deuteronomistic History." In *This Abled Body: Rethinking Disabilities in Biblical Studies*, edited by Hector Avalos et al., 104–13. Leiden: Brill, 2007.

Schmidt, Karl Mathias. "Bekehrung zur Zerstreuung: Paulus und der äthiopische Eunuch im Kontext der lukanischen Diasporatheologie." *Bib* 88.2 (2007) 191–213.

Schmithals, Walter. *The Office of Apostle in the Early Church*. Nashville: Abingdon, 1969.

Schmitz, Otto, and Gustav Stählin. "Menahem." In vol. 5 of *Theological Dictionary of the New Testament*, edited by Gerhard Friedrich, 773–99. Translated by Geoffrey W. Bromiley. Grand Rapids: Eerdmans, 1967.

Schnabel, Eckhard J. *Acts*. Edited by Clinton E. Arnold. Grand Rapids: Zondervan, 2012.

———. "Jewish Opposition to Christians in Asia Minor in the First Century." *Bulletin for Biblical Research* 18.2 (2008) 233–70.

Schneck, Richard. *Isaiah in the Gospel of Mark, I–VIII*. Berkeley: Bibal, 1994.

Schneider, Gerhard. *Das Evangelium nach Lukas*. 2 vols. Ökumenischer Taschenbuch-Kommentar 3. Gütersloh: Mohn, 1977.

———. "Der Zweck des lukanischen Doppelwerks." *Biblische Zeitschrift* 21 (1971) 45–66.

———. *Die Apostelgeschichte*. 2 vols. Teil. Freiburg: Herder, 1980, 1982.

Scholtus, Silvia. "Problemas eclesiásticos: Respuesta bíblica según Hechos 1–15." *DavarLogos* 5.2 (2006) 135–49.

Scholz, Daniel J. "'Rise, Peter, Kill and Eat': Eating Unclean Food and Dining with Unclean People in Acts 10:1–11:18." *Proceedings* 22 (2002) 47–61.

Schottroff, Louise. *Lydia's Impatient Sisters: A Feminist Social History of Early Christianity*. Louisville: Westminster John Knox, 1995.

———. *The Parables of Jesus*. Minneapolis: Augsburg Fortress, 2006.

Schreiber, Paul L. "Hosea 1:6–7 as Law-Gospel Dialectic." In *"Hear the Word of Yahweh": Essays on Scripture and Archaeology in Honor of Horace D. Hummel*, edited by Dean O. Wenthe et al., 13–22. St. Louis: Concordia Academic, 2002.

Schuele, Andreas. "Isaiah 56:1–8." *Interpretation* 65.3 (2011) 286–88.

Schulz, S. "Markus und das Altes Testament." *ZTK* 58 (1961) 184–97.

Schumacher, R. Daniel. "Saving Like a Fool and Spending Like It Isn't Yours: Reading the Parable of the Unjust Steward (Luke 16:1–8a) in Light of the Parable of the Rich Fool (Luke 12:16–20)." *Review and Expositor* 109.2 (2012) 269–76.

Schürer, Emil. *The History of the Jewish People in the Age of Jesus Christ*. Edited by Geza Vermes. New York: Bloomsbury T&T Clark, 2014.

Schürmann, H. *Das Lukasevangelium: Kommentar zu Kap. 1, 1–9:50*. Freiburg: Herder, 1969.

Schwartz, Daniel R. "Did the Jews Practice Infant Exposure and Infanticide in Antiquity?" *Studia Philonica Annual* 16 (2004) 61–95.

———. "Humbly Second-Rate in the Diaspora?: Philo and Stephen on the Tabernacle and the Temple." In *Envisioning Judaism: Studies in Honor of Peter Schäfer on the Occasion of his Seventieth Birthday*, edited by Ra'anan S. Boustan et al., 81–89. Tübingen: Mohr Siebeck, 2013.

Schweizer, Eduard. *The Good News According to Luke*. Translated by D. E. Green. Atlanta: John Knox, 1984.

Scobie, Charles H. H. "The Use of Source Material in the Speeches of Acts 3 and 7." *NTS* 25.4 (1979) 399–421.

Scott, Ian W. *Paul's Way of Knowing: Story, Experience, and the Spirit*. Grand Rapids: Baker Academic, 2008.

Scott, J. Julius, Jr. "The Cornelius Incident in Light of its Jewish Setting." *JETS* 34.4 (1991) 475–84.

Scott, James M. "Luke's Geographical Horizon." In *The Book of Acts in Its Graeco-Roman Setting*, edited by David W. J. Gill et al., 483–544. Vol. 2 of *The Book of Acts in Its First Century Setting*. Grand Rapids: Eerdmans, 1993.

Seccombe, David B. *Possessions and the Poor in Luke–Acts*. Louvain: Peters, 1982.

Seim, Turid Karlsen. *The Double Message: Patterns of Gender in Luke–Acts*. Nashville: Abingdon, 1994.

Seitzm Christopher R. "The Prophet Moses and the Canonical Shape of Jeremiah." *ZAW* 101 (1993) 3–27.

Segal, Alan F. *Paul the Convert: The Apostolate and Apostasy of Saul the Pharisee*. New Haven: Yale University Press, 1990.

Sell, Philip. "The Seven in Acts 6 as a Ministry Team." *Bibliotheca Sacra* 167.665 (2010) 58–67.

Serrano, Andrés García. "Anna's Characterization in Luke 2:36–38: A Case of Conceptual Allusion?" *The Catholic Biblical Quarterly* 76.3 (2014) 464–80.

Sewell, William H. "Some Reflections on the Golden Age of Interdisciplinary Social Psychology." *Annual Review of Sociology* 15 (1989) 1–16.

Shea, Chris. "Educating Paul." *Forum* 5.2 (2002) 225–34.

Sheeley, Steven. *Narrative Asides in Luke–Acts*. New York: Bloomsbury Academic, 2015.

Sheerin, Daniel. "St John the Baptist in the Lower World." *Vigiliae Christianae* 30.1 (1976) 1–22.

Shellberg, Pamela. *Cleansed Lepers, Cleansed Hearts: Purity and Healing in Luke–Acts*. Minneapolis: Fortress, 2015.

Sherif, Muzafer. *Intergroup Conflict and Cooperation: The Robbers Cave Experiment*. Norman: University Book Exchange, 1961.

Shiner, W. T. "The Ambiguous Pronouncement of the Centurion and the Shrouding of Meaning in Mark." *JSNT* 78 (2000) 3–22.

Shipp, Blake. *Paul the Reluctant Witness: Power and Weakness in Luke's Portrayal.* Eugene, OR: Wipf & Stock, 2005.

Shirock, R. J. "The Growth of the Kingdom in Light of Israel's Rejection of Jesus: Structure and Theology in Luke 13:1–35." *Novum Testamentum* 35.1 (1993) 15–29.

Shotter, John. *Texts of Identity: Inquiries in Social Construction.* Edited by Kenneth J. Gergen. Thousand Oaks, CA: SAGE, 1989.

Sick, David H. "Zacchaeus as the Rich Host of Classical Satire." *Biblical Interpretation* 24.2 (2016) 229–44.

Siegel, Daniel. *Mindsight: The New Science of Personal Transformation.* New York: Bantam, 2010.

Siegert, Folker. "Gottesfürchtige und Sympathisanten." *JSJ* 4 (1973) 109–64.

Sim, David C., and James S. Mclaren, eds. *Attitudes to Gentiles in Ancient Judaism and Early Christianity.* New York: Bloomsbury, 2013.

Simon, Marcel. "Saint Stephen and the Jerusalem Temple." *The Journal of Ecclesiastical History* 2 (1951) 127–42.

———. *St. Stephen and the Hellenists in the Primitive Church.* New York: Longmans, 1958.

Skarsaune, Oskar. *In the Shadow of the Temple: Jewish Influences on Early Christianity.* Downers Grove, IL: InterVarsity, 2002.

Sloan, Robert. "Signs and Wonders: A Rhetorical Clue to the Pentecost Discourse." *Evangelical Quarterly* 63.3 (1991) 225–40.

Smith, Abraham. "Do You Understand What You Are Reading?: A Literary Critical Reading of the Ethiopian (Kushite)Episode (Acts 8:26–40)." *JITC* 22.1 (1994) 48–70.

———. "'Full of Spirit and Wisdom': Luke's Portrait of Stephen (Acts 6:1–8:1a) as a Man of Self-Mastery." In *Asceticism and the New Testament*, edited by Leif E. Vaage and Vincent L. Wimbush, 97–114. New York: Routledge, 1999.

Smith, Daniel Alan. "Seeing a Pneu(matic Body) The Apologetic Interests of Luke 24:36–43." *Catholic Biblical Quarterly* 72.4 (2010) 752–72.

Smith, Daniel Lynwood. *The Rhetoric of Interruption: Speech-Making, Turn-Taking, and Rule-Breaking in Luke–Acts and Ancient Greek Narrative.* Berlin: de Gruyter, 2012.

Smith, Dennis E. "Table Fellowship as a Literary Motif in the Gospel of Luke." *JBL* 106 (1987) 613–28.

Smith, Eliot R., and Michael A. Zarate. "Exemplar and Prototype Use in Social Categorization." *Social Cognition* 8.3 (1990) 243–62.

Smith, Justin M. *Why Bios? On the Relationship between Gospel Genre and Implied Audience.* London: Bloomsbury, 2015.

Smith, Steve. *The Fate of the Jerusalem Temple in Luke–Acts: An Intertextual Approach to Jesus' Laments Over Jerusalem and Stephen's Speech.* New York: Bloomsbury T&T Clark, 2017.

Snodgrass, Klyne R. *Stories with Intent: A Comprehensive Guide to the Parables of Jesus.* Grand Rapids: Eerdmans, 2008.

———. "Streams of Tradition Emerging from Isaiah 40:1–5 and their Adaptation in the New Testament." *JSNT* 8 (1980) 24–45.

Snyder, Benjamin. "The 'Fathers' Motif in Luke–Acts." *The Journal of Inductive Biblical Studies* 2.2 (2015) 44–71.

Soards, Marion L. *The Speeches in Acts: Their Content, Context, and Concerns.* Louisville: John Knox, 1994.

———. "Tradition, Composition, and Theology in Luke's Account of Jesus before Herod Antipas." *Biblica* 66.3 (1985) 344–64.
Solevag, Anna R. "No Nuts? No Problem!: Disability, Stigma, and the Baptized Eunuch in Acts 8:26–40." *Biblical Interpretation* 24.1 (2016) 81–99.
Sorum, E. A. "The Roman Centurion." *Wisconsin Lutheran Quarterly* 109.2 (2012) 120–28.
Spence, Donald P. *Narrative Truth and Historical Truth: Meaning and Interpretation in Psychoanalysis*. New York: Norton, 1982.
Spencer, Aída Besançon. "Position Reversal and Hope for the Oppressed." In *Latino/a Biblical Hermeneutics: Problematics, Objectives, Strategies*, edited by Francisco Lozada and Fernando F. Segovia, 95–106. Atlanta: SBL, 2014.
Spencer, F. Scott. *Acts*. Sheffield: Sheffield, 1997.
———. *The Portrait of Philip in Acts: A Study of Role and Relations*. Sheffield: Sheffield Academic, 1997.
———. "Scared to Death: The Rhetoric of Fear in the 'Tragedy' of Ananias and Sapphira." In *Reading Acts Today: Essays in Honour of Loveday C. A. Alexander*, edited by Steve Walton et al., 63–80. London: T&T Clark, 2011.
———. "To Fear and not to Fear the Creator God: A Theological and Therapeutic Interpretation of Luke 12:4–34." *Journal of Theological Interpretation* 8.2 (2014) 229–49.
———. "A Waiter, a Magician, a Fisherman, and a Eunuch: The Pieces and Puzzles of Acts 8." *Forum* 3.1 (2000) 155–78.
Stagg, Frank. *The Book of Acts: The Early Struggle for an Unhindered Gospel*. Nashville: Broadman, 1955.
Stählin, Gustav. *Die Apostelgeschichte*. Das Neue Testament Deutch 5. Göttingen: Vandenhoeck & Ruprecht, 1962.
Stanley, Christopher. "Biblical Quotations as Rhetorical Devices in Paul's Letter to the Galatians." In *Society of Biblical Literature Seminar Papers, 1998, Part Two*, 700–730. Atlanta: Scholars, 1998.
Stanton, Graham N. *Jesus of Nazareth in New Testament Preaching*. Cambridge: Cambridge University Press, 1974.
Stanton, Graham N., and Guy G. Stroumsa, eds. *Tolerance and Intolerance in Early Judaism and Christianity*. Cambridge: Cambridge University Press, 1998.
Stendahl, Krister. "The Apostle Paul and the Introspective Conscience of the West." *HTR* 56 (1963) 199–215.
———. "Call Rather than Conversion." In *Paul Among Jews and Gentiles*, by Krister Stendahl, 7–22. London: Fortress, 1977.
Sterling, Gregory E. *Historiography & Self-Definition: Josephus, Luke-Acts & Apologetic Historiography*. Leiden: Brill, 1992.
Steuernagel, Valdir R. "Doing Theology Together with Mary." *Journal of Latin American Theology* 8.2 (2013) 9–49.
Stevenson, Walter. "The Rise of Eunuchs in Greco-Roman Antiquity." *Journal of the History of Sexuality* 5.4 (1995) 495–511.
Steyn, Gert J. "Trajectories of Scripture Transmission: The Case of Amos 5:25–27 in Acts 7:42–43." *HTS Teologiese Studies/Theological Studies* 69.1 (2013) 1–7.
Stock, A. "A Realistic Spirituality: Pathos in Luke Acts." *Journal of Spiritual Formation* 15.3 (1994) 321–22.
Stol, Marten. *Birth in Babylonia and the Bible: Its Mediterranean Setting*. Groningen: Styx, 2000.

Story, J. Lyle. "All is Now Ready: An Exegesis of 'The Great Banquet' (Luke 14:15–24) and 'The Marriage Feast' (Matthew 22:1–14)." *American Theological Inquiry* 2.2 (2009) 67–79.

———. "One Banquet with Many Courses (Luke 14:1–24)." *Journal of Biblical and Pneumatological Research* 4 (2012) 67–93.

Stowasser, Martin W. "Am 5,25–27; 9,11 f. in der Qumranüberlieferung und in der Apostelgeschichte: Text- und traditionsgeschichtliche Überlegungen zu 4Q174 (Florilegium)III 12/CD VII 16/Apg 7,42b–43; 15,16–18." *ZNW* 92.1–2 (2001) 47–63.

Strack, Hermann Leberecht. *Introduction to the Talmud and Midrash*. Minneapolis: Fortress, 1996.

Strauss, Mark L. *The Davidic Messiah in Luke–Acts: The Promise and its Fulfillment in Lukan Christology*. Sheffield: Sheffield Academic, 1995.

Streltsov, Alexei. "The Sacramental Character of Sharing Possessions in Acts." *Logia* 16.2 (2007) 13–19.

Stronstad, Roger. *The Prophethood of All Believers: A Study in Luke's Charismatic Theology*. Sheffield: Sheffield Academic, 1999.

Stulman, Louis. "Insiders and Outsiders in the Book of Jeremiah: Shifts in Symbolic Arrangements." *JSOT* 66 (1995) 65–85.

Sugawara, Yugi. "The Minor Characters in Mark's Gospel: Their Roles and Functions." *Annual of the Japanese Institute* 24 (1998) 66–82.

Sugirtharajah, R. S. "The Widow's Mites Revalued." *The Expository Times* 103.2 (1991) 42–43.

Sullivan, Roger W. "The Parable of the Great Supper (Luke 14:15–24)." *The Theological Educator* 56 (1997) 59–66.

Sweeney, James P. "Stephen's Speech (Acts 7:2–53) Is It as 'Anti-Temple' as Is Frequently Alleged?" *Trinity Journal* 23.2 (2002) 185–210.

Sweetland, Dennis M. "Following Jesus: Discipleship in Luke–Acts." In *New Views on Luke and Acts*, edited by Earl Richard, 109–23. Collegeville, MN: Liturgical, 1990.

Sylva, Dennis D. "The Temple Curtain and Jesus' Death in the Gospel of Luke." *Journal of Biblical Literature* 105.2 (1986) 239–50.

Tabb, Brian J. "Salvation, Spreading, and Suffering: God's Unfolding Plan in Luke–Acts." *Journal of the Evangelical Theological Society* 58.1 (2015) 43–61.

Tajfel, Henri. "The Achievement of Group Differentiation." In *Differentiation Between Social Groups: Studies in the Social Psychology of Intergroup Relations*, edited by Henri Tajfel, 77–100. London: Academic, 1978.

———. *Differentiation Between Social Groups: Studies in the Social Psychology of Intergroup Relations*. London: Academic, 1978.

———. "Experiments in Intergroup Discrimination." *Scientific American* 223 (1970) 96–102.

———. *Human Groups and Social Categories: Studies in Social Psychology*. Cambridge: Cambridge University Press, 1981.

———. "Intergroup Behavior II: Group Behavior." In *Introducing Social Psychology: An Analysis of Individual Reaction and Response*, edited by Henri Tajfel and Colin Fraser, 423–46. London: Penguin, 1978.

———. "Le Categorisation Sociale." In *Introductioin a La Psychologie Sociale*, edited by Serge Moscovici, 272–302. Paris: Larousse, 1972.

———. "Social Categorization, Social Identity, and Social Comparison." In *Differentiation Between Social Groups*, edited by Henri Tajfel, 61–76. London: Academic, 1978.

———. *Social Identity and Intergroup Relations*. Cambridge: Cambridge University Press, 1982.

Tajfel, Henri, and M. G. Billig. "Social Categorization and Similarity in Intergroup Behavior." *European Journal of Social Psychology* 3 (1973) 27–52.

Tajfel, Henri, and John C. Turner. "An Integrative Theory of Intergroup Conflict." In *The Social Psychology of Intergroup Relations*, edited by William G. Austin and Stephen Worchel, 33–47. Monterey: Brooks/Cole, 1979.

———. "The Social Identity Theory of Intergroup Behavior." In *Psychology of Intergroup Relation*, edited by William G. Austin and Stephen Worchel, 33–47. Monterey: Brooks/Cole, 1986.

Tajra, Henry W. *The Trial of St. Paul: A Juridical Exegesis of the Second Half of the Acts of the Apostles*. Tübingen: Mohr-Siebeck, 1989.

Talbert, Charles H. *Literary Patterns, Theological Themes, and the Genre of Luke–Acts*. Missoula, MT: Scholars, 1974.

———. *Reading Acts: A Literary and Theological Commentary on the Acts of the Apostles*. New York: Crossroad, 1997.

———. *What Is a Gospel? The Genre of the Canonical Gospels*. Minneapolis: Fortress, 1977.

Tannehill, Robert C. *The Acts of the Apostles*. Vol. 2 of *The Narrative Unity of Luke–Acts: Acts A Literary Interpretation*. Minneapolis: Fortress, 1990.

———. *The Gospel According to Luke*. Vol. 1 of *The Narrative Unity of Luke–Acts: A Literary Interpretation*. Philadelphia: Fortress, 1986.

———. "Israel in Luke: A Tragic Story." *JBL* 104.1 (1985) 69–85.

———. "The Lukan Discourse on Invitations." In *The Shape of Luke's Story: Essays on Luke–Acts*, by Robert C. Tannehill, 56–72. Eugene, OR: Cascade, 2005.

———. "The Magnificat as Poem." *JBL* 93 (1974) 263–75.

———. "The Story of Zacchaeus as Rhetoric: Luke 19:1–10." *Semeia* 64 (1993) 201–21.

Tannen, Deborah. "What's in a Frame?" In *Framing in Discourse*, edited by Deborah Tannen, 14–56. Oxford: Oxford University Press, 1993.

Tapie, Matthew A., and Daniel W. Mcclain, eds. *Reading Scripture as a Political Act: Essays on the Theopolitical Interpretation of the Bible*. Minneapolis: Fortress, 2015.

Tatum, W. B. "The Epoch of Israel: Luke I–II and the Theological Plan of Luke–Acts." *NTS* 10 (1964) 184–95.

Taylor, John. "The Gate of the Temple Called 'The Beautiful' (Acts 3:2, 10)." *Revue Biblique* 106.4 (1999) 549–62.

Taylor, N. H. "Stephen, the Temple, and Early Christian Eschatology." *Revue Biblique* 110.1 (2003) 62–85.

Thiselton, Anthony C. *New Horizons in Hermeneutics: The Theory and Practice of Transforming Biblical Reading*. Grand Rapids: Zondervan, 1992.

Thompson, Garrett G. "'Brothers and Fathers': The Polemic Cohesion of Stephen's Speech." *Pneumatika* 3.2 (2015) 52–66.

Thompson, Robin. "Diaspora Jewish Freedmen: Stephen's Deadly Opponents." *Bibliotheca Sacra* 173.690 (2016) 166–81.

Thornton, Claus-Jürgen. *Der Zeuge des Zeugen: Lukas als Historiker der Paulusreisen*. Tübingen: Mohr Siebeck, 1991.

Tiede, David L. *Prophecy and History in Luke–Acts*. Philadelphia: Fortress, 1980.

Tiemeyer, Lena-Sofia. "Death or Conversion: The Gentiles in the Concluding Chapters of Isaiah and the Book of the Twelve." *JTS* 68.1 (2017) 1–22.

Todorov, Tzvetan. *The Poetics of Prose*. Ithaca: Cornell University Press, 1977.

Toit, A. B. du. "A Tale of Two Cities: 'Tarsus or Jerusalem' Revisited." *NTS* 46.3 (2000) 375–402.

Tolmie, D. F. "Paulus se retoriese strategie in Galasiërs 3:1–14." *Verbum et Ecclesia* 23.1 (2002) 209–25.

———. "Paulus se retoriese strategie in Galasiërs 3:15–25." *Verbum et Ecclesia* 24.2 (2003) 515–32.

Toney, Carl N. "Paul in Acts: The Prophetic Portrait of Paul." In *Issues in Luke–Acts: Selected Essays*, edited by Sean A. Adams and Michael Pahl, 239–61. Piscataway, NJ: Gorgias, 2012.

Trebilco, Paul R. *Jewish Communities in Asia Minor*. Cambridge: Cambridge University Press, 1991.

Trible, Phyllis. *God and the Rhetoric of Sexuality*. Philadelphia: Fortress, 1978.

Trocmé, André. *Jesus and the Nonviolent Revolution*. Walden, NY: Plough, 2003.

Trompf, G. W. "On Why Luke Declined to Recount the Death of Paul: Acts 27–28 and Beyond." In *Luke–Acts: New Perspectives from the Society of Biblical Literature Seminar*, edited by Charles H. Talbert, 225–39. New York: Crossroad, 1984.

Trow, Martin W., ed. *Geneologies of New Testament Rhetorical Criticism*. Minneapolis: Fortress, 2014.

Trudinger, Paul. "St. Stephen and the ‹Edifice Complex›." *Downside Review* 104.356 (1986) 240–42.

Trumbower, Jeffrey A. "The Historical Jesus and the Speech of Gamaliel (Acts 5:35–9)." *NTS* 39.4 (1993) 500–517.

Tucker, J. Brian, and Coleman Baker. *T&T Clark Handbook to Social Identity in the New Testament*. London: Bloomsbury, 2014.

Tuckett, Christopher M. "The Christology of Luke–Acts." In *The Unity of Luke–Acts*, edited by J. Verheyden, 133–64. Leuven: Leuven University Press, 1999.

———. *Luke*. Sheffield: Sheffield Academic, 1996.

Turner, G. "Paul and the Globalisation of Christianity." *New Blackfriars* 86.1002 (2005) 165–71.

Turner, John C. "The Experimental Social Psychology of Intergroup Behavior." In *Intergroup Behavior*, edited by John C. Turner and Howard Giles, 66–101. Oxford: Blackwell, 1981.

———. "Henri Tajfel: An Introduction." In *Social Groups and Identities: Developing the Legacy of Henri Tajfel*, edited by William C. Robinson, 1–24. Oxford: Butterworth-Heinemann, 1996.

———. *Rediscovering the Social Group: Self-Categorization Theory*. New York: Blackwell, 1987.

———. "Social Categorization and the Self-Concept: A Social Cognitive Theory of Group Behavior." In *Key Readings in Social Psychology: Rediscovering Social Identity*, edited by T. Postmes and N. R. Branscombe, 243–72. Hove: Psychology, 2010.

———. "Social Comparison and Social Identity: Some Prospects for Intergroup Behaviour." *European Journal of Social Psychology* 5 (1975) 5–34.

———. "Some Current Issues in Research on Social Identity and Self-Categorization Theories." In *Social Identity: Context, Commitment, Content*, edited by Naomi Ellemers et al., 6–34. Malden, MA: Blackwell, 1999.

———. "Towards a Cognitive Redefinition of the Social Group." In *Social Identity and Intergroup Relations*, edited by Henri Tajfel, 14–32. Cambridge: Cambridge University Press, 1982.

Turner, John C., et al. "Self and Collective: Cognition and Social Context." *Personality and Social Psychology Bulletin* 20 (1994) 454–63.

Turner, Max. *Power From on High: The Spirit in Israel's Restoration and Witness in Luke–Acts*. Eugene, OR: Wipf & Stock, 2015.

———. "The Significance of Recovering the Spirit in Luke–Acts: A Survey of Modern Scholarship." *Trinity Journal* 2 (1981) 131–58.

———. "Spirit Empowerment in Luke–Acts: Some Linguistic Considerations." *Vox Evangelica* 12 (1981) 45–63.

———. "The Spirit in Luke–Acts: A Support or Challenge to Classical Pentecostal Paradigms." *Vox Evangelica* 27 (1997) 75–101.

Turner, Victor. *The Ritual Process: Structure and Anti-Structure*. Chicago: Aldine, 1995.

Twelftree, Graham H. *People of the Spirit: Exploring Luke's View of the Church*. Grand Rapids: Baker Academic, 2009.

Tyson, Joseph B. "From History to Rhetoric and Back: Assessing New Trends in Acts Studies." In *Contextualizing Acts: Lukan Narrative and Greco-Roman Discourse*, edited by T. Penner and C. Vander Stichele. 23–42. Leiden: Brill, 2003.

———. "Guess Who's Coming to Dinner: Peter and Cornelius in Acts 10:1–11:18." *Forum* 3.1 (2000) 179–96.

———. *Images of Judaism in Luke–Acts*. Colombia: University of South Carolina Press, 1992.

———. *Marcion and Luke–Acts: A Defining Struggle*. Columbia: University of South Carolina Press, 2006.

———. "Opposition to Jesus in the Gospel of Luke." *PRSt* 5.2 (1978) 144–50.

———. "Why Dates Matter: The Case of the Acts of the Apostles." In *Finding the Historical Jesus: Rules of Evidence*, edited by Bernard Brandon Scott, 59–70. Santa Rosa: Polebridge, 2008.

Ullendorff, Edward. *Ethiopia and the Bible: The Schweich Lectures*. Oxford: Oxford University Press, 1967.

Unnik, W. C. van. "Der Ausdruck ἕως ἐσχάτου τῆς γῆς (Apostelgeschichte 18) und Sein Alttestamentlicher Hintergrund." In *Evangelia, Paulina, Acta*, by W. C. van Unnik, 386–401. Vol. 1 of *Sparsa Collecta: The Collected Essays of W. C. van Unnik*. Novum Testamentum Supplements 29. Leiden: Brill, 1973.

———. "The 'Book of Acts': The Confirmation of the Gospel." *Novum Testamentum* 4.1 (1960) 26–59.

———. "The Redemption in 1 Peter 1:18–19 and the Problem of the First Epistle of Peter." In *1 Peter, Canon, Corpus Hellenisticum, Generalia*, by W. C. van Unnik, 1–82. Vol. 2 of *Sparsa Collecta: The Collected Essays of W. C. van Unnik*. Novum Testamentum Supplements 30. Brill: Leiden, 1980.

Upchurch, Cackie. "Hopeful Witness of Universal Salvation: The Canticle of Simeon, Luke 2:22–38." *The Bible Today* 50.6 (2012) 357–61.

Valentini, Alberto. *Il Magnificat: Genero letterario, struttura, esegesi*. Bologna: Dehoniane, 1987.

Valle, Acosta, and Martha Milagros. "Actes 10,1–11,18: Une Intertextualité Différée pour un Lecteur Davantage Impliqué." *Science et Espirit* 66.3 (2014) 417–31.

Vanhoozer, Kevin. *First Theology*. Downers Grove, IL: InterVarsity, 2002.

VanSeters, John. *In Search of History: Historiography in the Ancient World and the Origins of Biblical History*. New Haven: Yale University Press, 1982.

Varzi, Archille. "Boundary." *Stanford Encyclopedia of Philosophy*, October 10, 2013. Edited by Edward N. Zalta. Online. https://plato.stanford.edu/entries/boundary.

Vaughan, Curtis. "The Simeon Incident: An Interpretation of Luke 2:25–35." In *New Testament Studies: Essays in Honor of Ray Summers in his 65th Year*, edited by Huber L. Drumwright and Curtis Vaughan, 13–26. Waco, TX: Markham Press Fund of Baylor University Press, 1975.

Vaux, Roland de. *Ancient Israel: It's Life and Institutions*. Translated by John MacHugh. 2 vols. New York: McGraw-Hill, 1961.

Veltman, Fred. "The Defense Speeches of Paul in Acts." In *Perspectives on Luke–Acts*, edited by Charles H. Talbert, 243–56. Edinburgh: T&T Clark, 1978.

Venter, P. M. "Canon, Intertextuality, and History in Nehemiah 7.72b–10:40." *HTS Teologiese Studies/Theological Studies* 65.1 (2009). Online. https://doi.org/10.4102/hts.v65i1.135.

Vermes, Geza, ed. *The Complete Dead Sea Scrolls in English*. New York: Penguin, 1997.

Via, J. E. "An Interpretation of Acts 7:35–37 from the Perspective of Major Themes in Luke–Acts." In *SBL Seminar Papers 1978*, edited by P. J. Achtemeier, 209–23. Missoula, MT: Scholars, 1978.

Viljoen, François P. "Hosea 6:6 and Identity Formation in Matthew." *Acta Theologica* 34.1 (2014) 214–37.

Violet, Bruno. "Zum rechten Verständnis der Nazarethperikope Lc 4:16–30." *ZNW* 33.1 (1933) 251–71.

Volf, Miroslav. *The End of Memory: Remembering Rightly in a Violent World*. Grand Rapids: Eerdmans, 2006.

Völkel, M. "Freund der Zöllner und Sünder." *ZNW* 69 (1978) 1–10.

Waal, C. van der. "The Temple in the Gospel According to Luke." *Neotestamentica* 7 (1973) 49–59.

Wagemakers, Bart. "Incest, Infanticide, and Cannibalism: Anti-Christian Imputations in the Roman Empire." *Greece & Rome* 57.2 (2010) 337–54.

Walker, Peter W. L. *Jesus and the Holy City: New Testament Perspectives on Jerusalem*. Grand Rapids: Eerdmans, 1996.

———. "The Land and Jesus Himself." In *The Land of Promise: Biblical, Theological, and Contemporary Perspectives*, edited by Philip Johnston and Peter Walker, 100–120. Grand Rapids: InterVarsity, 2000.

Walker, William O. "The Portrayal of Aquila and Priscilla in Acts: The Question of Sources." *NTS* 54.4 (2008) 479–95.

Wall, Robert W. "Peter, 'Son' of Jonah: The Conversion of Cornelius in the Context of the Canon." *JSNT* 29 (1987) 79–90.

Wallace, Daniel B. *Greek Grammar Beyond the Basics: An Exegetical Syntax of the New Testament*. Grand Rapids: Zondervan, 1996.

Walters, Patricia. *The Assumed Authorial Unity of Luke and Acts: A Reassessment of the Evidence*. Cambridge: Cambridge University Press, 2009.

Warrington, Keith. "Acts and the Healing Narratives: Why?" *Journal of Pentecostal Theology* 14.2 (2006) 189–217.

Watson, Francis. *Paul, Judaism, and the Gentiles: Beyond a New Perspective*. Grand Rapids: Eerdmans, 2007.

———. *Paul, Judaism, and the Gentiles: A Sociological Approach*. London: Cambridge University Press, 1986.

Wattenmaker, William D., et al. "Linear Separability and Concept Learning: Context, Relational Properties, and Concept Naturalness." *Cognitive Psychology* 18 (1986) 158–94.

Watts, Rikki E. *Isaiah's New Exodus in Mark*. Grand Rapids: Baker Academic, 2001.

Webb, Robert. *John the Baptizer and Prophet: A Socio-Historic Study*. Eugene, OR: Wipf & Stock, 2006.

Wegener, Mark. "The Arrival of Jesus as a Politically Subversive Event According to Luke 1–2." *Currents in Theology and Mission* 44.1 (2017) 15–23.

Weinert, Francis D. "The Meaning of the Temple in Luke-Act." *Biblical Theology Bulletin* 11.3 (1981) 85–89.

Weissenrieder, Annette. "Searching for the Middle Ground from the End of the Earth: The Embodiment of Space in Acts 8:26–40." *Neotestamentica* 48.1 (2014) 115–61.

Welliver, Kenneth. "Pentecost and the Early Church: Patristic Interpretation of Acts 2." PhD diss., Yale University, 1961.

Wells, Peter S. *The Barbarians Speak: How the Conquered Peoples Shaped Roman Europe*. Princeton: Princeton University Press, 2001.

Welzen, Huub. "Vrede en oordeel in het Evangelie Volgens Lucas." *Hervormde Teologiese Studies* 71.1 (2015) 1–11.

Wendland, Ernst R. "'Blessed Is the Man Who Will Eat at the Feast in the Kingdom Of God' (Lk 14:15) Internal and External Intertextual Influence on the Interpretation of Christ's Parable of the Great Banquet." *Neotestamentica* 31.1 (1997) 159–94.

Wenell, Karen J. *Jesus and Land: Sacred and Social Space in Second Temple Judaism*. New York: Bloomsbury T&T Clark, 2007.

Wenkel, David. "From Saul to Paul: The Apostle's Name Change and Narrative Identity in Acts 13:9." *Asbury Journal* 66.2 (2011) 67–76.

Whitenton, Michael R. "Rewriting Abraham and Joseph: Stephen's Speech (Acts 7:2–16) and Jewish Exegetical Traditions." *Novum Testamanetum* 54.2 (2012) 149–67.

Wilckens, Ulrich. *Der Brief an die Römer*. 3 vols. Göttingen: Vandenhoeck & Ruprecht, 1978–82.

Wilcox, Max. "The 'God-Fearers' in Acts: A Reconsideration." *JSNT* 13 (1981) 107.

———. "Luke 2,36–38: 'Anna bat Phanuel, of the tribe of Asher, a prophetess . . .': A Study in Midrash in Material Special to Luke." In vol. 2 of *The Four Gospels 1992*, edited by F. van Segbroeck and C. M. Tuckett, 1571–79. Leuven: Leuven University Press, 1992.

Williams, Benjamin J. "Brotherhood Motifs in the Parable of the Prodigal Son." *Restoration Quarterly* 56.2 (2014) 99–109.

Williams, Margaret H. "The Jews and Godfearers Inscription from Aphrodisias: A Case of Patriarchal Interference in Early Third-Century Caria?" *Historia: Zeitschrift für Alte Geschichte* 41.3 (1992) 297–310.

Williamson, Rick L. "Singing: Luke's Songs as Melodies of the Marginalized." In *Vital Christianity: Spirituality, Justice, and Christian Practice*, edited by David L. Weaver-Zercher and William H. Willimon, 167–76. New York: T&T Clark, 2005.

Willimon, William H. *Acts*. Louisville: John Knox, 1988.

Wilson, Andrew. "Apostle Apollos?" *JETS* 56.2 (2013) 325–35.

Wilson, Benjamin R. "The Crucifixion Scene as the Climax of Lukan Inclusivity." *Expository Times* 127.9 (2016) 430–38.

Wilson, Brittany E. "Between Text and Sermon: Luke 1:46–55." *Interpretation* 71.1 (2017) 80–82.

———. "The Blinding of Paul and the Power of God: Masculinity, Sight, and Self-Control." *JBL* 133.2 (2014) 363–87.

———. "Hearing the Word and Seeing the Light: Voice and Visions in Acts." *JSNT* 38.4 (2016) 456–481.

———. "'Neither Male nor Female': The Ethiopian Eunuch in Acts 8:26–40." *NTS* 60.3 (2014) 403–22.

———. *Unmanly Men: Refigurations of Masculinity in Luke–Acts*. Oxford: Oxford University Press, 2015.

Wilson, Walter T. "Urban Legends: Acts 10:1–11:18 and the Strategies of Greco-Roman Foundation Narratives." *JBL* 120.1 (2001) 77–99.

Windisch, Hans. "The Case Against the Tradition." *Beginnings of Christianity* 2 (1922) 298–348.

Windsor, Lionel J. *Paul and the Vocation of Israel: How Paul's Jewish Identity Informs His Apostolic Ministry, with Special Reference to Romans*. Berlin: de Gruyter, 2014.

Winslow, Karen S. *Early Jewish and Christian Memories of Moses' Wives: Exogamist Marriage and Ethnic Identity*. Lewiston, NY: Mellen, 2005.

Winter, Bruce W. "Official Proceedings and the Forensic Speeches in Acts 24–26." In *The Book of Acts in Its Ancient Literary Setting*, edited by Bruce W. Winter and Andrew D. Clarke, 305–36. Vol. 1 of *The Book of Acts in Its First Century Setting*. Grand Rapids: Eerdmans, 1993.

Winter, Paul. "Magnificat and Benedictus-Maccabean Psalms?" *BJRL* 37 (1954) 328–47.

Wise, Michael O. "Dead Sea Scrolls: General Introduction." In *Dictionary of New Testament Backgrounds*, edited by Craig A. Evans and Stanley E. Porter, 252–66. Downers Grove, IL: InterVarsity, 2000.

Wisse, Jakob. *Ethos and Pathos from Aristotle to Cicero*. Amsterdam: Hakkert, 1989.

Witherington, Ben, III. *The Acts of the Apostles: A Socio-Rhetorical Commentary*. Grand Rapids: Eerdmans, 1997.

———. "Salvation and Health in Christian Antiquity: The Soteriology of Luke–Acts in Its First Century Setting." In *Witness to the Gospel: The Theology of Acts*, edited by I. Howard Marshall, 545–76. Grand Rapids: Eerdmans, 1998.

Witherup, Ronald D. "Cornelius Over and Over and Over Again: 'Functional Redundancy' in the Acts of the Apostles." *JSNT* 49 (1993) 45–66.

Wittgenstein, Ludwig. *Philosophical Investigations*. 3rd ed. London: Pearson, 1973.

Wolfe, Robert F. "Rhetorical Elements in the Speeches of Acts 7 and 17." *JOTT* 6.3 (1993) 274–83.

Woodington, J. David. "Charity and Deliverance from Death in the Accounts of Tabitha and Cornelius." *The Catholic Biblical Quarterly* 79.4 (2017) 634–50.

Worthington, Ian. *Voice into Text: Orality and Literacy in Ancient Greece*. Leiden: Brill, 1996.

Woude, Adam S. van der. "11Q Melchizedek and the New Testament." *NTS* 12 (1966) 301–26.

Wright, Addison G. "The Widow's Mites: Praise or Lament—A Matter of Context." *The Catholic Biblical Quarterly* 44.2 (1982) 256–65.

Wright, Christopher J. H. *God's People in God's Land: Family, Land, and Property in the Old Testament*. Grand Rapids: Eerdmans, 1990.

Wright, N. T. *The Challenge of Jesus: Rediscovering Who Jesus Was and Is*. Downers Grove, IL: IVP Academic, 1999.

———. "God's Way of Acting." *Christian Century* 115.35 (1998) 1215–17.
———. "Jerusalem in the New Testament." In *Jerusalem Past and Present in the Purposes of God*, edited by P. W. L. Walker. Carol Stream: Tyndale, 1992.
———. *Jesus and the Victory of God*. Minneapolis: Fortress, 1997.
———. *The New Testament and the People of God*. Minneapolis: Fortress, 1992.
Yadin, Y. "Aspects of the Dead Sea Scrolls." *Scripta Hierosolymitana* 4 (1965) 36–55.
Yamasaki, Gary. *John the Baptist in Life and Death: Audience Oriented Criticism of Matthew's Narrative*. Sheffield: Sheffield Academic, 1998.
Yoder, John Howard. *The Politics of Jesus*. Grand Rapids: Eerdmans, 1994.
York, John O. *The Last Shall be First: The Rhetoric of Reversal in Luke*. Sheffield: JSOT, 1991.
Young, Brad H. *The Parables: Jewish Tradition and Christian Interpretation*. Grand Rapids: Baker Academic, 2008.
Zadeh, Lofti. "Fuzzy Sets." *Informing and Control* 8 (1966) 338–53.
Zehetbauer, Markus. "Stephanus: der erste Heidentäufer?" *Biblische Zeitschrift* 57.1 (2013) 82–96.
Zlotowitz, B. M. "Rabban Simeon ben Gamaliel: A Mistaken Martyr." *CAAR Journal* 51.3 (2004) 164–68.

www.ingramcontent.com/pod-product-compliance
Lightning Source LLC
Chambersburg PA
CBHW080729300426
44114CB00019B/2529